s

EDINBURGH

CHARLIE GODFREY-FAUSSETT

About the author

Charlie Godfrey-Faussett first saw Edinburgh in the clear light of a summer dawn after hitchhiking up from London for the Festival at the age of 15. Since then, he hasn't been able to keep away from the place for long. Educated at Oxford, he lives in London and has also written the Footprint *London Handbook* and *England Handbook*.

Acknowledgements

Charlie Godfrey-Faussett would like to thank Emily Simpson, Thom Dibdin, Anne and John Simpson, Keith Coventry, Suzanna Beaumont, Richard Barlas, Callum Innes, Catriona Prebble, Aine Murphy and Addie Godfrey-Faussett for all their help, and Rhonda Carrier for her editorial patience.

About the contributors

Hugh Simpson, who wrote the history chapter, was born, brought up and educated in Edinburgh, where he unfortunately no longer lives.

Jonathan Glancey, who wrote the architecture chapter, is the Architecture and Design Editor of *The Guardian*, a post he previously held on *The Independent* from 1989 to 1997. His books include *The New Moderns* (1990), *Twentieth Century Architecture* (1999) and *London* (2001).

Richenda Miers, who wrote the day trips chapter, is a journalist and travel writer who has also written the Cadogan Guides *Scotland* and *Scotland's Highlands & Islands*.

Cadogan Guides
Highlands House, 165 The Broadway,
London SW19 1NE
info.cadogan@virgin.net
www.cadoganguides.com

The Globe Pequot Press
246 Goose Lane,
PO Box 480, Guilford,
Connecticut 06437–0480

Series design: Andrew Barker
Series cover design: Sheridan Wall
Art direction: Sarah Rianhard-Gardner
Photography: OLIVIA, © Olivia Rutherford
Maps © Cadogan Guides, drawn by Oxford Cartographers
Additional map work: Angie Watts

Managing Editor: Christine Stroyan
Editors: Rhonda Carrier and Mark Mann
Proofreading: Antony Mason
Indexing: Isobel McLean
Production: Navigator Guides Ltd
Printed in Italy by Legoprint
A catalogue record for this book is available from the British Library
ISBN 1-86011-892-5

Fredome
is a noble thing

John Barbour
(c.1320~1395)

Contents

Introducing

The Guide

Introduction

The most spectacular city in the British Isles has finally shaken off its proverbial provincialism. 'Fur coat and nae nickers' was once the cruel jibe directed at this venerable old lady of the north – it was considered a fine sight in most weathers, with the spires of the Royal Mile stacking up to the impressive Castle and the stately stone-built New Town overlooking the Firth of Forth, but there was somehow a sense of there being nothing much behind that imposing façade. In 1999, however, official confirmation of the renewed energy, optimism and Euro confidence that Edinburgh had been enjoying for at least the previous decade came when the Scottish Parliament reassembled here after a hiatus of 300 years.

A good deal of the impetus for this revival has come from the tourist industry. The city has been a popular destination since the early 19th century, when turmoil abroad made it an essential stop on the aristocratic Grand Tour, but the Victorians went further: with the melancholy imagination of Sir Walter Scott as their impetus, they developed an image of the Scottish capital that threw its turbulent history, tragic Queen and Highland dress-sense into Romantic relief.

Today, Edinburgh still panders to sentiment as the picturesque home of lost causes, from the Calvinists to the Jacobites, but this is tempered by a thoroughly modern outlook and a sense that the city belongs on the Continental map. With its biting winds, mellow twilights and long views, Edinburgh reconciles all its contradictions, and that is the best thing about it. A city of big skies, wide-open spaces and little dark corners, it demands exploration on foot. Much of it looks more like the stage set for an Italian opera than a contemporary urban environment, with the countryside and sea being so close at hand.

Take a stroll around the extinct volcano of Arthur's Seat in Holyrood Park and you'll see whole new districts taking shape below the Old Town, not least around the Scottish Parliament building itself. Head down to the docks in Leith and wonder at the 1950s homeliness of the Former Royal Yacht Britannia, berthed in the gleaming new Ocean Terminal shopping mall. These developments would certainly like to emulate the success of the Museum of Scotland – an ambitious framing of the whole country's history in a few thousand square feet of contemporary design. And then, of course, there's the city's world-famous arts festival in August, which is still going from strength to strength. Not for the first time in its long and colourful history, Edinburgh is undergoing a renaissance.

The Neighbourhoods

In this guide, the city is divided into the four neighbourhoods outlined on the map to the right, each with its own sightseeing chapter. This map also shows our suggestions for the Top Ten activities and places to visit in Edinburgh.

The following colour pages introduce the neighbourhoods in more detail, describing the distinctive character and highlights of each.

10 Royal Botanic Garden, p.113

Dean Village and Stockbridge

8 Dean Gallery, p.111

9 Following the Water of Leith walkway from Stockbridge to the galleries in Dean, pp.110–12

6 Exploring the architectural harmony of the New Town, pp.100–10

7 Scott Monument, p.96

3 Strolling down the Royal Mile, pp.63–76

5 Museum of Scotland, p.85

The New Town

The Royal Mile

The Old Town

2 Palace of Holyroodhouse, p.75

1 Edinburgh Castle, p.59

4 Greyfriars Kirkyard, p.84

Clockwise from top left: John Knox's House, High Kirk of St Giles, Writers' Museum, Palace of Holyroodhouse.

The Royal Mile

Lined with 17th-century high-rise housing, Edinburgh's ancient cobbled High Street and its offshoots (the Lawnmarket and Castlehill at the western end and Canongate to the east) run up a granite ridge to the dramatic nub of Edinburgh Castle and down to the monarch's Palace of Holyroodhouse, forming a Royal Mile from top to bottom and lending the city its famous skyline. Halfway up squats the High Kirk of St Giles, topped with its distinctively Scottish open-work spire. Thronging with people all year, the Mile's wide pavements lead into numerous steep, narrow and dark closes that once afforded the Edinburgh mob convenient escape routes and now give onto courtyards and unexpected views of the sea. All along its length, this old grey-stone high road bristles with reminders of Edinburgh's turbulent past and now bustles with hope for its future.

The Royal Mile
The Royal Mile chapter p.57
Hotels p.150 Restaurants p.159 Bars p.174

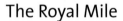

The Old Town

Located in the sunken valley south of the Royal Mile, the Old Town was long the dark side of Edinburgh. At its heart lay the Grassmarket, in the shadow of the hangman's noose, the sheer rockface of the Castle and grim Greyfriars Kirkyard. The gloomy approach along Cowgate was a dank rat-run bridged-over by polite society, who stepped from the High Street into the Southside without looking down. Nowadays, when the sun is shining the broad Grassmarket could almost pass for an Italian piazza, and Greyfriars Kirkyard is a surprising splash of green amid the grey. Cowgate, still faintly seedy, hosts a strip of not-entirely-tame nightclubs. Thanks largely to the presence of the University just up the hill, nightlife in the Old Town is alive enough for you to feel unwell in the morning.

Clockwise from top left: Greyfriars Kirkyard, Grassmarket and the Castle by night, The Scotsman Hotel, the Human Be-In.

Clockwise from top left: view over Princes Street, Monument to Dugald Stewart, a New Town terrace, George Street shopping.

The New Town

Mapped out with the aid of an architect's meticulous pen in the 18th century, the New Town is Edinburgh's neoclassical masterpiece, its stately stone-built terraces, crescents and circuses marching down the slopes north of the Royal Mile, stepping elegantly towards the Firth of Forth. When the stinking Nor'Loch beneath the Castle's cliff became the lovely Princes Street Gardens, the city's professional classes were quick to abandon their cramped tenements on the High Street. Recently they've even begun to relax their grip on their adopted home, with George Street in particular becoming home to a strip of designer shops and bars to rival any in Britain. Grand and spacious enough to lift the heart, the architectural legacy of the Enlightenment plays off beautifully against the fantastic Gothic skyline of the Old Town and the distant views over the Firth to the hills of Fife.

The New Town
The New Town chapter p.89
Hotels p.151 Restaurants p.165 Bars p.175

Dean Village and Stockbridge

Edinburgh's little river, the Water of Leith, babbles swiftly through a steep wooded valley northwest of the New Town. Once busy with mills and bakeries, Dean Village nestles in a quiet corner far below the massive Dean Bridge and makes a delightful central starting point for walks upstream to the galleries of modern art or downstream to dinky Stockbridge. This small town has been a desirable address since artist Henry Raeburn designed Ann Street for his wife high on the west bank in the early years of the 19th century. More recently, it has become an idiosyncratic haven for the city's chattering classes, clustered with quirky shops and restaurants and close to the colourful splendour of the Royal Botanic Garden.

Clockwise from top left: two of Stockbridge's independent shops, Royal Botanic Garden, Water of Leith walkway.

Outside the Centre

Visitors with time to spare are spoilt for choice when it comes to venturing further afield. Just to the east of the centre, next to the Palace of Holyroodhouse, the extinct volcanic uplands of Holyrood Park look down on Duddingston Village, snuggled beside its loch. To the northeast, beyond the late-night lights of Broughton, are the regenerated dockside towns of Leith and Newhaven, both once proudly independent entities, and further to the east the breezy seaside town of Portobello beckons. To the south, beyond the solid and genteel homes of Marchmont, The Grange and Morningside, splendid views and woodland walks are to be had on the Braid Hills and in the Hermitage. Westwards, the breweries of Fountainbridge unleash their malty smell, which spreads in the breeze over most of the city, but especially over the Hearts of Midlothian football terraces in Gorgie and Dalry. Further west still, Corstorphine is a polite old village suburb, home to the award-winning Edinburgh Zoo.

Clockwise from above: Bennet's Bar, Portobello, Duddingston, Leith.

Days Out
in Edinburgh

Couples' City p.10

Festival City p.18

Literary Edinburgh p.16

Indoor City p.12

Edinburghers' City p.14

COUPLES' CITY

The operatic setting, the sea views and the gentle twilights... Edinburgh could almost have been made to please strolling lovers. If the wind blows too keenly, every other corner hides a warm, cosy pub or an inviting restaurant. The city's traditionally buttoned-up, slightly stuffy reputation adds a daring frisson to public displays of affection, but it's easy enough to get away from it all, either in its green spaces or amidst its more secluded walks and wynds. Come the evening, the thriving late-night bar culture and entertainment scene will keep you up until the wee small hours.

One

Start: George IV Bridge.
Breakfast: Wake up gently over coffee in the busy back room of **The Elephant House**, with its views of the Castle.

Morning: Beat the coach tours into Edinburgh Castle first thing, enjoy the early-morning light and seek out the tiny **St Margaret's Chapel**.

Lunch: Head into subterranean cosiness at **Maxie's** wine bar, or enjoy a light meal on its sunny terrace overlooking busy Victoria Street and the Grassmarket.

Afternoon: Stroll down the Royal Mile towards the **Palace of Holyroodhouse** (*above, top left*), and if the sun's shining hike in **Holyrood Park** for more fabulous views.

Dinner: Catch bus no.35 from in front of the Palace of Holyroodhouse back up the Royal Mile and splash out on a candelit dinner at **The Witchery** (*above*).

Evening: Wander back down the Royal Mile and Cockburn Street to dance the night away at **The Massa** nightclub.

Two

Start: Princes Street.

Breakfast: Sample the fresh kippers in the city's most stylish bar, **Rick's** on Frederick Street.

Morning: Wander down through the elegant blocks of the New Town to bohemian **Stockbridge** and the **Water of Leith**.

Lunch: Walk upriver from Stockbridge along the Water of Leith's most delightful stretch for a wholesome lunch in the garden of **The Gallery Café** at the **Scottish National Gallery of Modern Art** (*above, top*).

Afternoon: Explore the gallery, and the Surrealist collection in the **Dean Gallery** (*above*) across the way. Catch the free 'artbus' back into town along Princes Street.

Dinner: Enjoy a candle-lit French dinner in the heart of the New Town at **Le Café St Honoré**.

Evening: Relax over some digestifs at the **Café Royal Bistro Bar**.

INDOOR CITY

Although it actually rains rather less here than elsewhere in Scotland, Edinburgh's biting winds can be enjoyably avoided in any number of salubrious restaurants, and its grey afternoons whiled away in a wealth of superb museums and galleries. The Museum of Scotland does a world-class job of telling a small country's history up to the present day, while the Royal Museum, Palace of Holyroodhouse and Former Royal Yacht Britannia are just three intriguing ways to keep out of the wet at the same time as gaining a glimpse into the life of the monarchy past and present.

Three

Start: Royal Mile.

Breakfast: Rev up with a warming cup of tea and a bacon roll in the **Lower Aisle Restaurant** beneath the High Kirk of St Giles.

Morning: Walk across George IV Bridge to explore the **Museum of Scotland** (*opposite, bottom right*) or its beautiful old neighbour, the **Royal Museum**.

Lunch: Get back to the Royal Mile for a proper Scottish lunch in the cosy basement at **Dubh Prais**.

Afternoon: Walk or take bus no.35 to Holyrood Park to experience the great outdoors indoors at **Our Dynamic Earth**.

Dinner: Experience the super-hip, Edward-Hopperesque and minimalist **Borough** (*above, top*).

Evening: By way of total design contrast, get snuggled into the cosy Victorian pub **Leslie's**, on Ratcliffe Terrace.

Four

Start: Top of Leith Walk.

Breakfast: **Valvona and Crolla**, one of the finest Italian delis in Britain.

Morning: Bus it down Leith Walk to the **Ocean Terminal** and explore the **Former Royal Yacht Britannia**.

Lunch: Take another bus along to The Shore for some fine seafood at **The Shore Bar** (*above, top right*).

Afternoon: Head back into the centre to see what life was like indoors in days gone by in **The Georgian House** and the **Charlotte Square Drawing Room Gallery** (*above, left*).

Dinner: Enjoy rooftop dining with a view in the designer surroundings of **Oloroso**, on nearby Castle Street.

Evening: Continuing the designer theme, drink and dance the night away at the **Opal Lounge** on George Street (*opposite, inset*).

EDINBURGHERS' CITY

Never boastful, of course, but tirelessly helpful, Edinburghers enjoy walking around their city as much as any visitor does. Though many do still live on the Royal Mile, it's just south and north of the centre that most can be found, taking their ease away from the tourist trail: in dinky Stockbridge, with its independent shops close to the much-loved Botanic Garden; in solid Bruntsfield, beyond the green acres of The Meadows; and in Leith, where they're Leithers, as they'll let you know for nothing, and not Edinburghers at all.

Five

Start: Canonmills.
Breakfast: Kick things off at **Au Gourmand** on Brandon Terrace, where the Auld Alliance is alive and well first thing in the morning.
Morning: Explore the book- and antique shops of **Canonmills** before heading to the **Royal Botanic Garden** (*opposite, left*) for a dose of contemporary art at **Inverleith House Gallery** and for some wonderful city views.
Lunch: Snack in style at **Hector's** in Stockbridge.
Afternoon: Browse the shops on **St Stephen Street** in Stockbridge (*above, left*), then amble through the New Town to **Broughton Street**, where you'll find more one-offs and a hip local scene.
Dinner: Have a cheerful, offbeat and inexpensive supper next to a laundromat at the **Lost Sock Diner**.
Evening: Catch the buzz on Broughton Street – at **Mezz** (*opposite, bottom right*), for instance, or in the more traditional **Cask and Barrel** (*above*).

Six

Start: Tollcross, at the top of the Lothian Road.

Breakfast: Seek out **Montpeliers**, the Morningsiders' favourite breakfast joint.

Morning: Wander through The Grange to play golf on **Bruntsfield Links** (courtesy of the Golf Tavern) or kick a ball about on **The Meadows**.

Lunch: Have an informal, healthy lunch with an Asian/Mediterranean bias at **The Apartment**, just by Bruntsfield Links.

Afternoon: Take a bus out to **Leith** and explore the up-and-coming area around The Shore and Commercial Street.

Dinner: Experience Edinburgh's finest gastronomic offerings at the **Restaurant Martin Wishart**.

Evening: Join the **Scottish Malt Whisky Society** and enjoy a few wee drams in their comfortable club-room.

Auld Reikie
wale o ilka tow
ROBERT FERGUSSON 1750-1774

LITERARY EDINBURGH

Perhaps because the Scottish capital was marginalized by the Union of 1707, and later thanks to the great publishing houses founded by the likes of Robert Chambers, Thomas Nelson and Alexander Black, Edinburgh has made the nurture of literary talent something of a speciality. Novelist Sir Walter Scott, easily the most popular and prolific of the city's literary sons, almost singlehandedly put his country on the world stage, though his path had been lit by the Scottish Enlightenment that shone so brightly in Edinburgh in the 18th century and still seems to glow round the town's old stones today. Philosophers such as David Hume and Adam Smith, biographers and drinkers as spirited as James Boswell, and poets of the calibre of Robert Burns and Robert Fergusson all made the place their playground. Robert Louis Stevenson loved and loathed it; Sir Arthur Conan Doyle grew up here; and, more recently, the likes of Irvine Welsh and Ian Rankin have secured its place on the literary map.

Seven

Start: **Makar's Steps**, at the top of The Mound, inscribed with quotes by Robert Burns and Hugh McDiarmid.

Breakfast: Take a light literary toast and tea in **Deacon's Café**, in the kitchen that once belonged to Deacon Brodie, inspiration for *Dr Jekyll and Mr Hyde*.

Morning: Doff your cap at the **statue of David Hume** wearing a toga at the top of the High Street, before ducking into Makar's Close, where there's plenty to read at the Writers' Museum.

Lunch: Restore your grey cells at **Clarinda's**, a sweet old-fashioned teahouse that was named after Burns' mistress.

Afternoon: Pay homage to Robert 'Auld Reekie' Fergusson at his tomb in **Canongate graveyard** (*above right*), then head to Princes Street via **Waverley Station** (the world's only station named after a novel) for spectacular views from the top of the **Scott Monument**.

Dinner: Partake of supper and a hearty 18th-century claret in **Whigham's Wine Cellars**.

Evening: Head back into the Old Town to join the **Scottish Literary Pub**

Tour, which sets out from the Beehive Inn.

Night: Carry on drinking at **Rutherford's**, Stevenson's favourite pub, seemingly little altered since his day. Then drop into the cramped confines of the **Royal Oak** for some impromptu folk ballads until late.

Eight

Start: South Bridge.

Breakfast: Make your way to the **Black Medicine Coffee Shop** for a fine cup of coffee beneath Nicolson's Restaurant (once the café where J. K. Rowling penned Harry Potter) and next door to Edinburgh's largest bookstore, **Blackwell's** (formerly James Thin's).

Morning: Tour the gruesome **Royal College of Surgeons**, where the model for Conan Doyle's Sherlock Holmes once lectured, then have a peep at the writer's old house at **No.23 George Square**.

Lunch: Check out the **City Café** (*right*), Edinburgh's original style bar, immortalized by Irvine Welsh.

Afternoon: Stroll down The Mound into Princes Street Gardens for a look at concrete poet Ian Hamilton Finlay's moving **tribute to Robert Louis Stevenson**. Then wonder at the number of great Scottish writers and scientists at the **Scottish National Portrait Gallery**.

Dinner: Get fishy at the **Café Royal Oyster Bar**, Hugh McDiarmid's formal favourite.

Evening: Take a tour of **Mary King's Close**, described by Iain Banks in his novel *Complicity* as the 'old void of disease, despair and death' at the heart of Edinburgh.

Night: Head back into the New Town for a pint at the **Oxford Bar**, favourite haunt of Ian Rankin's Inspector Rebus.

FESTIVAL CITY

Edinburgh's August arts festival (actually made up of various roughly concurrent festivals, most notably the International and the Fringe; *see* pp.38–9), has made a huge contribution to the city's renaissance since it began in 1947. Imagine about a million people in a beautiful city that is home to half that number, more than 500 shows performed in approximately a third the number of venues, and enough concurrent live entertainment, both in the venues themselves and on the streets, to make viewing options on American TV look parsimonious. Getting the best of the Fest in a single day is never really an option, but careful planning based around a few key venues guarantees you a good shot.

Nine

Start: Waverley Station.
Breakfast: Sample the very fine French-style sandwiches at **Duck's de la Gare**.
Morning: Make for the **Assembly Rooms**, the longest-established of the Fringe megavenues. Book tickets here for most of the other

venues too, after consulting the Daily Diary, then catch a show here or nearby.
Lunch: Head for **The Hub**, HQ of the International Festival, for further information, live music, food and very good coffee.
Afternoon: Amble down the Royal Mile, dodging performers trying to attract your attention, to **The Pleasance Cabaret Bar**, another very busy megavenue with an excellent reputation.
Dinner: Enjoy a cheap and cheerful Italian meal at **Il Castello**.
Evening: Savour the very best drama the Fringe is likely to have on offer at the **Traverse Theatre** (pre-booking essential).
Night: Check out some stand-up comedy, for instance at **The Stand Comedy Club**, or a one-off club night until late.

Roots of the City

Early Edinburgh

The focal point of the city has always been Edinburgh Castle, situated on **Castle Rock**, an extinct volcanic plug transformed by glaciation into a 'crag and tail', so that steep cliffs surround all but one side, making for an obviously defensible position. It is often said that the castle has not actually proven much of a stronghold, but while it has been captured – once supposedly by Robert the Bruce's nephew, climbing over the wall on a ladder – it has also survived siege. Stirling Castle, as the gateway to the north of Scotland, was strategically more important and saw action on several important occasions (the decisive battles of Independence against England, most famously Bannockburn in 1314), but Edinburgh Castle dominates the coastal plain south of the River Forth and has always been seen as the best way of controlling the city.

It is unlikely that the Romans ever occupied Castle Rock, though they did establish forts nearby, at Cramond and Inveresk. At the turn of the 7th century, the Rock is thought to have been a stronghold of the Britons. Since then, successive waves of conquerers and settlers have left traces of their language in the place names: Cramond from the Briton, Balerno from the Gaelic, Ravelston from the Anglo-Scandinavian.

One name that has defied explanation is Edinburgh itself. It's been suggested that the name is an anglicization of the earlier Briton name Din Eidyn (or Dunedin); certainly, 'burgh' was the English equivalent of the Briton 'Din', meaning a fortified place, but the 'edin' element remains elusive.

Early Edinburgh

Arthur's Seat, the city's very own extinct volcano, p.129.

Edinburgh Castle, occupying the site of a stronghold from at least the turn of the 7th century, p.59.

Museum of Scotland, tracing the story of Edinburgh from prehistory to the present day in a marvellous new building that is a sight in itself, p.85.

1018–1488

Holyrood Abbey, built in 1128 and the site of the coronation of Charles I in 1633, p.76.

Port of Leith, granted to the city for trade in 1329, now full of bars, restaurants and designer hotels after urban regeneration, p.118.

St Margaret's Chapel, Edinburgh's oldest church and one of Britain's smallest, p.62.

1018–1488: The Establishment of the Capital

By the 11th century, Gaelic-speaking kings had unified much of Scotland, and **Malcolm II** (1005–34) consolidated his hold on southeast Scotland at the battle of Carham on the Tweed (c. 1018). Edinburgh became an important centre, though the concept of a capital city was slow to emerge, as the court was constantly on the move in order to maintain law and order and not eat all the food at once. By the mid-13th century, **Edinburgh Castle** was the usual place from which government documents were issued when the court was in town, but it was only under **James III** (1460–88) that royal rule became concentrated on Edinburgh.

Malcolm III (1058–93), the milksop prince of Shakespeare's historically inaccurate *Macbeth*, actually established a dynasty that did much to modernize Scotland. The oldest remaining building in Edinburgh is the 12th-century **chapel** in honour of his wife Margaret, built by **David I** (1124–53), the youngest of their three sons. David also founded **Holyrood Abbey** in 1128, later to share its site with what is still a royal residence. It's pronounced to rhyme with Hollywood – appropriately, given the tragically glamorous cast that was to occupy Scotland's throne.

The Augustinian canons brought from St Andrews to occupy the abbey gained possession of land between it and Castle Rock, comprising the lower section of what is now known as the **Royal Mile**. The area became the burgh of **Canongate**, and its foundation charter seems to suggest that there was already in existence a royal burgh, in the modern sense of a town with legal trading rights, up the hill at Edinburgh. Edinburgh's earliest surviving charter dates from 1329, at the end of the reign of **Robert I** (Robert the Bruce). This charter asserts the 'ancient' rights of the burgh; it may replace an earlier, lost charter; or the canny citizens may have been laying claim to 'ancient' rights they had not previously possessed.

After the loss of Berwick – hitherto Scotland's premier trading port – to the English during the Wars of Independence (which broke out in 1296), Edinburgh emerged as Scotland's most important town. The 1329 charter also granted the city the use of the **port of Leith** so that it could engage in continental trade (Edinburgh was rare among European capitals in that it did not stand on a navigable watercourse). Leith later seceded from a bankrupt Edinburgh in 1833, only to be reunited in 1920 against the will of its people.

1488–1567

High Kirk of St Giles, the first parish church, former cathedral and site of stirring sermons by John Knox, p.67.
John Knox's House, though not necessarily ever inhabited by the preacher, has displays on his life and times, p.72.
Palace of Holyroodhouse, founded by James IV, reconstructed under Charles II, and still the Queen's official Scots residence, p.75.

1488–1567: Regicide and Religion

Scotland's government remained unstable throughout the **Middle Ages**, with a series of kings being killed and leaving infant successors. **James IV** (1488–1513), though involved in the coup that deposed his father James III, was in fact the only monarch in 150 years not to need a regent. The relative stability of his reign was the backdrop to a new intellectual

Herringbone and Mob – the Growth of the City to 1650

In its early years, the burgh of Edinburgh covered a small area below the castle, and by 1385, when the city was burned by Richard II of England, it consisted only of around 400 houses. Expansion was limited by marshy ground in the valleys on either side of what became the High Street. These marshes were probably the city's main defence until the **Kings Wall** was built in the early 15th century and strengthened in 1473. Part of the wall can be seen downhill from St Columba's Church in Johnston Terrace. After the Scots' defeat by the English at Flodden in 1513, the **Flodden Wall** was constructed in preparation for an attack that never materialized. Not finished until 1560, the wall, parts of which are still visible (*see* p.83), defined the limits of the city until well into the 18th century.

The city became a principal trading centre, but with an unusually limited trading area. The **High Street**, while probably wider than it is today, must still have been extremely busy. The now-familiar herringbone pattern was formed by the long gardens, later built over, running back at right angles from the High Street. Edinburgh became well known for its high-rise tenements or 'lands', which were prone to collapse and at risk from fire, even after large-scale rebuilding in stone in 1544.

With its narrow streets and high buildings, the city became known for the '**Edinburgh mob**', as it was easy to cause a disturbance and then slip away and disappear. The usual hallmark of the mob was that it was well organized, and prominent citizens often seemed to be involved: rather than merely being an unruly rabble, it acted as a crude instrument of social justice.

Scotland's urban population grew faster than England's; the city doubled in population between 1550 and 1620, and had tripled by 1650, without growing any larger geographically: it merely grew upwards. A population of more than 35,000 lived in a series of wynds (thoroughfares) and closes (cul-de-sacs) off one straight street. Population density was ridiculously high and conditions were insanitary to say the least.

The Suspicious History of the Summons of Plotcock

A story is told by the 16th-century historian Pitscottie that, as James IV was mustering his troops on the Boroughmuir before the fateful battle of Flodden, a cry was heard emanating from the Mercat Cross on the High Street at midnight, summoning men by name to appear within 40 days before the voice's master Plotcock, or Pluto King of the Underworld. One man heard the summons and crossed himself with a crown: he was the only man named to survive the battle the next day. Some have suggested that the event was stage-managed by the playwright Sir David Lyndsay, author of *Ane Satire upon the Three Estates*.

flowering in the city. James IV also founded the **royal residence at Holyroodhouse**, much to the displeasure of the monks next door.

After the death of James V in 1542, Henry VIII of England wished the infant **Mary, Queen of Scots** to be promised in marriage to his son. Mary was shipped off to France by her French mother and regent, Mary of Guise, returning in 1561 to find herself the Catholic queen of a Protestant country. Anti-Catholic agitation inspired by **John Knox**, the minister at **St Giles**, had led to the departure in 1560 of Mary of Guise's French allies and the declaration by Parliament of a Protestant Scotland. Mary's subsequent adventures – the murder of her secretary Rizzio, the explosion aimed at her husband Darnley, her abdication, imprisonment and execution – were in effect no more than a melodramatic interlude with a tragic central figure.

1567–1640: James VI, the Union of Crowns and Charles I

While the 16th century had seen conflict between Catholicism and Protestantism, the 17th century was characterized by conflict between different strands of Protestantism.

The reign of **James VI** (1567–1625) was one of great advances for Scotland in general and for Edinburgh in particular, with James dealing more successfully with the religious and financial problems facing the Crown than those who preceded or succeeded him. His reign also saw the foundation in 1582 of what was to become **Edinburgh University** – Scotland's fourth such institution at a time when England had only two.

The accession of James to the English throne as **James I** in 1603 (he retained his Scottish title), and the subsequent removal of much of the court to London, had surprisingly little effect on the prestige and status of Edinburgh; in fact, it was in 1633 that Edinburgh was first officially confirmed as Scotland's capital. James' religious beliefs were very much at odds with those of sections of the Scottish Church, but he seems to have avoided confrontation on the issue – unlike his son, the obstinate **Charles I** (1625–49). Charles' attempts to impose his religious views on the people led to riots in 1637, and his individual approach to taxation was also a source of discontent.

A **National Covenant** stating Scotland's right to civil and spiritual self-determination was read from the pulpit at **Greyfriars Kirk** and signed by ministers and local dignitaries (known as the Covenanters) in February 1638, in an act of clear defiance of the authority of the Crown, which helped bring about the **War of the Three Kingdoms** in the 1640s.

1567–1640

Canongate Tolbooth, the Canongate's equivalent of the Heart of Midlothian, now housing the People's Story relating everyday Edinburgh life through the ages, p.74.

George Heriot's School, a former orphanage and one of the city's most extraordinary buildings, p.83.

Gladstone's Land, the best surviving example of a 17th-century Edinburgh tenement, p.65.

Greyfriars Kirk, where the National Covenant defying Charles I was signed in 1638, p.83.

1640–89

Canongate Kirkyard, which has stunning views and more than its fair share of notable dead, p.75.

Royal Botanic Garden, with its splendid glasshouses full of exotic plantlife, p.113.

Witches memorial on Castlehill, a modern testament to the women burned because of the superstitions of others, p.60.

1640–89: Religion, Revolt and Revolution

At first the war made little impact on the city, aside from inciting fears that the Marquis of Montrose, Charles' Highland champion, would attack. Montrose's defeat at Philiphaugh preceded Charles' surrender to the Covenanters, who sold him to the English. Charles' execution in 1649 was badly received: he was, after all, King of Scotland. His son, later Charles II, negotiated with the Covenanters and made no attempt to halt the unpopular execution of Montrose, whose revolt had failed. The Covenanters were defeated at Dunbar in 1650, Scotland was incorporated into the Commonwealth set up by the victorious English Parliamentary forces under Oliver Cromwell, and Edinburgh, weakened by plague and war, was further enfeebled by Cromwell's crippling taxes.

The **Restoration** of 1660 saw the new **Charles II** (1660–85) forget about his agreements with the Covenanters. Revolts in 1666 and 1679 led to '**the killing times**', as Covenanters starved to death in Greyfriars Kirkyard or were executed. Charles' reign also saw the splendid reconstruction of the **Palace of Holyroodhouse** by Sir William Bruce of Kinross.

Charles was succeeded by his brother, **James VII and II** (1685–88), whose Catholicism led to his being replaced, in the so-called Glorious Revolution, by his daughter Mary and her husband **William of Orange** (1689–1702), who has become a hero or bogeyman to subsequent generations largely through being a Protestant. Thus ended a dynasty that had ruled Scotland for more than 400 years.

While the Covenanters who died after the revolts are often regarded as martyrs, they represented the extreme wing of the group and were few in number – certainly fewer than the number of unfortunates put to death for **witchcraft** at this time. Burning of witches, which was widespread during the war, continued in parts of Scotland until 1726.

As for the impact of the Covenant, it is still too early to tell: repercussions from religious debates of long ago are still keenly felt here. However, as recently as the 1930s Edinburgh, a city that often likes to believe itself above the sectarian disturbances that have plagued much of central Scotland, gave 30 per cent of the vote in city council elections to the anti-Catholic Protestant Action Party.

1689–1707: The End of an Old Song

The 1690s were a bad decade for the city: poor harvests led to famine, war between England and France affected trade, and the collapse of the attempt to found a Scottish colony at Darien led to financial ruin. All of this made some people better disposed to the idea of parliamentary **Union** with England, which occurred in 1707, though Union seemed to be a better idea for the English – who feared that Scotland would choose a Catholic monarch after the death of **Queen Anne** (1702–14), who could not produce a living heir – than the Scots.

Those who supported Union most strongly regarded it as the best of several bad choices; others were bribed, and the mob, violently opposed to Union but with no representation, rioted. 'The end of an old song' was how the Lord High Chancellor, Lord Seafield, put it at the time, and even the most fervent supporters of the Union have rarely had unmixed feelings about the events of 1707.

1689–1707

Parliament House, the walls of which are dotted with portraits of prominent Edinburgh lawyers, p.68.

The Union, and the loss of the parliament, had little effect on the social profile of the city. Scotland's own church, education and legal systems were safeguarded; indeed, lawyers were prominent in Edinburgh life and were credited largely with preserving the city and Scotland's character. The merchant class had also long been strongly represented: the peculiarly middle-class reputation with which Edinburgh has long been saddled was already present.

1707–66: A Hotbed of Genius

The 18th century is often described as the **Age of Enlightenment**, but in the case of Edinburgh the term could equally have applied to the vigorous intellectual life of the city in the century before Union. The 18th century was merely a continuation of this. Though no longer a political capital, the city was a renowned intellectual centre, home to such eminent figures as philosopher David Hume (*see* p.98), geologist James Hutton (*see* p.130) and philosopher, judge and anthropologist Lord Monboddo (*see* below).

Despite all this activity, the city was not democratic by any means. Its Member of Parliament was chosen by an electorate of 33 – namely the town council, who could also choose their own successors – and the treatment of radicals was notoriously harsh. Still,

---

1707–66

Goose Pie House, an octagonal dwelling built by 18th-century poet Allan Ramsay for himself, p.63.

Riddle's Court, where philosopher David Hume lived from 1753 and the site of lavish banquets held for James VI by a wealthy 16th-century burgess, p.65.

---

the 18th century was fairly calm, and even the Jacobite rebellion of 1745 – Bonnie Prince Charlie's doomed attempt to reclaim the crown in the name of his father, James VIII – had little impact on the city.

1766–1822: Sir Walter Scott and the New Town

By the mid-18th century, Edinburgh had become dangerously congested. The city was the second largest in Britain, despite being only a mile long and a quarter of a mile wide, and some buildings were 14 storeys high. The introduction of refuse collection in 1687 had alleviated some of the hygiene problems, but the citizens were still notorious for emptying human waste into the street. There was a lack of public buildings, and many houses were unsafe. The Lord Provost, George Drummond (*see* p.104), recognized the need for expansion and in 1766 young architect James Craig won the design competition for the **New Town**.

Lord Monboddo (1714–99)

James Burnett took his title from a small village in Kincardineshire. An eminent advocate, Greek scholar and early nudist, he became famous for his theory outlined in the *Origin and Progress of Language* (1776) – namely, that men used to have tails and were descended from orang utans. Darwin studied at Edinburgh University the following century and would certainly have heard of Monboddo's ideas.

Monboddo did not have a happy private life: his wife died in childbirth; his son, who had been examined in Latin by Dr Johnson

on his visit to Edinburgh, died in his teens; and his beautiful daughter, about whom Burns wrote, 'Fair Burnet strikes the adoring eye,/Heaven's beauties on my fancy shine,' died at the age of 25. An eccentric, he refused to use a carriage – which he called sitting 'in a box' – riding everywhere on horseback, even to London. On one of his visits there in his old age, the line-up of English lawlords, the King's Bench, quite literally collapsed. Monboddo didn't stir amid the confusion and debris, commenting that he'd thought the event must be an annual ceremony.

Its construction was both an architectural event of European significance and a turning point in the city's history, not least because, as the more well-heeled citizens moved out of the Old Town, Edinburgh lost its previously unique social mix, where people of all classes had shared the same buildings. The Old Town became more run-down, and, by the time of the great fire of 1824 (which led to the foundation of the world's first municipal fire service), the place had become a slum. Edinburgh was now two towns.

The impact of **Sir Walter Scott** (*see* p.97) on Edinburgh cannot be overestimated – and not just because of his monument. Not only did Scott revolutionize the role of the novelist in much of the Western world and have an incalculable effect on the Romantic movement, his novels also contributed massively to the Scots' image of themselves. Edinburgh is obsessed with its heritage, and much of its history comes from Scott rather than what actually happened. All of what is sometimes referred to as the 'shortbread and tea-towel' romantic vision of Scotland's past can, for better or worse, be said to have started with him.

Scott stage-managed the visit of **George IV** in 1822, the first visit by a monarch since 1651, commemorated by the statue at the intersection of Hanover Street and George Street. George was worried that his kilt was too short, but was reassured by a patriotic lady that 'we in Scotland could never see too much of your majesty'. This visit, signalling the establishment of Edinburgh as a magnet for romantic tourism and a place of pageantry rather than intrinsic importance, could be seen as the moment when Edinburgh began to disappear up its own kilt.

The 19th Century

The Disruption of 1843 – a split in the Church of Scotland caused by a dispute over whether congregations should have the right to choose their own clergy – led to the **formation of the Free Church**, commemorated by the statues of Dr Guthrie and Dr Chalmers facing each other along Castle Street. Otherwise, 19th-century Edinburgh was, by its own standards, uneventful, despite the presence of such luminaries as scientist James Clerk Maxwell (*see* p.105), novelist Robert Louis Stevenson (*see* p.69), and town planner Patrick Geddes (*see* p.34).

The advent in mid-century of the **Caledonian and North British Railways**, whose irrational rivalry produced ever faster trains south, and their famous eponymous hotels (now the Caledonian Hilton and the Balmoral, *see* p.151), did little to make the city more outward-looking. **Glasgow**, which could no longer be ignored after the opening of the Edinburgh–Glasgow railway in 1842, grew to twice Edinburgh's size and became the 'second city of the Empire', while Edinburgh clung to its status as the ancient capital, and settled into a cosy complacency.

Edinburgh failed to become as heavily industrialized as Glasgow or Dundee and did not suffer to anything like as great a degree from the slums and social engineering that accompanied their clearance, nor the Depression or the recent mass unemployment due to the decline of heavy industry. Yet the city's few **industries** have declined: printing and publishing, which produced names such as Chambers and Nelson, almost disappeared, and of the 20 breweries that existed as recently as the 1960s, only two recent micro-breweries and the award-winning **Caledonian Brewery** challenge the dominance of the Scottish Courage beer factory. The city continues to rely for employment and industry on law, banking (the **Bank of Scotland** was founded in 1695, the **Royal Bank of Scotland** 30 years later) and insurance (**Standard Life** was founded in 1825).

The 20th Century

For much of the 20th century Edinburgh traded on its past. Once a ridiculously packed city that you could walk around in half an hour, it became a sprawling place with many open spaces (not all of which are private golf clubs). Fortunately, post-1945 grandiose road and building schemes were dropped, though not before some of the city's more admired areas, including George Square (*see* p.87), were bulldozed. Councillor David Begg, one of the city's most controversial figures of recent years, has at last started to grapple with the **traffic problems** of a city which, like so many older cities in Scotland and England, was simply not designed for cars.

Edinburgh's profile was raised by the **International Festival**, founded in 1947 as a symbol of renewal in war-torn Europe. Nowadays it is the accompanying **Fringe** that captures the imagination, but the official Festival, even if it plays safe these days, should be honoured for bankrolling the event in the first place. Many Edinburgh citizens studiously avoid both.

The 20th Century

Dean Gallery, with the recreated studio of artist and Edinburgh institution Eduardo Paolozzi, p.111.

Scottish National War Memorial, with its shrine recording the names of the 150,000 Scots soldiers lost in the world wars, p.62.

Traverse Theatre, for superb entertainment in a wonderful purpose-built complex of theatres, bars and restaurants, p.181.

Edinburgh Today

Connected Earth, the Royal Museum's new space dedicated to the history of telecommunications from Bell to the Internet, p.85.

New Scottish Parliament, under construction to a design by Spanish architects Enric and Benedetta Miralles, p.76.

Playfair Project, a £27-million project to restore the Royal Scottish Academy and link it to the National Gallery, p.96.

The Scotsman Hotel, a stunning luxury hotel that opened in the former newspaper HQ in 2001 and symbolizes the city's confidence at the turn of the century, p.150.

Edinburgh Today

Edinburgh's complacency has been demonstrated in recent times by its lack of marketing acumen compared to Glasgow, which has shed its previous image problem and seen tourism mushroom as a result. The joke was that Edinburgh's response to Glasgow's once ubiquitous tourist slogan 'Glasgow's Miles Better' should be 'Edinburgh's Slightly Superior'.

Over the past few years, Edinburgh's cosy shortbread-and-tartan approach has been accompanied by *Trainspotting* chic – yet more evidence of the city's divided face. Scottish history has also seen the appearance of the *Braveheart* approach: Mel Gibson suggested that his 1995 film had helped to bring back the Scottish Parliament – a level of adherence to the facts matched only by that of the plot of the film itself.

Nevertheless, the **Scottish Parliament** has come back, and Edinburgh was the only realistic choice for its home. For this and for many other reasons besides, the city's future looks as exciting and unpredictable as ever.

Hugh Simpson

Art, Literature
and Architecture

ART

Edinburgh's proud indigenous fine art tradition stretches back centuries, but there are three local artists you should particularly look out for: **Allan Ramsay** (1713–94), son of the poet of the same name (*see* p.29) and one of the 18th century's most brilliant portrait painters, who much to the chagrin of Joshua Reynolds was appointed official portrait painter to George III; **David Wilkie** (1785–1841), who specialized in dramatic scenes satirizing the state of the nation after Union in 1707; and **Sir Henry Raeburn** (1756–1823), probably the finest portrait painter Scotland has ever produced, whose *Skating Minister* (*see* p.95) has become the city's logo. More recently, Leith-born artist **Eduardo Paolozzi** (1924–) has made a significant contribution to the city's street furniture, as has Scots concrete poet and artist **Ian Hamilton Finlay** (1925–).

Phoebe Anna Traquair (1852–1936)

The first woman to be elected an honorary member of the Royal Scottish Academy (*see* p.96), Phoebe Anna Moss came to Edinburgh from Dublin to marry palaeontologist Ramsay Heatley Traquair and became the city's foremost exponent of the Arts and Crafts movement, working in a wide range of media, including mural-decoration, painting, jewellery-making, enamelling, embroidery, bookbinding, and manuscript illumination and lettering. It was her work for the old Bellevue Reformed Baptist Church on Mansfield Place (*see* p.117) in the 1890s that sealed her growing international reputation.

Greatly influenced by poet/painters William Blake and Dante Gabriel Rossetti, Traquair counted among her friends and admirers W. B. Yeats and John Ruskin; the face of the latter appeared on many of her murals, as did those of Carlyle and Tennyson.

More of Traquair's work is on view in the National Gallery of Scotland (*see* p.92).

Contemporary Art

Following the lead of its sister college in Glasgow, Edinburgh College of Art (*see* below) has placed itself firmly behind the development of new talent, through the work of inspirational curators such as Mel Gooding. When the Stills, Collective and Fruitmarket galleries happen to open their new shows all at once of a Friday evening, a walk around Cockburn Street and Market Street proves that Edinburgh is capable of generating a considerable buzz about modern art.

Most of Edinburgh's commercial galleries are concentrated in the Dundas Street area of the New Town, though **Inverleith House** in the grounds of the Royal Botanic Garden (*see* p.113) is also worth a visit.

As well as *The List*, the *Edinburgh Gallery Guide* has free monthly **listings**, and the Collective Gallery's free *Scotland and Beyond*, published every two months, is available at most galleries. On the Internet, try *www.edinburgh-galleries.co.uk*.

Collective Gallery, *22–28 Cockburn St*, *t (0131) 220 1260*. Up-and-coming artists.

Doggerfisher, *11 Gayfield Square*, *t (0131) 558 7110*. Upcoming and outgoing British and European artists.

Dom, *8 Advocate's Close*, *t (0131) 225 9271*, *w www.dom-arts.com*. An ancient building hosting a changing roster of eclectic exhibitions by international artists and providing a platform for a new wave of primitivists.

Edinburgh College of Art, *Lauriston Place*, *t (0131) 221 6032*. Temporary exhibitions by students and visiting artists in the Old Town.

Edinburgh Printmakers, *23 Union St*, *t (0131) 557 2479*, *w www.edinburgh-printmakers.co.uk*. A good place to buy affordable prints, many by famous names.

Eye 2, *66 Cumberland St*, *t (0131) 558 9872*. The US and European arm of the Open Eye.

Fruitmarket Gallery, *45 Market St*, *t (0131) 225 2383*. A large, lively contemporary art space with a good café and bookshop.

Ingleby Gallery, *6 Carlton Terrace*, *t (0131) 556 4441*, *w www.inglebygallery.com*. Ground-breaking contemporary art for sale.

Finding Edinburgh's Art

City Art Centre, the City Council's collection, particularly strong on local topography, p.71.

Dean Gallery, world-renowned collection of Dada and Surrealist work, p.111.

National Gallery of Scotland, medieval and Renaissance masterpieces, Old Masters, and Impressionist and Scottish works, p.92.

Royal Scottish Academy, temporary exhibitions by Academicians and others, p.96.

Scottish National Gallery of Modern Art, the story after 1900, with increasing emphasis on contemporary Scottish art, p.110.

Scottish National Portrait Gallery, superb collection of painted Scots great and not so great, p.103.

Talbot Rice Gallery, Edinburgh University's impressive collection of Dutch Masters, plus exhibitions of contemporary art, p.88.

Merz Gallery, *87 Broughton St, t (0131) 558 8778*. A newish gallery injecting interesting contemporary art into Broughton.

Open Eye, *75–79 Cumberland St, t (0131) 557 1020, w www.openeyegallery.co.uk*. Contemporary British applied arts.

Patriothall Gallery, *The Wasp Studios, 48 Hamilton Place, t (0131) 225 1289*. Mainly shows artists who use its many studios.

Royal Fine Art Commission for Scotland, *Bakehouse Close, 146 Canongate, t (0131) 556 6699, w www.royfinartcomforsco.gov.uk*. Major Festival exhibitions plus smaller shows through the year, usually architectural.

Scottish Arts Club, *24 Rutland Square, t (0131) 229 1076/8157, w www.scotttishartsclub.co.uk*. Regular exhibitions by major contemporary artists in a private members' club.

Scottish Gallery, *16 Dundas St, t (0131) 558 1299*. A champion of Scottish painting and ceramics founded more than 150 years ago.

Sleeper, *6 Darnaway St, t (0131) 225 8444, w www.sleeper1.com*. Site-specific art space with mainly contemporary installations in an architect's office in the New Town.

Stills Gallery, *23 Cockburn St, t (0131) 622 6200, w www.stills.org*. An eclectic range of contemporary art spanning most media.

LITERATURE

Edinburgh has produced more than its fair share of famous writers. In 1508, one of the greatest of Scots poets, **William Dunbar**, became the first person to go on record with the comment that Edinburgh was a city with two faces. This duality, and the idea that there is a hidden side to the place, has informed much of the best literature associated with the capital. The most famous example, **Robert Louis Stevenson**'s *Dr Jekyll and Mr Hyde*, was written more than 400 years later, inspired by the nefarious activities of Deacon Brodie (*see* p.67), though half a century earlier **James Hogg**'s brilliant *Private Memoirs and Confessions of Justified Sinner* portrayed the evil that lurked in the heart of a good Calvinist.

The theme has recurred up to the present, most notably in **Irvine Welsh**'s portrait of the city's junkie culture in *Trainspotting*. Other contemporary writers to capitalize on the city's atmosphere of hidden menace are crime novelists **Ian Rankin** and **Christopher Brookmyre**, and racy fantasist **Iain Banks**.

The classic Scottish threesome, celebrated in the Writers' Museum (*see* p.66), consists of **Robert Burns**, **Sir Walter Scott** and **Robert Louis Stevenson**. Romantic lyricist Burns, lionized by high-society figures, was a frequent visitor to Edinburgh but is more closely associated with his native Ayrshire on the southwest coast. Stevenson loved and loathed his native city in equal measure, and left it to write his most famous works, though they all bear the stamp of his home town. Scott is little read these days, but his novels have inspired countless film and stage adaptations and his sensibility is alive and well in films such as *Braveheart*.

Other, less well-known poets and writers from Edinburgh deserve more recognition: **Allan Ramsay**, a poet and a wig-maker, founded the first circulating library in Britain and the first theatre in the city. His most famous poem is 'The Gentle Shepherd', but his 'Evergreen' and 'Tea-Table Miscellany' struck a new romantic note in 1724, paving the way for Burns and Scott. His statue, featuring his trademark bandage-like headgear is at the junction of Princes Street and The Mound, while you can still see his house, Goose Pie House, on Castlehill (*see* p.63).

Robert Fergusson, another beneficiary of Ramsay's influence, was born in 1750 in a close long since buried beneath North Bridge, and often enjoyed himself in a tavern now buried beneath South Bridge. The famous lines 'Reekie, farewell! I ne'er could part/ Wi' thee but wi' a dowy heart' bring his best-loved poem 'Auld Reekie' to a conclusion after painting a lively picture, written in robust Scots, of the city's daily life at the time. Sadly Fergusson himself was not so robust, falling down the stairs and in his delirium being incarcerated in the madhouse, where he died. Robert Burns described him as 'my elder brother in misfortune, by far my elder brother in the muse', and paid for his tombstone and epitaph in Canongate Kirkyard.

After Scotland's Union with England in 1707, Edinburgh experienced an extraordinary flowering of literary talent for the rest of the century. Among prominent figures were **David Hume** (*see* p.67), arguably the greatest British philosopher of all time, and his friend **Adam Smith** (*see* p.74), author of *The Wealth of Nations*. **James Boswell**, one of the most colourful and irrepressible of Edinburgh characters, was born into a well-to-do legal family but spurned the profession while he held out for a glamorous commission in the Guards in London. He relentlessly solicited the company of his elders and betters, most famously forming a close bond of friendship with Dr Johnson, and his *Life of Johnson* is acknowledged as being among

Literary Visitors

Many of the leading figures in English literature have been inspired by Edinburgh. The great Elizabethan poet, playwright and critic **Ben Jonson** walked to the city from London in 1618, at the age of 45. His greatest plays, *Volpone* and *Bartholomew Fair*, were already written, and he was on a generous pension as poet laureate and writer of masques in the court of King James I of England (VI of Scotland). After deciding to visit the land of his ancestors, he ended up staying for more than a year, despite pressing engagements in London, but only one line of his poem 'Edinborough' survives ('Edinborough – the heart of Scotland, Britaine's other eye...').

Daniel Defoe wrote his desert-island novel *Robinson Crusoe*, inspired by Alexander Selkirk of Largo, Fife, 20 years after making his name with *The True-born Englishman*, a scathing verse satire on xenophobia and the idea of pure Englishness. When his next satire landed him in prison, he was released on condition he went to Edinburgh to act as a spy for King William and later for Queen Anne, around the time of the signing of the Treaty of Union in 1707. Staying in the thick of things in Old Fishmarket Close (*see* p.70), he reported on the riots and cries of 'No Union, No Union' and 'English dogs'. Later he returned to the city briefly and edited the *Edinburgh Courant*, living in Moubray House (*see* p.72), the Royal Mile's oldest surviving house.

Percy Bysshe Shelley, the most radical of the young Romantic poets, honeymooned in Edinburgh after eloping with 16-year-old Harriet Westbrook in 1811. They were married illegally by the Reverend Joseph Robertson of Leith Wynd Chapel, at his house in Jack's Land on Canongate, where David Hume had also lived for a time, and for five weeks lodged on the ground and first floor of 60 George Street. Three years later, Shelley returned for two months with Mary Godwin and stayed at 36 Frederick Street, sorting out his debt problems; Harriet drowned herself in the Serpentine in Hyde Park.

Thomas De Quincey, author of the superb *Confessions of an Opium Eater*, may have written on a similar subject to Irvine Welsh but he didn't make quite as much money – after moving to Edinburgh in 1830 he frequently had to hide out in the debtor's sanctuary that surrounded Holyrood Abbey.

Edinburgh in Literature

From Sir Walter Scott to Ian Rankin and Irvine Welsh, Edinbugh has been home to many great writers, and has often featured on the pages of their novels.

Old Masters

Chambers, Robert, *Traditions of Edinburgh*, Chambers, 1824. Hugely entertaining stories of the Old Town told by one of its sons.

Cockburn, Henry, *Memorials of His Time*, Edinburgh, 1856. Witty, perceptive anecdotes of Edinburgh life in the late 18th century.

Defoe, Daniel, *A Tour Through the Whole Island of Great Britain*, Penguin, 1726. Includes a creative and far from impartial account of the city in the early 18th century.

Hogg, James, *The Private Memoirs and Confessions of a Justified Sinner*, OUP, 1824. Partly set in early 18th-century Edinburgh, about a Calvinist's brushes with Satan.

Scott, Walter, *The Heart of Midlothian*, 1830. Sir Walter's Edinburgh novel.

Smollett, Tobias, *Humphrey Clinker*, Penguin, 1771. Rollicking romp around early 18th-century Edinburgh and London.

Stevenson, Robert Louis, *Edinburgh*, 1879; *Catriona*, 1893; *Treasure Island*, 1883; *Dr Jekyll and Mr Hyde*, and *Kidnapped*, 1886. The central figure in *Dr Jekyll and Mr Hyde* was said to have been inspired by the prominent Edinburgh figure Deacon Brodie (*see* p.67).

Contemporary Writers

Banks, Iain, *Complicity*, Abacus, 1993. Gripping yarn about an Edinburgh journalist caught up in the paranoid delusions of a serial killer.

Boyd, William, *The New Confessions*, Penguin, 1987. An Edinburgh man hilariously reminisces on his extraordinary career.

Brookmyre, Christopher, *Quite Ugly One Morning*, Abacus, 1996. Violent, sharply written detective story set in the city today.

Gray, Alasdair, *Lanark*, Canongate, 1981. Bewildering, rococo novel that swings across Scotland's central belt.

Hird, Laura, *Nail and other Stories*, Canongate, 1997. Painfully astute short stories on the brutalities of everyday life in Edinburgh.

Linklater, Eric, *Edinburgh*, London, 1960; *Magnus Merriman*, Canongate, 1990. A city portrait and a comic novel satirizing the literati of the 1930s Scottish renaissance.

MacCaig, Norman, *Old Maps and New – Selected Poems*, Hogarth Press, 1978. Poems by Edinburgh's finest 20th-century lyric poet.

MacDiarmid, Hugh, *Scottish Eccentrics*, Carcanet, 1936. Prose essays on colourful Scots by the great 20th-century poet.

Meek, James, *McFarlane Boils the Sea*, Polygon, 1989. A surreal day in the life of Laura McFarlane in 1980s Edinburgh.

Rankin, Ian, *Hide and Seek*, Orion, 1997. Detective thriller set in the city by its best-selling crime writer.

Spark, Muriel, *The Prime of Miss Jean Brodie*, Penguin, 1961. Passion and fascism in the '30s.

Warner, Alan, *The Sopranos*, Jonathan Cape, 1998. Snappy novel about a teenage girl choir hitting town.

Welsh, Irvine, *Trainspotting*, Secker & Warburg, 1993. Cult Edinburgh drug-life novel that rapidly became a hit play and film.

---

the greatest of biographies, combining vividly reported conversation with canny sideswipes at its venerable subject.

It was a real coup when Boswell persuaded the great Scot-baiter – 'Ursa Major' as he was affectionately known – to travel to Scotland and undertake a tour of the wild Hebrides with him in 1773. 'I smell you in the dark' were Johnson's first words to Bozzy when the pair met on the Royal Mile. Welcoming him to his house in James Court, Boswell introduced the doctor to as many of his eminent acquaintants as he dared, with the notable exception of the Anglophobe atheist David Hume, and made special provision in his will for his young daughter because she had not been frightened by Johnson's terrible appearance. Boswell's wife was not so sanguine, being glad to see the back of the formidable but slovenly lexicographer when the pair took off on their extraordinary trip around the remote Highlands and Islands described in Boswell's *Journal of a Tour to the Hebrides* in 1785.

Hugh McDiarmid (1892–1978)

The greatest Scots poet of the 20th century was born Christopher Murray Grieve in Langholm in the Borders, and trained to be a teacher at Broughton High School in Edinburgh. He moved to Biggar in 1951 but spent a fair amount of time in the city, meeting his friends in one of three bars along Rose Street, depending on the seriousness of the occasion: the Café Royal (see p.175), the Abbotsford (see p.175) and Milne's Bar (see p.176), in descending order of gravitas.

In 1938 McDiarmid was expelled from the Communist Party for helping to found the Scottish National Party. Many of his best poems are in the purpose-built Scots dialect he invented to reinvigorate the language, such as his poem 'A Drunk Man Looks at the Thistle' (1926), which ranks with T. S. Eliot's 'The Wasteland' in scope and intensity.

More recently, the world has Edinburgh to thank for **Arthur Conan Doyle**, **Hugh McDiarmid** (see above) and **Muriel Spark** (see below). Conan Doyle, the creator of Sherlock Holmes, was born at 11 Picardy Place (which no longer exists) in 1859, and studied medicine in the city. His hawk-eyed detective was modelled on his tutor there, Dr Joseph Bell.

Muriel Spark (1918–)

Born in Edinburgh, Muriel Spark attended James Gillespie's School for Girls in Bruntsfield and later commented that she could always spot other former pupils from their use of the semi-colon, and that the city's most characteristic utterance is 'nevertheless' said with pursed lips and rhyming with 'lace'. In the 1950s she converted to Catholicism 'on the nevertheless principle'.

Her most brilliant creation has been Miss Jean Brodie, a spirited but misguided schoolteacher with a passion for art and a deeply suspect fancy for Mussolini. She was brought to cinematic life in an Oscar-winning performance by Maggie Smith. Both book and film draw an unsettling portrait of buttoned-up Edinburgh in the 1930s.

ARCHITECTURE

Edinburgh's setting is spectacular, rising on the back of volcanic hills in view of the sea. No modern city planner would choose this site, which is why so many modern cities are lifeless: the improbable geography and geology of Edinburgh afford it a majesty and a mystery few cities can begin to match.

Described in tourist brochures as the 'Athens of the North' (thanks to its hills and its many impressive Greek Revival buildings), it is no such thing. Unlike Athens, the setting and architecture of Edinburgh can be dark and brooding; and the buildings of the Old Town, with their vertiginous sandstone walls, gables and turrets, are like something from Mervyn Peake's *Gormenghast* trilogy. Auld Reekie is a city of the imagination; on a wretched, grey winter's day, when the damp and cold gnaw through the thickest tweeds, it can seem quite frightening.

And yet, spread out like some wondrous carpet less than 2 miles long and less than 1 mile wide, across the valley of what is now Princes Street Gardens (and what was the Nor'Loch), is the almost impossibly handsome New Town, a creation of the Age of Reason and showcase of Georgian architecture. The great American architectural historian Henry Russell-Hitchcock described it as 'the most extensive example of a Romantic Classical city in the world'.

Edinburgh, then, in terms of architecture and urban planning, is two cities, zipped together along Princes Street, the main east–west axis that every visitor will cross many times during their stay. Of course Edinburgh, like any thriving city, is also adorned and debased by modern buildings that interrupt the superficially seamless flow of the essentially 16th- and 17th-century stone architecture of the Old Town and the 18th- and 19th-century architecture of the New Town. It is also laced and lanced by suburbs, some picturesque, others banal, but never as grim as those that mar the entrances to most grand old cities. Its special virtue, aside from its operatic setting and the sheer quality of its architecture, is the fact that although it has several faces – darkness, reason and romanticism among them – this complex city does appear to hang together because of the magnificent and largely controlled use of local building materials.

Yes, there are some unforgivable concrete horrors (*see* below), yet, from the castle to the brand new Museum of Scotland, most of Edinburgh's buildings appear to owe as much to the skill of the stonemason as they do to the architect. You will find little brickwork in Edinburgh and not much, thankfully, in the way of garish post-modern architectural gimmickry in nursery colours. Instead, the city is composed, almost universally, of a silvery grey sandstone. When cleaned, this reveals, sadly, an unexpected rainbow of colours, from pinkish grey to dusty brown, that spoils the overall composition of the streets; over time, the local stonework blends into a uniform shade.

For the most part, too, Edinburgh is free from the sort of tweedy, herringbone brick pavements that have spoilt so many British town centres over the past 20 years; there is much pleasure to be had striding along grand old Edinburgh or Arbroath stone pavements, looking up at hardy, handsome, rainwashed grey stone buildings capped with lofty stone chimneys and shining slate roofs. And, if you are made of sturdy stuff, the city can look even better in the rain, or with its proud buildings braving it through autumn mists and winter snows.

Very Old Edinburgh

If you are a Goth by nature, then Edinburgh isn't really for you. There is a lively crinkle-crankle of 19th-century Gothic Revival buildings ranging from the gimcrack to the divine, but a paucity of medieval work and even less before that. If you must have a dose of Romanesque, then make for **St Margaret's Chapel** (not earlier than *c.* 1110; *see* p.62), occupying the topmost part of the unmissable Castle Rock.

As for Gothic, there's the impressive ruin of **Holyrood Abbey** (*see* p.76), and the **High Kirk of St Giles** (*see* p.67), a medieval jewel box redressed, unnoticed by most visitors, in what is effectively an 18th-century Gothic frock – the exterior walls – and with a heavily restored Victorian interior. Still, it looks all of a piece – unlike most British medieval cathedrals – even though it dates from the 12th century and incorporates major work from as late as 1910–11; and the graceful stone lantern that crowns its stubby tower is a late-medieval gem. Inside, don't miss the glorious late-medieval choir and wonderfully over-the-top Thistle Chapel by Sir Robert Lorimer (1910–11). If still in need of crockets and pinnacles, brave the suburb of **Corstorphine** (*see* p.122) where there is the cranky old parish church, added to and rebuilt many times since the 15th century. Otherwise, head for Salisbury or Cologne; you'll have more luck there.

Protestant Style

Now we're in business. The Reformation of 1560 redefined Edinburgh, its way of life and, ultimately, the way it looked, though the first 100% Protestant buildings, such as the rather bleak, late-flowering Gothic church of **Greyfriars** (1602–20; *see* p.83), show that it took architects and their clients some while to find a new style. The romantic pile of the **Tron Kirk** (*see* p.71) is a fine mix of Dutch, English and Italian styles bodged together happily; begun in the 17th century, it was rebuilt and added to many times.

Churches aside, this was the period during which the Old Town took on its particular character. The **Royal Mile**, running from the castle to the Palace of Holyroodhouse, has an exceptional array of fine 16th- and 17th-century townhouses: it would be invidious to pick one out in preference – it's the overall composition that counts (*see* p.58).

Although continuously built up by 1500, the Royal Mile was largely rebuilt after the sack of Edinburgh by the English under the Earl of Hertford in 1544. Fear of fire in the densely packed street led to the obligatory use of tiled or slate roofs on properties after 1621, and from 1674 all buildings had to be stonefronted. Many parts of the Palace of Holyroodhouse and the castle were rebuilt at this time, and Renaissance styling begins to appear in higgledy-piggledy ways – rarely artistically correct, but immense fun.

Buildings not to miss include **George Heriot's School** (*see* p.83); the plan is apparently based on a palazzo depicted in Serlio's seventh book of architecture (*c.* 1550), but the composition looks, happily, like a cross between Audley End in Essex and a Scottish baronial castle.

Prestonfield House, now a hotel (*see* p.155), was built for Sir James Dick, Lord Provost of Edinburgh, *c.* 1685–89 and represents a breakaway from traditional fortified houses to something more Dutch and domestic, with wayward Italian Mannerist interiors to boot. Who could resist the Leather Room, Dick's original bedchamber? (Before you get carried away, the red leather panelling is an exotic riot of snakes, shells, insects and cherubs.)

Rome Comes to Edinburgh

Crossing Princes Street Gardens from dark and claustrophobic Auld Reekie, you enter another world – that of the light, reasonable, horizontally planned **New Town**. These streets and squares, their gallant terraces and chaste, if noble, churches are, very possibly, the reason we can't help seeing Edinburgh as a fundamentally genteel city:

Sir Patrick Geddes (1854–1932)

The man who did so much to conserve the Old Town was initially a lecturer in zoology at the University. A property restorer and renovator, he lived in James Court and then in Ramsay Lodge, buying the Outlook Tower in 1892, where he opened the world's first environmental museum. In 1911 he mounted a landmark exhibition on cities and town planning, placing the emphasis firmly on the importance of community.

correct, well-mannered and more than a little superior to Glasgow and London, if not Paris and Rome.

The first quarter of the New Town was laid out from 1767, with gloriously uniform streets (although George Street, the central axis, is 100ft wide and the others only 80ft). What matters most here is not the individual buildings (they are all good) but the overall composition and the relationship of this Georgian streetscape to the dramatic architectural cliffs of the Old Town, framed beyond its regimented cornices and window lines. You'll feel very grand here even if you're down to your last wee bawbie.

The architect James Craig based his grid-iron plan on several sources – very probably the town of Richelieu in France, Inigo Jones's Covent Garden in London, and the planned Scottish town of Inverary in Argyll (1747). If you must single out the monuments, there's the church of **St Andrew's and St George's**, designed by Major Andrew Frazer (*see* p.101). The work of a military engineer, it has an interesting elliptical plan, a bold Corinthian portico that almost burrows into the pavement and a tall if not very graceful steeple.

The **Assembly Rooms and Music Hall** by John Henderson (*see* p.101) is an essay in Roman Classicism that was thought inelegant at the time but looks good enough today. **Old Register House** on Princes Street, designed by Robert Adam (*see* p.98), is a grandly austere *palazzo* built as a government office along the lines of Somerset House in London, and remarkably chaste and simple for an architect best known for his delicate and beautiful decorative touches.

Charlotte Square, which was also designed by Robert Adam, is a magnificent set piece and forms the highlight of the first New Town development (*see* p.93): the terrace on its northern side (Nos.1–11) is about as Georgian as architecture gets; the interior of No.1 is really quite superb. On the west side of the square is the bravura **West Register House**, originally St George's Church, designed by Robert Reid (*see* p.102). The mighty scale of the building topped with a lofty, copper-clad dome makes it look like an architectural refugee (or present) from St Petersburg.

Beyond the New Town confines are other important Georgian buildings, including the **City Chambers**, based on a design by John Adam (*see* p.70); the **Old Quad** at the Old College of the University of Edinburgh, by Robert Adam (*see* p.88); and **Parliament Square** by Robert Reid (*see* p.67). There are also many country houses on the city's outskirts. If you're a Georgian, it's as if Edinburgh was designed specially for you.

The 'Athens of the North'

Edinburgh has some of the finest Grecian buildings to be found anywhere. The joy for Hellenophiles is that the Greek Revival lasted here way after it had given way to sanctimonious Gothic south of the border and in the rest of Europe, so you are spoilt for choice. Gawp and give praise to these at least:

The **Royal High School** by Thomas Hamilton (*see* p.98) is a magnificent and magnificently sited Doric temple-style design that was a popular candidate as home for the new Scottish Parliament. The **Royal Scottish Academy** on The Mound, designed by William Playfair (*see* p.88), is a superb Doric temple that glows almost numinously at sunset. John Watson's School, Belford Road (now the **Dean Gallery**; *see* p.111), by William Burn was a suitably strict and muscular Doric design in which to educate unruly Scots boys.

Playfair's **Royal College of Surgeons** (*see* p.88) is an Ionic temple that looks as if it's pining for Greece. **St Bernard's Crescent** by James Milne (*see* p.113) is an impressive arc of late New Town housing. Last but not least, the **National Monument** on Calton Hill, by William Playfair and C. R. Cockerell (*see* p.99), is the summit of Greek Revival ambitions, the beginning (but nowhere near the end) of a re-creation of the Parthenon overlooking – wait for it – the Athens of the North. A monument to the fallen of the Napoleonic Wars, it was to have been a church.

Finding Edinburgh's Architecture

Very old Edinburgh: Corstorphine parish church, p.122; High Kirk of St Giles, p.67; Holyrood Abbey, p.76; St Margaret's Chapel, p.62.

Protestant style: Greyfriars Kirk, p.83; Palace of Holyroodhouse, p.75; townhouses of the Royal Mile, p.58; Tron Kirk, p.71.

Town planning: New Town, p.93.

Robert Adam: Charlotte Square, p.102; Old Quad at the Old College, p.88; Old Register House, p.98.

Robert Reid: Parliament Square, p.67; West Register House, p.102.

Doric designs: Dean Galley (formerly John Watson's School), p.111; Royal High School, p.98.

William Playfair: National Monument, p.99; Royal College of Surgeons, p.88; Royal Scottish Academy, p.88.

Victorian: Royal Museum, p.84; St Mary's Episcopal Cathedral, p.106.

Modern: Fruitmarket Gallery, p.28; Museum of Scotland, p.85; New Scottish Parliament, p.76; Playfair Project, p.96.

Anything Goes: Victorian to Modern

From the middle of the 19th century, Edinburgh was home to any number of architectural styles: Imperial Roman, demotic Greek, Gothic and free styles ranging from the highly romantic to the absolutely barking, but nearly all built sturdily in that local grey sandstone that has a tendency to keep the wildest building in order.

Goths will enjoy **St Mary's Episcopal Cathedral**, designed by George Gilbert Scott (*see* p.106). This triple-spired ecclesiastical dragon raises its elongated heads above the chaste Georgian and Italianate streets that pen it into its city site. **Fettes College**, by David Bryce (1864–70), is an unsurpassed Victorian shocker, a nightmare French Gothic-meets-Scottish Baronial monstrosity: hugely picturesque, vastly overscaled, utterly crackers and not to be missed.

Other essential viewing includes the **Royal Museum**, Chambers Street, designed by Francis Fowke et al (*see* p.84) and an intriguing light and spidery iron structure inside a plodding civic palace. More soberly, there are many decent **tenement blocks** dating from the 1880s; you will bump into them even when you're not trying.

Modern

The ungainly and ill-mannered **St James Shopping Centre** blights central Edinburgh as a Black Sabbath guitar solo might, inserted into a Beethoven piano sonata. (Sorry if this is unfair to Black Sabbath.) It's a classic example of how insensitive modern architecture can undermine the integrity of a traditional city, and it certainly gave modern architecture a bad name in Edinburgh.

Thankfully, there are several reasonably good modern buildings in Edinburgh (none a masterpiece) that go some way towards redeeming the sin of St James. The **University of Edinburgh Library** on George Square, designed by Basil Spence, Glover & Ferguson is a tolerable effort (in effect six gigantic concrete bookshelves), but was part of a concerted effort by the university, which really should have known better, to destroy the grace of George Square (*see* p.87). Sad.

One 20th-century building that adds to the city's magical skyline is **St Andrew's House** on Regent Road, designed by Thomas S. Tait. Part of the Scottish Office, this is a monumental combination of modern movement design, traditional materials and sense of place. Unlike many modern buildings in Edinburgh, it looks as if it has asked older buildings if it can join them, rather than barging its way in.

The complex and rather mind-blowing new **Museum of Scotland** is also definitely worth seeing (*see* p.85). Designed by Benson & Forsyth, this stone-clad collage of a building weaves and waves its way through the centre of the city and features an extraordinary variety of galleries, from the tiny to the awesome. The view from the roof is inspirational. Otherwise, there's the likeable **Fruitmarket Gallery** conversion, by local architect Richard Murphy, and the drum-like **Conference Centre** – one of the least ostentatious of recent buildings by the English post-modernist Terry Farrell.

Last, and certainly not least, is the **New Scottish Parliament** (*see* p.76). Designed by the Catalan architects Enrico and Benedetta Miralles, this composition of what should prove to be subtle interlocking fragments (based on the shape and memory of upturned boats on Scottish shores; don't ask why) will be as curious as anything the Victorians did, and perhaps as dark and brooding in its own way as the traditional architecture of Auld Reekie.

Jonathan Glancey

Edinburgh's Festivals

Edinburgh has become famous for its two great parties, in August and at the New Year. The annual summer Edinburgh Festival is a staggering convocation of nascent and professional performance talent, while Edinburgh's Hogmanay night, the focus for Scotland's traditionally riotous and convivial welcome to Ne'er Day, was voted second only to Sydney's at the Millennium.

It's hardly surprising that Edinburgh now styles itself a festival city year round. Okay, so things are quieter between the big events, but there are almost sure to be special events of one kind or another whenever you visit. Highlights include the International Science Festival; the International Children's Festival; the Jazz and Blues Festival; and the Scottish International Storytelling Festival.

THE EDINBURGH FESTIVAL

w *www.edinburgh-festivals.com.*

Every year, in the first week of August, the Athens of the North loses its marbles. The city has proved itself well suited to coping with the formidable explosion of performing talent that arrives on its doorstep: it's easy for audiences to find their way around; there is a multitude of performance spaces, from grand theatres and church halls to mountaintops and subterranean vaults; and the population is enlightened enough to tolerate, even welcome, hordes of hungry punters and half-crazed performers.

The Festival was born in the baking hot summer of 1947, a cultural manifestation of peace in Europe. Opera impresario Rudolf Bing (*see* box) organized various events, including the reunion of Jewish conductor Bruno Walter with the Vienna Philharmonic. Even then this was not just one festival – eight uninvited theatre companies also arrived, starting what became known as the Fringe. Today, though it may not be immediately obvious, the mayhem divides up into at least five distinct festivals.

Rudolf Bing (1902–97)

The man behind the idea for the Edinburgh Festival was an Austrian opera impresario who had been manager of Glyndebourne Opera prior to the Second World War and who became a British citizen in 1946. Three years after inaugurating the Edinburgh Festival with the symbolic reunion of Jewish conductor Bruno Walter and the Vienna Philharmonic Orchestra, Bing was made General Manager of the New York's Metropolitan Opera, a post that he fulfilled with flair until 1972. You can read about his life in his memoir *Five Thousand Nights at the Opera.*

International Festival

The Hub, Castlehill, **t** *(0131) 473 2000,* **f** *(0131) 473 2002,* **w** *www.eif.co.uk.* **Dates** *mid-Aug.*

This, the granddaddy of them all, has maintained its highbrow programme of performances by the world's finest artists. True to its operatic roots, music and singing usually feature strongly, and in recent years there has also been an interesting line-up of theatre based on great texts, and European dance and ballet. A recent development has been the instituting of late-night concerts at the Usher Hall, giving people a chance to see top-flight musicians for a fiver – a significant step towards popularizing classical music that everyone hopes will become a fixture.

The main venue is the modern Festival Theatre on Nicolson Street; other major venues are the Usher Hall, the King's, Lyceum and Playhouse theatres, and the Reid Hall, St Cecilia's Hall and Queen's Hall. The Festival's HQ, The Hub, is in the old Highland Tolbooth Kirk at the top of the Royal Mile. This is the place to book tickets, pick up programmes, see showcase performances and enjoy being at the centre of things over coffee or a meal.

The last week of the festival, when many of the fringe companies have gone home, is often much less hectic and more civilized. The Fireworks Concert in Princes Street Gardens (*see* p.41) brings the festival to its enormously popular climax.

Fringe Festival

Fringe Office, 180 High St, t (0131) 226 5257, centralized booking and ticket line t (0131) 220 4349, w www.edfringe.com. Dates 3wks in Aug.

There's so much going on in the city during August that it can ruffle the feathers of even the most sanguine culture vulture. The famous and by no means idle boast of the Fringe is that it is the largest festival of live performing arts in the world. In recent years it has come to be dominated by stand-up comedy, but theatre, dance, music and mime also vie for attention.

It's almost impossible to know what will really be worth seeing. *The Scotsman* drafts in legions of battle-hardened reviewers to cover the event, but by the time you've read all their opinions, you've either missed it or it's sold out. The answer is to keep a cool head and an ear to the ground. Gossip is the most reliable guide, as bar-stool critics turn their assessment of a show into an art form in itself.

The best thing about the Fringe is that anyone with the time, money and energy can join in. However, the core of the Festival has come to be dominated by the 'megavenues': the Assembly Rooms, the Pleasance and the Gilded Balloon (closed at the time of writing after damage in the Cowgate fire). They have a centralized booking system (*see* above), and their programmes are usually packed with surefire comedy hits.

The best place to find good theatre is still the Traverse (*see* p.181), which has gone from strength to strength since moving to its purpose-built complex in Cambridge Street. Along with the Assembly Rooms, the theatre's own mini-festival continues through the first week of September.

It's also worth looking out for site-specific fringe shows in places such as the Royal Botanic Garden and the city's underground streets. On one Sunday in the month, 'Fringe Sunday', performers gather in The Meadows to put on highlights from their shows. If the sun shines it makes for an excellent family day out, and it's just possible you'll spot something you'd like to see in its entirety.

With more than 1,500 shows taking place in hundreds of venues, you're spoilt for choice. The trick is learning to say no. A few carefully chosen and adventurous excursions are much more likely to be memorable than wearing out your wallet by cramming in as many shows as possible. Most venues stock copies of the *Daily Diary*, an invaluable information sheet for planning the day. *The List* magazine has also become expert at delivering previews, highlights and reviews.

Military Tattoo

Tattoo Office, 32 Market St, t (0131) 225 1188, w www.edintattoo.co.uk. Dates first 3wks Aug.

The Castle Esplanade is the extraordinary setting for this annual display of bagpipers, marching bands, acrobats and cheerleaders. If you can't get a ticket, listen from the top of Princes Street Gardens.

International Book Festival

Scottish Book Centre, 137 Dundee St, t (0131) 228 5444, w www.edbookfest.co.uk. Dates 2wks in Aug.

The world's biggest book festival, with debates, readings, lectures and workshops.

International Film Festival

Filmhouse, 88 Lothian Rd, t (0131) 221 8715, w www.edfilmfest.org.uk. Dates 2wks in mid-Aug.

Though based at the Filmhouse, the Film Festival also occupies various other venues. It has a reputation on the international circuit for inspired programming, as well as for its support for independent and Scottish films.

Television Festival

Information t (020) 7430 1333, w www.geift. co.uk. Dates 3 days in late Aug.

The *Guardian*'s international television festival is largely an insiders' event.

HOGMANAY

Programme from Hogmanay Box Office, The Hub (see p.65) from Nov, w www. edinburghshogmanay.org. Date Dec 31.

The Scots have always seen in the New Year in style. Traditionally 'the Daft Days' begin at Christmas and end on January 6, with Hogmanay (New Year's Eve) and Ne'er Day (New Year's Day) slap bang in the middle. The old habit of 'first-footing', when folk nipped in and out of each other's houses with a bottle of whisky and a lump of coal as midnight struck, has declined, but its convivial spirit survives. Indeed, the habit has been enshrined in the 'First-Foot Club' – often the only way for visitors to get tickets to the Royal Bank Street Party. Membership, available online or from The Hub, is £15 and offers various benefits, as well as admission.

In Edinburgh, until 1996, everyone gathered at Tron Kirk to wait for the clock's inaudible chimes – the cue to kiss as politely or as passionately as they cared. Sadly, bottles would inevitably end up in the air, while in 1996 the crush at the bottom of The Mound was so great that people nearly suffocated. As a result, the celebrations are now a well-managed, highly packaged six-day event.

The 150,000 tickets for the night of New Year's Eve are free but have to be booked well in advance. At about 7pm on December 31, checkpoints go up on streets around an 'exclusion zone' that usually includes George Street, Princes Street and its gardens, Waterloo Place, the Castle and the High Street. Ticket-holders are given an adhesive armband that allows re-entry into the zone.

The build-up to the big moment is formidable: all off-licences in the city are besieged until they close at around 8pm; pubs outside the zone usually close resignedly at around 10pm, and those inside are full to bursting. Waterloo Place is converted into a fairground for the four days leading up to Hogmanay, and a torchlight procession up Calton Hill starts the festivities on December 28. At least four large sound stages feature a range of world, Scottish and folk music, some cabaret-cum-street entertainment and appearances by washed-up 1980s popstars.

There are also extra ticket-only events around the city, including a smart ball in the Assembly Rooms and an alternative ceilidh, or knees-up, at the Traverse Theatre. The Tron still witnesses emotional but somewhat less dangerous scenes on the stroke of midnight. Events begin to wind down around 1.30am.

Before the City Council encouraged shops, restaurants and pubs to open on Ne'er Day itself, the place was a ghost town on the first day of the year. Now the festival continues, with concerts (often free), open galleries and an ice rink in Princes Street Gardens.

OTHER FESTIVALS

Edinburgh's one-time reputation as an austere place no longer holds true, and outside the two main celebrations the rest of the city's calendar is punctuated by smaller festivals dedicated to everything from science to storytelling.

January

Turner Watercolours
National Gallery of Scotland (see p.92). Dates throughout Jan.

The only chance in the year to view these exquisite paintings.

Burns Night
Throughout the city. Date Jan 25.

The Bard's birthday is generally celebrated by private gatherings during which a Burns supper of haggis, neeps and tatties (swede and potato) is consumed.

April

Ceilidh Culture Festival
Information: t (0131) 243 1442, w www. ceilidhculture.co.uk.

A new festival of traditional arts, including folk music, at various venues around the city.

International Science Festival

t (0131) 220 1882, w www.sciencefestival. co.uk. Dates 2wks in mid-April.

Shows, workshops, exhibitions, talks and tours for adults and kids in various venues.

Beltane

Beltane Fire Society, 19 Leven St, t (0131) 228 5353, w www.beltane.org. Date April 30.

Calton Hill is the scene of fertility and seasonal rites and torchlight processions.

Gay Film Festival

Filmhouse, 88 Lothian Rd, t (0131) 228 2688. Dates April/May.

A celebration of global gay cinema selected from the London Gay Film Festival on tour.

May

Scottish International Children's Festival

See p.198.

June

Caledonian Beer Festival

Caledonian Brewery, 42 Slateford Rd, t (0131) 337 1286, w www.caledonian-brewery.co.uk. Date usually 1st weekend in June.

A three-day celebration of beers and ales.

Royal Highland Show

Royal Highland Centre, Ingliston, t (0131) 335 6200.

Livestock, showjumping, crafts and so on.

Pride Scotland

The Meadows, t (0131) 556 8822. Date late June.

This gay and lesbian festival takes place in Edinburgh or Glasgow on alternate years and will next be held in Edinburgh in 2004.

July

Edinburgh International Jazz and Blues Festival

Information: Assembly Direct, 89 Giles St, t (0131) 467 5200, w www.jazzmusic.co.uk. Dates late July–early Aug.

The longest-running jazz festival in the UK usually attracts about 50,000 people. Concert halls, theatres, clubs and pubs feature all styles of jazz from international artistes, and there are open-air events too.

August

The Edinburgh Festival

See p.38.

West End Craft and Design Fair

St John's Church, Princes St, t (0131) 229 7565, w www.3d2d.co.uk. Date 3wks in Aug.

Contemporary Scottish craftwork for sale in the church grounds.

September

Fireworks Concert

Princes St Gardens, t (0131) 473 2001. Date last wk of International Festival (see p.38).

Tickets for bandstand seats sell out early, but good views of the spectacular display can be had from North Bridge, Calton Hill and even the hills of Fife.

Edinburgh Mela

Pilrig Park, Leith, t (0131) 473 3800. Date 1st wk in Sept.

A free, community-led South Asian festival, with floats and festivities, dancers and musicians, and more takeaway curries than you can shake a popadom at.

Doors Open Day

Information: Cockburn Association, Trunk's Close, 55 High St, t (0131) 557 8686/9387, w www.cockburnassociation.org.uk. Dates last weekend in Sept.

An opportunity to visit many of the city's buildings not usually open to the public, including the Christie Miller Mausoleum.

October

Sam'hain

Beltane Fire Society, 19 Leven St, t (0131) 228 5353, w www.beltane.org. Date Oct 31 (Halloween).

An extension of Beltane (*see* p.41), this is another excuse to gather on Calton Hill and enjoy displays of fire-eating, fireworks, dressing up and seeing out the old season in style.

November

Scottish International Storytelling Festival

Scottish Storytelling Centre, 43–45 High St, t (0131) 557 5724, w www.storytellingcentre. org.uk. Dates end Oct–early Nov.

Storytelling events for kids and adults across Edinburgh, the Lothians, Fife and the Borders.

December

Hogmanay

See p.40.

OUTSIDE THE CITY

Glasgow

For details of all events, contact the local tourist board (*t (0141) 204 4400*).

Celtic Connections

Dates Jan and Feb.

Musicians from the Celtic-speaking world descend on Glasgow for a celebration of traditional music at the Royal Concert Hall.

RSNO Proms

Dates 2wks in June.

Concerts by the Royal Scottish National Orchestra in the Royal Concert Hall.

Glasgow International Jazz Festival

Dates June and July.

Folk music and jazz indoors and out by groups from all over the world.

World Pipe Band Championships

Dates mid-Aug.

A stirring gathering on Glasgow Green of massed pipe bands and lone pipers from all over the world.

St Andrews

For details of all events, contact the local tourist board (*t (01334) 472021*).

Kate Kennedy Pageant

Dates mid-April.

A university rag held since 1849 in honour of the one-time niece of the local archbishop, or as a primitive spring welcome ceremony.

Annual Golf Week

Dates late April.

A promotional festival, with tournaments on each of St Andrew's five courses.

Highland Games

Dates late July.

Caber-tossing, rockthrowing, Scottish dancing and other kilted carry-ons on the North Haugh.

Lammas Fair

Dates Aug.

Scotland's oldest surviving medieval market, with stalls and booths in the streets. The colourful carnival lasts for two days.

Dunhill Nations Cup Golf

Dates late Sept–early Oct.

A pro-am championship friendly tournament played over 'The Old' course and at King's Barn.

St Andrew's Day

Date Nov 30.

Scotland's National Day, with bands, dances and fireworks. A week of celebrations takes place all over town during the run up.

Stirling

For further details, contact the local tourist board (*t (01786) 475019*).

Tartan Festival Fortnight

Dates July.

A celebration of all things Scottish, with dancing, ceilidhs, concerts, buskers, guided walks, medieval street stalls and people dressed in period costume.

Travel

GETTING THERE

By Air

There are direct flights from England and the Continent, but travellers from **North America** have to change at London or Amsterdam.

Within the UK

There are flights to Edinburgh from all **London** airports. Main airlines include:

Aer Lingus, t 0845 084 4444.
Air France, t 0845 084 5111.
British Airways, t 0845 773377.
British Midland, t 0870 607 0555.
KLM UK, t 0870 507 4074.
Lufthansa, t 0845 773 7747.

Discount Fares

Some of the best bargains are posted on the **Internet** (*see* box). See also the London *Evening Standard*, the Sunday papers or the back pages of London listings mag *Time Out*. The **Air Travel Advisory Board** (*t* (020) 7636 5000) lists travel agents offering good deals.

Student and Youth Travel

These agencies have branches in most UK cities or on university campuses:

STA Travel, t 0870 1 600 599, **w** *www.statravel.co.uk*.
Trailfinders, t (020) 7938 3939/7937 1234, **w** *www.trailfinders.com*.

No-frills Airlines

Low-cost carriers such as Ryanair and easyJet can offer great prices if you book well in advance (usually 2 months at peak times); fares booked last minute are not much cheaper than those of the major carriers. A discount is usually offered if you book on the Internet. Tickets have various conditions attached – for example whether you can get a refund or whether the date of the flight can be changed. All services may be less frequent in the winter.

At the time of writing, **Bmibaby** (*t* 0870 607 0555, **w** *www.flybmi.com*) had flights between Edinburgh and Cardiff, and Edinburgh and East Midlands; **easyJet** (*t* 0870 600 0000, **w** *www.easyjet.com*) offered flights between Edinburgh and Belfast International, Bristol, East Midlands, London Gatwick, London Luton and London Stansted; and **Ryanair** (*t* 0871 246 0000, **w** *www.ryanair.com*) had London Stansted and Bournemouth flights to and from Glasgow Prestwick (*see* p.45, 'Arrival').

From North America and Canada

There are no direct flights to Edinburgh. You can fly directly to **Glasgow Prestwick**, but it generally works out cheaper to fly to London and take a train or flight to Edinburgh. Flights from New York to Glasgow take about 6 hours, from LA it's 10; other cities linked to Glasgow include Boston, Chicago, Denver, Las Vegas, New Orleans, San Francisco, Seattle, Toronto, Vancouver and Washington.

Flights on the Internet

The best place to start looking for flights is the Internet – just about everyone has a site where you can compare prices (*see* below for examples), and booking online usually confers a 10–20% discount.

In the UK and Ireland

w *www.cheapflights.com*
w *www.ebookers.com*
w *www.flightcentre.co.uk*
w *www.lastminute.com*
w *www.skydeals.co.uk*
w *www.sky-tours.co.uk*
w *www.travelocity.com*
w *www.travelselect.com*

In the USA

w *www.air-fare.com*
w *www.airhitch.org*
w *www.expedia.com*
w *www.flights.com*
w *www.orbitz.com*
w *www.priceline.com*
w *www.smarterliving.com*
w *www.travellersweb.ws*
w *www.travelocity.com*

In Canada

w *www.flightcentre.ca*
w *www.lastminuteclub.com*
w *www.newfrontiers.com*

Airlines include:

Air Canada, t *0990 247 226.*
American Airlines, t *0345 789 789.*
Continental Airlines, t *0800 776 464.*

Student and Youth Travel

CTS Travel, t *1-877 287 6665,* **w** *www.ctstravelusa.com.*

STA Travel, t *1-800 329 9537,* **w** *www.statravel.com.*

Travel Cuts, t *1-866 246 8762,* **w** *www.travelcuts.com.*

By Rail

The **rail enquiries** number (**t** *08457 484950*) is generally satisfactory if you ask the right questions (i.e. check all the various permutations of route or time for your journey).

The main rail route to Edinburgh from London is the East Coast Line, now run by GNER (Great North Eastern Railways), whose track record in running trains on time at a reasonable rate is only marginally better than Virgin's dreadful West Coast Line to Glasgow. That said, the 4-hour journey from London (5 on a Sunday) is much more comfortable than travelling by coach, and door-to-door it's almost as quick as flying.

By Coach

Travellers from outside the UK can invest in advance in a National Express Explorer Pass, allowing an unlimited number of journeys around the country for a range of time periods. Passes must be bought outside Britain. National Express Tourist Trail Passes are a more expensive alternative if you've already arrived in the country.

Speedy connections from London and most other British cities are provided by:

National Express, t *08705 808080.*
Scottish Citylink, t *08705 505050.*

By Car

From the south, there are two main options: the A1 is slow but scenic, approaching the city from the east and offering stunning views of Lindisfarne and Holy Island from the attractive towns of Berwick-upon-Tweed and Alnwick; the M6 is quicker, especially if you take the A702 through Biggar.

If you have time, take the lovely A708, which leaves the M6 at Moffat and reaches Edinburgh via Selkirk, joining the A7 at Melrose.

Glasgow, Edinburgh and Edinburgh airport are straightforwardly connected via the M8.

TOUR OPERATORS

Bespoke Highland Tours, t *(0141) 342 4576,* **e** *bespoke.tours@virgin.net.* Tours include Edinburgh city breaks.

Ealasaid's Scottish Tours, t *(01261) 842249,* **w** *www.scottishtours.com.* 'Romancing the Highlands' tours taking in Edinburgh and more.

Ensemble Tours, t *(0131) 561 9513,* **w** *www.ensembletours.co.uk/edinburgh.* For both Fringe audiences and performing groups.

Fish Out Of Water, t *(0131) 669 6501,* **w** *www.fishoutofwater.net.* Includes culinary trips run in association with Malcolm Duck of Duck's at Le Marché Noir (see p.169).

Homemade Holidays, t *(01606) 835448,* **toll-free from USA/Canada t** *800 813 7352,* **w** *www.homemade-holidays.com.* Personalized holidays in England and Scotland, including 'Genealogy and Family Roots'.

Tayleur Mayde Golf Tours, t *(0131) 225 9114,* **toll-free from USA/Canada t** *800 847 8064,* **w** *www.tayleurmayde.com.* Customized golf tours, including Muirfield and Gullane.

ARRIVAL

By Air

Edinburgh Airport (**t** *(0131) 333 1000*) is at Turnhouse, about 15–20 minutes' drive west of the centre (allow half an hour at rush hour). A current revamp will open up the airport to transatlantic flights. For the moment, those flying from North America (and Ryanair passengers) arrive at **Glasgow Prestwick** (**t** *(0141) 887 1111*).

Getting to and from the Airports

There's no train from Edinburgh airport to the centre. The easiest option is to take an **Airport Taxi** (*t (0131) 344 3344/3153*), costing around £12 to the city centre depending on the time of day and the number of passengers. Travelling into Waverley Station and the city centre by **Shuttle Bus** takes slightly longer (around 30 minutes), but costs just £3.60 per person. Buses leave roughly every 15 minutes daily from 6.30am to 10.30pm.

For regular train services between **Glasgow** and Edinburgh, *see* p.140. Buses run by **Scottish Citylink** (*t 08705 505050, w www.citylink.co.uk*) take 90 minutes to 2 hours. **Taxis** cost at least £50.

Car hire firms at Edinburgh Airport include Avis (*t (0131) 333 1866*), Budget (*t 0845 606 666*), Europcar (*t (0131) 344 3114*), and Hertz (*t (0131) 344 3260*).

By Train

Trains from north and west Britain come in to **Waverley Station** at the east end of Princes Street – a memorable experience. Local services and connections to Glasgow and the north of Scotland operate from **Haymarket Station**, at the junction of Dalry Road and Haymarket Terrace.

By Coach

A new multi-million-pound bus station opened in early 2003 on **Elder Street** in the New Town, next to the site of the old station (replaced by Harvey Nichols).

ENTRY FORMALITIES

Passports and Visas

Britain has opted not to join the eight-strong group of European countries that practise an open-border policy, so **EU citizens** still have to bring their passports or ID cards. That means a few delays and detours, but basically they can expect to breeze through

Customs in a separate queue to avoid hold-ups. Anyone else can expect a fair grilling, particularly at airports.

If you are a national of the United States, Canada, Australia, New Zealand, South Africa, Japan, Mexico or Switzerland, you won't need a **visa** to get into the country if you are just on holiday or on a business trip. Other nationalities should check with their local British consulate (*see* p.52).

Customs

There are very few customs restrictions if you're coming **from another EU country**: you can bring any amount of wine, spirits, tobacco or perfume that you can reasonably argue is for your own personal consumption. There is no duty-free within the EU.

For those arriving **from outside the EU**, duty-free restrictions include 220 cigarettes or 50 cigars or 250 grams of tobacco; 2 litres of wine; 1 litre of spirits; 60ml perfume; 250ml toilet water. Anything above these limits must be declared.

Non-EU citizens generally face restrictions on how much they can return home with. If they have been away for more than 48 hours, Americans can take 1 litre of alcohol (over-21s), 200 cigarettes and 100 cigars home with them, plus $400 worth of tax-free goods, paying 10% tax on the next $1,000 worth of goods. After that, tax is worked out on an item by item basis.

US Customs, *P.O. Box 7407, Washington, DC 20044, t (202) 927 6724, w www.customs. ustreas.gov.* For more detailed information, visit the website or request the free booklet *Know Before You Go.*

Canadians can take back 200 cigarettes, 50 cigars, 200 tobacco sticks or 220 grams of manufactured tobacco; 1.5 litres of wine, 1.14 litres of spirits or 8.5 litres of beer. There is a $750 tax-free limit for trips of more than 7 days ($200 for 2–6-day trips).

Revenue Canada, *2265 St Laurent Bd, Ottawa K1G 4KE, t 800 461 9999, t (613) 993 0534, w www.ccra-adrc.gc.ca.* Provides a booklet, *I Declare*, with further information.

GETTING AROUND

Maps

It's worth going to a bookshop that stocks a full range, such as Ottokar's (*see* p.186), and choosing one to suit your purposes. The *A–Z Streetfinder* (map or book) is comprehensive but hard to read. Collins do a good (but unwieldly) full-colour fold-out city map. A great-value option is the charming *Edinburgh Central Area Street Map* by Ronald Smith. There is also a range of maps for cyclists and walkers, including a 'Seven Hills' map showing how to reach the city's main viewpoints.

By Rail

There are regular trains around the region (*see* p.135, 'Day Trips'). There's an information desk in Waverley Station, or call **National Rail Enquiries** (*t* 08457 484950).

By Bus

A variety of private companies run services throughout the city. For the newcomer it's easiest to stick to the maroon and white buses run by Lothian Regional Transport (**LRT**; *local calls t 0800 232 323, national calls t (0131) 225 3858*). If you don't have a token or travel pass, you need to have exact change at the ready. Timetables, passes and tokens are available at most newsagents and at **LRT Travelshops** (*27 Hanover St, t (0131) 554 4494, and Waverley Bridge, t (0131) 225 8616*).

Standard fares on LRT buses are 60p, 80p and £1. A **Day Saver pass** (£2.50, £1.80 off peak) is available on the bus and is useful if you're making more than five trips round the centre or travelling into town from a distance. The excellent **Ridacard** (£11) lasts one week and allows unlimited travel in the city (not buses to the airport) and discounts on night buses.

Night Buses

Night buses depart from Waverley Bridge between midnight and 4am, but they're not too frequent. There's a flat fare of £2.

Further Afield

FirstBus (*t (0131) 663 9233*) operates a variety of services around the region.

By Taxi

Hailing a taxi in the city centre in daylight hours shouldn't be a problem, but at the end of the evening it can be hard to find an empty cab (signalled by a yellow central light on the roof). If you haven't booked, your best bet is to start walking homewards; otherwise walk down any of the main routes out of the city and catch a cab coming back in.

Capital Cabs, t *(0131) 228 2555*.
Central Radio Taxis, t *(0131) 229 2468*.
City Cabs, t *(0131) 228 1211*.
Computer Cabs, t *(0131) 225 9000*.
Minicabs are cheaper and especially useful late at night, but remember that they're unlicensed and may be uninsured.

Any complaints should be addressed to the **Cab Inspector** (*t (0131) 529 5800*).

By Car

'**Greenways**' – green and red lanes reserved for buses and taxis at rush hour and peak times – were introduced in 1997 to ease congestion and pollution.

Driving is on the left, and at roundabouts (traffic circles) you should give way to vehicles coming from the right. It's illegal not to wear a front **seat belt**, and rear belts should be worn if available. **Speed limits** are: 30mph in built up areas; 40mph or 50mph on urban freeways; 60mph on dual carriageways and country roads; 70mph on motorways.

Parking

Parking in the city centre is very restricted; try to leave your car where you are staying and use public transport or walk. There's no parking at any time on **double yellow lines** and only after 6.30pm on **single yellow lines** from Monday to Saturday (otherwise parking restrictions may vary; details are displayed on posts on every street). A red line means no stopping at all.

Car Parks (24-hour)

Greenside, *Greenside Row*, *t (0131) 558 3518*.
NCP, *Castle Terrace*, *t (0131) 229 2870*;
St James Centre, *t (0131) 55 5066*; *St John's Hill*,
t (0131) 556 7886; *Elder St*, *t (0131) 558 8816*.
Waverley, *New St*, *t (0131) 557 8526*.

Car Hire

The following will pick up and deliver:
Arnold Clark, *t (0131) 444 1852*.
Hertz, *t (0131) 556 8311*.
National Car Rental, *t (0131) 333 1922*.
See p.46 for car-hire outlets at the airport.

By Bicycle

Cyclists can use the '**Greenways**' (*see* p.47,
'By Car') at any time, and many of the rail
lines that used to crisscross the area have
been turned into **cycle paths**.

Hiring a bike is the best way to explore
areas just beyond the immediate city centre.
Mountain-biking is popular but is not allowed
off the paths in Holyrood Park or the Braid
Hills. For real action head out to the Pentland
Hills (*see* p.125) or the Lammermuirs, both
just close enough for a day trip.

For **bike hire**, *see* p.193. Spokes at 232 Dalry
Road (*t (0131) 313 2114*) publishes a **cycle map**
detailing designated routes and paths.

By Motorbike

This option is for bravehearts only, but it's
much the speediest way of getting around.
Edinburgh Kawasaki, *195 Slateford Rd*,
t (0131) 444 1915. Hire from £50 a day, but you
need your own helmet and gear.

On Foot

Walking here is a pleasure, and many of the
city's major points of interest are within easy
walking distance. That said, the seven hills on
which it stands take their toll on the calves,
so remember the obvious: a good pair of
walking boots or shoes, and a light, weatherproof and, even more importantly, windproof
coat. Umbrellas are useless because of the
wind, so buy a snug-fitting hat.

GUIDED TOURS

Most tours are good fun, dwelling on a
cheerful mix of pubs, ghouls and tartan
kitsch: for a less macabre slant try the
Scottish Literary Pub Tour or Volcano Tours.

**Auld Reekie's Ultimate Ghost & Torture
Tour** (*£4*), *t (0131) 557 4700*. The underbelly of
Edinburgh, from haunted vaults to pagan
temples. Tours last 45 minutes and leave
several times daily from Tron Kirk on the
Royal Mile.

Discover Edinburgh (*£8.50*), *Guide Friday
Tourism Centre, 133–5 Canongate*, *t (0131) 556
2244*. Hop-on hop-off, open-topped
doubledecker bus tour taking in the Royal
Mile and the New Town.

Lothian Helicopters, *Edinburgh Airport*,
t (0131) 228 9999. Quarter-hour helicopter
flights over the city and the Forth Bridge,
from £50pp.

Mercat Tours (*£5–6*), *t (0131) 557 6464*,
w www.mercat-tours.co.uk. A good range of
atmospheric day and late-night tours
through the spooky underground vaults and,
in 2003, around the cellars of Mary King's
Close. Tours start at the Mercat Cross (*see*
p.70) at various times between 10.30am
and 9.30pm.

Scottish Literary Pub Tour, *t (0131) 226 6665*,
w www.scot-lit-tour.co.uk. Tours depart from
the Beehive Inn (18–20 Grassmarket) at
7.30pm most evenings in summer, on
Thursdays in winter, calling at the Ensign
Ewart (*see* p.182), Jolly Judge (*see* p.175) and
Milne's Bar (*see* p.176).

Volcano Tours (*£5*), *t (0131) 555 5488*,
w www.geowalks.demon.co.uk. Guided tours
of the extinct volcano at Arthur's Seat in
Holyrood Park (*see* p.128).

The Witchery Tour (*£7*), *352 Castlehill*,
t (0131) 225 6745, *w www.clan.com/
edinburgh/witchery*. A light-hearted look at
the impact of witchcraft, plague and torture
on the city. By appointment.

Practical A–Z

Climate

Scotland's capital is colder than you might expect, mainly because of the wind-chill factor. Surprisingly, it doesn't rain here as much as it does elsewhere in Britain, but the city is prone to *haars*, or sea mists, which roll in without warning from the Firth of Forth.

Late May to mid-July, when the evenings are longest and the sunsets at their most gradual and spectacular, are the sunniest periods. August is popular with tourists, but it's not necessarily the most clement month. September and October are full of the mists and mellow fruitfulness of the Scottish autumn: it's usually quite warm, and the soft colours of the trees, gardens and countryside can be breathtaking. November, when clear northern light casts the city's grey stone in sharp relief, is also often a good month.

In December and January the city is at its most atmospheric; the days are short and the wind blows hard, making the pubs and restaurants all the more welcoming. February is the most depressing month in the city calendar. When spring arrives suddenly, any time in March, April or early May, the sense of relief on the streets is palpable.

The key thing to remember about the Edinburgh weather is its unpredictability. Throughout any one day at any time of the year it's possible to experience a bewildering variety of conditions. The only answer is to wear layers, making sure one of them is light, waterproof and windproof, and – in a spirit of undying optimism – to pack your sunglasses.

Average monthly rainfall in inches

Jan	April	July	Oct
2.2	1.5	3.3	2.6

Crime

Edinburgh has its fair share of bagsnatchers and pickpockets, but the city centre is generally safe. Areas most likely to get rowdy at pub closing time (around midnight in the week, a hour or so later on Fridays and Saturdays) include the West End, the section of the Lothian Road between Bread Street and

Useful Telephone Numbers

Fire, Police or Ambulance, t *999.*
NHS Helpline, *0800 224 488*
Police Assistance Desk, *(7am–11pm)*
t *(0131) 311 5949.*
Police HQ, *(24hrs) Fettes Avenue,*
t *(0131) 311 3131.*
Post Office Helpline, t *0845 722 3344.*
Samaritans, t *(0131) 221 9999.*
Rape Crisis Centre, t *(0131) 556 9437.*
Victim Support, t *0845 303 0900.*
Lost Property, t *(0131) 311 3141.*
Rights Office, t *(0131) 667 6339.*
Weather check, t *0891 333 111, 50p/min.*

East Fountainbridge, and the Grassmarket and Cowgate. After dark it's also best to steer clear of The Meadows and green spaces such as Calton Hill and the Water of Leith walkway. Coburg Street in Leith is a notorious red-light district, but Leith generally is a lot less dangerous than it was (though not everyone you meet will be well-meaning or in their right mind, usually due to drugs or alcohol).

Drugs

All recreational drugs are illegal in Scotland. Unless you're carrying it in quantities that suggest intent to supply, cannabis will probably only attract a fine (plus a criminal record), but the penalties for possessing any other drug, including Ecstasy, acid, cocaine or heroin, are much more severe.

Disabled Travellers

Edinburgh is hardly wheelchair-friendly, thanks to its hills, steps, cobbles and narrow entrances and exits. That said, all new developments incorporate disabled access, and most public buildings have been modified.

Some buses in the city are low-loaders, and all black cabs are wheelchair accessible. Major road crossings have sound signals and most major attractions have guides in Braille. Induction loops in banks, theatres and cinemas are signalled by a big ear.

Throughout this guide we have noted if a major sight is wheelchair accessible.

Disabled Accommodation

Trefoil House, *Gogarbank, EH12 9DA, t (0131) 339 3148, f (0131) 317 7271, w www.trefoil.org.uk*. An adapted mansion in large grounds six miles from the centre, for adults and children.

Organizations in Edinburgh

The **Tourist Information Centre** (*see* p.56) can help with specific queries.

Lothian Coalition of Disabled People, *Norton Park, 5 Albion Rd, EH7, t (0131) 475 2360, f (0131) 475 2392*. Publishes a free *Access Guide* to Edinburgh.

Tripscope, *t 08457 585 641*. Extensive information on transport for the disabled, including wheelchair and scooter hire companies.

Organizations in the UK

Holiday Care Service, *2nd Floor, Imperial Buildings, Victoria Rd, Horley, Surrey, RH6 9HW, t (01293) 774535, f (01293) 771500, w www.holidaycare.org.uk*. Up-to-date information on destinations, transportation and suitable tour operators.

RADAR (Royal Association for Disability and Rehabilitation), *Unit 12, City Forum, 250 City Rd, London EC1V 8AF, t (020) 7250 3222, f (020) 7250 0212, w www.radar.org.uk*. Publishes several books with information for travellers with disabilities.

RNIB (Royal National Institute for the Blind), *224 Great Portland St, London W1T 5TB, t (020) 7388 1266, w www.rnib.org.uk*. Advises blind or partially sighted people about plane travel and accommodation.

RNID (Royal National Institute for the Deaf), *19–23 Featherstone St, London EC1Y 8SL, t 0808 808 0123, f (020) 7296 8199, w www.rnid.org.uk*. Has an information line with advice on travelling.

Tripscope, *The Vassall Centre, Gill Avenue, Bristol BS16 2QQ, t (020) 8580 7021, w www.justmobility.co.uk/tripscope*. Practical advice on travel for the elderly and disabled.

Organizations in the USA

American Foundation for the Blind, *15 West 16th St, New York, NY 10011, t (212) 620 2000, t 800 232 5463*. The best source in the USA for visually impaired travellers.

Mobility International USA, *PO Box 3551, Eugene, OR 97403, t (541) 343 1284, f (0131) 343 6812, w www.miusa.org*. Information, advice and tours. Annual membership is $35.

SATH (Society for Accessible Travel and Hospitality), *347 5th Avenue, Suite 610, New York, NY 10016, t (212) 447 7284, w www.sath. org*. Advice on all aspects of travel for the disabled. The website is a good resource.

Other Useful Contacts

Access Ability, *w www.access-ability.co.uk*. Information on travel agencies catering specifically for disabled people.

Access Tourism, *w www.accesstourism.com*. Pan-European website with information on hotels, guesthouses, travel agencies, specialist tour operators and so on.

ACROD (Australian Council for Rehabilitation of the Disabled), *PO Box 60, Curtin, ACT 2605, Australia, t (02) 6682 4333, w www.acrod.org.au*. Information and contact numbers for specialist travel agents.

Disabled Persons Assembly, *PO Box 27-524, Wellington 6035, New Zealand, t (04) 801 9100, w www.dpa.org.nz*. An all-round source for travel information.

Emerging Horizons, *w www.emerging horizons.com*. An international online travel newsletter for people with disabilities.

Irish Wheelchair Association, *Blackheath Drive, Clontarf, Dublin 3, t (01) 833 8241, w www. iwa.ie*. Guides for disabled holidaymakers.

Discounts

Most museums and sights offer discounts for **children** under 16, and many allow under-5s in free. **Pensioners** and **students** may be asked for proof (i.e. a passport or student card) before being allowed concessions.

Electricity, Weights and Measures

Like the rest of the UK, Scotland uses three-pronged, square-pin plugs. Adapters can be bought in any electrical shop. The supply is a mind-blowing 240V.

Clothing Size Conversion Chart

Women's Shirts/Dresses

UK	10	12	14	16	18
USA	8	10	12	14	16

Women's Shoes

UK	3	4	5	6	7	8
USA	4	5	6	7	8	9

Men's Shoes

UK	5	6	7	8	9	10	11	12
USA	7.5	8	9	10	10.5	11	12	13

Britain's slow but never-quite-halted adaptation to membership of the European Union is perhaps best reflected in its constant, confusing mixing of traditional Imperial (feet, miles, pints) and international metric (metres, grams, litres) measurements. Metric will (probably) eventually overcome Imperial, but as of now which system you use tends to vary according to what you want. Most ready-bottled products (milk, petrol/gasoline, paint, sugar) are sold and distributed in metric sizes, while more intimate things are still dealt with in Imperial – everyone says their own height in feet and inches, and draught beer is served in pints. In shops, markets and supermarkets, packaged goods are nearly all sold in metric, though no one will fail to understand if you ask for loose goods in Imperial. The road system, measured and signposted entirely in miles, is the one major area where the metric system has not yet made any impact, in part because changing would be horrifically expensive.

Note that the US and British Imperial liquid measures have never been the same in any case. One US gallon is equivalent to 0.83 of a British gallon, or 3.78 litres.

Embassies and Consulates

In Edinburgh

Canadian High Commission, 30 Lothian Rd, t (0131) 220 4333.

Dutch Consulate, 1 Thistle Court, Thistle St, t (0131) 220 3226.

French Consulate, 11 Randolph Crescent, t (0131) 225 7954, visas t 0891 600 215.

German High Commission, 16 Eglinton Crescent, t (0131) 337 2323.

US Consulate, 3 Regent Terrace, t (0131) 556 8315, visas t 0906 820 290, replacement passports t (020) 7499 9000.

Abroad

Canada British High Commission, 80 Elgin St, Ottawa, Ontario K1P 5K7, t (613) 237 1303, f (613) 237 6537, w www.britainincanada.org.

Ireland 29 Merrion Rd, Dublin 4, t (01) 205 3700, f (01) 205 3890, w www.britishembassy.ie.

USA 3100 Massachusetts Ave, Washington DC, 20008, t (202) 588 6500, f (202) 588 7870, w www.britainusa.com/consular/embassy.

Health, Emergencies and Insurance

Citizens of the EU and some Commonwealth countries get free medical care in Britain under the National Health Service. The days when you could get free treatment by just producing a passport are probably over, so you'll need to fill out the appropriate paperwork before you leave home (in the EU the form is called an **E111**). Thus armed, the only things you will have to pay for are prescriptions and visits to the optician or dentist, though these should not cost more than a few pounds. Be warned that the bureacracy is hellish, so consider taking out private travel insurance. Anyone else, and that includes visitors from the USA and Canada, should take out medical **insurance**.

If you need **urgent medical treatment**, go to the casualty department of the **Royal Infirmary** on Lauriston Place (t (0131) 536 4000).

For information on where to find a **doctor** (GP), contact the free **NHS Helpline Scotland** (t 0800 224 488, Mon–Fri 9am–8pm) or the **Primary Care Department** (Lothian Health, 555 Gorgie Rd, EH11, t (0131) 536 9000).

The generic sign for a **chemist** (pharmacy, drugstore) is a green cross on a white background. There's always at least one chemist open late-night in the city, and all chemists put details on their doors. **Boots the Chemist**, Britain's largest drug-dispensing chain store, has a late-night branch at 48 Shandwick Place off Princes Street (*t (0131)225 6757, Mon–Sat 8am–9pm, Sun 10am–5pm*).

Emergency dental treatment is provided by the Royal Infirmary (*see above, t (0131) 536 4900*), which also has an STD (Sexually Transmitted Disease) Clinic (*t (0131) 536 2103*).

Well Woman and Family Planning Clinic, *Dean Terrace Centre, 18 Dean Terrace, Stockbridge, t (0131) 343 1282/332 7941/343 6243*. Provides free treatment by appointment (emergencies Saturday 9.30am–12.30pm) and gives out free condoms.

Media, Internet and Libraries

Newspapers

Scotland has two quality broadsheets, the **Herald** (*w www.theherald.co.uk*), based in Glasgow, and **The Scotsman** (*w www. scotsman.com*), based in Edinburgh. Both are traditionally left of centre and at least as good as if not superior to their English equivalents, *The Times*, the *Daily Telegraph* and the *Guardian*. The main Scottish tabloid is the **Daily Record** (*w www.dailyrecord.co.uk*), published in Glasgow and just as bloodthirsty in its *Schadenfreude* as its southern counterparts. Its Edinburgh rival is the **Evening News** (*w www.edinburghnews.com*), while **The List** (*w www.list.co.uk*) is Glasgow and Edinburgh's events listings magazine, and the best place to find out what's going on at any time other than the Festival, when all the papers join in the jamboree and *The Scotsman* usually has the highest entertainment quotient.

Radio and TV

As elsewhere in the UK, local radio has proliferated.

BBC Radio Scotland 92.4–94.7 FM, 810 MW. Arts and music, including a Celtic music slot.

Radio Forth 97.3 FM, 1548 MW. Mainstream pop and regular travel updates.

Scot FM, 101.1 FM. Talk radio.

Internet Sites

The Scottish newspapers have excellent, up-to-date sites too (*see left*).

w *www.edinburgh-festivals.com*. The only official online guide to all the Edinburgh festivals; also has very good year-round eating, drinking, events and sightseeing reviews, and a superb design.

w *www.theoracle.co.uk*. A functional but comprehensive what's-on guide to Edinburgh.

w *www.edinburghguide.com*. Current cinema and theatre listings, and a handy web directory for Edinburgh and beyond.

w *www.eae-eventalert.co.uk*. An information service whereby you click on 'leaflets' to find out about upcoming events in the city.

w *www.edinburgh.org*. The Edinburgh and Lothians Tourist Board site; good on accommodation and with a useful links page.

w *www.edinburgh-galleries.co.uk*. The local gallery association's cultural listings.

w *www.ed.ac.uk/city/*. The University of Edinburgh's website, with very good links.

w *www.edinburgh.gov.uk*. The local council site; dull design but predictably strong on practical information.

w *www.scottish.parliament.uk*. All you could wish to know about the Scottish Parliament.

w *www.electrum.co.uk/pubs/*. An entertaining virtual pub crawl through Edinburgh.

w *www.holidayscotland.net*. The Scottish Tourist Board's well-designed site.

w *www.historic-scotland.gov.uk*. The national heritage site, with details of listed buildings and ancient monuments.

w *www.nts.org.uk*. The National Trust for Scotland site, with details of its conservation work and properties.

Local TV stations include the excellent **BBC Scotland** (for a baptism by fire try *Rab C. Nesbitt*), **Scottish ITV**, and **STV** (hobby-based programmes and Scottish sport).

Internet

Many of the central hotels offer internet access. Internet cafés in town include:

Pallas Athene, *28–30 Marchmont Crescent, t (0131) 667 7711, w www.pallas-athene.co.uk*.

That Café, *1a Brougham Place,* **t** *(0131) 229 0505,* **w** *www.ThatInternetCafe.net.*

Tinsley Lockhart Group, *44 West Preston St,* **t** *(0131) 466 7767,* **w** *www.t2lg.net.*

Web 13, *13 Bread St,* **t** *(0131) 229 8883,* **w** *www.web13.co.uk.*

Libraries

Central Library, *George IV Bridge,* **t** *(0131) 242 8000,* **w** *www.edinburgh.gov.uk/libraries;* **open** *Mon–Thurs 10am–8pm, Fri 10am–5pm, Sat 9am–1pm.* The flagship of Edinburgh City Libraries can provide details on local libraries around the city. The Edinburgh Room (reference only) is the place to go for all matters local and historical. If you want to borrow a book, you need to get temporary membership (refundable) in the Scottish Department.

National Library of Scotland, **t** *(0131) 226 4531,* **w** *www.nls.uk;* **open** *Mon, Tues, Thurs and Fri 9.30am–8.30pm, Wed 10am–8.30pm, Sat 9.30am–1pm.* Across the road from the Central Library, this is the country's reference copyright library. From here you can call up just about any book ever written in Scots or English, and all you need to join is a piece of ID such as a passport or driving licence, and a passport photo.

Money and Banks

Scottish one-pound notes are not legal tender in the rest of the UK, but all other denominations are (although shopkeepers in England may very well try to tell you differently). Otherwise, the currency is the same as the UK (i.e. the pound sterling, divided into 100 pence).

The major **credit cards** are widely accepted. For lost or stolen cards, call one of the following numbers:

American Express, t *(01273) 696 933/* **t** *(01273) 689 955.*

Diners Club, t *(01252) 513 500.*

MasterCard, t *0800 964 767.*

Visa, t *0800 895 082.*

Banks

Usual **banking hours** are 9am–4.30pm. The main banks are:

Bank of Scotland, *38 St Andrew Square,* **t** *(0131) 465 2500.*

Barclays, *1 St Andrew Square,* **t** *0845 600 0180.*

HSBC, *76 Hanover St,* **t** *0845 740 4404.*

Lloyds TSB, *28 Hanover St,* **t** *(0131) 226 4021.*

NatWest, *80 George St,* **t** *0870 240 3366.*

Royal Bank of Scotland, *142–44 Princes St,* **t** *(0131) 226 2555.*

Traveller's Cheques

Traveller's cheques and currency can be exchanged at most banks.

There are also **bureaux de change** in Waverley Station, at Edinburgh Airport, and in most large hotels.

Photography

Film can be bought or developed at most chemists (*see* 'Health', p.52). Some tourist shops on the Royal Mile also stock film.

The light in Edinburgh can be weak when it's not sunny, in which case you're best off using a higher ASA than usual.

Post, Fax and Telephones

The most **central post office** is at 8–10 St James Centre, EH1 3SR (*open Mon 9am–5.30pm, Tues–Fri 8.30am–5.30pm, Sat 8.30am–6pm*). Staff here will keep post addressed to you at **Poste Restante** for up to four weeks (if it's from overseas; for up to two weeks from the UK). You need a driver's licence or other form of ID to collect it.

You can **fax** from most photocopy shops, internet cafés, hotels and newsagents.

The **telephone code for Edinburgh** from within the UK is 0131. From abroad, dial the local international code (which from the USA and Canada is 00), then the UK code (44), then the Edinburgh code without the zero (131) and finally the seven-digit number.

The **international dialling code from Edinburgh** is 00, followed by the country code for the country you are dialling (1 for the USA and Canada, 353 for Ireland, 61 for Australia, 64 for New Zealand), followed by the local code with the first 0 missing.

For **Operator Services** call 100, for **Directory Enquiries** call 118500, and for the **International Operator and Directory Enquiries** call 118505.

Phonecards can be purchased at most newsagents and hotels.

Public Holidays

Scotland has public holidays – called bank holidays – on different days of the year from England and Wales. And different cities in Scotland also have their own bank holidays, which means that even when Edinburgh is closed for the day, shopaholics can nip over to Glasgow.

All banks and post offices are closed on public holidays, although ATM cash machines and *bureaux de change* will be open. Most shops, business and schools, plus some attractions, also close.

Jan 1 New Year's Day
Jan 2 Scottish holiday
April Good Friday
April Easter Monday
1st Mon in May May Day
last Mon in May Victoria Day (Edinburgh only)
last Mon in Aug late summer holiday
Dec 25 Christmas Day
Dec 26 Boxing Day

Smoking

Scotland is a nation of inveterate smokers (apparently more Scottish women smoke than women of any other nationality), and although a surprising number of smoke-free areas have been set aside in restaurants and hotels, to anyone with a horror of passive smoking, many Edinburgh pubs and bars will be an absolute nightmare. The Wetherspoon chain (which owns a couple of establishments in the city, including the Standing Order on George Street; *see* p.176) has made a point of providing no-smoking areas.

Public transport, some taxis, all museums and libraries and most visitor attractions are non-smoking.

Tax

In Scotland, as in the rest of Britain, consumer durables and comestibles are subject to Value Added Tax at 17.5% of their retail price. If you're canny and from overseas you can reclaim this at participating Tax-Free shops by completing a form on presentation of your passport.

Time

Scotland keeps the same time as the rest of Britain, Greenwich Mean Time (GMT), which is one hour behind the rest of Western Europe. New York is 5 hours behind GMT and San Francisco is 8 hours behind, while Tokyo and Sydney are 8 hours ahead.

British Summer Time is an hour ahead of GMT and lasts from about the last Saturday in March to the last Saturday in October.

Tipping

As in the rest of the UK, you should tip around 12%, though most **restaurants** already include a service charge of 12% in the bill – if so, you're not obliged to leave any extra. The service charge should be clearly stated, but some restaurants do their utmost to conceal it.

Hotels almost always include the service charge. Bellboys, doormen, bar staff, porters and ushers do not expect to be tipped but will appreciate the gesture. It's not uncommon to offer bar staff a drink of their choice on your first round.

Taxis are expensive enough already so tip at your discretion.

Toilets

Finding a toilet is not a problem: pubs, restaurants and hotels are usually happy to oblige, though it's polite to ask. All the national galleries are free and so are their facilities.

Disabled people using the National Key Scheme have 24-hour a day access to The Mound public lavatories on Princes Street.

Tourist Offices

In Edinburgh

Tourist Information Centre, *Waverley Market, 3 Princes St,* **t** *(0131) 473 3800;* **open** *Nov–March Mon–Sat 9am–6pm; April–Oct also Sun 1–6pm; May, June and Sept Mon–Sat 9am–7pm, Sun 11am–7pm; July and Aug Mon–Sat 9am–8pm, Sun 11am–8pm.*

Edinburgh Airport Information Desk, *Edinburgh Airport,* **t** *(0131) 333 1000,* **w** *www.baa.com;* **open** *April–Oct Mon–Sat 8.30am–9.30pm, Sun 9.30am–9.30pm; Nov–March daily 9am–5pm.*

In London

Scottish Travel Centre, *19 Cockspur St, London SW1 5BL,* **t** *0845 225 5121.* Provides help with routes, accommodation and so on.

British Travel Centre, *12 Regent St, Piccadilly Circus, London W1, no phone.* A complete booking service for rail, air and sea travel, sightseeing tours, tickets and accommodation.

Tracing Your Ancestors

Keeper of the Records of Scotland, *Scottish Record Office, Her Majesty's General Register House, Princes St, EH1 3YY,* **t** *(0131) 557 1022.* Contact them for advice and assistance.

Women Travellers

Edinburgh is generally a very safe city for lone women travellers, but the usual precautions associated with a big city should still be taken, especially after dark outside the centre and in parks or gardens.

Working and Long Stays

European Union citizens can enter the country with a passport and stay indefinitely. Visitors from the USA, Canada, Australia and New Zealand can stay for up to six months if they can prove they have a return ticket and sufficient funds to live on. For longer stays, visitors can apply to the British Embassy or High Commission in their own country for an Entry Clearance Certificate. If you are already in the UK and want to extend your visa, apply in writing to the Immigration and Nationality Department at Lunar House, Wellesley Rd, Croydon CR9 2BY (**t** *0870 606 7766*) several weeks before it runs out.

Citizens of most other European countries, with the exception of Albania, Bosnia, Bulgaria, Croatia, Macedonia, Slovakia, Yugoslavia and all the former Soviet Republics (other than the Baltic states), can enter Britain with just a passport and stay for three months.

For more information, contact your consulate. The **British Foreign Office** has a very useful website (**w** *www.fco.gov.uk*) that gives information on visa regulations, and you can also download the relevant application forms from it. The independent charity **Immigration Advisory Service** (*IAS, County House, 190 Great Dover St, London SE1,* **t** *(020) 7357 6917,* **w** *www.iasuk.org*) offers free and confidential advice to anyone seeking entry to the UK.

Residents of EU countries can legally work in the UK. Citizens from elsewhere will need a **work permit**, which, without the backing of an organization, can be very difficult to obtain. Young people aged 17–27 can apply for a Working Holiday-Maker Entry Certificate entitling them to stay in the UK for up to two years and take on casual work. These certificates are only available from British Embassies and High Commissions abroad and should be applied for in advance.

Full-time students in North America can apply for temporary UK work permits through **Bunac** (*PO Box 430, Southbury, CT 06488,* **t** *0 800 GO BUNAC,* **w** *www.bunac. org*). These are valid for six months, and Bunac can help organize accommodation and provide lists of possible employers.

Commonwealth citizens who have a parent or grandparent who was born in the UK are also entitled to work in Britain. Apply for a Certificate of Entitlement to the Right of Abode at the British Embassy or High Commission in your home country.

The Royal Mile

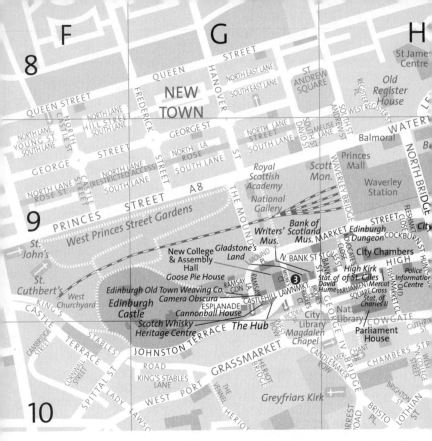

The Royal Mile

Tourists have been flocking to Edinburgh's historic High Street – once the most populous street in Europe – for 700 years, so it is somewhat surprising that this is still the living heart of the city. Inevitably, there are certain places where the idea of 'heritage culture' has been taken to extremes, but this nevertheless remains the centre of action.

The Royal Mile follows a virtually straight line downhill from Edinburgh Castle to the Palace of Holyroodhouse, passing the major sights of the High Kirk of St Giles and Parliament House. The main street, which changes its name from Castlehill to Lawnmarket to High Street to Canongate as you head east, is crowded with 'lands' (tenements) many storeys high, and punctuated by tiny cobbled 'closes' (alleys) off to each side.

1 Lunch

Dubh Prais, *123B High St*, **t** *(0131) 557 5732*. **Open** *for lunch Tues–Fri noon–2pm*. **Expensive.** Juicy game, venison and the likes in a cosy underground space.

2 Tea and Cakes

Clarinda's, *69 Canongate*, **t** *(0131) 557 1888*. **Open** *Mon–Sat 9am–4.45pm, Sun 10am–4.45pm*. A charming coffeehouse.

3 Drinks

Jolly Judge, *7 James Court*, **t** *(0131) 225 2669*. **Open** *Mon noon–midnight, Tues and Wed noon–11pm, Thurs–Sat noon–midnight, Sun 12.30pm–11pm*. A friendly, atmospheric pub hidden away down a narrow close but popular with literary tour groups.

You could stroll from castle to palace in half an hour, but there are enough sights along the way to occupy a whole day.

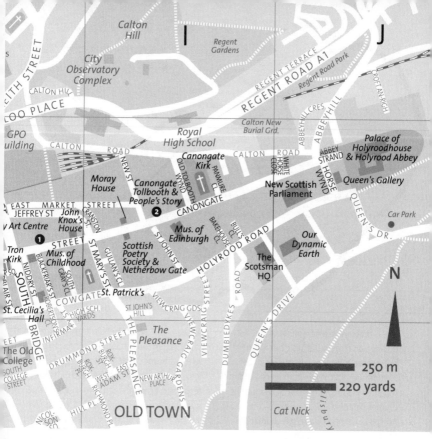

Highlights

Couples' City: Tiny St Margaret's Chapel, the city's oldest church, decorated with some beautiful modern stained glass, p.62

Indoor City: The Palace of Holyroodhouse, the grand setting for centuries of royal history, p.75

Edinburghers' City: The White Horse pub on Canongate, where time has stood still, p.175

Literary City: The Writers' Museum, where literary masters Scott, Burns and Stevenson are hailed, p.66

Festival City: The Hub, a sumptuous former church now home to the festival HQ, p.65

EDINBURGH CASTLE

*Castlehill, **t** (0131) 668 8800, **w** www.historic-scotland.gov.uk; wheelchair accessible. **Open April–Sept daily 9.30am–6pm, Oct–March daily 9.30am–5pm; closed 25, 26 Dec; adm £8. Audio tours.***

Though it was surprisingly unsuccessful as a defensive fortification, Edinburgh Castle is the country's most popular tourist attraction. It's a proper castle, with superb views, ruined walls, winding stairs, immense ramparts and lots of hiding places for kids to enjoy. Thanks to the romantic sensibilities of the Victorians, who restored St Margaret's Chapel, Edinburgh's oldest church (*see* p.62), and to the construction in 1927 of the awe-inspiring Scottish National War Memorial, the castle has also become something of a symbol of the nation's spiritual life.

Although it gets very crowded in the summer, the castle represents good value

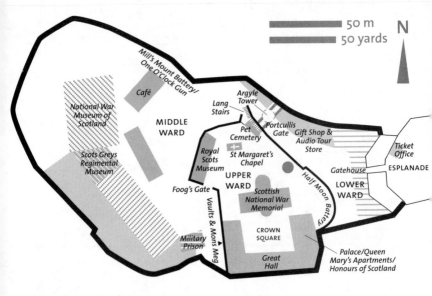

and is unlikely to disappoint. As well as buying you a melodramatic but informative self-guided audio tour, the ticket price includes access to the Honours of Scotland (the nation's crown jewels), St Margaret's Chapel, three military museums (the British Army's Lowland Brigade, which includes English and Scottish regiments, has its HQ at the castle, and different regiments in rotation provide the 12-man guard), the Great Hall and Queen Mary's Apartments, a Victorian military prison and a curious pet cemetery. You can also wander along parts of the battlements for great views across the city.

Esplanade G9

The old parade ground is now a grandly sited car park with magnificent views. During the Military Tattoo in August (see 'Edinburgh's Festivals', p.39), the massive banks of seating offer even more impressive views to ticket-holders but spoil the skyline for everyone else. Looking south, there's a great view of George Heriot's School (see p.83).

Avoid being run down by one of the frequent tour buses executing sweeping turns by sticking to the edge and mulling over some of the memorials. Most of them commemorate soldiers from different regiments who fell in the wars in South Africa.

At the entrance to Castlehill, on the left, is a sadly neglected modern memorial to the witches burned here until as recently as 1722. Nearby, Earl Haig, the field marshal responsible for the tactics that caused such appalling loss of life in the First World War, sits on his horse staring blankly into space.

Lower Ward G9

Gatehouse G9

The castle's impressive 19th-century entrance is guarded by two sentries and statues of Robert the Bruce and William Wallace. Look for the plaque on the gateway that commemorates the section of castle rock, now buried beneath the esplanade, that was legally granted to Nova Scotia in Canada by Charles I and has never been taken back. Above the gate an inscription reads *Nemo Me Impune Lacessit* – the royal motto that is also engraved on Scottish £1 coins, which roughly translates as 'no one messes with me and gets away with it'. The army joke is that here it simply means 'mind your head'.

Portcullis Gate G9

Past the gift shop, replete with teatowels, tartan and Historic Scotland merchandising, and the audio tour store, the Portcullis Gate stands guard over the entrance to the

Middle Ward. Built in the 17th century and capped in the 19th with the Argyle Tower, it was named after the fearless Archibald, ninth earl of Argyle, who was imprisoned on this spot the night before his execution and impressed his warders by enjoying a sound night's sleep.

Middle Ward F9–G9

Mill's Mount Battery G9

On the north side of Middle Ward next to the café, Mill's Mount Battery has great views over the New Town. The **One O'Clock Gun** here has been fired almost every day since 1861, and is now in the capable white-gloved hands of Tam the Gun, the longest-serving District Gunner in the British Army, who carries out his duties with impressive ceremony on the dot of 1pm every day, and at midnight on New Year's Eve.

National War Museum of Scotland F9

*t (0131) 225 7534, **w** www.nms.ac.uk. **Open** April–Sept daily 9.45am–5.30pm, Oct–March daily 9.45am–4.30pm; **adm** included in entry to castle.*

Formerly the United Services Museum, the National War Museum tells the story of the Scots at war over the last 400 years. Highlights include 'A Nation in Arms', describing the influence of war on the country's history, 'A Grand Life for a Scotsman', exploring daily life for a soldier down the ages, and 'Highland Soldier', examining that peculiar iconic breed.

Scots Greys Regimental Museum F9

See main castle listings for opening times and admission.

The Scots Greys, or Dragoon Guards, have their regimental headquarters at the castle. Next door to the National War Museum, this museum features lots of pictures of tanks, and a light tank, which must surely have been helicoptered into position, stands guard outside the front door.

Royal Scots Museum G9

See main castle listings for opening times and admission.

A small and old-fashioned but endearing exhibition on the regiment that was Britain's first standing army, which is also based here. Highlights include the seven Victoria Crosses won by Scottish soldiers in the First World War, pictures of soldiers being suckled by native Americans, and a display on how the regimental colours were discovered in a junk shop in Singapore. A chunk of the first aircraft shot down in the Second World War (at Humbie in Midlothian) is sometimes displayed.

The Vaults and Military Prison G10

Behind the Royal Scots Museum, below Foog's Gate, are the vaults in which French POWs were held while they were kept here laying the cobbles outside, and where people such as privateer John Paul Jones were dealt with (before he founded the US Navy), along with David Kirkwood, the 'Red Clydesider'.

Opposite, there's the opportunity to look around a perfectly preserved Victorian military prison, later used to lock up political prisoners such as the Marxist John Maclean.

Mons Meg

This famous cannon housed in the vaults is so big that someone once gave birth in its barrel. Supposedly named after the wife of its blacksmith from Mollance or Mons (although some contend that it was actually made in Mons, Belgium) and created for James II in 1455, it was used to subdue the Black Douglases in Threave Castle near Castle Douglas.

Whatever its origin, it was ceremonially fired when Mary, Queen of Scots married the French dauphin but was later neglected and ended up an awkward relic. It was Sir Walter Scott who had it reinstated in pride of place in the castle. In the 1980s it was sent to London to be restored, by coincidence at the same time as the statue of Eros from Piccadilly Circus was making the journey north to be restored in Edinburgh.

Upper Ward and Crown Square G10

St Margaret's Chapel G10

This beautifully simple building – one of the smallest churches in Britain and the oldest in Edinburgh – is in a spectacular position, commanding the best views northeast from the highest point on the castle rock. It was constructed on the orders of Queen Margaret, the saintly Saxon wife of Malcolm III Canmore, but not finished until about 20 years after her death in 1093.

Brought up in Hungary, Queen Margaret is credited with having brought some continental sophistication into Scotland and was renowned for her acts of charity – she regularly fed 300 beggars a day at the castle gates. Her son David I relocated the royal court here from Dunfermline and founded Holyrood Abbey (see p.76). Robert the Bruce had the rest of the castle destroyed by the Earl of Moray, but relented over the chapel and ordered its restoration. It has been restored several times since, most recently in 1993 to commemorate the 900th anniversary of Margaret's death.

The interior has not been radically altered since the days of David I. The shafts of the chancel arch are 19th-century, but the arch itself, with its zigzag teeth, is probably original. The beautiful stained glass is 20th-century, by Douglas Strachan, who also did much of the glass in the War Memorial (see below), and shows William Wallace in the company of saints Andrew, Ninian, Columba and Margaret.

Anyone called Margaret can join the St Margaret's Chapel Fellowship and contribute to the flowers placed in the chapel on her saint's day, 16 November.

Scottish National War Memorial G10

Adm free (ask at castle ticket office).

On the north side of Crown Square, the strong Gothic façade of the Scottish National War Memorial is unmistakable. Designed by Robert Lorimer in the 1920s on the site of the castle's church, the building has been described as a piper's lament in stone. It's a moving place that not even the muffled crackle of your fellow visitors' audio-guides will detract from.

Inside the Halls of Honour, the names of about 150,000 Scottish soldiers who lost their lives in the two world wars are recorded in leather-bound books beneath regimental bays illuminated by stained glass. The fine windows, many of them by Douglas Strachan, include the Women's Window showing a shell factory and workers in the fields, and dispassionate depictions of the machinery of war. Beyond, the heart of the memorial is founded on the solid castle rock, in the form of a shrine containing the names of the dead on Rolls of Honour.

The Palace and Honours of Scotland G10

Inside the palace, **Queen Mary's Apartments** have been restored to look as they did when James VI (later James I of England) last visited in 1617, and to include the tiny room where he was born to Mary, Queen of Scots. One of the old soldiers who act as guides will open the little window to reveal the vertical drop down which the baby was lowered to be baptised.

James himself was always unsure of his legitimacy, partly because he looked nothing like any of the other Stuarts. Further doubt arose in 1830 after a bad fire, when a small coffin was found in the wall of these apartments (though the bones were never formally identified as human). The coffin and its contents were put back in the wall. The smart money is on James being Lord Darnley's son by Mary; another theory notes James's resemblance to the son of the Countess of Mar, Mary's babysitter.

The rest of the palace is occupied by the **Honours of Scotland** exhibition, home of Scotland's crown jewels. Colourful murals and mock-ups tell the story of the Scottish crown as the queue twists towards the precious objects in their darkened room. Be warned: it can be slow going in peak season.

When you eventually reach them, the jewels are impressive. Part of the crown was used at the coronation of Robert the Bruce, making it far older than the one in London, and it was last worn by Charles II on 1 January 1651. The sceptre and its dazzling globe date from two centuries before that, while the intricately carved sword of state was a present from Pope Julius II to James IV.

The Stone of Destiny was used to solemnize the inauguration of Scots kings at Scone from the 9th century. The fact that it is a simple sandstone block has prompted claims that it's not the real thing, which was recorded as being richly carved. Various legends claim that the stone was Jacob's pillow when he dreamed about his ladder, and that the original is being kept in hiding until Scotland is a nation once again.

Original or not, the stone on display was taken by Edward I of England in 1296 and kept under the coronation chair in Westminster Abbey. In 1950 it was stolen by Scottish Nationalists, who carted it off in a battered van to Arbroath, slightly damaging it in the process. It was recovered and remained in London until 1996, when it was returned by the Conservative government.

Great Hall G10

Occupying the south side of the square, this was the home of the Scottish Parliament until shortly after James's son Charles I ascended the throne. Its splendid beamed ceiling was only uncovered in the late 19th century. The room now houses a formidable armoury of Scottish weapons.

Pet Cemetery G10

Immediately on your left at the top of the Lang Stairs into Upper Ward, which lead back down to Portcullis Gate, is the well-tended cemetery where the faithful companions of the castle's commanding officers are provided with a glorious resting place.

CASTLEHILL

Goose Pie House G9

Ramsay Garden, off Castlehill.

On the left as you leave the Esplanade is the house that 18th-century poet Allan Ramsay built for himself, known as Goose Pie House because of its octagonal shape, now much altered. Some of the extensions and alterations were undertaken by Patrick Geddes (*see* p.34), responsible for preserving much of the Royal Mile; he lived here towards the end of the 19th century.

Cannonball House G9

Corner of Castlehill and Castlewynd.

The starting point for volunteer-guided walks along the Royal Mile during the Festival. On the door of the house is a 'tirling pin' on its sounding bracket, as in the rhyme:

Wee Willie Winkie rins thro the toun
Upstairs and downstairs in his nicht goun
Tirlin' at the window, crying at the lock:
Are the weans in bed noo, for it's nigh on
    ten o'clock?

The Mile That Made the City

As the ice sheets moved east a few millennia ago, they dumped debris behind the hard volcanic plug of Castle Rock, leaving the distinctive 'crag and tail' formation. This landscape has defined the growth of the medieval city, with the Royal Mile itself running along the crown of the ridge that runs down from Castle Rock, and the Old Town on the ridge's southern slopes.

Below the cliffs on the steeper north side, the Nor' Loch for centuries prevented the city from spreading in that direction – until it was drained to allow the construction of the New Town in the 18th century. It is now Princes Street Gardens.

The Royal Mile echoes most impressively with the history of the 16th and 17th centuries – the Reformation, the struggles of the Stuarts to hang on to power, and the eventual loss of Scottish independence. Any melancholy that this last event might have provoked is rapidly being dispelled now that the city is once again Scotland's legislative capital.

This is a rare polite form of door knocker dating back to the days when people scratched at one another's doors instead of banging on them.

The house gets its name from a cannonball lodged above the first-floor window facing the castle. Legend has it that this was part of the barrage fired by government troops from the castle aiming to dent Bonnie Prince Charlie's bonnet at Holyrood. It's more likely that it marks the gravitational height of the water supply for the old reservoir over the road, a 19th-century tank for the water first pumped into the city in 1681, serving the wells all the way down the Royal Mile.

Edinburgh Old Town Weaving Company G9

555 Castlehill, **t** *(0131) 226 1555*, **w** *www. tartanweavingmill.co.uk.* **Open** *April–Oct daily 9am–6.30pm, Nov–March daily 9am–5.30pm (Sun from 10am); closed 25 Dec, 1 Jan;* **adm** *£4.50.* **Guided tours** *every 20mins, lasting 45mins.*

Here you can get your fill of all things tartan and see the great plaid in the process of manufacture. It's a noisy business, with the hall thrumming to the clickety-clack of the machines downstairs.

The tour seems designed to squeeze every last penny out of your curiosity instead of allowing you to select which aspects of the story you want to enjoy.

Scotch Whisky Heritage Centre G9

354 Castlehill, **t** *(0131) 220 0441*, **w** *www. whisky-heritage.co.uk.* **Open** *June–Sept daily 9.30am–6pm, Oct–May daily 10am–5.30pm; closed 25 Dec;* **adm** *£6.95.*

The centre offers 45-minute guided tours of its exhibition and a video on the history of the water of life, plus a 15-minute ride in a barrel (available separately but hardly worth it) around odorized, illuminated tableaux illustrating that story.

The slightly patronizing commentary obviously avoids the downsides of alcohol abuse; indeed, some of the scenes are quite comical (look out for Sir Walter Scott's horrified expression at the kilted King George IV's rubicund appearance). However, the whole experience should succeed in giving you a thirst for the stuff, which is – surprise, surprise – available in great variety at the themed bar downstairs. Your ticket entitles you to a free dram of the society's choosing, and there's also a decent café for lunch.

Camera Obscura and World of Illusions G9

549 Castlehill, **t** *(0131) 226 3709*, **w** *www. camera-obscura.co.uk.* **Open** *daily 9.30am– 6pm (July and Aug to 7.30pm);* **adm** *£4.95.*

These two early-17th-century tenements were added to by optician Maria Short in 1852 to become Short's Observatory, the crowning glory of which was the Camera Obscura. Patrick Geddes later bought the place and turned it into 'the world's first sociological laboratory' – an elaborate establishment that included a planetarium, a 'Scotland Room', an 'Edinburgh Room' and a 'World Room', which was intended to provide a lesson in environmental awareness. Nowadays the building plays a less earnest role, with the rooms off its winding stair crammed with freakish holograms and other diverting visual stunts.

The original **Camera Obscura** in the roof uses mirrors and lenses to project real-time scenes of the surrounding area on to a round white table. Before the invention of cinema, its live moving images must have been startling. For the full effect, visit near noon on a fine day, because bright sunshine is crucial for the projection of colour and detail. The display, involving a panorama of the city and demonstrations of a few entertaining tricks of the light, lasts about 20 minutes. During winter, there's also the rare opportunity to look directly at the sun, which is low enough in the sky at that time of year for the camera to pick out.

Outside, banks of binoculars and telescopes allow more long-distance voyeurism of the Royal Mile to the east and the Firth of Forth to the north; the powerful Russian binoculars let you glimpse what power-lunchers in the Princes Street clubs are eating.

The Hub G9

348 Castlehill, t (0131) 473 2000, w www.eif. co.uk. Open café and restaurant daily 9.30am–10pm (midnight during Festival).

This former church – which was once known as the Highland Kirk of Tolbooth St John's because it held services in Gaelic – is now the administrative headquarters of the Edinburgh International Festival and has a performance space where visiting artists strut their stuff (*see* p.183).

A richly decorated neo-Gothic marvel, it was designed in 1839 by James Gillespie Graham and Augustus Pugin, who gave the Houses of Parliament in London their distinctive look. With its steeple and spire, the tallest in the city (240ft), it was built on the site of the Victoria Hall, the Assembly Hall of the Church of Scotland during the Disruption.

LAWNMARKET

In the Middle Ages, this widening of the way was the place where cloth ('lawn') was sold, as well as 'butter, cheise, wool and sichlike gudis'. The market was only cleared away at the end of the 19th century.

Mylne's Court G9

Off Lawnmarket.

Now among Edinburgh's most attractive student halls of residence, this was once one of the smartest addresses on the Royal Mile. It was designed at the end of the 17th century by a mason who worked on Charles II's extension to Holyrood Palace and is probably the city's first proper square. It was sympathetically restored in the 1960s, down to the thick glass in the half-timbered windows.

Riddle's Court G9

Off Lawnmarket.

Riddle's Court gives an idea of what many of these courts looked like in the 18th century: note the doorway inscribed with '1726'. This is where David Hume bought his first house in 1753, and where he started his *History of Great Britain*.

Further into the court is the home of a wealthy 16th-century burgess John McMorran, who hosted lavish banquets here for King James VI. McMorran met an unexpected end on 15 September 1595, when he went to break up a sit-in by the sons of the gentry at the Royal High School (then in the Canongate), who were demanding a holiday. As he approached, they shot him in the head. By James VI's command the culprit was never brought to justice, probably because his father was the Chancellor of Caithness.

Gladstone's Land G9

477b Lawnmarket, t (0131) 226 5856, w www. nts.org.uk. Open April–Oct Mon–Sat 10am–5pm, Sun 2–5pm; last adm 4.30pm; adm £5.

This is the best surviving example of a 17th-century tenement (apartment block) in Edinburgh. Not connected with the British prime minister of the same name, it was bought in 1617 by a merchant called Thomas Gledstanes, who extended the 16th-century block at the front, supporting it on the two round arches that used to be a common feature of shopfronts on the High Street. The house demonstrates the way in which buildings were forced upwards because of the lack of space on the narrow ridge of the Royal Mile, while its stone frontage was a response to the frequent fires that broke out in the city.

In 1935, this became one of the first properties to be purchased by the National Trust for Scotland, which went on to restore it to its original state in the late 1970s. Externally, the semi-shuttered and fixed glass windows are the most obvious signs of this work, but it's worth venturing inside, not least to see the original decoration on the beamed ceilings: a painted profusion of flowers and fruits in mellow colours.

You pass through a reconstructed 17th-century shop to reach the welcoming, intimate house. The three rooms open to visitors are on the first floor, which would have been the smartest and most sought-after in the block. There's been some attempt to recreate the lack of light, but thankfully none to recreate the smell of the 'cruisie' lamps, which burned fish oil.

Interesting features include a sturdy little baby-walker and a large oak four-poster from Aberdeenshire. All the rooms would have been multi-purpose, hence the fold-up bed in the kitchen. Some of the ceilings are made of plaster, with mouldings of the same age as those in Moray House (see p.73) and Croft-an-Righ. Three of the ceilings have been painted freehand (rather than stencilled, as was more common). There's also a room decorated as it might have been in 1730, with green panelling, a mirror and sconces.

Well-informed volunteer guides are always on hand to answer any questions. There's also a one-bedroom holiday flat to let on the fourth floor (see p.157).

Luckless Lady Stair

Ladystair's Close is named after the beautiful but filthy-tongued Elizabeth, Lady Stair, who suffered badly at the hands of drunken men. After jumping from a window to escape her murderous first husband, Lord Penrose, she learned of his attempted remarriage abroad by seeing in a tinker's mirror a vision of her brother attacking him at an altar. Her brother returned from overseas and confirmed the story.

When the viscount died a few years later, in 1706, she vowed never to remarry, but was forced to save her reputation by marrying the Earl of Stair, who had contrived to appear half-naked at her prayer-window on the High Street. Only slightly less brutal than her first husband, the Earl thumped her hard enough to draw blood but then renounced any drink that was not offered to him by her fair hand.

Ladystair's Close G9

When The Mound opened at the end of the 18th century, this was the most direct route from the Old Town to the New Town. A plaque at its entrance commemorates the visit of Dick Steele, an early 18th-century wit and writer for the *Spectator*, who stood a banquet for some impoverished locals in a tavern, where he declared that he had 'drunk enough of native drollery to compose a comedy'. No record remains of his having done so.

Writers' Museum G9

Lady Stair's House, Makar's Close, Lawnmarket, **t** *(0131) 529 4901.* **Open** *Mon–Sat 10am–5pm, also Sun 2–5pm during Festival; last adm 4.45pm;* **adm** *free.*

Lady Stair's 17th-century home was heavily restored in the late 19th century and is now the Writers' Museum, celebrating the lives and works of Sir Walter Scott, Robert Louis Stevenson (see p.69) and Robert Burns with neatly laid out memorabilia and scribblings. Burns is supposed to have stayed here on his first visit to Edinburgh in 1786; his famous lines on global reconciliation ('Man to man the world o'er shall/Brothers be for a' that') are set in stone at the entrance to the close.

In the main ground-floor room, you can hear a mock-up of a slightly surreal conversation between Sir Walter and his publishers about concealing his identity, and then see his apotheosis in a scale model of his monument on Princes Street (see p.96). Up the stairs, which include a 'trip stair' to catch out strangers, are smaller rooms with pictures and mementoes of the great threesome.

The **Burns Room** is particularly interesting, with its slightly coy references to the poet's lascivious ways. This is not a museum to be hurried, and a visit is immeasurably enhanced by at least a little knowledge of the authors' works, though you don't have to read up before you arrive, as there are plenty of examples on display.

Outside, the steps leading up to the museum from The Mound, known as the

Makar's Steps, are inscribed with heartening quotations from other Scottish authors such as Hugh McDiarmid.

Brodie's Close G9

Deacon Brodie, famously the model for Stevenson's Jekyll and Hyde, was a respected town councillor in the late 1770s, and when the truth about him emerged no one could believe that someone so famous was a criminal. The way people still talk about him today, you might be forgiven for thinking he had been a murderer, not merely a thief: something about his veneer of respectability and his delight in dodging the law has made him a local hero. Now you can have a respectable cup of tea in his old kitchen (*see* Deacon's Café, p.164). Appropriately enough, a pub named after Brodie (*see* p.174) now stands opposite the criminal courts.

Statue of David Hume G9

This vague likeness, with its empty tablet and ironic classical pose, was commissioned by the Saltire Society and unveiled in 1997. Apparently the sculptor, Alexander Stoddart, proposed a Mount Rushmore-like piece carved out of Salisbury Crags, but this prime position at the start of the High Street is more appropriate to the philosopher's whole-hearted engagement with human affairs.

Although Hume, who was born in 1711 and died in 1776, was the *éminence grise* of Edinburgh in his day, the city of his birth and retirement was not quick to own its famous son: the greatest British philosopher of all time was refused a chair at the university that educated him, and at 41 was earning a pittance as Keeper of the Advocates' Library. In his charming ten-page autobiography, *My Own Life*, he famously described his first work, the *Treatise of Human Nature*, as falling 'dead-born from the press'. His controversial *History of England* was better received.

It has been suggested Hume's scepticism about the reliability of human knowledge initiated the thinking that gave rise to the modern science of psychology. He travelled abroad, earned sufficient independent means and was fêted in Paris. On his return to Edinburgh, he complained that his house in James Court, off the Lawnmarket, was too small for his cooking skills, although it did afford a view across the Firth to Kirkcaldy in Fife, where his friend Adam Smith was working on his *magnum opus*. Known as '*le bon* David' because of his mild manner and sometime popularity with the likes of Jean-Jacques Rousseau, he was one of the first to invest in the New Town, building a house for himself in South St David Street.

PARLIAMENT SQUARE

Parliament Square is set in solemn splendour around St Giles. The heart-shaped set of stones in the pavement just beyond the statue of the 5th Duke of Buccleuch is all that remains to mark the site of the 'Heart of Midlothian', Walter Scott's nickname for the old **Tolbooth**, a forbidding building that served as the council chambers, police station and town jail for several hundred years before being demolished in 1817. These stones are now the only place in Edinburgh where you're allowed to spit; in fact, it's meant to be positively lucky to do so.

The absence of the Tolbooth certainly affords plenty of room to appreciate the huge west front of the church, to which it was actually connected until 1632, when Charles I ordered 'an end to this profanation', giving the council cause to build Parliament House.

High Kirk of St Giles H9

*High St, t (0131) 225 9442, t (0131) 225 4363 (for church-related enquiries). **Open** April–Sept Mon–Sat 9am–7pm, Sun 1–5pm, Oct–March Mon–Sat 9am–5pm, Sun 1–5pm; **adm** free.*

Whether or not you find this edifice attractive, there's no denying its central place in Edinburgh's history. Supposedly constructed on the site of a chapel founded by monks from Lindisfarne in the 9th century, the huge building can be read as a miniature of the city as a whole, with its medieval tower standing proud above a smooth late-Georgian façade. The restored gilded finials on its famous crown spire, missing since about 1800, go some way towards giving the grey old pile a bit of dazzle and glory.

This was the medieval burgh's first parish church, begun around 1140. The only evidence of its origins is a single scallop capital, at the former north entrance to the nave on its northwest inside corner. The tower dates from the 14th and 15th centuries, and was capped with its distinctively Scottish crown spire in around 1486. But most of the present structure's ashlar exterior was the work of William Burn in the 1830s.

The kirk gets its name from the patron saint of cripples and lepers, though St Giles (c. 640–723) never actually visited Edinburgh. An Athenian orphan, he became a hermit in Provence, living off roots, berries and the milk of his pet deer, for which he was also made the patron saint of nursing mothers. Using his own body as a shield, he saved the life-giving animal from the huntsmen of the marauding Visigoths, whose chief was so impressed that he gave the monk land enough to found a monastery, still called Saint-Gilles. At the east end of the Preston Aisle, just before the Thistle Chapel, the oldest known example of the Edinburgh coat of arms features St Giles' pet hind.

The kirk was dedicated to St Giles in 1243. It once housed a piece of his armbone, mounted in gold with a diamond ring on one finger, which was donated to the church in 1454 by William Preston. It is still often known as St Giles' Cathedral, though strictly speaking it hasn't been one since 1689, when the Church of Scotland did away with bishops.

Interior

The interior is generally older than the exterior. The four stone pillars supporting the tower are all that remains of the Norman church destroyed by Richard II of England in 1385, but much of the rest of the interior is

15th-century. In the Reformation, the most illustrious period in St Giles' history, John Knox (see p.73) preached here to more than 3,000 people, inveighing against the idolatry of St Giles. His statue stands forbiddingly by the front door. Later, one Jenny Geddes famously threw her stool at a preacher using Laud's liturgy, part of the attempt to impose the English prayer book, shouting 'Does the false loon dare say Mass at my lugg?'

In the **north aisle** are the tombs of the leaders of the bitter religious wars: Argyll, the famous Covenanter, and Montrose, the leader of the Royalists. Characters commemorated on the right side of the nave include Thomas Chalmers and Robert Fergusson, and there's a plaque reading 'Thank God for James Young Simpson's discovery of chloroform anaesthesia' (see p.103).

Robert Lorimer's **Thistle Chapel** (1910) is worth seeking out. The Order of the Thistle was created in the 15th century by James III, and the chapel features fine stained glass by Douglas Strachan. There is other noteworthy stained glass by socialist artist William Morris and the pre-Raphaelite William Burne-Jones.

Beneath the cathedral there's an unpretentious **café** where you can take shelter and tea in the company of women of a certain age and lawyers from Parliament House.

Parliament House H9

Parliament Square, t (0131) 225 2595. **Open Tues–Fri 10am–4pm; adm free.**

This is an accessible piece of the historic city that is still very much alive. The parliament for which it was built lasted 68 years, before the Act of Union in 1707.

At the Last Riding (opening) of parliament, the procession up the street from Holyrood must have been spectacular: first came the commissioners for burghs (each with an attendant); then came the commissioners for shires (each with two attendants); the barons, viscounts and earls followed (each with a train-bearer and three attendants); then came the heralds, with splendid tabards, riding in front of the Honours of

Robert Louis Stevenson (1850–94)

Valiant in velvet, light in ragged luck,
Most vain, most generous, sternly critical,
Buffoon and poet, lover and sensualist:
A deal of Ariel, just a streak of Puck,
Much Antony, of Hamlet most of all.

W. E. Henley (1849–1903)

Edinburgh's most celebrated and brilliant prose writer came from a family of respected engineers, memorably portrayed in Bella Bathurst's book *The Lighthouse Stevensons*. Robert Louis himself was a fragile young man with a voracious sexual appetite, and most of his writings bear the stamp of his explorations around the seamy side of his birthplace: although *The Strange Case of Dr Jekyll and Mr Hyde* is set in London, it reeks of Edinburgh. In 1874 Stevenson was moved to write to a friend that he 'hates the place to the backbone', but much later, after he had gone to Samoa in the South Pacific in the hope of curing his tuberculosis, he still harked back to his roots.

His early *Picturesque Notes* remain some of the most evocative writing on the city, and his romantic novel, *Catriona*, also contains imaginative descriptions of the city before the building of the New Town. A monument to Stevenson by the artist Ian Hamilton Finlay, in the form of a stone path, a memorial slab and several birch trees, now stands in West Princes Street Gardens near the Ross Bandstand, although the writer's 'heritage trail' crops up all around the city.

manner. The roof is the best-preserved part of the original building; the front was remodelled by Robert Reid in the early 19th century, in imitation of Robert Adam, for the Court of Session – the function the place still serves.

Apart from the roof, other things to look out for include the small late-19th-century fireplace with bas-relief scenes from Shakespeare's *The Merchant of Venice*. The statues of justice and mercy by Alexander Mylne (1637) outside the south door were originally over the main entrance. Most unusual of all, perhaps, is the scene that the journalist James Bone described in 1926:

Counsel themselves when not in court or consulting near their box are walking up and down their ancient hall where once the Scottish Parliament sat. The ritual is to march in pairs facing towards one another at the turn like officers on board ship. Up and down they go...the tragedy and the comedy of the Scots Bar.

Around the walls are portraits of the 18th- and 19th-century lawyers who took hold of the reins of power when the parliament was dissolved – men such as Monboddo, Kames, Hailes, Dundas of Arniston and Henry Dundas, Henry Erskine and even, unsuccessfully, Robert Louis Stevenson (*see* box). There are two particularly fine statues: one of Duncan Forbes by Roubiliac, which was probably the first marble statue in Scotland, and one of Walter Scott at his ease.

Statue of Charles II H9

The oldest lead statue in Britain, put up in 1685, was originally going to be of Oliver Cromwell, but the council hastily changed their plans at the Restoration. Later, in the 18th century, they painted it white, prompting James Boswell to write:

The milk-white steed is well enough
But why thus daub the man all over
And to the swarthy Stuart give
the cream complexion of Hanover.

The statue is nicknamed 'Two-faced Charlie' because of the little face attached to the buckle on the back of his suit of armour.

Scotland (the crown, sword and sceptre), each carried by their hereditary bearer; next came the Lord High Commissioner, the Duke of Queensberry and the dukes (with gentleman train-bearers and eight attendants each), followed by the marquises (with their six attendants); the Duke of Argyle brought up the rear with a squadron of horse guards. The new parliament has vowed that there will never be such ceremony again.

Inside, the hammerbeam ceiling is a wonder, its great beams of Danish oak pointing down with their decorative corbels in a threatening

Mercat Cross H9

Just behind the cathedral, the Mercat Cross was the stone symbol of the medieval Burgh's trading privileges. The capital of the present cross is early-15th-century, with dragons emerging from the foliage, but otherwise it's a 19th-century replica or as good as, paid for and positioned by British prime minister W. E. Gladstone and, like many of its type, not really a cross at all, as it is topped with the unicorn of Scotland.

In its original position at the top of Fishmarket Close, the cross would have witnessed just about every event of royal importance that happened in the city: it flowed with wine when James IV rode into the city with his new bride in the early 16th century; some years later, the man who had held the castle for his granddaughter Queen Mary, Kirkcaldy of Grange, was hanged at it.

Royal proclamations have always been made from it, notably that of Charles II's accession in 1649 on condition that he accepted the National Covenant. Two years later the anti-Covenanting General Montrose was hanged in front of it, a year before the Royal Arms was torn down by an angry mob. Another couple of years and Cromwell was proclaimed protector at the cross, only for the basin's spouts to flow with claret again six years later when the monarchy was restored in 1660. All the magistrates drank to the king on bended knee, throwing the glasses over their shoulders and breaking '300 dozen'. But then in 1682 the Solemn League and Covenant was ceremonially burned by the hangman here, and seven years later William and Mary were proclaimed king and queen from it.

Finally it was used in 1745 to proclaim James VIII as king, with Bonnie Prince Charlie standing by to press the claim, though later in the year the Jacobite standards were burnt at its foot. It's not that surprising perhaps that it fell over ten years later and had to wait for the reformer Gladstone to bring it back, after an absence of more than a hundred years.

THE HIGH STREET
Upper High Street H9

The building of the **City Chambers** as the Royal Exchange in the mid-18th century (a plaque states that it went up over Craig's Close, site of the Cape Club frequented by poet Robert Fergusson), was a sign of a new security in the city after the upheaval of the '45 uprising. Even so, dealers, used to conducting their business in the open air, were initially reluctant to use it. It provides the first hint of the Georgian developments that were to come in New Town in the valley below, though the arcaded screen you now see on the streetfront, with its simple war memorial, is a much more modern addition.

Beneath the building are the spooky underground vaults and cellars of **Mary King's Close**, one of Edinburgh's 'buried streets'. Guided walks by Mercat Tours (see p.48) leave regularly from the Mercat Cross, taking you on an atmospheric journey spiced with horrible tales of people with the plague being sealed up alive, wading through human excrement and hanging one another from meathooks.

The remarkable statue in the courtyard, *Alexander Taming Bucephalus* by John Steell, made the sculptor's reputation and ensured that he was given plenty of work adorning the New Town.

On the opposite side of the street, **Old Fishmarket Close** was once home to the English spy and novelist Daniel Defoe. According to the eminent 19th-century judge and memoir-writer Lord Cockburn, this was:

where fish were thrown out on the street at the head of the close, whence they were dragged down by dirty boys and dirtier women, and then sold unwashed – for there was not a drop of water in the place – from old rickety, scaly, wooden tables, exposed to all the rain, dust and filth: an abomination the recollection of which greatly impaired the pleasantness of the fish at a later hour of the day.

Police Information Centre H9

*188 High St, **t** (0131) 226 6966, **w** www.lbp. police.uk. **Open** daily March, April, Sept, Oct 10am–8pm, May–Aug 10am–9.30pm, Nov–Feb 10am–6pm; closed 24–26 Dec; **adm** free.*

This working police station has a small exhibition of nasty weapons and a wallet made from the skin of the left hand of Burke, Edinburgh's most famous serial killer and Hare's right-hand man. There are also displays charting the history of the Lothian and Borders police force.

Just beyond the police station, **New Assembly Close** contains a surprising Georgian building, with Roman Doric columns that look quite out of place in this part of town. Designed in 1813 by Gillespie Graham, as St David's Masonic Chapel, it is home to the Law Society of Edinburgh.

Cockburn Street and Market Street G9–H9

Named after the judge, memoir-writer and wit Lord Cockburn, **Cockburn Street** twists down from the Royal Mile to Waverley Bridge. Lined with cafés, art galleries and trendy clothes shops, it really comes into its own at weekends. About halfway up the street, on the right, the back of the 12-storey City Chambers (*see above*) towers up.

Several steep flights of steps through narrow closes make their way up to the High Street on the right and down to **Market Street** on the left. At the end of Market Street, the **Playfair Steps** lead down to the National Gallery of Scotland and Royal Scottish Academy (*see p.96*) at the bottom of The Mound. Spread out beyond Princes Street Gardens is the New Town and, beyond, the sea with the hills of Fife in the distance. When they look close, it's said to presage rain.

To the left, on Mound Place, rear the twin towers of the **New College** and **Assembly Hall**. They too were designed by Playfair for the Free Church in the mid-19th century, the

Tudor front intended to line up with his Royal Scottish Academy building below and, when viewed from below, to frame the spire of the Church of Scotland's Assembly Hall in the Highland Tolbooth Kirk. The Assembly Hall was a temporary home to the Scottish parliament before it moved to Holyrood Road.

City Art Centre G9

*2 Market St, **t** (0131) 529 3993, **w** www.cac. org.uk. **Open** Mon–Sat 10am–5pm, also Sun noon–5pm during Festival; **adm** free.*

The Art Centre houses the City Council's fine art collection – some 4,000 paintings (including an impressive holding by the Scottish Colourists), drawings, sculptures, prints and photographs, mostly by Scottish artists, from the late 17th century on. The licensed café on the ground floor features a mural by William Crosbie, depicting aspects of the city's life and history.

Bank of Scotland Museum G9

*Bank of Scotland HQ Building, The Mound, **t** (0131) 529 1288, **w** www.bankofscotland. co.uk. **Open** mid-June–early Sept Mon–Fri 10am–4.45pm; **adm** free.*

This small museum in the vaults of the impressive and spectacularly sited headquarters of the Bank of Scotland (now officially called HBOS, having merged with the Halifax building society) charts the history of money. Displays include early coinage (including a Scottish coin from 1136), and forgery.

Purchased in 1800, the building has a Roman Baroque design that includes a green dome topped with a great gilded statue of Fame, which was largely the work of David Bryce towards the end of the 19th century.

Tron Kirk and Old Town Information Centre H9

*Corner of High St and South Bridge, **t** (0131) 225 8408, **w** www.blackhart.uk.com. **Open** daily April–Oct 10am–6pm, Nov–March noon–5pm; **adm** free.*

The Tron stands at the busiest crossroads on the Royal Mile, where traffic thunders over the bridges. Much altered since it was first built in the early 17th century to absorb some of St Giles' congregation, the church is named after the market weighbeam that stood in Hunter Square behind it. Services here were known as 'the Maiden Market' because of their popularity with the fashionable set of the day. A fire in the 1820s destroyed the original steeple, permanently silencing the bell that poet Robert Fergusson described as a 'wanwordy, crazy, dinsome thing'.

This was the traditional place to see in the New Year, before the celebrations became more professionally packaged (*see* p.40). The church is now occupied by the **Old Town Information Centre**, during excavations for which another old close was discovered, named **Marlin's Wynd** after the Frenchman who claimed to have paved the High Street. With a little imagination on the part of the visitor, it affords a glimpse into what 17th-century Edinburgh streets were really like.

Hunter Square, behind the church, has been the subject of an urban renewal scheme, and boasts some bronze fruit baskets by Scottish artist Ian Hamilton Finlay. Somewhere beneath is the **Union Cellar**, where nobles signing the Treaty of Union were forced to flee from disgruntled crowds.

Brass Rubbing Centre H9

Trinity Apse, Chalmers Close, High St, t (0131) 556 4364. **Open** *April–Sept Mon–Sat 10am–4.45pm, also Sun noon–4.45pm during Festival;* **adm** *free.*

Trinity Church, once one of the grandest churches in Edinburgh, was founded in 1462. In 1848 it was demolished to make way for Waverley Station and rebuilt in Chalmers Close some 20 years later, with the original stones after they had been (not very carefully) stored on Calton Hill. It was partly demolished again soon after that and only the apse now survives in the medieval stone. Two-thirds of the original altarpiece are housed in the National Gallery on The Mound.

The main reason to visit is the **Brass Rubbing Centre**, run by helpers and offering a variety of patterns and figures, from the impossibly complex to the very simple. It's not a bad introduction to church history either.

Museum of Childhood H9

42 High St, t (0131) 529 4142, w www.cac.org. uk. **Open** *Mon–Sat 10am–5pm, also Sun noon–5pm during Festival;* **adm** *free.*

Though founded by a man who hated children and who was keen to emphasize the difference between a Museum of Childhood and a museum for children, this place now happily fulfils both functions. Younger children may get frustrated by the tempting array of toys behind glass, but the activity area and fun library should make up for it. Nostalgic thirtysomethings will be delighted to recognize some of their childhood toys and intrigued by examples of the toys their grandparents might have played with.

At the end of the close facing the museum, **Moubray House** was built around 1462 and is distinguished by its outside stair. This is one of the oldest houses on the Royal Mile, with some 16th and 17th-century additions and alterations. Daniel Defoe briefly edited the *Edinburgh Courant* here in 1710.

John Knox's House H9

43 High St, t (0131) 556 9579, w www. storytellingcentre.org.uk. **Open** *July Mon–Sat 10am–5pm and Sun noon–4pm, Aug Mon–Sat 10am–7pm and Sun noon–4pm, Sept–June Mon–Sat 10am–5pm;* **adm** *£2.25.*

Saved from destruction by its association with the famous preacher (*see* box), this house juts into the High Street as obstinately as Knox expounded his beliefs. It's not even certain that Knox ever lived here, though it is claimed it is the house to which he came to to die. By way of compromise, the exhibition inside also features the man who certainly did own the place in the 16th century, James Mosman, a Catholic goldsmith hanged for his allegiance to Mary, Queen of Scots.

John Knox (1513–72)

The great Protestant reformer, a high-profile public figure and a driven man who famously feared none but the Lord, has received much bad press over the years, but his life was by no means all doom and gloom: aged 59 he married 17-year-old Margaret Stewart, and the two rode up the Canongate on their wedding day in splendid style.

Knox first appears in the records with a double-edged broadsword, acting as bodyguard to Protestant heretic preacher George Wishart at St Mary's Haddington, the village of his birth. Wishart was burned at the stake in front of Cardinal Beaton, who was himself then assassinated by Protestants.

Knox's first book, memorably entitled *The First Blast of the Trumpet against the Monstrous Regiment of Women*, was directed against the rule of the Catholic 'Bloody Mary' Tudor and Mary of Guise (Mary, Queen of Scots' mother) and was not a misogynist rant against ranks of amazons. But Elizabeth I never forgave him for it and Mary, Queen of Scots was not allowed to forget it.

Three years later, Knox's *First Book of Discipline* was instrumental in laying the foundations of literacy in Scotland, and is said to have started the strong Scottish tradition in education. Knox is famous for preaching to congregations of more than 3,000 people in the High Kirk of St Giles.

CANONGATE

The Netherbow Centre, and the appropriately named World's End pub, marks the point where the burgh of Edinburgh ends and the burgh of Canongate begins. Surprisingly perhaps, Canongate's name has nothing to do with military ordinance, but actually refers to the Canons of Holyrood Abbey at the bottom of the hill and the 'gait' (street) on which they lived. Their founder David I authorized the separate burgh in 1143 and it was only just over 500 years later that Edinburgh acquired feudal superiority over it.

Edinburgh's acquisition of Canongate in the 17th century provided new space for the city's nobility to construct grand houses with large gardens. Once such was **Moray House**, built for Mary, Countess of Home and later bought by the Earl of Moray. Its balcony demonstrates how these stone buildings initially imitated wooden construction techniques, supported on stone 'beams'. It was from here that the Covenanting General Argyll looked down during a wedding reception to see his arch enemy Montrose being wheeled to the scaffold.

The house has been a teacher-training college since the 19th century, but it's still possible to find the little summer house where the Treaty of Union with England was plotted, hidden away among the college's ugly buildings through the arch.

Scottish Poetry Society and Netherbow Gate 19

5 Crichton Close, t (0131) 557 2876, w www.spl.org.uk. Open Mon–Fri 11am–6pm, Sat noon–4pm; closed local public holidays (call for details) and Dec 24–Jan 2.

This wonderful purpose-built, free **lending library** has a wide range of Scottish and international poetry that is available to borrow (with proof of address).

In its courtyard, some of the old city wall can still be seen, including the **Netherbow Gate**, the great gate that marked the eastern

Knox, Mosman and Mary make an interesting trio, which is well exploited: there's a reconstruction of Mosman's workbench; the rather bare interior echoes to the sound of recreated arguments between Knox and Mary; and the walls are lined with well-presented historical panels and glass cabinets displaying objects relating to their lives.

The house gets across some idea of what 17th-century living quarters might have been like. The beams and ceilings are crudely patterned in a style familiar from Gladstone's Land (*see* p.65). On the ground floor some recently excavated medieval 'luckenbooths' (lockable shops) tell the story of the Netherbow Port that adjoined the house.

boundary of the old city. It was demolished 250 years ago to ease the flow of traffic, though it had long been more useful as an excise checkpoint than as a defensive barrier: a couple of decades before it was taken down, Charles Stuart's Highlanders had simply pushed their way through into the city when the gates were opened to let a carriage leave. Its speedy demolition was also an indication of how rapidly things settled down after the '45 uprising.

A carving above **No.9 High Street** gives a more accurate impression of how the gate might have looked than the fanciful bronze sign outside the **Netherbow Centre** next door. The bell from the gate can be seen in the courtyard of the centre.

Canongate Tolbooth and People's Story 19

163 Canongate, t (0131) 529 4057, w www.cac. org.uk. Open Mon–Sat 10am–4.45pm, also Sun 2–5pm during Festival; closed 25, 26 Dec; adm free.

The **Tolbooth**, with its protruding clock, was built in the French style in 1592 as Canongate's equivalent of the Heart of Midlothian. It now houses the **People's Story**, which paints a vivid picture of life as it has been lived by Edinburghers through the ages, through a wealth of information and artefacts.

The first floor has displays dedicated to the city's various trades, with the famous sign of penmakers McNiven and Cameron declaring:
They come as a boon and a blessing to men,
The Pickwick, the Owl, and the Waverley Pen.
The story becomes more entertaining the nearer the top of the building you climb, as the displays approach the present day: eavesdrop on the men in the Empire Bar, Potterow, as they make their way to a football derby between Hearts and Hibs in 1933, or on their wives in the genteel surroundings of Fergusson's Tearoom, then meet seventeen-year-old punk rock mannequin Rodney Relax, who liked to hang out at Clouds disco in Tollcross in the late 1970s. A video room on the top floor brings the story up to date.

Museum of Edinburgh 19

Huntly House, 142 Canongate, t (0131) 529 4143, w www.cac.org.uk. Open Mon–Sat 10am–4.45pm, also Sun noon–5pm during Festival; adm free.

Edinburgh's main museum of local history is rather disappointing. The 16th-century house (three townhouses joined together) is more interesting than many of the displays, which are of the old-school glass-cabinet variety. That said, it does paint a full picture of Edinburgh's history. Some of the exhibits are highly symbolic, such as the National Covenant; others are highly sentimental, such as Greyfriars Bobby's collar (*see p.84*).

Canongate Kirk 19

Opposite Huntly House, t (0131) 662 9025. Open Sun 9.30am–12.30pm, also June–Sept Mon–Sat 10.30am–4.30pm.

Built in 1688 as the parish kirk of Canongate when the Abbey Church of Holyrood was remodelled by James VII as a Catholic Chapel Royal, this church has a peculiar Dutch gable that can be explained by the close trading links the burgh had with the Low Countries in the 17th century. After his victory at Prestonpans in 1745, Charles Stuart

---

Adam Smith (1723–90)

Stolen by the gypsies as a three-year-old but recovered unharmed, the author of *The Wealth of Nations* (1776) established the very ground rules of economics, with his concepts of the division of labour and laissez-faire. Even in his own time, such ideas were enthusiastically adopted and Smith rose to become Commissioner of Customs, drawing a considerable salary.

Towards the end of his life, he bought a house in Panmure Close in Canongate, where despite his wealth he sneakily stole sugar from behind his housekeeper's back. His mutterings were famously considered by a couple of passing fishwives to make him a candidate for the asylum.

held English officers captive here; they could probably have heard the Jacobite celebrations going on down the road in Holyrood Palace.

The **graveyard** more than makes up for the plain interior, with great views of the Greek buildings on Calton Hill (*see* p.99) and more than its fair share of notable dead: Adam Smith's grave is left of the gate as you enter; further on is that of poet Robert Fergusson, with its inscription by Robert Burns, who paid for the stone; Burns' beloved 'Clarinda' is here under her real name (Mrs Agnes McLehose), then there's George Drummond, six times Lord Provost and the driving force behind the New Town. More controversially, a stone slab against the church's east wall claims to mark the grave of David Rizzio (*see* Palace of Holyroodhouse, below).

On the streetside of the graveyard is the original **Canongate Mercat Cross**, which once stood outside the Tolbooth up the road, plus a modern sculpture of the mythical chimera.

Just beyond the Kirk, **Dunbar's Close** has a well-kept Edinburgh secret in the form of a lovely little reconstruction of a 17th-century garden. In neighbouring Panmure Close is **Panmure House**, where economist Adam Smith (*see* box) lived from 1778 to 1790.

HOLYROOD

Palace of Holyroodhouse and Holyrood Abbey J9

Holyrood Rd, t (0131) 556 1096/7371, w www. royal.gov.uk; wheelchair accessible by prior arrangement. Open daily April–Oct 9.30am– 6pm, Nov–March 9.30am–4.30pm; last adm 45mins before closing; guided tours only in winter; garden open summer only; adm £6.50.

Colloquially known as Holyrood Palace, this building more than any other makes the mile royal. First opened to the public in summer 1909, it's still the official residence of the Queen in Scotland, although the royal family spend more time at Balmoral in the Highlands.

Opened in honour of the Queen's Golden Jubilee, the new Queen's Gallery, an outpost of the revamped Royal Collection in London, can now be seen in the old Duchess of Gordon's School, near the front entrance to the palace. A rolling selection of Old Master paintings are on display and entrance is available both separately and as part of the ticket price to the palace.

Exterior

As you approach the main entrance, passing the 19th-century **fountain** (modelled on that at Linlithgow Palace), the battered stonework of the left-hand tower with the conical turrets looks much older than the one on the right – and is so, being the famous apartments of Mary, Queen of Scots, built by her father James V in 1535. He also began the west front with its heraldic decoration, but the right tower didn't go up until more than a century later, under Charles II.

State Apartments

Inside the palace, the first thing you come to is the **great stair**, with its extraordinary Baroque plaster ceiling boasting ring upon ring of delicately modelled flowers and foliage, supported by four angels waving the symbols of monarchy. It forms a sumptuous prelude to Queen Victoria's **dining room**, relatively modest in its neoclassicism and still used by Queen Elizabeth II, and the **throne room**, where George IV was presented with the Scottish crown.

These rooms are followed by five that are still decorated much as they would have been in the time of Charles II, leading to his **bedroom**, where the ceiling has an *Apotheosis of Hercules* complete with the king's favourite pet spaniels.

Linking the two towers is the **Great Gallery**, lined with a bizarre array of portraits of Scottish monarchs down the ages, all with Charles II's nose. The collection, commissioned by Charles to reinforce the monarchy's divine right to rule after the War of the Three Kingdoms in the 1640s, was turned out at a phenomenal rate of about a painting a week over two years, by Dutchman Jacob de Witt.

The portraits would have looked down on the splendid scenes at the palace when Bonnie Prince Charlie briefly brought life to the place again for five weeks after his victory at Prestonpans in 1745. Reproached for his lack of attention to the ladies, he pointed to his Highland soldiers and said, 'These are my beauties!' Not much later many of them were lying dead at Culloden.

Historical Apartments

The tour concludes with the apartments that were home to Charles II's great-great-grandmother, Mary, Queen of Scots. It's easy to picture her in the tiny ante-room, vainly shielding her favourite David Rizzio from her drunken husband's murderous intentions. The two rooms in the top of the tower have been a shrine to Mary for at least the last 200 years, making them probably the most visited place in Edinburgh. It's disappointing to discover that the bed and much of the furniture is not original, and any trace of the blood from Rizzio's 51 stab wounds disappeared long ago, but the poky rooms make it easy to imagine the young Frenchwoman's dark days and long nights and to envisage her son James VI running down the stairs in his underwear to receive the news, brought to him by a man who had covered 400 miles on horseback in two and a half days, that he was king of England too.

Holyrood Abbey

The ruined abbey, used for the coronation of the doomed King Charles I in 1633, is much older than the palace, though only a tiny part of the church founded by David I in 1128 survives. It's difficult to visualize today just how grand the abbey would have been in the Middle Ages. The story goes that David I founded it after falling from his horse when it reared before an angry stag; he looked up, saw a shining cross between its antlers and vowed to found a chapel on the spot.

As you come in from the palace, turn right to reach the door of the original church, which leads into the roofless nave from the cloisters. There's also an excellent view of the nave from the gardens.

Mary, Queen of Scots (1542–87)

The roller-coaster life of Scotland's favourite ill-fated queen began in Linlithgow Palace. 'Roughly wooed' as a child by Henry VIII for her hand in marriage to his six-year-old son, Edward, she was instead married to the French *dauphin* at the age of 15, thus becoming queen of France as well.

Three years later, after her husband died, she landed in Leith and was forced to justify her Catholicism to John Knox in Holyrood Palace. She married her megalomaniac cousin Lord Darnley, only to see him murder her Italian secretary, David Rizzio. Darnley was then murdered himself, possibly with Mary's knowledge. Mary was married to the Earl of Bothwell, forced to abdicate in favour of her infant son, imprisoned by her cousin Elizabeth I of England and finally beheaded.

New Scottish Parliament J9

Designed by Spanish architects Enric and Benedetta Miralles, this complex of buildings deliberately avoids the look of pompous palaces of power (it actually promises to resemble a group of upturned boats). *The Scotsman* newspaper has also moved into a vast new HQ on Holyrood Road, which will itself undergo extensive development.

Queensberry House

The last great townhouse constructed in Edinburgh before the Union, this has been turned into one of the entrances to the new Scottish parliament building, attracting some criticism from architectural historians.

On the day that the Duke of Queensberry was out of the house signing the Treaty of Union, his son's keeper left his post to join in the street protest. The son, a monstrous brute who suffered an extreme form of the family's congenital insanity, escaped and made a hearty meal of a servant boy on the kitchen spit. The family failed to hush the incident up, and inevitably the public came to regard it as divine retribution for the duke's part in selling out to the English.

The Old Town

1 Lunch

Blonde, 75 St Leonard's St, **t** (0131) 668 2917. **Open** Mon 6–10pm, Tues–Sun noon–2pm and 6–10pm. **Moderate**. A locals' favourite, cooking up Scottish recipes based around fresh local ingredients.

2 Tea and Cakes

The Elephant House, 21 George IV Bridge, **t** (0131) 220 5355. **Open** Mon–Fri 8am–11pm, Sat and Sun 9am–11pm. A student haunt with a view of the castle from its back room.

3 Drinks

Bow Bar, 80 West Bow, **t** (0131) 226 7667. **Open** Mon–Sat noon–11.30pm, Sun 12.30–11.30pm. A traditional pub famed for its award-winning beer and whisky. Don't expect to find a seat.

The Old Town

... the city lies under such scandalous inconveniences as are, by its enemies, made a subject of scorn or reproach; as if the people were not as willing to live sweet and clean as other nations, but delighted in stench and nastiness: I believe this may be said with truth, that in no city in the world do so many people live in so little room as at Edinburgh.

A Tour through the Whole Island of Great Britain, Daniel Defoe, 1726

In medieval times Edinburgh's grandest folk lived in the Old Town beneath their poorer neighbours up on the Royal Mile, in fine houses along Cowgate and the Grassmarket. During the 18th century, however, anyone with money moved to the open spaces of the New Town, and the narrow closes that ran south between the towering blocks on the High Street became a stinking warren riddled with disease. As recently as 50 years ago, the dark side of Edinburgh lurked here in the heart of the Old Town.

The area is now the lively old heart of the city, with Arthur's Seat watching over it from the east, the green expanse of The Meadows to the south and the protective presence of the castle above. The tall buildings and bridges thrown over the valley from the Royal Mile two hundred years or so ago still plunge its ancient thoroughfare into subterranean gloom, yet it remains home to some of the city's hidden gems, some excellent museums and a host of offbeat shops and cafés.

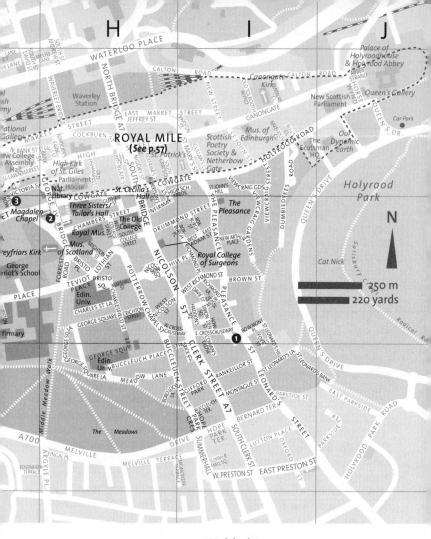

Highlights

Couples' City: Casey's, a charming old-fashioned sweet shop, p.188

Indoor City: The Museum of Scotland, an exciting look at the country's history, p.85

Edinburghers' City: The Meadows, a green expanse perfect for strolls and picnics, p.87

Literary City: No.23 George Square, one-time home to Sir Arthur Conan Doyle, p.87

Festival City: The Pleasance Cabaret Bar, one of the main fringe venues, p.183

COWGATE

To look over the South Bridge and see the Cowgate below full of crying hawkers, is to view one rank of society from another in the twinkling of an eye.

Robert Louis Stevenson, 1876

As the name suggests, this was once the route by which cattle were driven into the city to market. The finest houses in town used to line the street because it was much more accessible to the carriages of the nobility than the steep-sided High Street above, but after the building of George Square to the south and the New Town to the north the area declined into poverty. The hawkers have now given way to crowds of drunken students, especially on Friday and Saturday nights, when the whole length of Cowgate and Grassmarket becomes Edinburgh's late-night party rendezvous.

Such revelry nearly put paid to many of the Old Town's historic buildings a few weeks before Christmas 2002, when the biggest fire in the city's history broke out in Cowgate by South Bridge. Eleven buildings were destroyed and Edinburgh's nightlife was deprived of a number of top venues, including the Gilded Balloon. There has been fierce debate about how the hole left in this historic part of the Old Town should be filled, but with any luck the architects will remain true to the area's vibrant atmosphere.

St Patrick's Roman Catholic Church I9

*Cowgate, t (0131) 556 1973. **Open** Mon–Fri 11.45am–1.15pm, Sat 8am–6pm, Sun 8.30am–5pm.*

Formerly the Cowgate Chapel, an extravagant Episcopalian church, St Patrick's hides behind a pompous 1920s façade. Inside, some interesting 18th-century murals by the painter Alexander Runciman are being restored after having been painted over. The church is affectionately known as St Paddy's, testament to the area's strong Irish presence.

St Cecilia's Hall/Russell Collection of Early Keyboard Instruments H9

*Niddry St, Cowgate, t (0131) 650 2805, w www. music.ed.ac.uk/russell/. **Open** Russell Collection Wed, Sat 2–5pm, during Festival Mon–Sat 10.30am–12.30pm; **adm** £3. Collection closed for essential works until July 31 2003.*

Tucked beneath South Bridge, **St Cecilia's Hall** is one of the last vestiges of Cowgate's glory days and a must-see for music lovers. In 1821 Lord Cockburn said of it:

... there have I myself seen most of our literary and fashionable gentlemen, predominating with their side curls, and frills and ruffles and silver buckles; and our stately matrons stiffened in hoops and gorgeous satin; and our beauties with high-heeled shoes, powdered and pomatomed hair, and lofty and composite head dresses. All this was in Cowgate!

From the outside it looks like an anonymous brick warehouse, but inside is the first purpose-built concert hall in Scotland (and only the second in the UK). It was commissioned in the mid-18th century by the well-to-do aficionados of the Musical Society of Edinburgh, for whom Robert Mylne designed a well-proportioned lozenge-shaped hall, windowless to block out distracting sounds from the street but lit from above by a shallow, oval glass dome.

In its lifetime the hall has been used as a school, a Baptist chapel, a boxing academy and a Freemasons' hall, but in the late 1950s the University of Edinburgh bought it with the specific aim of restoring it to its original design and function. Concerts are now regularly held here, often organized by the Georgian Concert Society (*3 East Castle Road, EH10 5AP, t (0131) 229 8018*). See also p.183.

St Cecilia's is home to the **Russell Collection of Early Keyboard Instruments**, one of the world's most important historical collections of instruments. The displays have little explanation, but if you're lucky volunteer guide Lilian Cameron or assistant curator John

Raymond will be on hand to elucidate the collection's finer points and demonstrate the sound of some of the 51 antique harpsichords, spinets, virginals, clavichords and grand pianos.

By the entrance stands the earliest English grand piano in existence, belonging to the family of the Duke of Wellington since the 18th century. This is the instrument that sounded the death knell for the harpsichord, whose simple plucking action was super-seded by the piano's more versatile and expressive hammer action. Other highlights include the collection's oldest piece, a 16th-century Italian virginal strung parallel to the keyboard to make it a more convenient shape for domestic use, and 'the green Taskin' (1769), the world's most-copied harpsichord, which experts itch to test out with the *Goldberg Variations*. There are also harpsichords that could well have been played by Handel or Mozart, and virginals of the kind played by Queen Elizabeth I and Mary, Queen of Scots.

Some of the instruments are decorated with beautifully painted patterns, landscapes or roses; some are looking their age. At the time of writing they were arranged shoulder to shoulder in reverse chronological order, but their presentation was due to be revamped as part of the overhaul of the building taking place in the first half of 2003.

South Bridge to George IV Bridge H9–10

South Bridge was finished in 1789, a couple of decades after North Bridge. It had to be built sloping downhill from the High Street because the wealthy residents in the squares already developed at the bridge's southern end complained that otherwise it would obstruct their views. The bridge has 19 arches, but the arch you see here is the only one visible, all the others being built into the tall buildings along its length. Looking up, you can see how the original bridge was widened a span towards the west in 1929.

Just before the monumental modern arches at the back of **Sheriff's Court**, the **Tailor's Hall** (H10), the longest-surviving fine

building on Cowgate, has been reincarnated as the Three Sisters Pub and Tailor's Hall Hotel (*see* p.151). The hall was built for the Guild of Tailors in the early 17th century, and in the 18th century it was adapted for use as a theatre. When the theatre was closed down, after the licensing of the Canongate Playhouse, the hall was taken over by Campbell's Brewery, once one of more than 50 breweries in the area. None remains, but there are still plenty of places down here to stop for a drink.

Crossing the west end of Cowgate, **George IV Bridge** was named after George's visit to Edinburgh in 1822. On the right of the bridge, looking up from Cowgate, is the 1930s bulk of the **National Library of Scotland** (*see* p.54) on its seven-storey book-stack below the bridge. Opposite it is the **City Library** (*see* p.54), built in the deco-rative French style of the late 19th century. The latter's Edinburgh Room is a good place to glean information on local history.

Magdalen Chapel H10

Cowgate, at the foot of Candlemaker Row.
Open Mon–Fri 9.30am–4pm.

In the gloomy shadow of George IV Bridge, this tiny chapel is Cowgate's last bit of medieval history. Built in 1541 on the site of a church dedicated to St Mary Magdalene, it has four beautifully preserved and surpris-ingly sophisticated stained-glass roundels from the mid-16th century, representing the only complete stained glass in the whole of Scotland to have survived the Reformation.

Set in a square, the Royal Arms of Scotland and the Arms of Queen Mary of Guise sit above the Arms of Macqueen (the merchant who founded the chapel) and the combined arms of Macqueen and Kerr, the family of his wife, Janet Rynd, who ensured the comple-tion of the chapel after her husband's death. Her tomb can be found tucked into the corner below the windows.

After Janet's death the patronage of the chapel was granted to the Corporation of Hammermen, a medieval guild that added the tower and the façade facing Cowgate; its insignia can be seen above the entrance. The interior of the chapel is strikingly adorned with dark wooden tablets or 'brods', each recording a donation by a Hammerman to his less fortunate brethren.

Down the years the chapel has been used as a meeting place by many different denominations, including Baptists and Methodists. In the 19th century it was sold to the Protestant Institute of Scotland, which merged with the Scottish Reformation Society in 1965. The chapel is now its head-quarters. Reverend Sinclair Horne is happy to discuss the building's past and the intricacies of Scottish church history with visitors.

VICTORIA STREET AND GRASSMARKET

Victoria Street G9

...all these streets on the southern slope of the hill... are throughout of a low and repulsive character and are among the worst things of their kind that I have ever seen. The most notorious places in London are habitable and inviting in comparison.

Theodor Fontane (1858)

Since Fontane's time the construction of the terraced sweep of Victoria Street, designed by 'High School' Hamilton, happily put paid to some of the grimmest housing in Edinburgh. Indeed, Victoria Street is now one of the most prettified shopping streets in the whole city, its specialist stores including a broom-seller, a cheesemonger, various Latin-American gift shops and a joke shop (*see* 'Shopping').

All that remains from the time of those twisting slums are some gabled late-17th- and 18th-century buildings at the bottom of the street, where it becomes the **West Bow** (pronounced as in 'take a bow'). This was once the main approach to the Lawnmarket from the west, ascending in a sharp Z from here up to Castlehill.

Getting it in the Neck

The Grassmarket's most famous hanging was of a certain Captain Porteous, an over-bearing officer in charge of the city guard. While overseeing the execution of a popular smuggler called Wilson (at a time when smuggling was regarded as a patriotic activity), Porteous ordered his men to fire on the crowd, who were trying to make off with the corpse. Porteous was tried for murder and sentenced to death, but Queen Caroline ordered a stay of execution. This was inter-preted as a reprieve, and an infuriated mob broke into the Tolbooth where Porteous was being held, seized him and hanged him from a dyer's pole in the Grassmarket.

It has long been suspected that respected pillars of the community disguised them-selves in order to join in the lynching. As Theodor Fontane also noted: '...you will hear people tell this story with an expression on their faces that seems to say, "Those were the kind of people we were and if necessary will be again."'

Making off with corpses seems to have been the norm at one time: in the early 20th century a skeleton found immured in a house in Dalry was recognizable by the pistol still attached to its neck as that of one John Chiesly, who had shot the Lord President of the Court of Session; Maggie Dickson, or 'half-hangit' Maggie, had a pub in Grassmarket named after her, in honour of her sudden resurrection while being carted off for burial.

Many Covenanters were hanged for their beliefs on the spot outside The Last Drop pub, now marked by a memorial. In fact, so many were executed for their stand against episcopacy that these were known as the 'killing times' (*see* Greyfriars Kirk, p.83).

Grassmarket G10

On summer afternoons and evenings, the café-lined Grassmarket puts on a passable imitation of an Italian piazza, and year-round its string of historic pubs become loud and jolly at night. Even so, the place hasn't quite managed to shake off the shadow of the hangman's noose or the memory of the crowds that gathered to watch him work.

From the far end there are impressive views up to the castle and the half-moon battery, just above the northwest corner of the Grassmarket beyond Johnston Terrace. In the southwest corner, beyond the Fiddler's Arms, is **West Port** (G10), where the serial killers Burke and Hare lived early in the 19th century. The West Port was once the western gate in the city wall.

The Vennel G10

The flight of stairs leading up from the southern end of the Grassmarket is called The Vennel; halfway up it on the left is a surviving fragment of the **Flodden Wall**, hastily put up in 1513 after the disastrous defeat by the English (although in reality the enclosure of Cowgate and the Grassmarket was more useful as a protection against smugglers than against the English). The crenellated bastion with its two gunloops is original.

Further up, the **Telfer Wall** was erected in 1620 to enclose 10 more acres that had just been bought by the town. For some time these walls restricted the growth of the city to the south, which was one reason for the High Street's over-development skywards. The red sandstone building peeping between the other buildings at the top of the steps on your right is the **Edinburgh College of Art**.

GREYFRIARS AND THE MUSEUMS

George Heriot's School G10

Lauriston Place, t (0131) 229 7263. Open by appointment only.

The school is one of Edinburgh's most extraordinary buildings. George Heriot was goldsmith and jeweller to King James VI at the beginning of the 17th century. When the court moved down to London, 'Jinglin' Geordie' went too, safeguarding his lucrative royal patronage. He became one of the richest men in the kingdom but in his will remembered his home town, leaving money for the establishment of a hospital 'for the care and education of the orphans of freemen of the City of Edinburgh'.

The building was begun in 1628 by the builder William Wallace and completed by the end of the century. The school is now fee-paying and private, so unless it happens to be having an open day there is little chance for visitors to explore the splendid interior. Even so, its fine Scots Renaissance style can be well appreciated from a distance.

This side of the building is grand enough for it not to be immediately obvious that you are in fact looking at the back. The best view of the front is from the Castle Esplanade (*see* p.60). The sturdy, turreted gatehouse on Lauriston Place was designed by William Playfair in 1829.

In 1785 the Italian balloonist Lunardi took off from here to fly across the Firth of Forth. He landed near Ceres in Fife, much to the disappointment of the god-fearing locals, who had apparently mistaken him for the Angel Gabriel.

Greyfriars Kirk H10

Entrance off Candlemaker Row, t (0131) 225 1900, w www.greyfriarskirk.com. Open April–Oct Mon–Fri 10.30am–4.30pm, Sat 10.30am–2.30pm, Nov–March Thurs 1.30–3.30pm.

As you enter this rather grisly place, the monument to James Borthwick sets the tone, with its rampant skeleton festooned with surgical instruments. This was the first church built in the city after the Reformation, on the site of the old Greyfriars monastery, which had been given to the city by Mary, Queen of Scots. The eastern part, although heavily restored, is the oldest (1620); the western side was completed a century later by architect Alexander McGill. The entire church was much restored in 1938 but is well worth exploring, if just for its atmosphere.

Greyfriars' principal claim to fame, however, is as the place where the National Covenant was signed in 1638, in defiance of Charles I's imposition of the *Book of Common Prayer*. (The covenant itself is on display in the Museum of Edinburgh, *see* p.74.) The first person to sign was the Marquess of Montrose, followed by thousands of people – rich and poor – some of whom signed their names in blood.

Greyfriars Kirkyard

A sublime cemetery, yet I sud'na like to be interr'd in't. It looks sae dank and clammy and cauld.

Christopher North

This unexpectedly large and grassy grave-yard is a peaceful oasis from the bustle of George IV Bridge, where you can wander among the graves accompanied by birdsong and enjoy the excellent views into the Old Town down the hill. A board at the gate lists the famous people who are buried here: the likes of architects William Adam and James Craig, designer of the New Town; scientists Joseph Black and James Hutton; and the poet Allan Ramsay.

In the **Covenanters' Prison** in the south-west corner of the kirkyard, 1,184 Covenanters captured at the battle of Bothwell Bridge were held for five months without shelter, and with only one penny loaf each a day to eat. The tomb of 'Bloody George Mackenzie', who prosecuted the Covenanters mercilessly, is also in the kirkyard, which has long been believed to be haunted by his uneasy spirit. He was an enlightened man who gave 1,500 books to found the Advocates' Library, which later became the National Library of Scotland (*see* p.54).

Royal Museum H10

Chambers St, t (0131) 247 4027, w www.nms. ac.uk; wheelchair accessible. Open museum Mon–Sat 10am–5pm, Tues 10am–8pm, Sun noon–5pm, closed 25 Dec; Café Delos daily 11am–4pm; Soupcon tearoom daily 10am– 4.30pm; adm free; guided tours; audio tours.

The Royal Museum, purpose-built in 1861, is the largest all-encompassing museum in Britain, combining the curatorial responsibili-ties of the V&A, the Natural History Museum and the Science Museum in London. Long steps lead up to its large and airy entrance hall, made more soothing still by the trickle of water from the fountains in its two fish-ponds. Elegant cast-iron columns soar upwards, supporting delicate balconies laden with fascinating treasures, the whole space flooded with natural light.

Broadly speaking, the **Natural World** is on your left as you enter, in the building's east wing, and the **Decorative Arts** are on the right. Curving staircases at either end of the balconied main hall run up to two more floors.

To help make sense of the museum, it's worth picking up one of the **self-guided audio tours**. The highlights tour begins on the second floor, with the working 19th-century planetarium, an extraordinary mossy agate casket, and a painted stone statue of the fearsome Chinese warrior Wei T'O. It then

Greyfriars Bobby

The best-known resident of the Greyfriars Kirkyard is Bobby, whose status as the world's most famous Skye terrier is thanks largely to the Walt Disney film of his life.

When Bobby's master John Gray, a farmer from Midlothian, died one market day in 1858, his loyal little dog refused to leave his graveside in the kirkyard for 14 long years. Bobby was fed by locals, who also gave him a collar (now on display in the Museum of Edinburgh, *see* p.74), and the Lord Provost himself issued a licence to prevent him being put down as a stray, albeit reluctantly.

However, when his own time came, poor Bobby could not be buried next to his master; he was laid to rest in another part of the graveyard, in a patch of unconsecrated ground. There's a life-size statue of him just outside the churchyard at the corner of Candlemaker Row and George IV Bridge.

Sadly, in recent times some doubt has arisen as to whether Bobby's mourning was focused on the correct grave.

moves downstairs to the blue whale and the world's smallest bird, which sounds like a purring bumblebee. Next up is Princess Pauline Borghese's luxurious travelling service and Napoleon Bonaparte's tea set. It finishes on the ground floor with a look at that doomed flightless creature, the dodo. The tour takes in only a fraction of the different displays but does involve most of the rooms. There's a longer tour that goes into more detail.

In autumn 2003, a major new gallery called **Connected Earth** will open as part of BT's programme to distribute its vast heritage collections to museums around the country. The new gallery, located on the first floor of the museum, will cover the history of telecommunications from telegraphs to the internet and mobile phone, with a particular focus on the legacy of Alexander Graham Bell, inventor of the telephone (*see* p.102).

Museum of Scotland H10

Chambers St, **t** *(0131) 247 4027,* **w** *www.nms. ac.uk; wheelchair accessible.* **Open** *museum Mon and Wed–Sat 10am–5pm, Tues 10am– 8pm, Sun noon–5pm; Tower Restaurant Mon– Sat 10am–11pm, Sun noon–11pm;* **adm** *free.*

Opened to great fanfare on St Andrew's Day 1998, the Museum of Scotland really is something to get excited about. With six floors of exhibits, it weaves a compelling story of Scottish life through the ages, with up-to-the-minute displays and an intriguing collection of objects found on Scottish soil. The building itself is striking: the pink sandstone fortress, with its distinctive tower, was inspired by the country's brochs, castles, towerhouses and tenements. Individual stones of different hue were hand-picked and placed in the cladding in positions selected by the architects, Gordon Benson and Alan Forsyth.

Inside, the museum aims to tell the history of Scotland from prehistory to the present day. The exhibits, all ingeniously displayed, are designed 'to be comprehensible to an intelligent 10-year-old', which could explain some of the rather whimsical, patronizing wall blurbs, which include such comments as 'we cared about what we ate' when introducing evidence of early agriculture. That said, it's quite an achievement that the museum even comes close to its ambitious goal of telling the story of life on Earth from a distinctly Scottish perspective. Although criticisms have focused on its absorption with artefacts from around Scotland and on significant omissions such as the lack of any exhibit relating to national hero William Wallace, the museum offers up an entertaining, persuasive and important vision of cultural identity.

Level 0:
Early People and Beginnings

The ground floor has 12 rather disturbing abstract sculptures by Edinburgh artist Eduardo Paolozzi, on themes relating to Scotland's mysterious early inhabitants. Each figure incorporates the display of a historical artefact; highlights include a well-preserved bow and arrow found in a bog, a hoard of Roman silver, and an elongated wooden figure from about 600 BC, found at Ballachulish near Inverness.

The story proper starts with 'Beginnings', a colourful and action-packed display on the geology of the country more than 650 million years ago. Its later stages include howling wolves and a reconstruction of the growth of the forests and their flora and fauna, which children find intriguing.

Levels 1 and 2:
The Kingdom of the Scots

The towering Hawthornden Court on the ground floor leads straight into an exhibit on the birth of the Scottish nation. For many this will prove the most rewarding part of the visit, because it explains why this museum exists at all.

At its entrance, in 'Scotland Defined', pride of place is given to the 8th-century Monymusk reliquary or Brec Bennoch ('speckled peaked one' in Gaelic). This little metal casket for religious relics is associated with St Columba and was carried in front of the victorious army of Robert the Bruce.

Because the latter had been excommunicated by the Pope, the Declaration of Arbroath asserting Scottish independence that adorns the walls here had to be put forward by nobles of the ilk of William Wallace. Another object related to the Bruce on this level is the Bute mazer, a lovely 14th-century drinking bowl made shortly after Bannockburn.

This part of the museum takes the story of Scotland up to Union in 1707, and includes 12th-century chessmen found on the island of Lewis; a section on the Gaels, with dirks, brooches and the *Red Book of Clanranald*, the earliest Gaelic history book; the Scottish Renaissance Cadboll cup; the grisly Maiden, a guillotine designed by the Earl of Morton that also did for him; and the extraordinary Fetternear Banner from 1520, the only church banner to have survived from medieval Scotland, made for the Confraternity of Holy Blood who worshipped in St Giles' Cathedral.

Level 3: Scotland Transformed

Level 3 continues the nation's story after union with England. Power here is given literal expression by the huge Newcomen steam engine from Kilmarnock, built into the heart of the museum. It's surrounded by evidence of the industrial revolution, including the collar of a coalminer and a photo of the 'iron ring', the men who controlled iron production in the country. When one of this select group of capitalists took heed of his afterlife and gave a large donation to the Church of Scotland, his gift was described as 'the most expensive fire insurance ever'.

Elsewhere on this level are displays on the Jacobites, the Church and 'the spirit of the age', which includes some fine painted panelling from Riddle's Court in the High Street (*see* p.65).

Level 4: Industry and Empire

Level 4, dedicated to Scotland's industrial evolution, is dominated by the steam locomotive *Ellesmere*, built in Leith in 1861.

Level 5: Twentieth Century

The top floor is the most idiosyncratic gallery in the museum, taken up with a completely random selection of more than 300 20th-century items chosen by Scottish celebrities and by the public at large. Newsreader Kirsty Wark chose her Saab convertible; more meaningfully perhaps, a mother chose her baby son's life-saving incubator. Whatever you make of the logic behind the collection, the range of choices is certainly intriguing.

Outside, the roof garden provides fine views over Edinburgh and its surroundings.

THE SOUTHSIDE

Royal Infirmary G10

Lauriston Place.

Founded in 1729, this was Scotland's first hospital specifically intended for the care of the sick poor, and it soon acquired a Royal Charter from George II, whose statue can be seen outside the main entrance. Funded by voluntary public subscription, it remained dependent on charitable contributions until 1948, when it became part of the National Health Service.

The hospital was originally located in Robertson's Close, just off Cowgate. The first patient, Elizabeth Sinclair from Caithness, was admitted into a small rented house that had been converted into an infirmary of around six beds and was known locally as the 'Little House'. She was treated by members of the Royal College of Physicians and Incorporation of Surgeons, who served the hospital free of charge.

The hospital has been in the current Scottish baronial building for more than 100 years. The older part is a series of surgical and medical pavilions, or ward blocks, joined by connecting corridors. This pavilion layout was promoted by Florence Nightingale, who had been the inspiration for the Infirmary's nurse training school.

It's worth taking a quick look inside the hospital's foyer, entering by the gate beneath the Clock Tower through the 'Ever-Open Door'. Immediately to the right of the entrance is a model of the Adam building that housed the Infirmary before it moved here. It is currently in the process of moving to vast new premises on the outskirts of the city, towards Dalkeith – the fourth time it will have moved.

The Meadows G11–H11

In spring, when the cherry blossom is out, or on long summer evenings, the expanses of The Meadows are a delightful place on which to read, walk or picnic. Both Edinburgh's professional football teams once used this turf as their home ground, now trodden by countless amateur teams on Sunday afternoons. After dark, though, anywhere away from the lamplit paths is best avoided.

The Meadows were once under water, forming the Southside's equivalent of the Nor'loch, Borough Loch. In the 18th century they were partially drained by Sir Thomas Hope of Rankeillor and renamed Hope Park, and in 1886 Edinburgh's answer to London's Great Exhibition was held here. A great glass pavilion was constructed on a similar scale to the Crystal Palace in London's Hyde Park, and was visited by about 18,000 people a day over six months. When it closed, riots broke out, with students locking the manager in his office; he had to be rescued by the police.

Buccleuch Place H11

Part of the nerve centre of the University of Edinburgh, this row of houses was built by James Brown shortly after he built George Square and is an imposing piece of Scottish vernacular classicism. At **No.18** is a plaque commemorating the founding of the *Edinburgh Review* by Francis Jeffrey and Henry Brougham in 1802. This was much more than just a literary journal: it was a free-thinking supporter of the Whig reform movement of which Walter Scott said, 'its left leg was literature, but its right leg was politics'.

On **Buccleuch Place Lane** the original stone slab set into the cobbles was placed there to make it easier for street-sweepers to clear away the mire for the well-heeled. The latter

may have been making their way to No.15 Buccleuch Place (the house jutting out more than the others), where the aristocracy, often target of the *Review*'s polemics, would have graced the **George Square Assembly Rooms**, the last ballroom in the Old Town.

George Square H10–11

Built by architect James Brown in 1766, and named after his brother, this was once Edinburgh's most prestigious address, the largest and smartest development outside the Old Town's city walls before the coming of the New Town. In the 1960s Edinburgh University was somehow allowed to demolish three sides of the square to make room for several large, ugly buildings, but the surviving west side, which houses some of the university's arts departments, gives an idea of how the square would have looked.

Almost every house that remains is associated with some great historical figure: at **No.22**, young Jane Welsh secretly met historian Thomas Carlyle for the first time in 1821; **No.23** is where Sherlock Holmes' creator, Sir Arthur Conan Doyle, lived for four years some sixty years later; at **No.24** lived Henry Erskine, the great lawyer and poor man's friend, who pressed a coin into Boswell's hand when he met him with Dr Johnson, whispering 'for the sight of the bear'; Sir Walter Scott was brought up in **No.25**; at **No.27** lived General Sir Ralph Abercromby, who used to walk the square with a pet ape sporting a cocked hat; Robert McQueen, Lord Braxfield, the type for Robert Louis Stevenson's 'Weir of Hermiston', lived at **No.28**; and Henry Dundas, 'the Dictator of Scotland', died in his house here in 1811.

Other noteworthy residents included Admiral Duncan of Camperdown, lexicographer John Jamieson, and Lady Don, a fierce 'Directrix' of society balls and the last person in Edinburgh to keep a sedan chair. Her neighbour might have been the Duchess of Gordon, the beautiful patroness of Robert Burns, who had attracted attention as a girl by riding down the High Street on a pig.

Edinburgh University Collection of Historical Musical Instruments H10

*Reid Concert Hall, Bristo Square, **t** (0131) 650 2423. **Open** Wed 3–5pm, Sat 10am–1pm, also Mon–Fri 2–5pm during Festival; **adm** free.*

Though it's one of Edinburgh's most old-fashioned museums, this and the Russell Collection (*see* p.80) together make up the UK's most comprehensive display of historical instruments. Early bagpipes are a highlight.

Royal College of Surgeons H10

*Entrance at 9 Hill Square, **t** (0131) 527 1600, **w** www.rcsed.ac.uk. **Open** Mon–Fri 2–4pm; **adm** free*

The college is in an Ionic temple purpose-designed by William Playfair (*see* box below) in the early 19th century, a grand edifice befitting the prestige that the medieval craft guild (founded in 1505, when the Town Council of Edinburgh granted a Charter of Privileges to the Barber Surgeons) had acquired.

Sir Jules Thorn Exhibition of the History of Surgery and Dental Museum

The ground floor has a rather traditional display on the story of surgery; upstairs is a more accessible and highly instructive exhibition on modern surgical methods. Exhibits in the adjacent Dental Museum include extracting keys, vulcanite dentures and some fearsome-looking hand drills.

Playfair Pathology Museum H10

*18 Nicolson St, **t** (0131) 527 1649; **tours** apply in writing.*

This itself is housed in the handsome classical **Playfair Hall**, whose shelves are stacked with a gruesome array of pickled lungs, limbs, bones and even babies. According to the guide, 'the beauty of the collection is that you can see tumours of a size they would never achieve today' (beauty, in this case, being strictly in the eye of the beholder).

Old College H10

*South Bridge, **t** (0131) 650 2252. **Free tours** Mon, Wed, Fri during Festival; phone for details.*

This building – Robert Adam's largest and most spectacular public commission, begun in 1789 but not completed for many years – houses the University of Edinburgh's administrative HQ and part of its Law Faculty, plus a section of its library in the beautiful Playfair Hall. At the rear the **Talbot Rice Gallery** (*t* (0131) 650 2211, *w* www.trg.ed.ac.uk; **open** Tues–Sat 10am–5pm, also Mon–Sat 10am–5pm and Sun 2–5pm during Festival) has a small permanent exhibition of Dutch and Italian Old Masters, the university collection, and galleries that hold excellent exhibitions of contemporary art (*see* p.29).

The Old College was originally known as the New University, as the old university had been founded here some two centuries earlier. This was also the site of Kirk o'Field, the house where Lord Darnley, husband of Mary, Queen of Scots, narrowly escaped death from an explosion suspected to have been caused by the Earl of Bothwell. Darnley was subsequently strangled in the garden.

Inside the front gate, the **Old Quad** is another sensitive piece of work by Playfair. The college dome, topped with an Art Nouveau gilded youth clutching the torch of Learning, was added in the late 19th century.

> ## William Playfair (1789–1857)
>
> The son of London architect James Playfair, William first came to Edinburgh as a boy to live with his uncle, the mathematician Professor John Playfair, and went on to leave his mark on the city in the form of countless prestigious buildings.
>
> Along with his rival, Thomas Hamilton, Playfair transformed the rambling organic growth of the Old Town with a number of stately classical buildings, including the Royal Scottish Academy, the Royal College of Surgeons, and the National Monument on Calton Hill. In fact, it was largely thanks to Playfair's buildings that Edinburgh came to be dubbed 'The Athens of the North'.

The New Town

The New Town

Elegant, imposing and harmonious, the New Town is the largest expanse of Georgian architecture in Europe, rivalled in Britain only by that of Bath, Cheltenham and York. Originally a speculative property development for wealthy citizens, it was primarily intended as a residential area, but many of its streets have come to be dominated by shops, banks and grand business headquarters. It is still the preserve of the well heeled, but ever-increasing numbers of trendy shops, restaurants and bars are opening up, and in doing so broadening its social mix. Like the Old Town, the New Town with its neoclassical streets has been a UNESCO World Heritage Site since 1995.

Highlights

Couples' City: Le Café St Honoré, a secluded brasserie with a French feel, p.165

Indoor City: The Georgian House, the National Trust for Scotland's showcase period residence, p.102

Edinburghers' City: Rick's, the trendiest bar and restaurant in town, p.166 and p.176

Literary City: The Scott Monument, a Gothic landmark hailing the city's famous son, p.96

Festival City: The Assembly Rooms, a grand venue oozing with history, p.101 and p.182

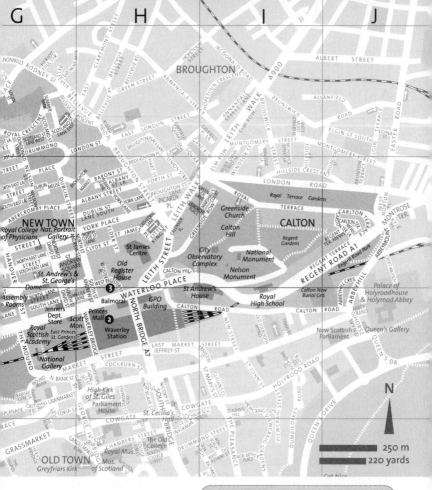

1 Lunch

Mussel Inn, *61–65 Rose St*, **t** *(0131) 225 5979.*
Open *daily noon–10pm.* ***Moderate.*** Fresh
shellfish served up in a bright, modern
atmosphere. Booking advisable.

2 Tea and Cakes

Duck's de la Gare, *on the Waverley Steps*,
t *(0131) 557 8887.* ***Open*** *Mon–Fri 7am–7pm, Sat
9am–6pm, Sun 11am–5pm.* Great French-style
coffeeshop near the station, with good-value
sandwiches, croissants and cakes.

3 Drinks

Café Royal, *17–19 West Register St*, **t** *(0131)
556 1884.* ***Open*** *Mon–Thurs and Sun
11am–11pm, Fri and Sat 11am–1am.* Choose
between the smart Circle Bar with its leather
seats, Doulton portrait tiles and island bar,
or the more restrained Bistro Bar.

PRINCES STREET AND THE MOUND

Princes Street F9–H9

Edinburgh's main shopping drag allows for the city's most memorable views of the Castle. Buildings (much ruined by the shopfronts) line its north side from near the Caledonian Hilton hotel at its western end to Waterloo Place and the foot of Calton Hill, but the views to the south across Princes Street Gardens, created after the draining of the Nor'Loch in the 18th century, are compensation enough.

St John's and **St Cuthbert's** (F9), the churches at the western end of Princes Street Gardens, are worth a look if they're open. The Episcopalian St John's is the older, designed by William Burn in 1816. On the corner of King's Stables Road is a round tower that originally protected the **West Churchyard** from grave-robbers. The churchyard itself contains some notable graves, including those of Dr Jamieson (of the Dictionary), George Meikle Kemp (architect of the Scott Monument), Thomas De Quincey and John Napier, the inventor of logarithms. In the corner, just under Castle Rock, the tombstone of someone called Jekyll is said to be where Robert Louis Stevenson got the name for Mr Hyde's alter ego.

National Gallery of Scotland G9

The Mound, t (0131) 624 6200, w www. nationalgalleries.org; wheelchair accessible. Open Mon–Sat 10am–5pm, Sun 2–5pm; extended hours during Festival; adm free.

The National Gallery of Scotland was opened just under 150 years ago in William Playfair's second Greek temple on this prime site, tucked behind his first effort on Princes Street, which is now the Royal Scottish Academy (*see* p.96). In fact this building was meant for both the Academy and the new National Gallery, which explains its unusual set of four Doric porticoes, one on each façade, giving grand entrances for the Academy on the east side and the National Gallery on the west. Trains now rumble beneath on their way through Princes Street Gardens to Waverley Station, and the gallery's main entrance is through the building's northern end, facing the paved area at the bottom of the Playfair Steps.

Given that it was not even awarded a grant until the start of the 20th century, some time after similar galleries in Liverpool and Manchester, its collection – and those of its extensions, the Scottish National Portrait Gallery (*see* p.103) and the Scottish National Gallery of Modern Art (*see* p.110) on Belford Road – are all the more astonishing. The three galleries are all run by the National Galleries of Scotland, which is funded by central government, and more recently also by the Heritage Lottery Fund, with an annual purchase grant of little more than £1.5 million.

Only a selection of the gallery's wonderful collection can be hung at any one time, but many paintings are in storage at The Mound and staff are usually delighted to show visitors specific items. Others are held at the National Gallery's two outstations: **Paxton House** (*t (01289) 386291*), a Palladian mansion near Berwick-upon-Tweed with a grand collection of Chippendale furniture and about 70 appropriate paintings; and, further afield, **Duff House** (*t (01261) 818181*), an extraordinary Baroque palace in Banff, designed by William Adam.

The neat set of **ten octagonal galleries** on the ground floor was refurbished according to Playfair's original plan, with claret walls, rich green carpets and paintings hung two or three deep in the traditional manner, which gives the place the masculine air of a gentlemen's club. Friendly staff in smart tartan trousers greet visitors on arrival in the lobby, where you can pick up an audio highlight guide and a very basic floorplan.

Immediately after the Second World War the gallery's collection was considerably enhanced by the long-term loan of the

The Growth of a Vision

The New Town's evolution was different in every respect from that of the Old Town with its slow organic growth. It was first formally proposed in 1753, by the city's six-times Provost, George Drummond, after one of the stacked-up 'lands' on the High Street collapsed with considerable loss of life. Six years later Drummond began the work of draining the Nor' Loch – the lake beneath Castle Crag, where Princes Street Gardens now stand, which had long been an obstacle to the northwards expansion of the city. In 1763 work began on the North Bridge to link the historic High Street to the New Town area (and to the road to Leith). And in 1766 a competition for the design of the New Town was won by 23-year-old James Craig.

The young architect's rectangular design formed the basis of the first New Town: George Street along the top of the natural ridge, the 'Lang Gait' (now Princes Street)

running parallel to it to the south, and Queen Street parallel to it to the north. These three straight streets, which end in St Andrew Square in the east and Charlotte Square in the west, were named in honour of George III and his family.

Almost at once Edinburgh saw a 'great flitting' of the gentry from their crumbling piles on the hill into the stately new homes of the New Town, leaving the Old Town to sink into squalor. By the 1820s, a 'Second New Town' had gone up further down the hill to the north, where Drummond Place and Royal Circus were linked by Great King Street. The second development, with its grand, showy circuses, was less austere and has largely stayed true to its residential intentions.

In a final wave of construction, the Earl of Moray caved in to the temptation to develop for profit the land he owned to the west, which he did in some style in the streets surrounding the monumental Moray Place.

private collection of the Duke of Sutherland (a different branch of the family from the Dunrobin Sutherlands notorious for their Highland Clearances). This had originally been part of the Royal Collection, brought together by the Duc d'Orléans in the early 18th century. It's probably the finest private collection in the UK and still forms the core of the gallery's Old Masters. It's also bound to be on display at any given time because it never goes out on loan. (The gallery's most famous sculpture, Antonio Canova's *Three Graces*, is shared on a seven-year rotation with the Victoria and Albert Museum in London, where it will be until 2006).

Main Floor: East Wing

Two of the main octagonal galleries are devoted to 16th-century Italian paintings and include five Titians and a Tintoretto. Titian's late *Three Ages of Man* is a superb allegorical portrait of maturity, old age and infancy, with its subjects rapt in a landscaped dream of sex, death and love. Also in these rooms are Titian's mythological paintings, *Diana and Callisto* and *Diana and*

Actaeon. Beyond are Velázquez's exceptional *Old Woman Cooking Eggs*, an interesting Goya done for a tapestry design, and a very popular El Greco.

Main Floor: Central Gallery

On their own in a small gallery, at the heart of the collection, are some of its most prized exhibits – the second series of Nicolas Poussin's *The Seven Sacraments*, painted in the mid-17th century. Described as 'one of the most profound achievements of European post-Renaissance art', this sombre and restrained series of paintings depicts the rituals of the early Christian church, from Baptism to Extreme Unction. They form an extraordinary set of historically researched dramatic tableaux, each a crowded but carefully staged moment of high religious significance.

The ground-floor galleries also contain some Flemish and Dutch 17th-century paintings, including a Rembrandt self-portrait, several paintings by Rubens and the largest and probably earliest Vermeer in existence, *Christ in the House of Martha and Mary*.

Main Floor: West Wing

The highlights of the museum's small English collection – Thomas Gainsborough's *The Hon. Mrs Graham*, Joshua Reynolds' *The Ladies Waldegrave* and John Constable's beautiful *Denholm Vale* – are in the west wing. There are also two fascinating paintings relating to the Jacobite cause, one by Agostino Masucci showing the Old Pretender, Prince James Francis Edward Stewart, marrying the Polish princess Clementina Sobieska in 1719, and the other by Pier Leone Ghezzi of the baptism of their son, Bonnie Prince Charlie, the following year.

In the last room is the American painter Benjamin West's vast picture with the self-explanatory title *Alexander III of Scotland rescued from the fury of a stag by the intrepidity of Colin Fitzgerald*. Two other interesting pictures painted by Americans are John Singer Sargent's *Lady Agnew of Lochnaw* and Church's *View of Niagara Falls from the American Side*.

Standing guard as you leave the galleries in the west wing are two superb full-length portraits by Sir Henry Raeburn (*see* box 'Edinburgh's Logo on Ice'): one of a kilted Highland chieftain, Colonel Alastair Macdonell of Glengarry, whose friend Sir Walter Scott declared him to have lived a century too late; and the other of Sir John Sinclair of Ulster, an eminent statistician and agriculturalist from Caithness, in the uniform of the regiment he temporarily raised for prime minister William Pitt during the Napoleonic Wars.

Upper Floor

On the south side of the upper floor are the gallery's most popular paintings – some fine examples of the work of Delacroix, Van Gogh, Degas, Gauguin and the French Impressionists and postimpressionists.

On the north side are highlights of the gallery's Renaissance paintings, including the Trinity Altarpiece, on long-term loan from the Queen, and the finest piece of 15th-century painting to survive in Scotland, created for the altar of the Holy Trinity Collegiate Church, which once stood on the site of Waverley Station, by Netherlander Hugo van der Goes. The panels show the church's provost, Sir Edward Bonkil, kneeling in adoration of the Father, Son and Holy Spirit; on the back of the panels are portraits of James III, his wife Queen Margaret of Denmark, St Andrew and St Canute.

In the same room are Raphael's *Holy Family with a Palm Tree* and his later *Virgin and Child*, known as the 'Bridgewater Madonna', both magnificently cleaned and restored.

Lower Floor: The Scottish Collection

The national galleries' collection of Scottish painting and sculpture is divided between the main buildings across the city; the main National Gallery on The Mound is home to a comprehensive selection of Scottish art from the end of the 16th century until about 1920.

Left of the entrance are a selection of early still lifes; then you arrive at David Allan's *Pittcairn Family*, an early example of the conversation-piece group portrait that became so popular in the 18th century.

Down the steps are some early and late examples of the work of the brilliant portrait painter Allan Ramsay. Ranked alongside Joshua Reynolds, he has many more in the National Portrait Gallery on Queen Street (*see* p.103). Here you can see his intriguing painting of Romantic French philosopher Jean-Jacques Rousseau in Armenian garb, commissioned by his friend David Hume.

Possibly the most influential Scottish painter of all was David Wilkie, whose genre paintings of ordinary Scottish life are wonderfully busy studies of people's facial expressions and mannerisms. His *Pitlessie Fair* and *Distraining for Rent* dramatize contemporary social history, while his *Letter of Introduction*, with the house dog suspiciously sniffing the stranger's trouser-leg, was based on his own experience of arriving in London. A measure of Wilkie's influence can be seen in Sir George Harvey's picture of people enjoying the sport of curling on a frozen loch.

Edinburgh's Logo on Ice

You're likely to have seen the image before, but coming face to face with Sir Henry Raeburn's *Skating Minister* in the Scottish Collection of the National Gallery is quite a surprise: it's small, the dark figure's forward-leaning energy is all the more striking for being so contained, and you can even make out the tracks of skates on the frozen loch.

The picture has long been a puzzle to art historians, and was only really 'discovered' in 1949. Most do believe it to be by Raeburn, who probably painted it in 1795, but some are only half convinced that it is the Reverend Robert Walker, though all agree that the figure could well be skating on Duddingston Loch at the foot of Arthur's Seat. Ironically, though it is by no means a typical Raeburn portrait it has become easily his most famous, perhaps because of the minister's dignity on the ice.

Another strength of Scottish painting was in landscape: Horatio McCulloch's *Inverlochy Castle* and Alexander Nasmyth's *Tantallon Castle* are good examples. Also look out for Nasmyth's picture of Princes Street in 1825, showing the original North Bridge, some typical streetlife of the time, and the half-built columns of the Royal Scottish Academy.

Possibly the most popular pictures in the collection are Sir Joseph Noel Paton's fairy paintings, illustrations of Shakespeare's *A Midsummer Night's Dream*. Visitors have been so amazed by their obsessive detail and by the not entirely benign activities going on in the undergrowth that Oberon and Titania's quarrel and reconciliation had to be glazed over to protect them from being pawed.

Edinburgh and Scottish history receive almost as vivid treatment at the hands of William Allan in his *Murder of Rizzio*, and in the next generation with James Drummond's loving recreation of the Grassmarket in the Old Town as the setting for his *Porteous Mob*, from Walter Scott's *Heart of Midlothian*. It's hard to overestimate the influence of Scott's *Waverley* novels on Scottish painting, and you're likely to see other illustrations of scenes from his work in the galleries.

Another great illustrator of literature was William Dyce, whose *Francesca da Rimini* was inspired by an episode in Dante's *Inferno*. All that has remained of Francesca's elderly husband's murderous intentions since the picture was damaged and reframed is a sinister hand creeping in on the left.

The great landscape and seascape painter William McTaggart is represented by his early work, *Spring*, and by *The Storm*, painted much later in 1890. This tremendous studio painting of a sea rescue off the coast of Kintyre was acquired by Andrew Carnegie and given to the gallery by his widow on the centenary of the births of both her husband and the painter in 1935. The rescuers and their lifeboat putting out for a threatened fishing boat are almost swallowed up by the raging elements.

As you approach the 20th century, a complete change of style is marked by the work of the Glasgow School, the best examples of which are Sir James Guthrie's solid, earthbound *Hind's Daughter*, of a farm labourer's heavy-headed child among cauliflowers, William York MacGregor's *Vegetable Stall*, with the stallholder eerily painted out, and James Paterson's heart-stopping landscape *Autumn in Glencairn, Moniaive*.

In contrast, at the end of the gallery are some delightfully colourful works by Celtic revivalist John Duncan; *The Progress of the Soul*, a series of four hung in rotation, by Phoebe Anna Traquair (*see* p.28); and Robert Burns' decorations of *Diana and her Nymphs* for Crawford's tearooms.

Prints and Drawings

The National Gallery's excellent collection of prints and drawings, some of which may be in storage at any one time, includes some beautiful examples of the visionary poet William Blake's work, as well as the Henry Vaughan bequest of J. M. W. Turner's watercolours. Only shown in January, when the light is at its weakest, their colours have been wonderfully preserved since 1900.

The Playfair Project

The National Gallery of Scotland and its neighbour, the Royal Scottish Academy, are being joined together beneath Princes Street Gardens as part of the most extensive re-development in their history. The £27-million project also involves the restoration and refurbishment of the Royal Scottish Academy building (see below), providing a spacious glass-fronted concourse area and a sculpture court overlooking East Princes Street Gardens.

Inevitably the work has proved controversial among preservationists, but it is hoped that the new restaurant and café with views of the Gardens, the introduction of some sophisticated IT signing, the new lecture theatre and education suite and an enlarged galleries shop will all help underpin the future of these venerable institutions. The link building is scheduled to open in 2005.

Royal Scottish Academy G9

The Mound, t (0131) 225 6671/5945, w www. nationalgalleries.org. Open Mon–Sat 10am–5pm, Sun 2–5pm; closed for refurbishment until Aug 2003; adm free.

The RSA, now a temporary exhibition space that is being managed and redeveloped by the National Galleries of Scotland (see above), has been housed in one of William Playfair's Greek temples on The Mound since 1919. The current renovation work is scheduled for completion in August 2003, and the event will be marked by the exhibition Monet: the Seine and the Sea.

Although the Academy sounds terribly establishment, it was born of revolt, when in 1826 11 artist members of the Royal Institution for the Encouragement of the Fine Arts in Scotland declared themselves fed up with the Royal Institution's autocratic and aristocratic administration. In founding their new Academy, they laid out five simple objectives for the benefit of the artists: to have an annual exhibition; to instruct students free of charge; to open a library

dedicated to the fine arts; to provide funds for artists in need; and to admit Honorary Members on the strength of their talent. Broadly speaking, that is still what the Academy does today. It hosts the annual exhibitions of the Royal Scottish Society of Watercolourists (usually in winter) and the Society of Scottish Artists (in autumn), as well as the bi-annual shows of the Royal Academicians themselves.

On top of the Academy you can see the 25-ton statue of Queen Victoria dressed up as Britannia by John Steell, who also designed the Scott Monument.

Scott Monument G9

East Princes Street Gardens, t (0131) 529 4068/ 3993, w www.cac.org.uk. Open March–May and Oct Mon–Sat 9am–6pm, Sun 10am–6pm, June–Sept Mon–Sat 9am–8pm, Sun 10am–6pm, Nov–Feb Mon–Sat 9am–4pm, Sun 10am–4pm; adm £2.50.

Love it or loathe it, the Scott Monument is probably the second most famous of Edinburgh's landmarks. In 1847 Dickens wrote to a friend:

I am sorry to report the Scott Monument a failure. It is like the spire of a Gothic church taken off and stuck in the ground.

Yet it is its very Gothic excess that contrasts well with the clean classicism of the New Town, as well as being entirely appropriate to the romantic imagination of the city's most famous son (see box).

In John Steell's statue, Scott sits wrapped in his shepherd's plaid, a book on his knee, his faithful deerhound Maida casting up an enquiring glance at her master, who is more than twice lifesize. His pose is unheroic but also suggestive of what some resent about him: his love of the rustic squirearchy and promotion of a kind of 'tartan idyll'. Decorating the monument are 64 statuettes of characters from the novels and from Scottish history. The most clearly visible are the four on the first gallery: Bonnie Prince Charlie, the Lady of the Lake, Meg Merriless and the Last Minstrel.

Sir Walter Scott (1771–1832)

The influence of eminent advocate and prolific writer Sir Walter Scott on his country's reputation is hard to overestimate. Though nowadays few read his works for pleasure, he was instrumental in partially reviving the capital's lost pride by organizing George IV's visit in 1822, by restoring the crown jewels and by celebrating the city in prose and verse, and the favour was returned by the city when his famous monument was restored at great expense.

Counting the likes of James Fenimore Cooper and Pushkin among his admirers, Scott published his first work in 1802 and wrote about 20 books in half as many years, enabling him to build a fantasy home for himself at Abbotsford in his beloved Borders. Though he was cursed with a limp from the polio he contracted as a child, and though there was a melancholy strain in all he wrote, he was an energetic supporter of other Scottish writers, especially James Hogg, who called him 'Wattie'.

As an engineering feat alone, the monument was quite an achievement. Its architect was an unknown called George Meikle Kemp, whose ambitious design, modelled on the author's beloved Melrose Abbey, was assured of stability by the sinking of a shaft 52ft down to the solid rock to support a structure just under four times that height. Sadly, Kemp never saw his great project finished: he drowned in the Union Canal one dark night in 1844, just before its completion.

Buried in the foundations of the monument, along with some coins, newspapers, maps and medals in a glass jar, is a bronze plaque declaring that Scott's writings 'were then allowed to have given more delight and suggested better feeling to a larger class of readers, in every rank of society, than those of any other author, with the exception of Shakespeare alone'.

There are 287 steps up to the highest gallery, which offers panoramic views over the city and out to sea.

Around North Bridge H8–9

On the west side of the bridge, the lumbering but impressive **Balmoral Hotel** (*see* p.151) with its bloated clock tower was built in 1902 as the North British Railway Hotel and is now one of the most luxurious hotels in the city. Beside it, the often windy **Waverley Steps** lead down to **Waverley Station** (H9), which is the only station in Britain to have been named after a novel. British Rail attempts to rename it were successfully opposed.

Before the Battle of Waterloo, the area in front of Old Register House was called Shakespeare Square and was famous for its Theatre Royal, where the most celebrated actress of the day, Sarah Siddons, appeared in 1784. Nothing daunted by her initial failure to draw the expected applause, she continued with her performance, and in one of the silences that followed a voice was heard to murmur, 'That's no' bad!', which provoked a thunderous ovation. Walter Scott's dramatised version of *Rob Roy* was another highlight that saved the theatre's by-then ailing fortunes, but it was a short reprieve.

In 1859 the theatre was demolished to make way for the new **General Post Office** (H9), the large Italianate building now standing empty on the North Bridge opposite the Balmoral; Prince Albert laid its foundation stone in 1861. The enormous building is currently being converted into offices, but the familiar façade of the much-loved East End landmark will be saved.

By the GPO on the corner of North Bridge is one of the city's more dramatic public monuments, the **Wellington Statue** (H9), unveiled on the 37th anniversary of Napoleon's defeat at Waterloo (18 June 1852). The entire weight of the sculpture balances on the horse's hind legs and tail – which is made even more remarkable, as one contemporary observed, by the fact that the horse has no hocks. Moves to have the statue taken down because of its British Tory associations have been unsuccessful.

Old Register House H8

2 Princes St, t (0131) 535 1314, w www.nas.gov. uk. Open Mon–Fri 9am–4.30pm; adm free.

This grand domed building forms arguably the finest example of Robert Adam's neo-classical architecture. Begun to his design in 1774 but not completed for nearly 30 years, it was significant at the time on three counts: it was the first public building in the New Town, designed to encourage further private investment and to provide a welcome as you came off North Bridge; it was the first building in Edinburgh to be graced with a dome (partly hidden behind the pediment); and it was the first purpose-built repository for records in the Western world.

Since then it has altered remarkably little, and is still the HQ of the **National Archives of Scotland**. Visitors are welcome to explore the temporary historical exhibitions held in the foyer and, if they ask, to have a quick look at the splendid domed interior. To use the reading rooms, you have to apply for a ticket.

CALTON

Waterloo Place H8–9

Waterloo Place crosses the **Regent Bridge**, which has a triumphal arch depicting scenes from Waterloo. The bridge was engineered by Robert Stevenson (grandfather of Robert Louis) in order to connect the New Town to the new Calton Jail. Enormously expensive, it ploughed right through part of the **Old Calton Burial Ground**, whose prominent obelisk is the **Martyrs' Memorial**, erected in 1844 by the Complete Suffrage Association.

Abraham Lincoln casts a sympathetic eye on the memorial from over the way on the **Emancipation Monument**, which commemorates the Scottish-American dead of the American Civil War. Next to it is the **David Hume mausoleum**, Robert Adam's great, round, Roman-style mausoleum for the great, round sceptical philosopher. On his burial in 1776, Hume's friends kept vigil for eight nights by the gloomy tomb – some said

this was to prevent the devil coming for his atheist soul, but it was more likely to have been to prevent medical students from coming for his valuable corpse. Also buried here are the painter David Allan, and Thomas Hamilton, the architect of the Martyrs' Memorial, the Royal High School (*see* below) and much else in the city.

On the site of old Calton Jail, **St Andrew's House** was modelled on the UN building in Geneva. Opened as the new Scottish Office on the day Britain declared war in 1939, it still houses some of its departments.

The Terraces I8–J8

Regent Terrace, Carlton Terrace and Royal Terrace form a loop around the bottom of Calton Hill.

At the start of **Regent Terrace**, the home of foreign consulates and private art galleries, is the **Royal High School** with its colonnaded façade. The building, by Thomas Hamilton, is the most complete contribution to the Greek Revival in Edinburgh. Although the building dates from 1825, the school itself is the city's oldest, founded in 1519. Former pupils include Walter Scott and at least three future lord chancellors of England. In 1968 the school moved out to the genteel suburb of Barnton to become one of the city's better state schools and the building currently stands empty, although it nearly became the seat of Scotland's parliament when the government was casting around for a site in the 1990s. In front of the school stands Hamilton's **monument to Robert Burns**.

As Regent Terrace rounds the bend it turns into the elegant curve of **Carlton Terrace** (spelt with an 'r' – it was named in the 19th century after the Prince Regent's London home, Carlton House). As it heads back towards Leith Walk and Broughton, the road then becomes **Royal Terrace**, the city's grandest and most spectacularly sited residential street. The simple form of **Greenside Church**, with its square steeple topped with four tall pyramids, beckons you from the end of the street.

Calton Hill H8–I8

Calton Hill offers one of the finest views of the city, with the Forth road and rail bridges in the distance. The root of the name Calton is less august than this landmark deserves, being derived from the old Gallic word for a hill with scrubby bushes on top, where folk used to hang out their washing. Many of the structures on the hill were designed by the tireless William Playfair (*see* p.88).

Nelson Monument I8

*t (0131) 556 2713. **Open** April–Sept Mon 1–6pm, Tues–Sat 10am–6pm, Oct–March Mon–Sat 10am–3pm; **adm** £2.*

This 106ft signal tower, designed by Robert Burn, was built in memory of Admiral Nelson after his death in 1805, and its flags still fly the signal 'England expects that every man will do his duty' on the anniversary of that death, 21 October. The foundation stone was laid two years after construction and in great secrecy, the authorities fearing that a crowd of Nelson's admirers might fall off the cliff.

A climb to the top of the steep, narrow staircase is bracingly rewarding, and if the wind is strong, admiring the view over the low parapet can be quite hair-raising. The 'time-ball' on the mast drops at 1pm every weekday, in conjunction with the One O'Clock Gun fired from the castle. This was set up in 1852 for the benefit of skippers on the Firth of Forth and used to be linked to the castle by the longest telegraph wire in the world.

City Observatory Complex I8

*Summit of Calton Hill. **Open** for group visits by prior arrangement with the Astronomical Society of Edinburgh, t (0131) 667 0647.*

Calton Hill's walled observatory complex comprises a number of buildings. At its heart is the domed **City Observatory**, designed by William Playfair in 1818 to provide accurate time-readings. Inside is the two-faced 'Politician's Clock'; one side faces into the observatory, the other faces out, to allow ships' captains to set their timepieces.

The Gothic style of the battlemented **Old Observatory House** in the southwest corner of the complex was designed to complement the old Calton Jail down the hill. Built for the optician/astronomer Thomas Short from 1776 to 1792, it is almost the only surviving work of James Craig, the planner of the New Town.

In the northeast corner, the **City Dome** (1895) has been the venue for various astronomical attractions but currently stands empty. Playfair's **Doric Monument** to his mathematician uncle John Playfair (the president of the Astronomical Institution, which awarded him the contract for the City Observatory) stands in the southeast corner.

National Monument I8

Astronomical is the only word to describe the cost of the scheme proposed by, among others, Scott, Cockburn and Lord Elgin (the one with the Marbles): a replica of the Parthenon to commemorate the fallen of the Napoleonic Wars. The National Monument was started in 1826 but ran out of funds three years later. Something of an embarrassment to the city (known as 'Edinburgh's Folly'), it inspired various early 20th-century schemes to complete it: as a National Gallery, as a celebration of 200 years of the Union, or even as part of yet another new parliament building. All came to nothing. Now the great blocks beneath its 12 Doric columns provide a very solid viewpoint, regularly mobbed at events such as the Festival fireworks.

Monument to Dugald Stewart H8

Playfair's finishing touch on Calton Hill was his spectacularly positioned circular **monument to Dugald Stewart**, the professor of moral philosophy, a more exact copy of the Lysicrates monument, put up only a year after Hamilton's monument to Burns (*see* p.98). If it looks familiar, it may be because TV journalists seem fond of using it as the backdrop for reports on the latest developments on the Scottish political scene.

At the bottom of the steps to the left, hidden in the ivy, you can find the unusual **memorial to Saint Wolodymyr the Great**, ruler of Ukraine.

GEORGE STREET, QUEEN STREET AND THE SQUARES

St Andrew Square G8–H8

Little of the original character of the first square to have been built in Craig's New Town has survived, although the houses along the north side do give a rough idea of what it all would have looked like. The rest of the square has been largely swallowed up by grandiose financial institutions. However, the exterior of the elegant Palladian country house that is now the **Royal Bank of Scotland**'s headquarters would still just about be recognizable to its 18th-century owner, Sir Laurence Dundas, Commissary-General in the British Army. In 1774 Dundas pipped the city council to the post by buying this site before they could build St Andrew's Church here (forcing the church to be built on George Street, *see* p.101). Inside, the building has been much altered, but it's worth taking a look at the starry 19th-century dome in the telling room. The reckless Sir Laurence later lost the house one night in a bet, but rather than move out built his creditor another house in Drummond Place.

The 150ft **column** that stands in the middle of the square dominates its surroundings as surely as the man on top held the reins of power in late 18th-century Scotland. This was Henry Dundas, first Viscount Melville, who was dubbed 'Harry IX, uncrowned King of Scotland' and described by Cockburn as 'the absolute dictator of Scotland'. Dundas served as prime minister William Pitt's right-hand man, keeping rigorous control over the voting of peers into Westminster and wielding the kind of power that was only finally done away with by the 19th-century reform acts. The column, which was modelled on Trajan's in Rome, was erected in 1823, some two decades before Nelson's Column in London.

The six elongated figures that sit on top of the **Bank of Scotland**, which is located next door to its rival, represent Navigation, Commerce, Manufacture, Art, Science and Agriculture – the interests at the time of the British Linen Bank, which commissioned the building in 1846.

Moving clockwise round the square, you'll find a plaque on the wall at **21 St David's Street** marking the place where David Hume's house once stood. One of the first people to move into the New Town, the philosopher is supposed to have taken it in good part when the daughter of a judge graffitied his wall with 'St David'. He replied that many a worse man had been canonized, and the name has stuck for the street. Ironically, given Hume's atheism, the house was later used for the first meetings of the Bible Society of Scotland.

George Street F9–G8

Once the city's financial centre, George Street has now become its most lively upmarket shopping street. All along the street, you'll see flashy new bars and restaurants jostling for position with many of the city's most illustrious shops, and some of Edinburgh's grand bank buildings have now become spectacular, echoing drinking halls.

Unlike those of Princes Street, George Street's Georgian origins are still clearly visible if you look above the shopfronts. Over the first building on the north side of the street, the **Standard Life Assurance** building, the original pediment (1839) includes Steell's sculpture of the Wise and Foolish Virgins. Next door is another more modern interpretation of the parable in bronze relief.

Walking down George Street from St Andrew Square, you will be more or less following the line of the New Town's early development: the first cross-street, **Hanover Street**, was begun in 1784, the second, **Frederick Street**, in 1786, and the third, **Castle Street**, six years later.

One of the joys of George Street is the changing panorama: the green dome of West Register House in Charlotte Square (see p.102) is like a beacon at the far end of the street; looking south down Hanover Street, the Royal Scottish Academy (see p.96) is backed by the Assembly Hall's twin towers (see p.71) and the spire of the Highland Tolbooth Kirk, now The Hub (see p.65); and to the north the New Town slopes down to the Firth of Forth and the hills of Fife beyond, a view enhanced at Frederick Street by Playfair's church of St Stephen in Stockbridge (see p.112).

St Andrew's and St George's Church was forced to make do with its constricted site after being displaced from St Andrew Square (see p.100). The New Town's first parish church, its shape is reminiscent of Bernini's St Andrew's in Rome's Quirinale. The elliptical sweep of the interior is certainly beautifully proportioned, and contains modern stained glass and the original boxed pews.

The church is most famous for being the scene of the Disruption in 1843, when Thomas Chalmers (whose statue stands at the crossroads of Castle Street and George Street) led 407 ministers out of the Church of Scotland's annual assembly to set up the Free Church – free, that is, from the interference of patronage and the Civil Courts. When the churches reunited again in 1929, they met here for the first time. In 1964 St Andrew's was amalgamated with St George's in Charlotte Square, when the latter was converted into West Register House (see p.102).

Opposite is the **Dome**, the largest of George Street's bank-turned-bars, on the site of the old Physician's Hall. Its magnificent interior is hidden behind a grand columned portico.

On the north side at No.45 stands the former premises of *Blackwood's Magazine*, which counted George Eliot among its contributors. The English essayist Sydney Smith, one of the editors of the first number of the *Edinburgh Review*, stayed next door at No.46 and described Edinburgh as a place of 'odious smells, barbarous sounds, bad suppers, excellent hearts and most enlightened and cultivated understandings'.

Just before Frederick Street and the statue of William Pitt, **No.60** has a plaque commemorating the 1811 visit of radical romantic poet Shelley, on honeymoon with his first wife Harriet Westbrook, who committed suicide shortly afterwards. Continuing along the right side of the street, you pass two Edinburgh institutions: **Aitken & Niven** (see p.186), outfitters to the gentry, and **Hamilton & Inches**, the city's finest jewellers (see p.186).

North off George Street, **39 North Castle Street** (virtually unaltered since the late 18th century) was once home to Sir Walter Scott and has a miniature of the statue on the Scott Monument over the door.

Assembly Rooms G9

54 George St, t (0131) 220 4349, w www. assemblyroomsedinburgh.co.uk.

This splendid building opened for magnificent society gatherings at the end of the 18th century and is still serving much the same purpose today, albeit with considerably less formality. Its pompous portico by William Burn was a later addition to John Henderson's austere essay in continental classicism.

The last 200 years have witnessed a procession of the famous and wannabe-famous through its doors. Sir Walter Scott announced himself to be the author of the Waverley novels here (everyone already knew), and William Makepeace Thackeray was nearly lynched here when he disparaged Mary, Queen of Scots. Dickens gave hugely popular public readings in the Music Hall behind the Assembly Rooms – so popular that in 1861 the organizers oversold tickets several times over and several people nearly suffocated in the crush. He gave the reading anyway and commented on the attentiveness of the audience in such discomfort.

No such mishap could occur today: the Assembly Rooms are efficiently run as a year-round venue for a wide range of events, from club nights to poetry readings. They really come into their own, however, at the Festival, when the splendid rooms are converted into a theatrical Fringe megavenue (see p.39).

Charlotte Square F9

A masterpiece of Georgian design, Charlotte Square was created by Robert Adam. Though he never saw the finished effect, it is his work on the north and south of the square that is responsible for its unity and poise.

On the west side, St George's Church, designed by Robert Reid to Adam's instructions, became West Register House in the 1960s. Its distinctive green dome is modelled on St Paul's in London and is topped with an illustration of the natural order as it was held to be at the time: a gilded cross on top of the earth on top of the imperial crown.

From 1959 to 1999, No.6 was the Edinburgh residence of the Secretary of State for Scotland; since 1999 it has been the official residence of Scotland's First Minister.

The Georgian House F9

7 Charlotte Square, t (0131) 226 3318, w www.nts.org.uk. Open daily April–Oct 10am–6pm (last admission 5.30pm), Nov, Dec, Feb, March 11am–4pm (last admission 3.30pm); adm £5.

This is the National Trust for Scotland's showcase Georgian residence, and the New Town's partner to Gladstone's Land on the Royal Mile (see p.65). Volunteer guides are on hand in the five main rooms (ground-floor bedchamber, basement kitchen, drawing room, dining room and parlour) to answer any questions you might have. The furniture is of particular interest, being distinctively Scottish, with the best examples in the dining room and parlour.

One of the few original features of the house is the stone-compartmented wine cellar in the basement. It's worth looking at this first and then watching the 20-minute video reconstruction of a day in the life of the house. Another short film on New Town architecture also sets the house in context.

The immaculately clean kitchen is one of the most popular rooms, with its boiling range, rotating roasting spit (powered by the fire) and baking range. Here the food would have been prepared for the informal but gigantic suppers that were a feature of the Scottish enlightenment, and very different from prim Victorian dinner parties.

Charlotte Square Drawing Room Gallery F9

28 Charlotte Square, t (0131) 243 9300. Open Mon–Sat 10am–5pm, Sun noon–5pm; adm free.

The National Trust has also furnished a room on the south side of Charlotte Square as it might have been shortly after the square was built. Elegant furniture complements the fine proportions of a room decorated with antique prints and paintings, while downstairs the tinkle of coffeespoons adds to the refined ambience. There's also a restaurant popular with an older crowd.

Queen Street F8–G8

Queen Street looks much as Princes Street must have done when it was first built. Most of this long terrace of grand townhouses is now occupied by the offices of insurance companies, accountants, land agents, surveyors and civil engineers, and this has left it little altered externally.

For a few years after it went up, rough gorse would have sloped down from here to the mills on the Water of Leith; today the tops of these slopes are the more formally landscaped **Queen Street Gardens**. Once the private gardens of the Earls of Wemyss (whose townhouse was at No.64), these are still reserved for local keyholders.

Discovery Room F8

*52 Queen St, t (0131) 225 6028. **Open** Easter–Oct Thurs 10am–noon, or by appointment; **adm** free.*

This was the home of Sir James Young Simpson (1811–70), pioneer of anaesthesia and the first Scottish doctor to be knighted. One dark afternoon in November 1847, Simpson and his assistants Dr Keith and Dr Duncan were discovered sprawled unconscious beneath his dining room table. Upon recovery, Simpson described his first experiment with chloroform:

> Before sitting down to supper we all inhaled the fluid, and were all under the mahogany in a trice, to my wife's consternation and alarm.

Born in Bathgate in West Lothian, Simpson had a long struggle against the prejudice of the clergy and his obstetrician colleagues to get the practice of anaesthesia accepted. Both groups considered pain to be a natural part of giving birth, and it was only after he successfully kept Queen Victoria under during labour that the outlook for his innovation improved. He also invented the obstetric forceps named after him, wrote several classic medical textbooks and was a keen archaeologist. The full story can be explored in the Discovery Room, which also affords a rare glimpse inside a New Town property of the period.

Royal College of Physicians G8

*9 Queen St, t (0131) 225 7324, w www.rcpt.ac.uk. **Open** group visits by prior arrangement.*

Now the HQ of the Royal College of Physicians, this house, one of the first on the street, was designed in 1771 by Robert Adam and re-designed in the neoclassical style by Thomas Hamilton when the college moved down from George Street in 1844. The grand portico at Nos.9 and 10, with its three health-related statues of Hygeia flanked by Aesculapius and Hippocrates, stands out solidly from the rest of the street. The library is accessible to anyone with an interest in matters medical, but more general group tours of the spectacular interior are by arrangement only.

Beyond the college at No.4 are the headquarters of **BBC Scotland**, on the site of the Philosophical Institution founded in 1848 with Thomas Carlyle as its first president.

Scottish National Portrait Gallery G8

*1 Queen St, t (0131) 624 6200, w www. nationalgalleries.org; wheelchair accessible. **Open** Mon–Sat 10am–5pm, Sun noon–5pm, and extended hours during Festival; **adm** free.*

National portrait collections seem to be a distinctly 19th-century British idea, and Scotland's was the second of only four in the world – the others being in London, Dublin and, since 1962, Washington.

Founded in 1882, the Scottish NPG was the dreamchild and gift to the city of John Ritchie Findlay, philanthropist and proprietor of *The Scotsman* newspaper. The building, designed by Robert Rowand Anderson and completed in 1890, was intended to be different from Playfair's classical galleries on The Mound, drawing its inspiration from the Doge's Palace in Venice, and its red Dumfriesshire sandstone and Gothic revivalist style are in striking contrast to the Craigleith stone and classical proportions of Queen Street.

Anderson also incorporated an impressive array of sandstone historical figures into his design, though sadly they're not labelled. The first group, at the northwestern corner as you approach the gallery from the east along Queen Street, consists of a sailor, a soldier, a philosopher and a political economist: Adam Duncan of Camperdown, Sir Ralph Abercromby, David Hume and Adam Smith respectively. On the front façade, John Knox

George Drummond (1687–1766)

Six times Lord Provost of Edinburgh, George Drummond was instrumental in founding the Royal Infirmary (see p.86) and St Cecilia's Hall (see p.80), and supported the proposals for the New Town in 1753. Though the competition for the design of the latter was not held until 10 years after his death, he had already had the Nor'Loch (now Princes Street Gardens) drained and laid the foundations of North Bridge.

In the '45 rebellion Drummond marched out against the Jacobites as captain of the College Company, but little by little his men flitted away down the narrow closes off the West Bow, until he was left at the gate with only a handful, including the philosopher David Hume.

stands steadfast in the fourth niche along. Next to him towards the entrance is the Good Sir James Douglas, standing above and to the right of Robert the Bruce, whose heart he took with him in a box on the Crusades. High up on a pinnacle above the main entrance is History; below her, Scotland sits crowned in the central arch behind; and she in turn is supported by Industry and Religion.

Past the main entrance, James VI and I stands next to Malcolm III, followed by earlier Scottish kings. On the corner of Queen Street and North St Andrew Street stand geologist James Hutton; surgeon John Hunter; artist Sir Henry Raeburn; 17th-century lawyer James Dalrymple, 1st Viscount Stair, who wrote the 'Institutions of the Law in Scotland; and John Napier, the 16th-century inventor of logarithms.

Round the corner, in the middle of the eastern wall on North St Andrew Street, is Mary, Queen of Scots, supported by her defenders John Lesley and William Maitland. At the top corner nearest St Andrew Square are four poets from the 14th to 16th centuries: John Barbour, William Dunbar, Gavin Douglas and Sir David Lindsay.

En masse the statues introduce the formidable processional frieze in the Gallery's Central Hall, where the figures all appear again, contributing to a still more expansive Victorian celebration of great Scots, which even includes Edward I of England, three Vikings and a Druid.

Completed in 1898 by artist William Hole, the frieze is as informative on Scottish costume down the ages as it is on the protagonists of the country's history. The first of the large murals to be completed, in 1901, was the depiction of St Columba's mission to the Picts; Hole carefully researched the history and even gave Columba the correct Celtic hairstyle. His attendant's crozier is the still-extant example reputed to have belonged to St Fillan. (It's also a reminder that the building was once the home of the Museum of Antiquities, now removed to the Museum of Scotland; see p.85).

Scotland has turned out a disproportionate number of great men and women, and most can be found inside the Gallery. The earliest portrait is of James III on a coin (1485), while the most recent subjects are still key players in Scottish political, sporting and commercial affairs. Unfortunately the texts for the pictures are models of brevity, so invest in the museum's excellent 'Companion Guide' to find out more about the sitters' lives.

Particularly worth looking out for are David Allan's William Inglis, the golfing surgeon; Allan Ramsay's David Hume, whose contentment is so great that the master painter clearly struggled to depict the slightest trace of intelligence in his face; Alexander Nasmyth's Robert Burns, unfinished to preserve the fleeting delicacy of the likeness; and Henry Raeburn's striking portraits of the tartan-trousered fiddler Niel Gow and the sarcastic judge Lord Elgin, who looks as if he's just eaten a lemon. More recent highlights include Oscar Kokoschka's spirited expression of the characters of amateur boxer Douglas Douglas Hamilton and his wife Elizabeth; Alexander Moffat's restrained picture of Muriel Spark wearing a red scarf; and Avigdor Arikha's feathery portrait of the Queen Mum.

On the ground floor there are special exhibitions, a good bookshop and an excellent non-smoking café.

OUTER NEW TOWN

North of Queen Street and west of Charlotte Square are the grand squares and gracious curves of the 'Second New Town', which was added to the original New Town grid from 1801 onwards.

North New Town F8, G8–9

The first extension to the original rectangular grid were the streets sloping away down the hill to the north of Queen Street. **Abercromby Place** (named after General Sir Ralph Abercromby, who gave up his blanket to a cold soldier as he lay dying himself at Aboukir Bay in the Napoleonic Wars) was the first curved street in town and its construction drew astonished crowds. **No.17** was home to architect William Playfair (see p.88) and is now an upmarket guesthouse (see p.152). At **No.3** a plaque commemorates Marie Stopes, pioneer of birth control.

Named after the Lord Provost George Drummond (see box, p.104) who proposed the building of the New Town, **Drummond Place** was the second phase's equivalent to St Andrew Square, and it too has its share of distinguished former residents. **No.38** was home to Adam Black, another Lord Provost of Edinburgh, who bought the rights to the *Encyclopaedia Britannica* in 1827 and is commemorated with a huge statue in Princes Street Gardens. Sir Robert Lorimer, architect of the National War Memorial and the Thistle Chapel in St Giles, altered **No.4** for his brother John Henry Lorimer, introducing curves to the panelled front door and a scroll above it. As a plaque records, this was also the home of painter Sir William McTaggart. Finally, **Nos.31 and 32** were the home of Sir Compton 'Whisky Galore' Mackenzie until 1972, and only just managed to accommodate his library of 12,000 books.

To the west of Drummond Place, **Great King Street** was completed in around 1820. Named, like George Street, after 'mad'

George III, it consists of four palace-fronted blocks that are divided in the middle by Dundas Street. J. M. Barrie, the author of *Peter Pan*, lodged at **No.3** as a struggling young journalist. Earlier in the century, Thomas de Quincey, author of *Confessions of an Opium Eater*, stayed in the brand new block at **No.9** for four years.

The corner of Great King Street and **Dundas Street** is the spot where the last sedan chair in Edinburgh was available for hire until 1870. Half a century earlier, there were more than a hundred of these single-seater, two-man-powered weatherproof boxes for the well-to-do plying the city streets. Today rickshaws, pulled by English-speaking rugby players, have emerged as their environmentally friendly replacement.

James Clerk Maxwell (see box) was born at what is now the **International Centre for Mathematical Sciences** at 14 India Street (closed to the public). In **Jamaica Street**, Kay's Bar (see p.176) is a cosy pub housed in the last surviving early 19th-century house in the street.

James Clerk Maxwell (1831–79)

Brought up on the family estate of Glenlair in Galloway, James Clerk Maxwell returned to the city of his birth to attend the Edinburgh Academy, where he was nick-named 'Dafty' because of his stammer and strong regional accent. But he was far from dim: at the tender age of 15 he presented his first paper to the Royal Society of Edinburgh in George Street.

This was the start of a career in science that was to see him take up the first ever professorship of experimental physics at Cambridge in 1871. There he developed his revolutionary ideas on electromagnetic radiation – his 'Maxwell equations', which laid the foundations of subsequent theories of electronics.

He died just eight years later, but his work was important enough for him to be hailed the 'father of modern science', and for his contribution to be ranked alongside the discoveries of Newton and Einstein.

Moray Place F8

The last and most impressive of the New Town developments, **Moray Place**, **Ainslie Place** and **Randolph Crescent** were built by the Earl of Moray between 1822 and 1855, with the benefit of lessons learned from the first two developments: there is less uniformity and a reduction in the number of straight lines, and even stricter instructions on admissible designs were put in place.

Moray Place, an enormous 12-sided Roman Doric circus, was the glorious centrepiece of the development. Enough of its original appearance (right down to the cobbles and the paving stones) has survived for it to be a favourite location among film-makers, and it has stood in as a generic early-19th-century 'grand address' for any number of great Western European cities.

The Earl of Moray ensconced himself firmly at **No.28**, while religious reformer Thomas Chalmers lived at **No.3** from 1831 to 1835. Some of the houses are now smart offices; those that aren't probably belong to millionaire lawyers. On the north side, spectacular private gardens are visible from Doune Terrace slope down to the Water of Leith.

The West End D9–E10

For visitors arriving from the airport, the West End is often their first impression of the city, and it's not an entirely happy one, bordering as it does Haymarket – Edinburgh's junior train station and an ugly great road junction to boot. Shandwick Place establishes the heavy Victorian tone of the area, with its rank of imposing stone-fronted tenements backed up by the spooky twin neo-Gothic towers of St Mary's Cathedral, the area's only real sight.

For the best glimpse of this strangely contradictory area, explore the alleyways behind West Register House on Charlotte Square and stroll up the grand boulevard of Melville Street towards the cathedral to see how the 19th-century interpreted the neoclassicism of the 18th.

St Mary's Episcopal Cathedral E9

Palmerston Place, t (0131) 225 6293, w www. cathedral.net. Open daily 7.15am–6pm (to 9pm in summer).

Built between 1874 and 1917, St Mary's contrasts dramatically with Melville Street's classical lines. The architect, George Gilbert Scott, considered it one of his finest works., and it undeniably possesses a solemn dignity. The stone buttresses supporting the 270ft main spire can also be seen on the inside of the church.

The twin spires of the cathedral (known as Barbara and Mary after the Walker sisters, who left money for the church's completion) completely upstage the **statue of Robert Dundas** halfway down the street.

Dean Village
and Stockbridge

06

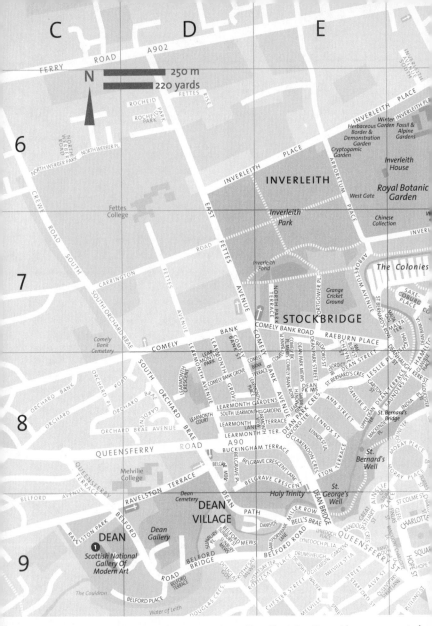

Dean Village and Stockbridge

A little stonemill village on the Water of Leith, Dean Village sits snugly in its wooded valley just a few minutes' walk west of the New Town, way beneath the towering Dean Bridge. Once bustling with bakers and millers, these days it provides an unexpected treat on the romantic walk upriver from Stockbridge to the Scottish National Gallery of Modern Art and the Dean Gallery. These two treasure troves of artistic endeavour are best reached from the riverbank via the Dean Cemetery, an atmospheric Victorian graveyard above the village, with monuments to, among others, architect William Playfair and memorialist Lord Cockburn.

1 Lunch

The Gallery Café, *74 Belford Rd*, **t** *(0131) 332 8600*. **Open** *daily 10am–4.30pm*. The Scottish National Gallery of Modern Art's café has a terrace overlooking the Sculpture Garden that's a great spot for lunch on sunny days.

2 Tea and Cakes

Au Gourmand, *1 Brandon Terrace*, **t** *(0131) 624 4666*. **Open** *Mon–Sat 9am–6pm, Sun 10am–5pm*. A French café/deli near the river providing excellent snacks for office workers by day. By night (Wed–Sat 7–10.30pm) it's an idiosyncratic *haute cuisine* restaurant.

3 Drinks

The Bailie Bar, *2–4 St Stephen Street*, **t** *(0131) 225 4673*. **Open** *Mon–Thurs 11am–midnight, Fri and Sat 11am–1pm, Sun 12.30–11pm*. A cosy, welcoming spot that draws an eclectic mix of locals. Food is good and reasonably priced.

Highlights

Couples' City: The walk from Stockbridge along the Water of Leith to the galleries, p.110–112

Indoor City: The Scottish National Gallery of Modern Art, strong on French art, p.110

Edinburghers' City: The tranquil delights of the Royal Botanic Garden, p.113

Literary City: The eerie Dean Cemetery, p.111

Festival City: The Theatre Workshop, p.112

The quirky little town of Stockbridge boasts some interesting independent shops and restaurants serving contemporary cuisine. A highlight is the delightful Ann Street, designed by artist Sir Henry Raeburn, in honour of his wife.

A short walk north downstream are the horticultural glories of the Royal Botanic Garden, with their superb views towards the distant skyline of the Royal Mile.

DEAN VILLAGE

Scottish National Gallery of Modern Art C9

*75 Belford Rd, **t** (0131) 624 6200, **w** www. nationalgalleries.org; wheelchair access. **Open** Mon–Sat 10am–5pm, Sun 2–5pm; extended hours during Festival; **adm** free.*

The National Gallery of Modern Art was founded in 1959, after more than half a century's determined lobbying. First housed in Inverleith House (*see* p.113) in the Botanic Garden, it was the UK's first national gallery devoted to modern art. Inverleith House was always intended to be temporary, but it took another 25 years, until 1984, for the government to provide a permanent home here, in William Burn's 1825 neoclassical building first erected for John Watson's School for the fatherless children of professionals.

Lawn and Sculpture Garden

The **front gardens** have recently been transformed by US landscape artist Charles Jencks' *Landform*, a stepped S-shaped mound of grass next to shallow crescent-shaped pools of water that just about manages to avoid municipal ordinariness. The ducks love it. Viewed from the first-floor windows of the gallery, *Landform* provides a satisfying link with Dean Gallery over the road (*see* p.111).

At any one time you might find work by Jacob Epstein, Eric Gill, Henry Moore and Eduardo Paolozzi on display in the **Sculpture Garden** at the rear (overlooked by the terrace of the gallery's excellent café; *see* p.169).

Inside the Gallery

What you will see is difficult to predict: the gallery has a reputation for inspired hangings of selections from its collection of more than 800 paintings and 200 sculptures on a two- or three-monthly rotation. However, if a work you want to see is not on display, staff will let you view it in storage on request.

The gallery plays to its strengths: the opening of the offshoot Dean Gallery has provided a new home for its outstanding

array of Dada and Surrealist work, but Cubism, the Scottish Colourists and German Expressionism are still strongly represented here, as is modern French art in general.

An almost continuous series of **special exhibitions** are mounted, usually in Rooms 1–6, where you can pick up a regularly updated floorplan. The gallery has rooms of varying sizes, which allows the wide range of its collection to be divided up into manageable and accessible groups and periods, and also makes it simple for visitors to navigate.

One good place to start is with the **early 20th-century French art**. These are works that fall into something of a grey area between this gallery's collection and that of the National Gallery on The Mound (*see* p.92), but they are anything but grey themselves: examples include Fauvist work by Henri Matisse and Andre Dérain.

Edouard Vuillard's shimmering, softly charged interiors and still lifes are some of the paintings most recently transferred from the National Gallery, and form part of Sir Alexander Maitland's important 1960 gift. One of that collection's most popular works is Picasso's melancholic *Mère et Enfant* (1902–3) from his 'Blue Period', prompted by the suicide of a close friend.

Surprisingly perhaps, the National Gallery has a lot of work by **20th-century Scottish artists** – prior to 1960 the gallery had a rule that no work be purchased by living artists or artists who had been dead less than ten years. Among the earliest to look out for are the Colourists, including F. C. B. Cadell, John Fergusson and George Hunter, who shared a love of colour informed by their enthusiasm for French paintings.

Their works are often hung in such a way that you can explore the development of their different styles over time. The portraiture of Cadell, for instance – who had his studios in Ainslie Place – displays an interesting progression: his nude, *The Model* (1912), employs a vague, impressionistic style and cunningly incorporates a mirror; *Portrait of a Lady in Black* (Miss Don-Wauchope; 1921) is much simpler, sharper and more definite.

The gallery also has a representative selection of the work of the **Edinburgh School**, William Gillies, Anne Redpath and William McTaggart (grandson of the 19th-century landscape painter). More recent Scottish artists such as Ken Currie and Ian Hamilton Finlay are also well represented, and there's a significant and evolving collection of work by younger Scottish and British artists, such as Callum Innes and Rachel Whiteread.

Dean Gallery D9

73 Belford Road, t (0131) 624 6200, w www. nationalgalleries.org. Open Mon–Sat 10am–5pm, Sun 2–5pm; extended hours during Festival; adm free.

An extension of the Gallery of Modern Art, the Dean Gallery is housed in a building converted from an old school, the Dean Orphanage, built by Thomas Hamilton in 1833, with a Tuscan portico flanked by peculiar open chimney towers. The clock on the front was taken from the old Netherbow Port on the Royal Mile, which was demolished in 1764. From its lawns you also get a good view of another palatial school building in the area – the Jacobean-style Melville College, still a private school for boys.

Through the front entrance on the right is the **Eduardo Paolozzi Gallery**, which includes a recreation of the artist's own London studio. Something of an Edinburgh institution in his own right, Paolozzi was a close friend of the Gallery of Modern Art's most significant benefactor, the champion golfer Gabrielle Keiller (*see* above). A significant proportion of Keiller's collection, which includes pieces by Man Ray, Miró and Tanguy, is now on display in the Dean's ground-floor galleries, as are 26 drawings and paintings from the collection of the artist and great promoter of Surrealism Sir Roland Penrose, including works by Delvaux and Ernst.

Upstairs is a space for temporary exhibitions of modern art and photographs. The Dean also has a large library and archive of artists' books, catalogues and manuscripts; works can be consulted by appointment.

> ## Gabrielle Keiller (1908–95)
>
> Edinburgh owes the extraordinary contents of the Dean Gallery to the discerning eye of one 20th-century woman. Born in North Berwick while her American father was on a golfing holiday, Gabrielle Keiller went on to become a championship golfer herself. It wasn't until the death of her third husband, fellow golfer and eminent archaeologist Alexander Keiller, however, that Keiller's dedication to art collecting began. She subsequently became the close friend and patron of Leith-born artist Eduardo Paolozzi, and amassed a formidable number of works by her favourite Dada and Surrealist artists.

Dean Cemetery D9

Dean Path. Open 9am–5pm (to dusk in winter).

Dean Cemetery is the nearest Edinburgh comes to Père Lachaise in Paris – not so much in scale as in the quality and profusion of its statuary. Look out for the mausoleum to Glasgow magnate James Buchanan, which echoes Playfair's monument to Dugald Stewart on Calton Hill (*see* p.99), and, at the far end of the cemetery, for the monuments to William Playfair (*see* p.88), to memorialist extraordinaire Lord Cockburn, and to Lord Jeffrey of the *Edinburgh Review*.

Continuing round to the north wall, you'll find memorials to Robert Reid, architect of St George's in Charlotte Square (*see* p.14), and publisher Alexander Black.

Dean Village and Estate D9

Secluded Dean Village is a short, steep climb up Bell's Brae from the busy West End, but down by the old bridge you'd never know it. Once the city's most important flour-milling area, the area no longer feels much like a village: many mills have been refurbished as residential accommodation and smart offices for architects, and at any time except rush hour, when office workers stream back and forth, the place is eerily deserted.

Dean Village D9

Well Court (E9), the red stone fantasy on Damside, was constructed at the end of the 19th century for John R. Findlay, owner of *The Scotsman* and a philanthropist who wanted to provide work for redundant mill workers. He also wanted a fine view from his house high up in Rothesay Terrace to the south.

Bell's Brae was once the main road out of Edinburgh. The early 18th-century house on the right is **Bell's Brae House** (E9), the first in the village to be restored (in 1948). Next door is **Baxter's Incorporation Granary**, a restored 17th-century building with the insignia of the Baxters (or Bakers) over the door. Between the two is Hawthornbank Lane; from here steps lead up to Belford Road and the **Drumsheugh Baths** (E9), an 1882 swimming club decorated with Ottoman motifs; it's worth a look if you can persuade someone to let you in.

Dean Estate E8–9

Dean Bridge (E9) was part of a speculative project in 1831 by the Lord Provost, John Learmonth, to replicate the success of the Raeburn Estate (*see* p.113), and remains one of Scottish engineer Thomas Telford's finest works. The superb views are blocked by a parapet put up in 1912 to deter would-be suicides. The church and spire at its north end is **Holy Trinity** (E8), built in 1837.

The **riverside path** (*see* p.132) beneath the bridge is something of a lovers' lane. Sheltered in winter, dappled and lined with bluebells in summer, and spooky after dusk, it has lovely hanging gardens (private) that slope down from the elegant early-19th-century estates above. Further north along the path are **St George's** and **St Bernard's Wells** (*see* p.133).

STOCKBRIDGE

Stockbridge, which spans the Water of Leith around the old Stock Bridge on Deanhaugh Street, occupies a rough square north and west of the New Town's Royal Circus. The **Stock Bridge** replaced a ford and footbridge in 1786, but the present bridge dates from 1900.

The neighbourhood still has the air of a small country town, but in the last 20 years it has become one of the most fashionable parts of the city, and is one of Edinburgh's trendiest quarters for bars and cafés. The likes of Marianne Faithfull and Warhol's rock-chick Nico are rumoured to have stayed here, and since Raeburn's time the area has been a magnet for artists and creative types who can't quite afford a place in the New Town.

Deanhaugh Street and **Raeburn Place** (E7), Stockbridge's main drag, have good shops and cafés. On the northwest side of the river, southern Stockbridge is taken up by the Raeburn Estate (*see* below). Along the south bank runs **Hamilton Place** (F7–8), with the old fire station (now a public toilet) on the left and the **Theatre Workshop** (*see* p.181) in what was once the Wesley Hall.

The neat little houses and streets of **The Colonies** (F7), between Glenogle Road and the river, were an experiment in housing for working-class artisans, but their charm and location have made sure they've never been affordable to those they were intended for.

South of Hamilton Place, **St Stephen Street** (F8) has quirky clothes and antique shops with two-tiered frontages. The south side, with steps going up and down to the small shops, restaurants and bars, is an extended example of an architectural arrangement once common in Edinburgh. In the 1970s, the street was at the forefront of Stockbridge's transformation into a trendy area for artists and students (and more recently for yuppies).

Further along on the right is the Georgian arched gateway to **Stockbridge Market** (F8), which announces the availability of 'Butcher Meat, Fruits, Fish and Poultry'.

Described by one academic of the time as 'a mouth without cheeks', **St Stephen's Church** (F8) is a landmark. It was originally intended to stand in Royal Circus but, like St Andrew's before it, ended up in a much smaller site. Step forward William Playfair (*see* p.88), who rose to the challenge by building an unusual square church at a diagonal to the corner, with a Baroque tower and yawning entrance monumental enough to draw the eye from

George Street far up the hill. The church's cavernous but plain interior, which has always been too large for its congregation, was divided in two in the 1950s. It's now a community centre.

Over the road, the comparatively tiny late-19th-century **St Vincent's Episcopal Church** (F8), still a place of worship, has connections with the Knights Hospitallers of Jerusalem.

Raeburn Estate E8

Henry Raeburn (1756–1823) was the finest portrait painter Scotland has produced: his famous *Skating Minister* is in the National Gallery of Scotland (*see* p.95). Born in Stockbridge, Raeburn bought a large house overlooking the Water of Leith when he became successful, and it was he that was behind this early 19th-century development southwest of Deanhaugh Street, designed to tempt wealthy residents away from the New Town. Raeburn insisted that there be no shops or taverns, that the balconies be copies of those in Northumberland Street, and that the railings be like the ones in Heriot Row.

The estate's showpiece is **Ann Street**, named in memory of Raeburn's wife. A gem of Georgian architecture, it is one of Edinburgh's most desirable addresses thanks to the comparative delicacy of its neoclassicism, its human scale and its hilltop site. The houses on this street are also unique in the New Town for having front gardens, which have created a community spirit seldom found in Edinburgh's smarter addresses. The publisher Robert Chambers lived at No.4, while in 1829 Thomas de Quincey lodged at No.29 in the headiest phase of his opium-eating.

Built a decade later, the grand, open sweep of **St Bernard's Crescent** extends on either side of a pretty central garden. It's worlds apart from from the quiet intimacy of Ann Street. In **Danube Street**, No.7 was home to landscape-painter Horatio McCulloch. Until the 1980s, house prices on this street were a little depressed by the activities of a madam, though she apparently ran her establishment with the dignity her address commanded.

Royal Botanic Garden E6–F7

*Entrances on Arboretum Place and Inverleith Row, t (0131) 552 7171, w www.rbge.org.uk; wheelchair accessible. **Open** daily April–Sept 10am–7pm, March, Oct 10am–6pm, Nov–Feb 10am–4pm; closed 25 Dec, 1 Jan; **adm** free. **No picnics**.*

Edinburgh's second most popular tourist attraction, the Botanics – as they are known locally – have a special place in the hearts of Edinburghers. Some people remember being allowed to run around them freely as small children, others return to stroll along the rolling paths or just to sit and admire the fine views of the city. Whatever the season, the gardens contain within their modest confines a fascinating and astonishing variety of trees, shrubs and flowers from all over the world.

Founded in 1670 by two doctors as a Physic Garden attached to the Palace of Holyroodhouse, the gardens are one of the oldest institutions in the world specifically established as a centre for research into the life of plants. Since then, however, they have moved three times, to Trinity Hospital (roughly where Platform 11 of Waverley Station now stands), on to the then-purer air of Leith Walk, and finally to their present location in 1822, using specially designed carts to transport the mature trees.

Inverleith House F6

*Arboretum Place, t (0131) 248 2943. **Open** same hours as Botanic Garden; **adm** usually free.*

In the centre of the gardens, facing north, this austere mansion housed the National Gallery of Modern Art (*see* p.110) from 1960 to 1984. Something of its spirit at that time survives in the cutting-edge art exhibitions mounted in the Inverleith House Gallery. The south lawn of the house, next to the Terrace Café, is one of the best places from which to appreciate the Edinburgh skyline.

When it was built at the end of the 18th century, the house was inhabited by James Rocheid and his mother, who won a reputation for her exaggerated formality.

The Glasshouses F6

Today the most exotic residents of the Botanics are in the splendid glasshouses. The oldest is the octagonal **Tropical Palm House**, or 'Palm Stove' (1834), home to a 200-year-old cabbage palm. Viewed from the gardens, the building is hidden by its grander Roman Doric neighbour, the **Temperate Palm House**, Britain's tallest glasshouse (70ft). Even at that height, it wasn't tall enough for one of its resident palms, which tried to break out in the early 1980s and had to be cut down to size.

These iron and glass pavilions are the highlight of the 'Glasshouse Experience', which starts out in the more efficient and user-friendly hothouses put up in the mid-'60s. Pick up an explanatory leaflet as you enter.

The tour kicks off in the relative cool of the **Temperate House** – a climate favoured by the likes of the Australian bottlebrush and extraordinary she-oak. Keep an eye out too for the Australian grass tree, which only flowers when it gets burnt in bushfires.

Kids love the small **aquarium**, which also lets you see the bottom of the pool in the next house, the **Tropical Aquatics**. In this dense rainforest, Amazonian water lilies, cocoa plants, rice and bananas flourish.

The **Fern House** is next, full of nodding, prehistoric, bracken-like plants on the scale of triffids. Their close relatives can be found in the less humid **Orchid and Cycad House**. Some of the primitive, slow-growing cycads you can see here are more than 200 years old and are endangered in their natural habitat. Your average dinosaur would recognize them instantly. By contrast, the orchids are so varied and complex that roughly a tenth of all flowering plants in the world are reckoned to be orchids.

Beyond the **South American Aquatic House**, home to the bromeliads and epiphytes, the **Cactus and Succulent House** is a luxuriant, prickly desert. It's worth completing the tour with a visit to the latest greenhouse, set apart from the others and divided into the **Peat House** and **Tropical Rock House**. This is where some of the garden's 400 or more species of rhododendron are to be found.

The Gardens E6–F7

In the other corner of the garden's east end is the **Rock Garden**, a landscaped area with a scree slope and a mountain stream twisting through a profusion of upland, Arctic and Mediterranean plants. The beds are divided into areas of origin, with the highest point given over to Scottish plants. The short climb up to it gives fine city views over the garden wall past St Colm's church. Looking the other way, over the **Heath Garden**, the countless varieties of heather are spectacular in autumn.

Past the **Caledonian Hall** on the left, once home to the Edinburgh Horticultural Society, is John Muir's Grove in the **Woodland Garden**. Planted early in the 20th century, this was dedicated in 1990 to the pioneer conservationist and founder of Yosemite National Park. Its Sierra redwoods are examples of the largest known living organism on the planet.

Back near the Glasshouses in the **Fossil Garden** you can see Scotland's largest fossil – a tree trunk that lived 320 million years ago, surrounded by examples of some of the most ancient tree species, such as the monkey puzzle and the dawn redwood.

Nearby is the extraordinary little **Alpine Garden**, with a greenhouse full of tiny, exquisite flowers, including primulas, cyclamens and crocuses. Beyond it, heading west, is the **Winter** or **Silver Garden**, whose plants are best viewed during the winter months.

From May to October the **herbaceous border** is a riot of colour. Behind it to the north, an ecological garden is under development, next to the educational **Demonstration Garden**, laid out in the 'order beds' once used to train students in plant classification.

At the far western end of this area, the unique **Cryptogamic Garden** is an area of scrubby woodland scattered with dead wood to support the growth of elusive fungi.

Another development on the other side of the garden is the **Pringle Chinese Collection**, with a pavilion on a pool of contemplation. Paths twist through its south-facing slopes, planted with specimens from four vegetation zones. The garden here has the best collection of Chinese plants outside China.

Outside the Centre

INNER AND SUBURBAN EDINBURGH

Spreading well beyond the historic Old and New Towns, Edinburgh has grown over the past 100 years or so to embrace a number of once-distinct towns and villages. Leith and Duddingston are the most obvious examples, as well as the seaside resort of Portobello, but even Broughton, just five minutes' walk downhill from Princes Street, was once a small village in its own right. To the west, Corstorphine too has been subsumed into Edinburgh's metropolitan orbit but still has a discernible village centre, church, dovecote and green.

These days the majority of these areas have blended more or less seamlessly with the city's more anonymous and genteel middle-class districts. These are interspersed with various depressed housing schemes, such as Craigmillar and Granton, home to 'schemies' and to Irvine Welsh's *Trainspotting* junkies.

Further out, on the fringes of town, there are a number of worthwile destinations, most of them accessible by a short bus or train journey from town centre. Visitors who haven't feasted sufficiently on Edinburgh's rich history can seek out the imposing ruined castle at Craigmillar, the Roman remains at Cramond, or – for history of a sporting nature – Bruntsfield and Leith Links, which both claim to be the original home of golf.

Broughton H7–I7

At the eastern end of the New Town and home to some of the city's hippest shops, bars and restaurants, Broughton likes to think of itself as Edinburgh's Greenwich Village. The curve of the main thoroughfare, Broughton Street, betrays its origins as a country road through the estate of Bellevue House, which stood in Drummond Place. Now the street and its side-streets are the liveliest in north Edinburgh, making the area popular with students and the city's gay community.

At the bottom of the hill, on Mansfield Place, the old **Bellevue Reformed Baptist Church** contains some remarkable murals by the largely overlooked Arts and Crafts artist Phoebe Anna Traquair (see p.28), reminiscent of William Blake's visionary drawings. The murals have been restored but at the time of writing could not be viewed owing to the ongoing development of the church.

From the foot of Broughton Street, it's a 10-minute walk down Bellevue to up-and-coming **Canonmills** with its designer media offices and souped-up sandwich bars on an attractive stretch of the Water of Leith close to the Royal Botanic Garden (see p.113).

Holyrood Park and Arthur's Seat J9–K11

Queen's Drive (closed to traffic on Sundays) circles the hill; you can park at its highest point by Dunsapie Loch, from where it's a 20min walk up a grassy slope to the summit. See also 'Walks: Holyrood to Duddingston via Arthur's Seat', p.128.

The ideal place to get away from the crowds, Holyrood Park is one of the best things about Edinburgh. Few cities, after all, can boast their own miniature Highland mountain and extinct volcano. The profile of **Arthur's Seat** seen from the west has been compared to that of a crouching lion, and, however easy the ascent may look, the Scottish weather can turn a harmless ramble up its flanks into a terrible ordeal. But on a fine day the climb to the top is rewarded by a magnificent 360-degree view of the city, with the sea to the north and east and the Pentland Hills to the west.

The park was first properly enclosed by James V and named after his palace beside it. Mystery surrounds the origin of the name 'Arthur's Seat'. In the earliest records it's just called 'the Crag', and it's been suggested that the romantic name may be a corruption either of the Gaelic Ard-na-Said, meaning 'height of arrows', referring to the dark-age hill fort and hunting grounds, or of Ard Thor, meaning 'the height of the thunderer'.

It's been a long time since the hill really did thunder: it was last active 350 million years ago, when Scotland was on the Equator. The Edinburgh Geological Society publish an excellent illustrated guide to the park's geology, *Discovering Edinburgh's Volcano.*

Salisbury Crags and the Radical Road J10

The most obvious of the park's geological features is the long line of cliffs called Salisbury Crags, formed by a great layer of solidified lava or basalt intruded into sandstone. At sunset they often look as if they're made of gold. It was at the southern end of these crags that James Hutton developed his 'Theory of the Earth' in 1788, which helped lay the foundations of modern geology.

At the bottom of the Crags is the Radical Road, built at Walter Scott's instigation by unemployed weavers from west Scotland.

Leith and Newhaven J4–K4

Leith

Bus nos.10, 12, 16 and 17 from Princes St, or a 30min walk down Leith Walk.

What first seemed an unlikely boom in upmarket waterside eateries and refurbished pubs has changed the once seedy docklands of Leith out of all recognition. The focus of this development is **The Shore**, the old harbour. Its pubs and restaurants come to life in the evening, but there's much to explore in the surrounding streets during the day.

The docks, usually windy and forlorn, burst into life with the arrival of some navy or other. The most memorable occasion is when the tall ships' race stops here, the resulting forest of masts conjuring up images of the port over the centuries.

Leith's first recorded mention was in 1128, when it was referred to as Inverleith – the mouth of the Water of Leith. The ruins of some of its oldest buildings can still be seen along The Shore and in Tolbooth Wynd. In time the harbour was widened and dredged, and in the first year of the 19th century Leith Docks began to be built. The original iron swing bridge from 1801 is still in place, though it no longer swings.

George IV landed here on his historic visit in 1822, to be greeted by Sir Walter Scott and 2,000 spectators in temporary seating: a plaque on The Shore marks the spot. The last shipbuilding yard closed as recently as 1984.

The rivalry between Edinburgh and Leith is legendary. Until the 1920s the latter was an independent town controlling much of its larger neighbour's seagoing trade. In the 19th century it even bailed the bigger burgh out of bankruptcy. A line down the middle of the Boundary Bar on Leith Walk marked the frontier between the rivals: until 1920, when it was incorporated into the capital, you could buy a drink later in the Leith half of the bar, though the proud citizens of Edinburgh rarely availed themselves of the opportunity. If they had, they would no doubt have failed the Edinburgh police's famous test for drunkenness: asking suspects to repeat clearly after them, 'The Leith Police dismisseth us.'

East of Constitution Street, the rather desolate city park behind the Leith Academy is **Leith Links**, one of the more serious contenders for title 'birthplace of golf'.

The latest regenerative development to join this dockland boomtown is the grandly monikered **Ocean Terminal**. Designed by Sir Terence Conran on the western harbourside, this much-hyped shopping mall and entertainment complex sits in magnificent windswept isolation just off Commercial Street. Every American will be familiar with the concept, but Ocean Terminal has the added frisson of being the new home for the Former Royal Yacht *Britannia*. Even if you don't want to board this dinky vessel, there are very good views of her from department store Debenham's Britannia View restaurant.

Former Royal Yacht *Britannia* I3

Ocean Terminal, **t** *(0131) 555 5566,* **w** *www. royalyachtbritannia.co.uk.* **Open** *daily April–Sept 9.30am–4.30pm, Oct–March 10am–3.30pm;* **adm** *£7.75.*

Unless photos and intimate details of the life of the current Royal Family make you queasy, you'll enjoy the latest addition to Edinburgh's line-up of regal heritage. Built in 1954 on the Clyde, it's an undeniably handsome little ship, decommissioned in 1997 after taking part in the ceremonial handover of Hong Kong to China.

The Queen is quoted as saying that the Royal Yacht *Britannia* was 'the one place where I can truly relax'. That wouldn't be true any more, now that glass panels have been fitted into the walls of her bedroom so the public can peer through at her deep double-tucked bedspread. The Duke of Edinburgh's room has received the same treatment, causing one Scottish visitor to observe that he slept in 'a wee bed for a big man'. In fact the tour is cunningly designed to reveal the elegant and homely 1950s style of the yacht's interior – not a gaudy floating palace at all – before you arrive at the stately dining room, where just about every major political figure on the international scene over the last 40 years has been formally wined and dined.

On your way round, the audio handset tour supplies rather coy details of life on board this seagoing embassy dedicated to 'the British way of doing things'. Look out for the suburban-looking garage doors on the starboard side, where the Rolls-Royce, or latterly the Land Rover, was kept.

Newhaven Heritage Museum G3

24 Pier Place, Newhaven, t (0131) 551 4165; bus nos.10, 11, 16, 17 and 22 from Princes St. **Open** *daily noon–5pm; adm free.*

Newhaven has yet to catch up with its big brother next door. The little fishing village saw much better days during the herring fishery boom, which only really collapsed in the 1950s, but a few net-drying huts and distinctive fishermen's houses on the quayside still contribute to its charm, and many of the old-timers in the village remain fiercely independent of both Leith and Edinburgh. There are also fine views across to the Fife coastline on a clear day.

This one-room museum of local history shares the old fishmarket building with Harry Ramsden's fish restaurant. With its lively interactive displays, it's good for kids as well as grown-ups, and the local volunteers who run it are more than happy to enliven a visit with reminiscences of their own.

It is the fisherwomen who made Newhaven famous: the doughty females who used to think nothing of carrying at least their own bodyweight in creels (baskets) of fish on their backs all the way up to the Royal Mile each day. Part of the exhibition is made up of recordings of the fishwives' famous song, and you can also try on their clothes for size: they are supposed to have worn at least eight petticoats to protect themselves from the chilly brine seeping out of their creels – during the late 19th century this voluminous style was adopted by fashionable women up and down the UK.

The fishwives were the backbone of an introverted matriarchal community that grew up around the little harbour, established in the 16th century. Since the discovery of herring in the Firth of Forth in 1793 until as recently as 1950, the fishing village was responsible for much of the Firth's character.

It was at Newhaven in 1511 that James IV ordered the construction of a warship, the *Great Michael*, on a scale to astonish all Europe – it was claimed that it took all the oak in Fife to provide the ship with its 10ft thick cladding. A massive vessel capable of carrying 1,000 troops, the *Great Michael* was put under the command of the poet-sailor Sir Andrew Wood but never saw active service and was sold to the French after Flodden, rotting away in Brest. There's a model of it in the **Olde Peacock Inn**.

Duddingston Map p.117

Bus nos.4, 44, 45 and 106 from Princes St.

Duddingston is the best-preserved example of a self-contained feudal village to be found within the city limits. Nestling on the edge of Holyrood Park, and linked to the Queen's Drive by a flight of steps that is known as **Jacob's Ladder**, it is best approached from Arthur's Seat, and makes a good walk from the Royal Mile (*see p.57*). It can also be approached along the **Innocent Railway** – so called because it used horses instead of steam – which is now a cycle path beginning at the southern foot of Salisbury Crags and running round the far edge of Duddingston Loch.

The **loch** is largely responsible for the charm of the village's position. It used to be a popular spot for skating, even by moonlight, and if Raeburn's famous (reputed) portrait of the Reverend Robert Walker in the National Gallery is to be believed (see p.95), even ministers of the kirk partook of the sport. Today the reedy loch is enjoyed by a tremendous variety of waterbirds, especially swans, which complete the picturesque view of the small 12th-century church perched above. By the church gate is a 'loupin-on-stane', a 17th-century platform for mounting horses.

The **Sheep Heid Inn** on The Causeway, once visited by both James VI and Bonnie Prince Charlie, is a pleasant, busy village pub with a skittle alley.

Portobello Map p.117

Bus no.46 from St Andrew Square (no.42 for the return journey).

A visit to Portobello, just beyond Duddingston, feels like a trip to the seaside. Until the 1960s, this was a Victorian beach resort town popular with Edinburghers, who would happily take holidays here. (To some extent, North Berwick further along the coast still plies this holiday trade.) Not surprisingly perhaps, this was the birthplace of music-hall comedian Harry Lauder.

The architectural traces of its glory days give Portobello an edge, and it is now going through a further wave of gentrification with the arrival of young professionals and their families. The beach is still a fun place for kids, though they're more likely to be interested in the amusement arcades than having a swim.

Craigmillar Castle Map p.117

t (0131) 661 4445; bus nos.33 and 82 from North Bridge. Open April–Sept daily 9.30am–6.30pm, Oct–May Mon–Wed and Sat 9.30am–4.30pm, Thurs 9.30am–12.30pm, Sun 2–4.30pm; adm £2.50.

This tremendous old ruined fortification has proper battlements, impressive curtain walls and good views of Arthur's Seat and the Royal Mile. Mary, Queen of Scots ensured its lasting fame by spending a few nights here, and the shell of the room where she is supposed to have slept can be viewed. In a field at the back you can still make out the old fishpond in the shape of a 'P' for her hosts, the Prestons. The castle is popular with medieval re-enactment societies.

The castle can be approached from the back via a fairly long uphill walk; it's also within cycling distance of the city. Craigmillar itself has one of the city's most depressing housing schemes and is not safe to wander around.

Marchmont, The Grange and Morningside Map p.116

South of The Meadows stretch rolling acres of polite suburbia made up of elegant villas and grand 19th-century tenement blocks. **Marchmont** is popular with students; further up the hill, **The Grange** is the preserve of bankers, lawyers and chartered accountants, while **Morningside** has given its name to a whole social manner and accent, known as 'douce', characterized by rather sedate, prim and proper, comfortable respectability laced with lashings of vicious gossip.

As much a frame of mind as a place on the map, Morningside is also known in the city as the temporary home of sadly lost minds receiving psychiatric treatment at the **Royal Edinburgh Hospital**. These days the purple rinses aren't quite as severe as they used to be, the net curtains don't twitch as suspiciously as they once did, and not every visitor is rhetorically asked, 'You'll have had your tea, then?' The invincible ladies taking tea in the guesthouses on the slopes of the Braid Hills were satirized in Muriel Spark's *The Prime of Miss Jean Brodie* (see p.32), and the author herself attended **James Gillespie's school** in Bruntsfield, the gateway to Morningside.

Bruntsfield Links, one of the earliest golf courses in Edinburgh, is still a pitch and putting green (with clubs and balls available from the Golf Tavern in the summer). Rumour has it that a plague pit was also once located here.

Holy Corner, at the crossroads of Morningside Road and Colinton Road, is the site of four churches, just by the Churchill Theatre, the alleged location of the stone in which James IV is supposed to have planted the Scottish standard when rallying his troops for the disastrous battle of Flodden. On Newbattle Terrace there is a splendid Art Deco cinema, the Dominion, which is still run as a family business.

Royal Observatory Map p.116
Blackford Hill, **t** *(0131) 668 8100; visitors' centre* **t** *(0131) 668 8405,* **w** *www.roe.ac.uk;* **bus** *nos.41 and 42 from The Mound.* **Open** *Mon–Sat 10am–5pm, Sun noon–5pm; adm £2.60.*

Overlooking The Grange on Blackford Hill, this large museum will interest anyone with a passing interest in astronomy, although it is mainly orientated towards school parties and children. The spectacular views north of Edinburgh from Blackford Hill are worth the trip in themselves.

The exhibition commences with a temporary exhibition centre giving interesting sketches of stargazers' lives down the years. At the top of a spiral staircase is a huge telescope, and on the rooftop are further powerful telescopes allowing visitors to spot people struggling up the slopes of Arthur's Seat. It's also here that you'll find the computer gallery: an array of computer games, videos and interactive exhibits with stars and planets, including our own, as their theme.

Braid Hills and Hermitage
Map p.116
Bus *nos.11, 15, 16, and 17 to the junction of Comiston Rd and Greenbank Crescent.*

On a sunny day there are lovely walks to be had in the Braid Hills, with their fine views, and in the **Hermitage of Braid**, a deeply wooded dell complete with a delightful burn, a little late 18th-century mansion (now a teashop and countryside education centre) and a dilapidated 'doocot' (dovecote). The hermitage has well-marked nature trails winding through the trees – quite a surprise within such easy reach of the city centre.

The path alongside the little Braid Burn eventually comes out at the foot of Blackford Hill, a short steep climb below the Royal Observatory (*see* above). Alternatively, it makes a pleasant cycle route to Craigmillar Castle (*see* p.120).

Fountainbridge, Dalry and Gorgie Map p.116
Bus *nos.3, 30, 33, 61, 65 and C5 from Princes St.*

Southwest of the Lothian Road, this area is known for its breweries, as well as for Tynecastle Park, home of Heart of Midlothian Football Club. Many of its 19th-century working-class tenements have survived and, unlike some of the poverty-stricken modern housing estates on the outskirts of the city,

---

Sean Connery (b.1930)

Most famous for his role as British secret agent 007, Sean Connery once did the milk round near Fettes College, the city's most exclusive private school – and also the school from which Ian Fleming had his character, James Bond, expelled.

He was born in Fountainbridge, and it was from this Edinburgh district that he took the name for his US film production company. Other early jobs in the city included being a labourer, a lifeguard and a male model at the Edinburgh College of Art, and he was also once asked by Matt Busby to play football for Manchester United.

Connery's witty contribution to the Museum of Scotland's 20th-century gallery (*see* p.86) is a milk bottle containing a copy of the Declaration of Arbroath, the earliest assertion of Scottish nationhood on record, and he has long dedicated himself to the cause of the Scottish Nationalist Party.

In 1992 the actor was made a Freeman of the City of Edinburgh, and for some years now he has been involved in discussions with Sony to open a £90-million film studio near the city, though he has as yet expressed no intention to return from his home in Spain to live there.

the area has maintained a strong sense of community and much of its character.

Indeed, the whole area stills bears the mark of its industrial past, with the Union Canal (very spooky after dark) slicing through it on its way to Scottish Courage's Fountain Brewery. This massive complex is largely responsible for the characteristic sweet smell of malt that comes and goes across the city.

On Roseburn Street, **Murrayfield Stadium** is the scene of international Rugby clashes and Union matches (*see* p.192).

Caledonian Brewery Off maps

42 Slateford Rd, t (0131) 337 1286, w www. caledonian-brewery.co.uk; details of tours from Caledonian Events, t (0131) 226 5113.

The Caledonian offers a taste of the local brew and an interesting tour of a still opera-tional 19th-century brewery. It also holds Saturday night ceilidhs throughout the year and a three-day beer festival in June (*see* p.41).

Fountainpark Leisure Complex E11

130 Dundee St, t (0131) 229 0300. **Open** *Mon 2.30–9.30pm, Tues–Thurs noon–7pm, Fri–Sun noon–9.30pm;* **adm** *£3.*

This huge shopping mall and entertainment complex was built on the site of a brewery and contains a version of Scottish history for the MTV generation in the form of **Shaping a Nation**, featuring a cross-section of personal-ities from Robert the Bruce to Dolly the Sheep, plus lots of computer games.

Water of Leith Walkway Visitor Centre Off maps

Lanark Rd, t (0131) 455 7367, w www. waterofleith.eden.org. **Open** *April–Oct daily 10am–4pm, Nov–March Wed–Sun 10am– 4pm;* **adm** *£1.90.*

At the western end of Gorgie and Dalry, towards Slateford, you can pick up the Water of Leith through Craiglockhart to walk to Colinton (*see* p.125) or back into town; from Craiglockhart out to Colinton takes about 20 minutes, back into town about half an hour. The visitor centre provides information on the history and wildlife of the river.

Corstorphine Map p.116

Bus nos.26, 26A, 31, 63, 69 and 86.

One of Edinburgh's oldest villages, this is now a sprawling suburb on the west of the city beyond Murrayfield Stadium. The area is a quiet backwater that's popular with young families and the retired, and fashionable Scots brought up here might even be a little embarrassed about its quiet gentility. Substantial traces of the old village can still be found just off the main Glasgow–Edinburgh and airport road, especially its famous medieval church with its heavy slabbed roof, the village green and some old houses in the main street. On Dovecote Road, quite close to the consulate of the Republic of China, is a 16th-century beehive 'doocot' (dovecote).

Corstorphine Hill Map p.116

It's well worth the climb to the top of this hill for the spectacular views that it affords south across the city to the Pentland Hills. At the top is yet another monument to Walter Scott, this time a simple tower erected among the trees by one William Macfie in 1871 to commemorate the centenary of the author's birth. Also sited on the hill is **Edinburgh Zoo** (*see* p.197).

Cramond Map p.116

Bus no.41 from George St. For Cramond Island safe crossing times call the Forth Coastguard, t (01333) 450 666.

This is the place to come for a walk on the beach and a blast of sea air within a bus ride from the city centre. Once a small fishing village, it sits on two estuaries where the River Almond flows into the Firth of Forth.

It also used to be the largest Roman fort in the area, capitalizing on its superb defensive position, the site of which has been carefully excavated and preserved. Only a few years ago a trawler captain made himself a small fortune when he caught in his nets an extraordinary stone carving of a Roman lion eating a woman. It is now in the Museum of Scotland (*see* p.85).

Cramond is one of Edinburgh's smartest suburban enclaves, but the preservation of the village has left much of its charm intact. A small ferry crosses the river in summer, opening up superb walking possibilities along the Firth to Dalmeny House (*see* p.126). Alternatively, you can head upstream alongside the Almond to the **Old Cramond Brig** (bridge), or downstream along the promenade beside the Firth of Forth, past Lauriston Castle to Granton, Newhaven and Leith. This last walk is good for a fine day, but takes at least two hours and passes through some pretty desolate areas.

Cramond Island Off maps

Cramond has its own deserted island across the tidal causeway – the ideal place to build a miniature Mont St Michel. The crossing can be slippery and muddy, much to the delight of the chatty lugworm-diggers you pass along the way, but the wild island itself is a safe and pleasant place to explore, and from its summit there are good views of the Forth bridges, Edinburgh Castle and North Berwick Law, way off in the distance. Keep an eye on the tide unless you want to be stranded here for eight hours.

Lauriston Castle Map p.116

Cramond Rd South, Davidson's Mains, t (0131) 336 2060. Open for guided tours only (at 15mins past the hour) April–Oct Mon–Thurs, Sat, Sun 11am–5pm, Nov–March Sat, Sun 2–4pm; adm £4.50.

This 16th-century towerhouse was given to the city by its owners, the Reids, in the 1920s. There are fine views of Cramond Island and the Firth from the extensive gardens, and it houses one of the world's most important collections of Sicilian furniture.

Architect William Burn (also responsible for the look of the High Kirk of St Giles, *see* p.67) added to the original house, and the ship's library was an even later addition. The Reids furnished the house in line with their business, a ship and train outfitters. The dining-room chairs, for instance, were originally made for rail travel.

John Law (1671–1729)

Educated at the Royal High School, John Law led an extraordinary life, becoming at different times a goldsmith, a banker and a scientific gambler. After killing a love rival in a duel, he was sentenced to death, pardoned and then re-imprisoned. He escaped, was quickly captured but fled once more, this time to Holland, from where he set out for Genoa and Venice, speculating in foreign currencies and picking up a wife on the way.

In 1703 he returned to Edinburgh to live at Lauriston Castle and dream up the concept of banknotes. In 1716 France adopted his scheme for a national bank and he became a Frenchman. By now a very wealthy man through his involvement with the French East India Company, he was in a position to order the construction of what was to become New Orleans.

In 1720 Law converted to Catholicism and became Controller General of Finance for France. Following that country's economic collapse, he died in genteel poverty in Venice.

The guided tour emphasizes both Mr Reid's practical interests as one of the first people in Scotland to specialize in architectural reconstruction and interior design, and the pragmatic personality of Mrs Reid. The pair amassed an important collection of clocks, prints and engravings, plus a large number of Crossley Wool Mosaics from the late 1850s – a peculiar type of mass-produced popular painting and the forerunner of modern reproductions (found in the hall). The 1896 Broadwood boudoir grand in the front room and the silk damask wallpaper are typical of the Reids' unassuming but luxurious tastes.

The view from Lauriston Castle has not much changed since they lived here. Their living room was in the original towerhouse, which was once the home of the father of John Napier, the inventor of logarithms. The banker John Law (*see* box), who was the first person to propose the use of banknotes (though his idea wasn't adopted at the time), also lived here.

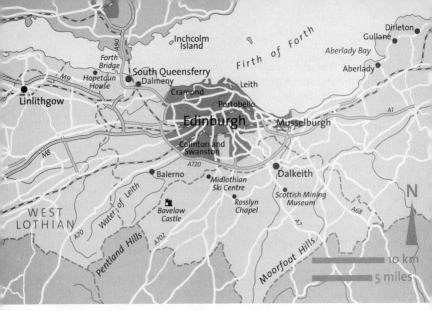

OUTSIDE THE CITY

Several destinations just beyond the city limits can make for a rewarding afternoon or full day out. To the east, Musselburgh is the first distinctly independent place on the Firth of Forth and gives a good taste of a provincial Scottish town. Dalkeith is another satellite town of Edinburgh, with a proud mining heritage and a country park. Six miles southwest of the town, the Rosslyn Chapel is a 15th-century masonic mystery close to a charming woodland glen.

Continuing clockwise round the city lie polite suburban enclaves in the lee of the Pentland Hills. Stretching southwest of Edinburgh for about 20 miles, the Pentlands provide wild walking and mountain biking opportunities.

Back on the Firth of Forth, to the west of Edinburgh, are the settlements of Dalmeny, with its adorable little church of St Cuthbert's, and South Queensferry, with its boat trips to islands in the Firth. They're nestled at the southern end of the spectacular Forth Bridges, close to the stately splendours of Hopetoun House.

Musselburgh Map above

Known as the 'Honest Toun' for refusing to claim the bounty on the body of the Earl of Moray, this is a dignified but slightly dilapidated East Lothian town. Sights include its tiny Victorian harbour at Fisherrow, the 16th-century bridge across the Esk, and the larger 19th-century bridge designed by John Rennie, the model for London's original Waterloo Bridge. The other main draws are the imposing 17th-century Tolbooth on the town's typically wide High Street, the racetrack, and the ancient Musselburgh Links.

Dalkeith Map above

Dalkeith itself is not much to look, but on its outskirts it does have an absorbing industrial heritage museum, as well as a splendid country park (**t** *(01316) 541666*).

Scottish Mining Museum
Map above
Lady Victoria Colliery, Newtongrange, **t** *(0131) 663 7519,* **w** *www.scottishminingmuseum.com;* **bus** *nos.86, 89, 95, 29, 3a from Haymarket or Princes St.* **Open** *daily March–Oct 10am–5pm, Nov–Feb 10am–4pm;* **adm** *£4.*

Newtongrange was one of the largest pit villages in the country, and this museum gives you a good idea of miners' daily lives, with two floors of exhibitions and a 'magic helmet audio tour' that delights kids (included in the admission fee).

Colinton and Swanston Map left

Bus no.5 from North Bridge or no.17 from Princes St to Colinton.

The posh suburb of Colinton sits on the southern outskirts of the city, just inside the ring road. The prettiest way to reach it is via the **Water of Leith Walkway** (*see* p.122) through the wooded Colinton Dell. With its welcoming restaurants and pubs, the place exudes the atmosphere of a well-ordered village, aspiring perhaps to be something like the suburban equivalent of Stockbridge, with the manicured grounds of private school **Merchiston Castle** setting the tone.

Just outside the ring road further to the east is **Swanston House and Farm**, where R. L. Stevenson spent his childhood summers, though its peace is now spoiled by the bypass. The house can be seen if not visited, though it is only really accessible by car.

Pentland Hills Map left

The Pentlands, the closest hill range to Edinburgh, are flanked by the A702 and A70: the most easily accessible by bus, the A702 heads out of town past the Hill End dry ski slope to Castle Law Hill, where there's an easy climb up to an Iron Age fortification; but more satisfying walking can be found off the A70 beyond Balerno – the turning second on the left after the village leads out to a farm called Listonshiels, from where there are challenging walks up to Thriepmuir Reservoir and the Black Hill (5,367ft), and on to the Glencorse Reservoir.

Both routes require a good map, wet-weather gear and hiking boots, but the effort is rewarded with glimpses of some of the last remnants of the Great Caledonian Forest and Bavelaw Castle, and with spectacular views right across Edinburgh towards the Highlands, just about visible on clear days.

Rosslyn Chapel Map left

*Chapel Loan, Roslin, **t** (0131) 440 2159, **w** www. rosslyn-chapel.com; **bus** nos.315 or 37 then L1 (or £12 taxi ride one-way). **Open** Mon–Sat 10am–5pm, Sun noon–4.45pm; **adm** £4.*

Following in the footsteps of such illustrious tourists as Robert Burns, Walter Scott, the Wordsworths, and Dr Johnson and James Boswell (who scratched their names on the 18th-century windows of the local inn), you'll come away from the mysterious Rosslyn Chapel with more questions than answers. Was this the last resting place of the Holy Grail? Is the Lost Gospel buried beneath it? Why are there so many carvings of little green men?

Speculation apart, the sheer quantity of gorgeous medieval carved stonework here is breathtaking, and though the entire 15th-century edifice has been canopied for protection, the walkway beneath the eaves provides great views over the deep little valley of the North Esk.

Trails lead down to the river from the chapel if you want to escape the crowds of other wonderers (the aura of mystery surrounding the chapel and its carvings can seem a little contrived). Funnily enough, it was near here that a piece of modern scientific history was made, when Dolly the sheep was cloned at the Roslin Research Institute.

Dalmeny and South Queensferry Map left

Train to Dalmeny from Waverley and Haymarket (20mins), bus no.43 to South Queensferry from the bus station or Princes St.

The town of Dalmeny is strung out along the Firth between the gigantic Forth Rail Bridge (*see* p.126), an indispensable monster from the age of steam, and the more graceful suspended lines of the Forth Road Bridge. You can cross the latter on foot, but it's longer than it looks. If you're feeling hearty, you could walk across to North Queensferry and take the train back to Edinburgh from there. Another option is to take the footpath alongside the railway in the direction your train was travelling. A steepish, often muddy, track leads down to the Hawes Inn at South Queensferry.

In the summer months there are boat-trips around the islands in the Forth from the harbour of South Queensferry: *Maid of the Forth* from the Hawes pier (*t (0131) 331 4857, w www.maidoftheforth.co.uk*) does jazz cruises and ceilidh nights, as well as trips out to Inchcolm.

Church of St Cuthbert Off maps

This adorable 12th-century village church a five-minute walk from Dalmeny station is the most complete example of Romanesque architecture in Scotland. The simple arched door in the southern wall is carved with an elaborate, well-weathered procession of mythical beasts, figures and faces. Inside, the carvings, complete with grotesque heads and faces, are just as impressive, covering the vaulting arches over the nave. Look out for the muzzled bear on the south side.

You might need to ask for the key to the church in one of the cottages over the road. There's an excellent 20p guide to the church by Ian G. Lindsay.

Firth of Forth Rail Bridge

Map p.124

The world's first really large structure made entirely of steel, at more than a mile in length, the bridge was constructed between 1882 and 1890, engineered by Sir John Fowler and Benjamin Baker. Its three double cantilevers were designed to carry much more weight than necessary in the light of the Tay Bridge disaster of 1879. More than 50 lives were lost during the Forth Bridge's construction, and maintenance teams are continuously employed re-painting the metal behemoth.

Dalmeny House Off maps

Dalmeny Park, t (0131) 331 1888, w www.dalmeny.co.uk. Open July–Aug 2–5pm Sun–Tues; adm £4.

Still very much a family home, Dalmeny House is most famous for its Old Master paintings and its French Napoleonic furniture collections. A visit here is like being welcomed into another century.

Inchcolm Island and Abbey

Map p.124

Reachable by boat from the Hawes pier, Inchcolm Island is an atmospheric rock in the middle of the Forth, its most prominent feature the gaunt ruins of **St Colm's Abbey**. This very fine Augustinian priory was founded in the Middle Ages and is a great place for kids to scramble about and explore.

Hopetoun House Map p.124

South Queensferry, t (0131) 331 2451, w www.hopetounhouse.com. Open daily April–Sept 10am–4.30pm, Oct 11am–3.30pm; adm £5.30.

A fair 2-mile walk west along the shore beyond South Queensferry (there's also road access from the town; the house is signposted from the road bridge), this huge stately home was largely the work of William Adam in the 18th century and is now the residence of the Marquess of Linlithgow. It contains an impressive collection of paintings, tapestries and chinaware, although if the weather is fine the deer park and shoreline may be more appealing. The harebells and daffodils in the woodlands around the house are spectacular in springtime.

Walks

08

Map showing the route from Holyrood to Duddingston via Arthur's Seat, with grid references J–M and 9–11.

HOLYROOD TO DUDDINGSTON VIA ARTHUR'S SEAT

The small mountain in some 650 acres of rough parkland 10 minutes' walk east of the Royal Mile ranks as Edinburgh's most surprising and delightful natural asset. About 350 million years ago, when Scotland was somewhere near the equator – and enjoying a similar climate to the West Indies – Arthur's Seat was an active volcano. Now its craggy plug makes up the impressive back garden of the Palace of Holyroodhouse.

This walk begins in front of the palace and heads up to the summit via holy wells, a ruined chapel and a miniature Highland col. It then descends into the little village of Duddingston for lunch, returning via the royal park's most striking geological features, the birthplace of modern geology, and more views embracing Edinburgh's spectacular position on the Firth of Forth. It's a treat for both naturalists and botanists, who can expect to find a wide variety of Scottish wildflowers. Arthur's Seat also has noteworthy literary associations.

Begin the walk outside the front gates of the Palace of Holyroodhouse, at the foot of the Royal Mile, on Abbey Strand. Look for the brass letter S set into the road right on the roundabout, which marks the extent of the debtors' sanctuary that embraced Holyrood Abbey until as recently 1881. The sanctuary provided refuge from the law for Napoleon's relatives and Thomas de Quincey, among many others with money problems. 'Inmates' were allowed out with guaranteed impunity on Sundays to visit friends and family.

Through the gates of the palace, Queen Mary's apartments are on the second floor of the left-hand tower, where her Italian lover David Rizzio was stabbed in front of her by her husband. The tower still looks pretty as much it would have done in the 16th century, as do the houses on the left of the gates, now offices for Historic Scotland.

Walk right, down Horse Wynd, and you'll pass the recently opened outstation of the Royal Collection, the Queen's remarkable private collection of Old Master paintings and Renaissance art (see p.75). In its ground-floor reception area, an 'e-gallery' gives information and examples from the entire Royal Collection; upstairs three spaces stage two or three small exhibitions a year of works selected from the collection in London.

Walk down to the end of the road, and at the junction of Holyrood Road, in Holyrood Lodge, the **Royal Park's Information Centre** (*t* (0131) 556 1761) can provide a variety of guides to different aspects of Arthur's Seat – 'Discovering Edinburgh's Volcano' is particularly good. The centre is run by the **Holyrood Park Rangers Service** (*t* (0131) 652 8150) who care for the park and its occupants, animal, mineral and vegetable.

From here the walk heads out on to the hill. Cross the car park and make your way past the no-entry sign and the 15th-century **St Margaret's Well**, originally from the village of Restalrig and rescued from the depradations of railway-builders by enthusiastic Victorian antiquarians. Make for the ruined **St Anthony's Chapel**, clearly visible beyond **Haggis Knowe**. This rocky knoll provides the first of the park's superb viewpoints, sitting on top of rudimentary lava columns of the type most spectularly seen at the famous Giant's Causeway in Northern Ireland.

From here you'll be following in the footsteps of one of the protagonists of James Hogg's *Confessions of a Justified Sinner*, where he 'found his way into that little romantic glade adjoining to the saint's chapel and well. He was still involved in a blue haze, like a dense smoke, but yet in the midst of it the respiration was the most refreshing and delicious.' Robert Fergusson praised the healing powers of St Anthony's Well (now dammed) with the lines:

*On May Day, in a fairy ring
We've seen them round St Anton's Spring
Frae grass the caller dew-drops wring
To weet their een
And water clear as crystal spring
To synd them clean.*

St Anthony's Chapel, ruined for two centuries, was probably founded in the early 1400s to defend the holy well just down the hill. From here, walk straight up the **Dry Dam** towards the summit of Arthur's Seat. On the left above, **Pulpit Rock** was formed by a subsidiary crater on the lip of the volcano.

From the grassy col at the top of the Dry Dam, it's a short steep scramble to the top

Start: Abbey Strand at the bottom of Canongate, in front of the Palace of Holyroodhouse.

Finish: Either back on Abbey Strand or, if you don't walk the Radical Road, at Dumbiedykes Road, near St Leonard's Street and The Pleasance, from where you can take bus no.21 back to Princes Street.

Alternatively, bus no.42 runs from Duddingston to George Street via Buccleuch Street (be aware that it also passes through Craigmillar, one of the city's more dangerous housing schemes).

Walking time: About 3 hours, not including lunch in Duddingston.

Suggested start time: 10am.

Lunch/drinks stop: Sheep Heid Inn, *see* p.178.

and some of the finest views of Edinburgh's spectacular position. You're standing only 823ft above sea level in the middle of a 9th-century hill fort. To the west, the spine of the High Street runs up to the Castle; to the north lies the glinting sliver of the Firth of Forth; to the east there's the distinctive blue cone of North Berwick Law. Closer by in the same direction, the slopes running down to **Dunsapie Loch** are marked by Bronze Age and medieval cultivation terraces. The picturesque little loch was created when Queen's Drive was built in the 19th century.

Cross Queen's Drive near the car park south of the loch and continue across Dunsapie Bog to find a path through the rough grass that leads to **Jacob's Ladder**, a flight of steps descending into Duddingston. The steps give good views over the village and its wide **loch** – the only natural one in the park and a haven for wildfowl. The village has preserved its medieval pattern: it's an assemblage of church, manor and main street, with the ancient **Sheep Heid Inn** (*see* box), a good spot for some well-earned refreshments.

After lunch, either head back into the city on the bus, or take the lochside road out of the village past the church, which runs beneath **Samson's Ribs**, a craggy cliff of basalt columns similar to the famous ones in Fingal's Cave on the island of Staffa. Follow the foot of the cliffs round to the right to emerge at the end at The Hause beneath the **Gutted Haddie**. This is one end of the **Radical Road** that runs along the feet of **Salisbury Crags**, an igneous basalt intrusion that is one of the most prominent Edinburgh landmarks. The road beneath, constructed by unemployed weavers at Sir Walter Scott's instigation, provides more superb city views.

A hundred yards from the start of the path, **Hutton's Section** is a quarry in the cliff where Sir James Hutton devised his revolutionary geological theories (*see* box). The road's highest point is directly below the **Cat Nick**, a fault in the cliff top that is weathered into a small notch. Beware here of both rock falls and the spitting fulmars that nest in the crevices above.

The Radical Road descends beyond the Cat Nick and leads back to the car park near the Palace of Holyroodhouse.

THE WATER OF LEITH AND ROYAL BOTANIC GARDEN

The Water of Leith, once Edinburgh's major industrial waterway, is now in places barely more then a babbling brook, yet its course through the city provides an almost unbroken stripe of countryside, complete with birdsong, sometimes only a few yards from the hard city pavements.

The Water may not be on the scale of the Hudson, Seine or Thames, but in its time Edinburgh's little river has worked as hard as any of them, playing a surprisingly large role in the city's livelihood and prosperity. By the early 19th century it was powering at least 70 mills and providing a thriving international seaport on the Firth of Forth at Leith.

Not much remains of all that activity. For many years the river was less a free-flowing watercourse than a sluggish, clogged-up ditch; then, for much of the 19th century, it was an open sewer. In the First World War German zeppelins found it a useful marker for finding their way in to town to drop their bombs. Today it is quiet and rural, cleaned up and used by city-dwellers for leisure pursuits.

Walking at a leisurely pace but without stopping too often, Canonmills can be reached in about two hours, Newhaven in about three. If you have children with you, there are excellent opportunities for playing pooh-sticks off the bridges along the way.

Since most of the walk is outside, it's worth checking the weather forecast before you set out – this is a beautiful walk on a sunny day but could be miserable if it's raining. Most of the walk runs along tarmac paths, but there are patches that might be muddy.

The walk begins at **Roseburn Terrace**, to the west of Haymarket Station along Haymarket Terrace and West Coates. Take any bus bound for Corstorphine from Shandwick Place in the West End and get off at Coltbridge, at the end of Roseburn Terrace. Cross the road at the lights, and you'll see the little 18th-century bridge at an angle to its larger replacement, put up in 1841. Walk back a little way towards town and you'll find a pair of heavy squat gateposts topped with pyramids at the entrance to **Roseburn Cliff**. Go through the gateway and turn left down to the river.

This part of the Water is barely more than a stream where ducks come to paddle and grassy meadows stretch out to the right. You'll be struck here by the sound of bird-song and (in spring and summer) the scent of meadow flowers.

It is a gentle 5-minute stroll from here to the **Scottish National Gallery of Modern Art** (see p.110), passing under the first of two great **viaducts** spanning the Water's narrow breadth. Originally constructed for the North Edinburgh Railway, the first viaduct now carries the **North Edinburgh Cycleway** between Dalry, Davidson Mains and Granton.

As you round a bend in the river, the ground opens up and you approach **The Cauldron** – the rather dramatic name for a widening of the water at a tangled thicket of deadwood. You might be lucky enough to see a heron lift lazily into the air. Up on the left bank, there's the stump of a windmill that used to grind gorse for horse fodder in the 19th century; on the right you can see the three distant spires of St Mary's Episcopal Cathedral (see p.106) above the treetops.

A little further along you will come to a small wooden bridge over the river. Cross the bridge and climb the steep flight of steps on the other side to reach the Scottish National Gallery of Modern Art (this entrance closes at 4.45pm or dusk, whichever is earlier).

Alternatively, from the stone tower topped with a thistle that stands 100 yards further along the river on the right, you can make the steep, sometimes slippery, climb up through the woods to **Donaldson's College for the Deaf**, one of Edinburgh's most impressive buildings. On his death in 1830, James Donaldson, proprietor and editor of the *Edinburgh Advertiser* (the *Daily Mail* of its day), left money for the building and endow-ment of a school, built by William Playfair

> **Start**: Roseburn Terrace, just west of Haymarket Station.
> **Finish**: Canonmills, from where bus nos.8 and 17 lead back into the centre, or Newhaven, from where bus nos.10, 11, 16, 17 and 22 take you back to town.
> **Walking time**: About 2 hours to Canonmills, 3 hours to Newhaven, not including lunch or drinks stops.
> **Suggested start time**: 11am.
> **Lunch/drinks stop**: The Northern Bar, see p.177.

from 1841 to 1851. Queen Victoria is said to have been so miffed at not getting the building for herself that the curtains on her carriage windows always had to be drawn when she went past.

Continuing along the river, take the bridge across to the west bank. Beyond the **Belford Bridge** (decorated with the city arms), the river flows meditatively through a narrow, wooded valley. After about a quarter of a mile, take the steps up the slope on the left and turn left along the road (Dean Path); a little way along on the left is the entrance to **Dean Cemetery** (see p.111).

After wandering around the cemetery for a while, return to the river path, which continues past the roaring waters of Damhead Weir. Where the iron footbridge crosses the river, the path is diverted through **Dean Village**, a secluded treasure (see p.111). Follow **Damside** round to the right until you reach the junction with Dean Path and Bell's Brae; it's just a short, steep climb up Bell's Brae to the busy West End, but down here by the old bridge you would never know it. Have a peek inside **Well Court** (see p.112) on Damside as you pass.

As you approach the stone bridge, the former **Dean Primary School** (1874) is on the right, with its sculpted roundel relief of Education doing her gracious best for two enquiring youngsters. Cross the bridge into **Bell's Brae**, where **Bell's Brae House**, **Baxter's Incorporation Granary** and **Drumsheugh Baths** (for all, see p.112) can be admired.

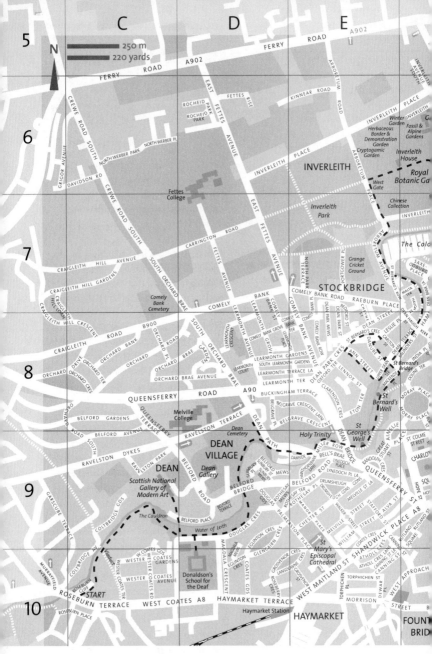

To continue the walk, turn left down **Miller Row**. On your left is a grotty picnic area with three old millstones and a fine view of the river and the enormous **West Mill**. To your right, the strange castellated building was built as a racquets court by publisher Thomas Nelson in 1912. From here there's also a good view of Kirkbrae House reaching up to the southern end of the massive **Dean Bridge** (see p.112).

Follow the path beneath the bridge with the river rushing along below to your left. The next section of the walk is the most charming and individual, with lovely (sadly private) hanging gardens sloping down to the river on both sides. A little way along the

enshrines a full-size statue of Hygeia, the Roman goddess of Health, celebrating the well's alleged healing properties. Legend has it that the founder of the Cistercian Order, St Bernard of Clairvaux, was shown the miraculous spring by some small birds while hiding near here in the 12th century. It remained hidden until three boys out fishing stumbled upon it in 1770. The temple was built 20 years later and restored in 1887 by one of the Nelson family. Earlier this century, the well was declared potentially toxic because river water had got in. To view the interior of the wellhouse, you need to call **t** (0131) 332 2368 at least seven days ahead.

Go down the steps by the temple to the riverside path and turn right past a roundel with a bas-relief of the Nelson family. Carry on a little way to **St Bernard's Bridge**, climb its mock-Jacobean steps and turn left into **Dean Terrace**, formerly called Mineral Street in honour of the well water's composition. By way of introduction to **Stockbridge** (see p.112), turn left along Upper Dean Terrace and walk up the hill and round the corner into the elegant curves of the **Raeburn Estate** (see p.113), then return to the river.

The path runs along a short stretch of river backed by ugly offices and housing to reach **Falshaw Bridge**. To reach the **Royal Botanic Garden** (see p.113), climb the steps up to the bridge, then turn left and follow the road right, taking you around the corner and through the gateposts topped with weathered Chinese lions (once marking the entrance to Inverleith House and supposedly from the Castle) into Arboretum Avenue. From here it's a short climb uphill past Grange Cricket Ground into Arboretum Place and the garden's main West Gate, where there's a shop and café (open in summer).

Leave the garden by its East Gate and turn right down **Inverleith Row** towards the river. A little way along on the left, past an impressive series of Georgian villas, is **No.8 Howard Place**, where RL Stevenson was born in 1850. Just across Inverleith Row, Stevenson's family also lived briefly at **No.1 Inverleith Terrace** before moving to Heriot Row.

river to the north, **St George's Well** is a simple stone hut with '1810' carved above the door; it's so modest you might not notice it at all. The same cannot be said for **St Bernard's Well**, an huge circular Roman temple with ten columns and a lead dome that sits quite unexpectedly and incongruously on top of another wellhouse a little further along. It

Ahead of you, across the bridge, is **Canonmills**, of which unfortunately nothing survives to remind the visitor of its milling history. From here it's a short walk or bus ride back into the centre.

If you want to continue to the coast, turn left into **Warriston Crescent** before you reach the bridge. Chopin stayed at No.10 on a visit in 1848; piano concerts were once given in the house on the anniversary of his visit, and private concerts still take place on occasion.

At the end of the crescent bear right and take the steps up to the Edinburgh, Leith and Granton Railway, now a cycle path between Canonmills and Granton. Turn left at the top of the steps and fork right between the twin pillars of J. Dick Peddie's grand neo-Tudor bridge (1845) to reach **Warriston Cemetery** (there's a gap in the wall on the right at the end of the bridge).

An underground tunnel connects the north and south parts of the cemetery, Edinburgh's version of London's Highgate Cemetery (and equally popular with gay men). Many of its extraordinary monuments, testaments to the piety, wealth or vainglory of a multitude of worthy citizens, have been swallowed up in the greenery or vandalized, but they still constitute an impressive collection, and on a sunny day the cemetery is very tranquil. And there's an upside to its neglect in the abundance of wildlife, including badgers and owls.

Coming out of the tunnel into the main northern section brings you to the **war memorial**, a large, simple stone cross inset with a sword. Beyond and behind it to the right is a sad Doric column in a grove of yew trees, commemorating local building contractor Alexander Wilson. Keep left to reach the impressive façade of the **catacombs** – buildings fine enough for the living, let alone the dead, but now sadly bricked up. Above their west end on the left, there's an unmarked recumbent figure in a bed of moss – all that remains of the **'pink lady'**, who used to lie in a bizarre Gothic mortuary chapel made of white marble, with red glass that bathed her in an eerie light. At the other end, look for the sumptuous Iona cross in memory of poet and essayist Alexander Smith. Other notables commemorated with obelisks, crosses and urns include James Young Simpson, the pioneer of anaesthesia; and painters Horatio MacCulloch and Adam Black.

In the southern section is found the grave of 'Dr Syntax', aka John Sheriff, a much-loved character of the 1840s who, according to T. M. Tod in his *Random Notes and Recollections of Edinburgh*, used to sport 'an antiquated riding coat of enormous size and a broad-brimmed hat...green spectacles and a staff of large proportions'.

An unusual detour here is **Lady Haig's Poppy Factory** (*9 Warriston Rd, t (0131) 556 5262*), set up by Earl Haig's wife in 1926 (it moved here from Canongate in 1965) and the nursery of the paper poppies, put together by ex-servicemen, that spring up in November to commemorate the fallen of the two world wars. On display are some early, very faded examples of the crêpe flowers and, most moving of all, some of the standard-issue bronze medals and offical Royal commiserations sent by King George V to the families of those that died.

Return to the cycle path at the bridge and **turn right** along the long straight path ahead (with bridges visible in the distance), which continues to Granton and Newhaven. From here it is a lovely half-hour walk to the sea at Newhaven, along an open grassy path that passes under several bridges. Apart from a few dog-walkers and plenty of birdlife, you may well have it to yourself. It's from Granton that the world's first train ferry crossed the Firth to Burntisland in Fife.

The path ends on Trinity Road. Turn right around Trinity Crescent and you will come to Drew Nichol's at the Old Chain Pier (*see* p.178), a lovely pub overlooking the water. Continuing along the road, keeping the sea on your left, will bring you to **Newhaven Harbour** and the excellent **Newhaven Heritage Museum** (*see* p.119).

From Newhaven you can catch a bus back into the city centre or along the edge of the docks to the **Former Royal Yacht *Britannia*** and **Leith** (*see* p.118).

Day Trips

09

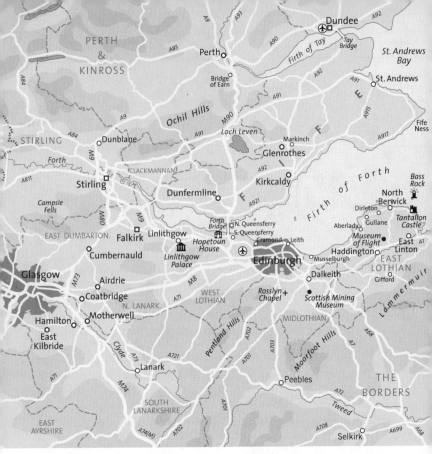

Edinburgh's great rival, Glasgow, may lack the former's castle and spectacular setting, but it makes up for those omissions in some style with wonderful architecture, internationally respected galleries, museums and theatres, some top-class restaurants, great nightlife and the famously warm welcome of its citizens. Less than an hour by train to the west, across Scotland's crowded central belt, it boasts among its attractions the Burrell Collection and Pollok House, a pair of world-class art galleries in Pollok Country Park. More centrally, you'll find the Centre for Contemporary Arts, the Gallery of Modern Art and the venerable Hunterian Museum and Art Gallery. *The List* magazine (*see* p.53) also covers events in Glasgow.

Also just under an hour away by train from Edinburgh, Stirling is a small university town with an even more impressive castle housing famous Renaissance apartments. Nearby is the National Wallace Monument in memory of the nation's medieval liberator, who was memorably caricatured by Mel Gibson in the film *Braveheart*.

Marginally further from Edinburgh to the northeast, on the coast, is Scotland's most ancient university at St Andrews. This is also the spiritual home of the nation's patron saint and of the national game of golf. As well as cathedral, castle and picturesque harbour, the 15th-century university quads are worth exploring.

A 20-minute train journey west of Edinburgh, Linlithgow rewards a visit with its ruined and evocative royal palace. Meanwhile, along the coast east of the city stretches a string of sleepy towns and port villages: dinky Aberlady, golf-crazy Gullane, pretty Dirleton with its castle, and North Berwick – a seaside resort to rank with Portobello. Further east still, the seabird-spotted Bass Rock squats offshore, close by the magical clifftop ruins of Tantallon Castle.

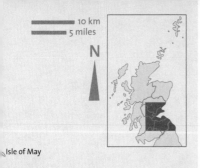

GLASGOW

Edinburgh was for many years lulled into a complacent acceptance of its role as the cultural centre of Scotland, but that complacency has been exploded: quietly, almost stealthily, Glasgow has moved up, to the point where it now vies with its grand rival for international attention. Indeed, Glasgow celebrated its reign as Cultural Capital of Europe in 1990 and was the City of Architecture and Design in 1999.

It's a remarkable turnaround for a city that was once the ugly, boisterous, working-class hub of redundant Scotland; because of the flourishing Clydeside shipyards and all the associated heavy industry that grew up after the Industrial Revolution, the city was particularly badly hit by the Depression. Glaswegians themselves, however, remain unfazed and even unsurprised by this change in fortunes.

The Burrell Collection

Pollok Country Park, 3 miles southwest of the city, **t** *(0141) 287 2550.* **Open** *Mon–Sat 10am–5pm, Sun 11am–5pm;* **bus** *no.45 from Queen St Station or Union St;* **adm** *free.*

Opened in 1983, this is Glasgow's greatest treasure, attracting thousands of visitors from all over the world. The collection was given to the city by the wealthy industrialist Sir William Burrell (1861–1958) in 1944, and the breadth of Burrell's taste is astonishing. He was a traditionalist, with no time for the avant garde, but within that scope his eye was caught by almost anything: prehistoric artefacts, Oriental art, stained glass, porcelain, silver, paintings, sculpture, carpets, crystal and tapestries. The 1970s building, designed by Barry Gasson, has won prestigious architectural awards.

There are objects from the ancient civilizations of Egypt, Iraq and Iran, Greece, the eastern Mediterranean and Italy. But almost a quarter of the collection is Oriental: Chinese ceramics include polychrome figures from the Tang Dynasty (AD 618–907) and porcelain from 14th-century Yuan and 15th-century Ming dynasties. There are also Japanese prints, ceramics from the Near East, and Near Eastern carpets.

Medieval church art and sculpture are also well represented. Burrell saw his medieval tapestries as the most valuable part of his collection. Look for the 15th-century *Ferret Hunt* and *Hercules Initiating the Olympic Games*. Another relic from the Middle Ages is stained glass, some of it from churches but also some vignettes of everyday life.

Burrell started his collection with paintings and was still buying them two years before he died, 80 years later. As with the rest of his treasures, he appears to have had an astonishingly catholic taste, ranging from Degas and Cézanne to Bellini and Hans Memling. Among the sculpture on show is Rodin's *The Thinker*, a bronze from one of the many casts of this best known of his works, in the original size.

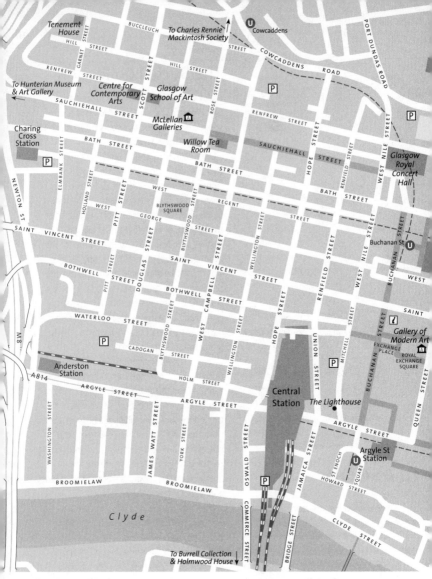

Centre for Contemporary Arts

*350 Sauchiehall St, **t** (0141) 332 7521, **w** www. cca-glasgow.com. **Open** Tues, Wed and Fri– Sun 11am–6pm, Thurs 11am–8pm; **adm** free.*

Founded in 1975, the biggest contemporary arts centre in Scotland has galleries, a theatre, a bookshop, a café and a bar. Its 30 or so annual exhibitions tour internationally, and it also hosts drama, music, readings, talks, films and festivals. It's housed in a building designed by Alexander 'Greek' Thomson in 1865.

Gallery of Modern Art

*Royal Exchange Square, **t** (0141) 229 1996. **Open** Mon–Wed and Sat 10am–5pm, Thurs 10am–8pm, Fri and Sun 11am–5pm; **adm** free.*

The gallery opened in 1996 in one of the grandest of the tobacco merchants' houses. The exhibition is loosely divided into earth, air, fire and water themes, and the imagination is stretched – which may be the point. Despite objections by conservationists over the contemporary mosaic on the pediment outside, the opening of the gallery has given a new focus to the square.

George Square

This square at the heart of the city is a popular venue for demonstrations and is dominated by a **statue of Sir Walter Scott** on an 80ft column (first intended for a statue of George III). Scott towers over Victoria and Albert, Robert Burns, James Watt and others, his plaid across the wrong shoulder as was his custom. On the eastern side of the square are the Italian Renaissance-style **City Chambers**, the offices of Glasgow City Council, of which there are free guided tours (**t** (0141) 287 2000).

Glasgow Cathedral

*Castle St, **t** (0141) 552 0988. **Open** April–Sept Mon–Sat 9.30am–6pm, Sun 1–5pm, Oct–March Mon–Sat 9.30am–4pm, Sun 1–4pm.*

The city's parish church is on the site of a church built by St Mungo, and Glasgow grew up around it. There are still traces of the original stone building, dedicated in the presence of King David I in 1136 and rebuilt in 1197. The crypt, choir and tower were built in 1233; the rest was added at stages in the succeeding years. It's one of the best examples of pre-Reformation Gothic architecture in Scotland.

Charles Rennie Mackintosh (1868–1928)

One of the city's most talented sons, Mackintosh was a leading exponent of 'the Glasgow Style', which influenced the modern movement. His local work includes **Mackintosh House** (attached to the Hunterian Museum; *see* right); **Glasgow School of Art** (*see* below); the interior of the **Willow Tea Room** (217 Sauchiehall Street); the **HQ of the Charles Rennie Mackintosh Society** (in the former Queen's Cross Church, 870 Garscube Road); **House for an Art Lover**, based on an unrealized 1901 design (Bellahouston Park, Dumbreck Road), **Scotland Street School** (225 Scotland Street), **The Lighthouse**, now an architecture and design centre with a Mackintosh interpretation centre (Mitchell Street), and **The Hill House**, Helensburgh.

Opposite is **Provand's Lordship**, dating from 1471 and the city's oldest house. Built for a priest, it's now a museum with 17th- and 18th-century furniture, tapestry and pictures.

Glasgow Royal Concert Hall

2 Sauchiehall St, t (0141) 353 8000, w www.grch.com.

Designed by Sir Leslie Martin in 1990, the Glasgow Royal Concert Hall has a 2,500-seat auditorium and two good restaurants. Leading international orchestras perform classical music and jazz concerts here, and the Royal Scottish National Orchestra and City of Glasgow Philharmonic play here too.

Glasgow School of Art

167 Renfrew St, t (0141) 353 4500, w www.gsa. ac.uk. **Tours** *Mon–Fri 11am and 2pm, Sat 10am; adm £5.*

Believed by many to be Mackintosh's supreme architectural achievement, the School of Art, viewable by guided tour only, was constructed in 1896. One of the best things about it is that it is still being used for the purpose for which it was built.

Hunterian Museum and Art Gallery

Hillhead St, t (0141) 330 4221 (museum), t (0141) 330 5431 (gallery), w www.hunterian.gla.ac.uk. Open Mon–Sat 9.30am–5pm; adm free.

The **museum** (Scotland's first public museum) opened in 1807 and contains the eponymous 18th-century physician's fine collections of coins, paintings, prints, books and manuscripts, and zoological, mineral and medical specimens. The **gallery**'s collection of work by Whistler is rivalled only by the collection in Washington's Freer Gallery. There are also paintings by Rembrandt, Chardin, Stubbs, Pissarro, Ramsay, Reynolds, Sisley and more. It also boasts a comprehensive collection of work by Mackintosh (*see* left).

The attached **Mackintosh House** (*Mon–Sat 9.30am–12.30pm and 1.30–5pm*) is a reconstruction of nearby No.6 Florentine Terrace, now demolished, where Mackintosh lived from 1906 to 1914.

Getting There

Trains from Edinburgh's Waverley Station and Haymarket Station to Glasgow's Queen Street leave every 15mins and take 50mins (t 08457 484950). **Buses** run from Elder St in Edinburgh to Buchanan Street bus station (t (0141) 332 7133).

Tourist Information

11 George Square, t (041) 204 4400, w www. seeglasgow.com. Open May, June and Sept Mon–Sat 9am–7pm, Sun 10am–6pm; July and Aug Mon–Sat 9am–8pm, Sun 10am–6pm; Oct–March Mon–Sat 9am–6pm.

Eating Out

Di Maggio's Pizzeria, *Royal Exchange Square, t (0141) 248 2111.* Delicious, unusual pizzas and pasta. Set meals in the basement cost under a fiver.

Rogano, *11 Exchange Place, t (0141) 248 4055.* Renowned for its atmosphere and seafood, Rogano dates from 1876 but was remodelled in 1935 in the Art Deco style. Downstairs, Café Rogano is cheaper but the food is as good.

McLellan Galleries

*270 Sauchiehall St, **t** (0141) 331 1854. **Open** varies with exhibitions; **adm** varies.*

Built in 1854, these galleries were designed for touring and temporary exhibitions, but until 2006 they will be home to highlights from the collections belonging to **Kelvingrove Museum and Art Gallery**, Scotland's most popular free visitor attraction, which is closed for a huge refurbishment. Kelvingrove Museum has engineering and archaeological collections, and ethnological, natural history and social history exhibits; the Gallery claims to have one of the best collections of paintings owned by any city, with the works of 'The Glasgow Boys' particularly well represented. There are also sculptures (including some Rodins), ceramics, jewellery and furniture displays (including work by Mackintosh).

Merchant City

Just off George Square beyond the City Chambers, the gridded streets of the old Merchant City were created *c.* 1750 for the tobacco lords, who built their mansions and warehouses here. Now a focus for inner-city regeneration, the area has seen many of its fine buildings restored. **Merchant Square** (71–3 Albion St), is a vibrant hub, with bars, restaurants and shops, and regular events year-round. A *Merchant City Trail* leaflet is available from the National Trust centre in **Hutcheson's Hall** at 158 Ingram Street.

Pollok House

*Pollok Country Park, **t** (0141) 616 6410. **Open** daily 10am–5pm; **bus** no.45 from Queen St Station or Union St; **adm** £5 April–Oct, free Nov–March.*

Pollok House, in the same grounds as the Burrell Collection (*see* p.137), was built in 1750 for the Maxwell family and has one of the UK's finest collections of Spanish paintings. There are also many works by other European masters, and 18th- and 19th-century furniture, silver, ceramics and crystal.

St Mungo Museum of Religious Life and Art

*2 Castle St, **t** (0141) 553 2557. **Open** Mon–Thurs and Sat 10am–5pm, Fri and Sun 11am–5pm; **adm** free.*

The world's first museum of religion has three galleries, as well as a Buddhist Zen garden. The *pièce de résistance* is Dali's *Christ of St John of the Cross*.

The Tenement House

*145 Buccleuch St, **t** (0141) 333 0183. **Open** March–Oct daily 1–5pm; **adm** £3.50.*

This restored first-floor flat in an 1892 tenement gives an insight into the living conditions of the lower-middle-class family who lived here in the early 20th century.

STIRLING

Its strategic position made Stirling a fortress town in earliest times, and seven battlefields, including Bannockburn, lie in its shadow. Today it has flung itself into tourism with gusto, and in summer hums with every sort of entertainment, exhibition and event.

Stirling Castle

*Top of Castle Wynd, **t** (01786) 450000. **Open** April–Sept daily 9.30am–6pm, Oct–March daily 9.30am–5pm; **adm** £7.50.*

Legend credits King Arthur with taking this castle from the Saxons; what is certain is that Alexander I died here, Henry II took it as part-payment for the release of William the Lion after the Battle of Alnwick, and William died here in 1214. In those days it was built of timber, superseded by masonry in the 13th century. Continual alteration and restoration have resulted in today's castle, most of it 15th- and 16th-century, with Renaissance architecture added by James IV and James V. Nine-month-old Mary was crowned Queen of Scots in the Chapel Royal in 1543.

Getting There

Trains (t 0845 748 4950) run from Waverley Station in Edinburgh every hour or so and take just under an hour. Citylink (t 08705 505050) run hourly **buses** from Elder Street, which also take about an hour.

Tourist Information

41 Dumbarton Rd, t (01786) 475019, w www. visitscottishheartlands.org. **Open** daily May, June, Sept and Oct 9am–5pm, July and Aug 9am–7pm, Nov–April Mon–Sat 10am–5pm.

Eating Out

Golden Lion Milton Hotel, King St, t 0808 100 5556. Good food in a glitzy environment.
Park Lodge, 32 Park Terrace, t (01786) 474862. Haute cuisine in a charming hotel overlooking the park and the castle.
Stirling Highland, Spittal St, t (01786) 272727. There's a choice of restaurants at this luxury hotel in the old High School.

The Old Town

The old part of Stirling is clustered up the hill towards the castle. Some historic buildings line the steep, narrow streets, including the **Church of the Holy Rude**, built uphill with the choir elevated, where James VI/I was crowned. **Argyll's Lodging** in Castle Wynd (included in castle admission) is a splendid example of a complete 17th-century townhouse. **Stirling Old Town Jail** in St John Street has 'living history performances', original cells and a good view from the roof.

Bannockburn Heritage Centre

Glasgow Road, t (01786) 812664, w www.nts. org.uk; **bus** Midland Bluebird or Strathclyde from Stirling bus station. **Open** site 24hrs; heritage centre, shop and café daily April–Oct 10am–5.30pm, Nov–March 11am–4.30pm; **adm** £3.50.

The Battle of Bannockburn between Robert the Bruce and the English in 1314 took place over an area that is now mostly housing, less than 2 miles from Stirling. The heritage centre has an audiovisual theatre that gives a history of the battle, and if you walk through the hedge from the car park you come to the imposing Robert the Bruce Memorial Statue.

National Wallace Monument

Abbey Craig, t (01786) 472140. **Open** daily March–May and Oct 10am–5pm, June 10am–6pm, July and Aug 9.30am–6.30pm, Sept 9.30am–5pm, Dec–Feb 10.30am–4pm; **adm** £5.

1½ miles northeast of town, this Victorian monster of a tower, 220ft high with a mighty bronze statue of Wallace set in its wall above the door, is almost as much of a landmark as the castle. The five floors contain a 'battle tent' with the talking head of Wallace, his sword, and the story of the Battle of Stirling Bridge in 1297, which he is said to have directed from the top of Abbey Craig (not quite as in the film Braveheart). There is a Hall of Scotland's Heroes, with marble busts, and a 360° diorama of the surroundings with a description of their history.

ST ANDREWS

According to legend, St Rule, custodian of St Andrew's remains in Patrae some time between the 4th and 8th centuries, had a vision telling him to take five of the saint's bones, sail to the western edge of the world and build a city in his honour. Rule set off and was shipwrecked just to the west of today's harbour. Hurrying ashore, he enshrined the relics on the headland where the ruins of the 12th-century cathedral now stand. St Andrew became Scotland's patron saint; his white cross on a blue ground became the national flag (the 'silver saltire'); and the city where his remains lay became the ecclesiastical capital of Scotland. Don't miss its picturesque **harbour** – the main pier was rebuilt in the 17th century with stones from the ruined cathedral and castle.

The University

Scotland's oldest university, founded in 1411, is the living heart of St Andrews. Tours usually take place twice a day from June to August (*t (01334) 476 161*). On Sundays you might catch students processing from the chapel in the medieval scarlet gowns introduced so they could be seen entering brothels (divinity students wear black gowns: presumably they were above suspicion.) Or you might glimpse Prince William, who is reading for a degree here.

Among the many fine university buildings is the **Church of St Salvator**, founded as the University Chapel by Bishop Kennedy in 1450. The pulpit was the one John Knox preached from, carried here from the parish church.

St Andrews Cathedral

On seafront at head of North St, t (01334) 472563, w www.historic-scotland.net. **Open** *daily April–Sept 9.30am–6.30pm, Oct–March 9.30am–4.30pm; adm £2.50 (£4 with castle).*

Founded in 1160, this was once the largest cathedral in Scotland, with medieval pilgrims praying in their thousands at its 31 altars. When you stand in front of the remains of the high altar, remember that Robert the Bruce stood here at the consecration of the cathedral in 1318, 160 years after building began. In 1559 zealous reformer John Knox preached on the 'cleansing of the temple', rousing his congregations to such hysteria that they stripped the cathedral of its embellishments, leaving it to decay into ruin.

Yet even as a ruin it is magnificent. A great twin-towered façade soars towards the sky, surrounded by neat green turf, graves, the foundations of the priory, a few massive walls and a Norman arch. The **Cathedral Museum** is full of interesting relics, including a unique sarcophagus.

St Rule's Tower, also within the precinct, is where the holy relics of St Andrew were kept until the cathedral was completed. If you climb its 158 steps you'll be rewarded by wonderful views of the town and out to sea.

Getting There

Trains from Edinburgh's Waverley Station to Dundee and Aberdeen stop at St Andrews' Leuchar Station (1hr 45mins). Express **buses** run from Elder Street every hour and take 2 hours (*t (01383) 621249*).

Tourist Information

70 Market St, t (01334) 472021, w www. standrews.com. **Open** *April–June daily 9.30am–5.30pm, July and Aug daily 9.30am–7pm, Sept daily 9.30am–6pm, Oct–March Mon–Sat 9.30am–5pm.*

Eating Out

Brambles, *5 College St, t (01344) 475380.* Traditional homemade Scottish bistro food.
Rusacks, *Pilmour Links, t (01344) 474 321, w www.heritage-hotels.com.* A prestigious hotel overlooking 'The Old' course (*see* p.144), serving excellent food.

The **Pends**, now roofless, was the vaulted gatehouse entrance to the cathedral precinct, dating from the 14th century. It is said it will collapse when the wisest man in Christendom walks through the arch.

St Andrews Castle

On seafront just off North St, t (01334) 477196, w www.historic-scotland.net. **Open** *daily April–Sept Mon–Sat 9.30am–6.30pm, Oct–March 9.30am–4.30pm; adm £2.50 (£4 with cathedral).*

Northwest of the cathedral on a rocky headland overhanging the sea beyond a deep moat, the castle, now a ruin, was built as the Bishop's Palace at the end of the 12th century and witnessed some extremely nasty incidents in the bloodstained history of the Scottish Church, including the burning at the stake of ardent Protestant reformer George Wishart in 1545. It fell into ruin in the 17th century but you can still see the **Bottle Dungeon**, where a lot of the Reformers were imprisoned; it is hard to believe that many can have survived. Also look out for the **mine and counter mine**, tunnelled through the rock during the siege of 1546–7.

British Golf Museum

Bruce Embankment, t (01334) 460046, w www.britishgolfmuseum.co.uk. Open Easter–mid-Oct daily 9.30am–5pm, Nov–Easter Mon and Thurs–Sun 11am–3pm; adm £4.

The Golf Museum is opposite the famous Royal and Ancient Golf Club, which determines the rules of the game (though it's by no means Scotland's oldest club). It's a must for golfers, featuring everything you didn't know about the history of golf going back to its conception 500 years ago.

The R&A's club house is open to members only. The autumn Golf Meeting at the end of September is the main event of the year. Of its four courses, 'The Old' is the most famous.

EAST OF EDINBURGH

The coast east of Edinburgh is a paradise for naturalists, with nature reserves, sandy beaches, rugged rocks and a wealth of birds. The seaside towns are like English resorts, with rows of villas staring out to sea, while romantic ruined castles punctuate the area.

Aberlady

This straggling seaside village was a thriving trading port until the Peffer Burn silted up. Pantiled cottages border its main street, alongside the Quill Gallery, some inns, and a **mercat cross** that lost its top in the Reformation. The **church** with its 15th-century tower and vaulted stone basement houses part of an 8th-century Celtic cross with interwoven bird carvings. The original 'louping-on stane' at the gate was the mounting block.

Gullane

Church land until the Reformation, this town became a holiday centre for the wealthy genteel, with the famous **Muirfield** (where the Open is regularly held; *see* p.192) among its golf courses and a sandy beach for non-golfing visitors.

Nearby Gullane Hill was formed by wind-blown sand – a process that continues. Sand has silted up Aberlady Bay on the west side of the hill and created a **bird sanctuary and nature reserve** boasting more than 200 recorded species of birds, including five species of tern. A footbridge leads from the roadside car park into the reserve.

Dirleton

Three miles west of North Berwick, this is one of the prettiest villages in the area, with pantiled cottages, a 17th-century church, a session house, an old school and inns grouped around two wide, tree-lined greens.

Dirleton Castle and Garden (*t (01620) 850330*) is a 13th-century ruin overlooking the upper green from a rocky mound in the middle of the village. The last castle in the south of Scotland to resist Edward I, it was demolished by General Monk, for Cromwell, in 1650. Surrounded by lawns, a fine garden and a 17th-century bowling green, it has a 17th-century doo'cot with 1,100 empty nests – a relic from when pigeon meat was a food supplement in the lean winter months.

Yellow Craig, a sandy beach studded with dunes and backed by woodland, is reached by a lane leading a mile seawards from the eastern edge of Dirleton. It has a caravan park, picnic sites and a nature trail. The small hillock rising from the trees was the model for Spyglass Hill in Robert Louis Stevenson's *Treasure Island*. The sandy bay overlooks Fidra Island, a lump of eroded black basalt rock.

North Berwick

North Berwick developed into a holiday and golf resort during the 19th century. A compact, sunny town flanked by two bays with a rocky headland between, it teems with holidaymakers in summer. **North Berwick Law**, a volcanic rock, towers above the town. Climb its steep flank for a view out to sea, over to the hills of Fife and across the Lothian plain to the Lammermuirs, Moorfoots and Pentlands. One of a chain of warning beacons in the Middle Ages, it is crowned by a Napoleonic Wars watchtower. There is also an arch made from a whale's jawbone.

The **Scottish Seabird Centre** on the harbour (t *(01620) 890202,* **w** *www.seabird.org*), opened by the Prince of Wales, is a splendid place for ornithologists of all ages. Spy cameras on the Bass Rock relay live pictures of puffins, gannets and so on.

Bass Rock

A mile and a half offshore, this volcanic plug is 350ft high and a mile in circumference, its sheer-walled wedge forming a reference point for sailors. Boat trips from North Berwick cruise around it, but permission is needed to land. St Baldred the hermit died on the rock in the 7th or 8th century, and you can just make out where his cell was, on a terrace on the south side. Bass Rock is now a gannetry, as well as a haven for gulls, kitti-wakes, puffins, fulmars and guillemots.

Tantallon Castle

3 miles east of North Berwick off the A198, t (01620) 892727. **Open** *April–Sept daily 9.30am–6.30pm, Oct–March Mon–Wed and Sat 9.30am–4.30pm, Thurs 9.30am–noon, Fri and Sun 2–4.30pm;* **adm** *£3.*

This dramatic 14th-century ruin on the edge of a sheer cliff overhanging the sea between two bays was a stronghold of the powerful Douglas family, who ruled their domains with a total disregard for authority. They lived as they pleased – especially when Margaret Tudor, devious widow of James IV, married their leader, the Earl of Angus, in 1514, and they became arch manipulators in the power struggle over the boy-king, James V. Tantallon was a perfect stronghold, its massive curtain walls cutting it off on its headland and making it impregnable against the impotent batterings of rivals, and the family built on to it and strengthened it. Seen silhouetted against the sea, this is one of Scotland's most heart-stopping ruins.

Dunbar

This was an important fishing port 300 years ago, and smuggling also flourished here: 8,000 pounds of contraband tobacco passed through the town in 1765. Today it is a rapidly developing holiday resort with reput-edly the lowest rainfall and highest sunshine in Scotland. Edward I defeated the Scots here in 1295, and in 1650 Cromwell defeated the supporters of Charles II in Dunbar, killing 3,000 and taking 10,000 prisoners.

Dunbar Harbour has cobbled quays around an outer and inner basin, restored ware-houses, a coastguard station, working fishing boats, piles of netting and lobster creels, pleasure craft and the ever-vigilant lifeboat.

Getting There and Around

Trains from Haymarket Station and Waverley Station (t *0845 748 4950*) to North Berwick take 40 minutes and stop at various coastal points. There's a good **bus** network across the area, with buses from Edinburgh departing from Elder Street (t *(0131) 663 9233*).

Tourist Information

Dunbar: *143 High St, t (01368) 863353, w www.dunbar.org.uk.* **Open** *Easter–Oct Mon–Sat 9am–5pm, Sun 10am–3pm.*

North Berwick: *Quality St, t (01620) 892197.* **Open** *April–Sept Mon–Sat 9am–5pm, Sun 10am–3pm, Oct–March Mon–Sat 9am–5pm.*

Eating Out

Cuckoo Wrasse, *Dunbar, t (01368) 865384.* A quayside bistro where delicious fresh seafood is served.

Greywalls Hotel, *Muirfield, Gullane, t (01620) 842144, w www.greywalls.co.uk.* When King Hussein and Queen Noor of Jordan ate here, the only Lutyens house in Scotland and now one of its best hotels, they pinched the chef; luckily, the replacement has proved superior.

Open Arms Hotel, *Dirleton, t (01620) 850241.* An upmarket inn on the edge of the village green, overlooking the castle. People drive out from Edinburgh to eat here.

The town sprawls around a wide High Street, squared off at the north end by **Lauderdale House**, built by Robert Adam. The 16th-century steepled **Town House** in the middle of the High Street is the oldest civic building in constant use in Scotland, with a local history and archaeology museum.

The best view of **Dunbar Castle** is from above, at the edge of Lauderdale House barrack square. One jagged, fang-like tower and a few scattered stones are all that remain of what was an extensive fortress guarding the gateway to the eastern plain. The original castle was built in the 11th century for Cospatrick, Earl of Northumbria. When Bothwell abducted Mary, Queen of Scots in 1567, he brought her to Dunbar Castle. It was demolished by Mary's half-brother, Moray, after her final defeat. Later, Cromwell used its stones to improve the harbour.

John Muir Country Park

Belhaven Bay, t (01620) 827423. **Open** *24hrs;* **adm** *free.*

This park on the western outskirts of town is named after the Dunbar-born 19th-century conservationist and explorer who founded America's national parks. Acres of wild coastland surround the mouth of the Tyne, where you can walk along the cliffs, fish, sail, surf, ride, play golf, and enjoy the wildlife.

Museum of Flight

East Fortune Airfield, north of the A1 near Haddington, t (01620) 880308, w www.nms.ac.uk/flight. **Open** *daily Easter–Oct 10.30am–5pm (to 6pm in July and Aug), Nov–Easter 10.30am–4pm; during Oct–March bottom hangar only is open;* **adm** *£3.*

This museum is at the airfield from which the airship R34 made the first double crossing of the Atlantic. It displays about 50 antique and modern aircraft, as well as the world's most extensive British rocketry collection. The tiny de Havilland Puss Moth is the type of plane in which Amy Johnson's husband Jim Mollison made the first east–west solo flight across the Atlantic, in 1932.

LINLITHGOW PALACE

In Linlithgow, off the M9, t (01506) 842896, w www.historic-scotland.gov.uk. **Open** *April–Sept daily 9.30–6.30, Oct–March Mon–Sat 9.30–4.30, Sun 2–4.30;* **adm** *£4.*

There was a Pictish settlement here before the Romans came, and the first royal palace was recorded in the 12th century. Edward I had his headquarters in Linlithgow in 1301 and David II built a royal manor, destroyed by fire in 1424. The following year work began on the present palace, which is one of the country's most poignant ruins.

The elaborate fountain in the quadrangle is said to have run with wine when James V gave it to Mary of Guise as a wedding present in 1538. Four years later their daughter was born in one of the upper chambers – ill-fated Mary who was proclaimed Queen of Scots within a week of her birth. Over-enthusiastic fuelling of domestic fires, possibly with bedding straw, by General Hawley's troops garrisoned here on the night of 31 January 1746 reduced the palace to a smouldering shell. The swans on the loch add a royal touch: it is said they flew away when the Roundheads arrived and returned the day that Charles II was crowned at Scone in 1649.

Getting There

There are five **trains** an hour from Waverley Station (**t** 0845 748 4950), taking 17–21mins, and **buses** every 15mins from Waterloo Place, taking about an hour (**t** 0870 608 2608).

Tourist Information

Burgh Halls, The Cross, t (01506) 844 600. **Open** *Easter–Sept daily 10am–5pm.*

Eating Out

The Four Marys, Main St, **t** (01506) 842171. A popular pub serving good food.

Livingston's, 52 High St, **t** (01506) 846565. A bistro-style cottage with a conservatory, serving good food at reasonable prices.

Where to Stay

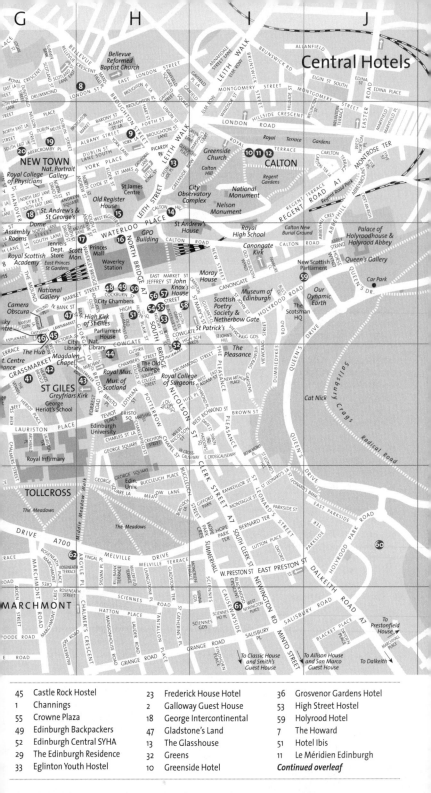

Central Hotels

45	Castle Rock Hostel	23	Frederick House Hotel	36	Grosvenor Gardens Hotel
1	Channings	2	Galloway Guest House	53	High Street Hostel
55	Crowne Plaza	18	George Intercontinental	59	Holyrood Hotel
49	Edinburgh Backpackers	47	Gladstone's Land	7	The Howard
52	Edinburgh Central SYHA	13	The Glasshouse	51	Hotel Ibis
29	The Edinburgh Residence	32	Greens	11	Le Méridien Edinburgh
33	Eglinton Youth Hostel	10	Greenside Hotel	*Continued overleaf*	

Not so long ago it was nigh on impossible to find a room in the middle of Edinburgh between June and October without booking months in advance. However, so many hotels have sprung up all over the city that nowadays there's a good chance of your finding somewhere central even at the last minute. The Festival and New Year will always remain the exceptions to this reassuring rule, but it is largely thanks to those occasions (as well as the arrival of the Conference Centre and to the coming of the new Parliament) that options throughout the year have improved.

The really outstanding hotels in the city are still the two old station hotels that lord it over either end of Princes Street – the Balmoral and the Caledonian Hilton. Yet there are some less expensive hotels that also have a distinctive Edinburgh character. The Town House group of hotels in the New Town – The Howard,

Map Key (cont'd)

The Bonham and Channings – are the best examples, as is historic Prestonfield House Hotel beneath Arthur's Seat. The Point Hotel is unique for its ultra-modern design, combined with a lively restaurant and bar, while Malmaison in Leith has been voted UK Hotel of the Year in the *Observer/Guardian* Travel Awards for the past four years.

Less expensive accommodation comes in the form of a multitude of bed and breakfast guesthouses and backpackers' hostels. The tourist board (*see* p.56) can provide details and booking for many of these.

Price categories for a double room per night in high season:

luxury	£200 and above
expensive	£100–200
moderate	£70–100
inexpensive	less than £70

The Old Town

Luxury

The Scotsman Hotel H9
20 North Bridge, **t** *(0131) 556 5565,* **f** *(0131) 652 3652,* **e** *reservations@ thescotsmanhotel.co.uk,* **w** *www.thescotsmanhotel.co.uk.*
A stylish conversion of the old *Scotsman* newspaper building in a spectacular position at the top end of the North Bridge. The best rooms have great views towards Calton Hill, Leith and the Firth of Forth. Amenities include discreet 'privacy hatches' to prevent those annoying room service intrusions, a buzzy bar and brasserie (*see* p.162, North Bridge Brasserie), a gourmet restaurant (*see* p.162, Vermilion), a stunning stainless steel and slate swimming pool, a spa area and a gym.

Expensive

Apex City G10
61 Grassmarket, **t** *0845 608 3456,* **f** *(0131) 226 5345,* **e** *city@ apexhotels.co.uk,* **w** *www. apexhotels.co.uk.*

This four-star addition to the Apex group of budget-hotels-turned-would-be-designer-boltholes shares the castle views of its sister and near-neighbour, the Apex International (*see* p.151). All the rooms have widescreen TVs, CD and DVD players, and some have cinema surround sound. The Agua restaurant, decorated in sumptuous reds and burgundies, offers a global take on local cuisine.

Best Western Edinburgh City Hotel G10
79 Lauriston Place, **t** *(0131) 622 7979,* **f** *(0131) 622 7900,* **e** *reservations@ bestwesternedinburghcity.co.uk,* **w** *www.bestwesternedinburghcity. co.uk.*
An elegantly converted maternity hospital with 52 no-frills rooms, some on the ground floor.

Carlton Hotel H9
North Bridge, **t** *(0131) 472 3000,* **f** *(0131) 556 2691,* **e** *carlton@ paramount-hotels.co.uk,* **w** *www.paramount-hotels.co.uk.*
A large, recently refurbished hotel orientated towards business travellers, with the usual facilities.

Crowne Plaza H9
80 High St, **t** *(0131) 557 9797,* **f** *(0131) 557 9789,* **e** *rescp edinburgh@allianceuk.com,* **w** *www.crowneplazaed.co.uk.*
Housed in a modern old-style building that caused great debate when it went up, this comfortable, efficient American-owned hotel has just about blended into the Royal Mile. It has two good restaurants and a piano bar.

Holyrood Hotel I9
Holyrood Rd, **t** *(0131) 550 4500,* **f** *(0131) 550 4545,* **w** *www. macdonaldhotels.com.*
A new hotel that's warming up for the opening of the Parliament building just down the road. Apart from the eagerly awaited executives and politicos, it caters to a good few tourists, with its comfortable, understated décor and fairly expensive Scottish-French food in Flint's restaurant

downstairs. Suites have views over Salisbury Crags, and the sixth-floor Executive Club comes with personal butler service.

The Witchery by the Castle G9
Boswell's Close, Castlehill,
t *(0131) 225 5613,* **f** *(0131) 220 4392,*
e *mail@thewitchery.com,*
w *www.thewitchery.com.*
Situated right next to the Castle Esplanade, this celebrity magnet had six opulent suites filled with antiques and boasting open fires, Bose sound systems and large rolltop baths, making it the ideal place for a romantic break. Champagne and breakfast in bed come as part of the deal; dinner can be enjoyed in one of The Witchery's atmospheric dining rooms (*see* p.162).

Moderate

Apex International G10
31–35 Grassmarket, **t** *0845 608 3456,* **f** *(0131) 220 5345,*
e *international@apexhotels.co.uk,*
w *www.apexhotels.co.uk.*
Formerly a pair of bland budget hotels, the Apex mini-chain (*see also* Apex European, p.154, and Apex City, p.150) has been injected with a large dose of contemporary chic, with prices upped accordingly. The International's 175 rooms have DVD and CD players and, usually, two double beds, and some have great castle views, as does The Heights restaurant. There's also a three-storey bar and brasserie.

Bank Hotel H9
1 South Bridge, **t** *(0131) 622 6800,*
f *(0131) 622 6822,* **e** *bank@festival-inns.co.uk,* **w** *www.festival-inns.co.uk.*
A Scottish-themed hotel in a former bank, with the busy Logie Baird's Bar (*see* p.175) on the ground floor. Nine rooms, some en-suite.

Tailors Hall Hotel H10
139 Cowgate, **t** *(0131) 622 6800,*
f *(0131) 622 6818,* **e** *tailors@festival.inns.co.uk,* **w** *www.festival.inns.co.uk.*

A fairly sensitive conversion of what was once the Cowgate's grandest building (*see* p.81). The courtyard is also the busy beer garden of the Three Sisters pub.

Inexpensive

Hotel Ibis H9
6 Hunter Square, **t** *(0131) 240 7000,* **f** *(0131) 240 7007,* **w** *www.ibishotel.com.*
A bright, clean chain hotel, the Ibis may not have a great deal of character but it represents good value in terms of location.

The New Town

Luxury

Balmoral Hotel H9
1 Princes St, **t** *(0131) 556 2414,*
f *(0131) 557 3747,* **e** *reservations@thebalmoralhotel.com,*
w *www.thebalmoralhotel.com.*
Its clock tower dominating the east end of Princes Street (the clock is kept a couple of minutes fast for the benefit of train travellers), this is the grandest and most expensive hotel in Edinburgh. In the galleried entrance hall, a huge chandelier hangs above a stairway leading up to rooms with some of the best views in the city. The impressive facilities include several noteworthy restaurants (including Number One, *see* p.165).

Caledonian Hilton Hotel F9
Princes St, **t** *(0131) 222 8888,* **f** *(0131) 222 8889,* **w** *www.caledonian.hilton.com.*
Expensively refurbished and now part of the Hilton chain, this much-loved grand hotel is gentlemanly, understated and very welcoming. The best rooms have enchanting views over Princes Street Gardens. Though it's largely orientated towards functions and conferences, it's very comfortable and welcoming to all comers, and is apparently the favoured stopover of Sean Connery. The Pompadour (*see* p.165) is a

magnificent formal dining room, Chisholm's is more laid-back, with an international menu and charming service. There's a busy basement fitness centre and swimming pool.

The Howard G8
34 Great King St, **t** *(0131) 315 2220,*
f *(0131) 557 6515,* **e** *reserve@thehoward.com,* **w** *www.thehoward.com.*
Set in one of the New Town's showpiece streets, this is the grandest and most 'country house' of the Town House hotels (*see also* The Bonham, below, and Channings, p.153). The 15 rooms of various sizes are furnished in an old-fashioned style, with rolltop baths and writing desks. Some are on the ground floor. The design of its popular restaurant, 36, is in deliberate contrast to the rest.

Expensive

Albany Hotel H8
39–43 Albany St, **t** *(0131) 556 0397,*
f *(0131) 557 6633,* **e** *info@albanyhoteledinburgh.co.uk,* **w** *www.albanyhoteledinburgh.co.uk.*
Despite its chintzy feel, the Albany is popular with youngish travellers who want to be in a Georgian residence near Broughton Street. Breakfasts are expensive, but there are plenty of other options nearby. Some ground-floor rooms.

The Bonham E9
35 Drumsheugh Gardens, **t** *(0131) 623 6060,* **f** *(0131) 226 6080,*
e *reserve@thebonham.com,*
w *www.thebonham.com.*
A stylish conversion of a huge Victorian house near the West End, with bold colours and fancy lighting. Some rooms are palatial (one has an Italian waterjet bath), and there are some on the ground floor. The restaurant doesn't quite match those at its older sister hotels, The Howard (*see* above) and Channings (*see* p.153), but the Californian-style menu is an interesting alternative to the usual Scottish-French theme. Room service is impeccable.

The Edinburgh Residence E9

7 Rothesay Terrace, t (0131) 622 5080, f (0131) 226 3381, e reserve@ theedinburghresidence.com, w www.theedinburghresidence.com.

Newly set up by the Town House Company, which also owns the Howard (*see* p.151), The Bonham (*see* p.151) and Channings (*see* p.153), this consists of 29 luxury suites in a series of West End townhouses. Three of the Classic suites have their own entrances, the eight Townhouse Apartments have an average floorspace equal to that of a tennis court, and all have an *armoire* with microwave, mini-fridge and food preparation area. There's also a Drawing Room with an honesty bar.

George Intercontinental G8

19–21 George St, t (0131) 225 1251, f (0131) 226 5644, e edinburgh@ interconti.com, w www.edinburgh. interconti.com.

The haunt of the establishment before the war, this is now part of the Intercontinental chain. A popular business hotel all year round, it still has plenty of character and regularly hosts bonanzas for the TV festival in August.

The Glasshouse H8

Omni Complex, Greenside Place, t (0131) 525 8200, e resglasshouse@ theetongroup.com, w www. etontownhouse.com.

This boutique hotel by the group behind London's Threadneedles was scheduled to open as we went to press, offering 66 sixth-floor rooms and suites with great views and a rooftop bar. Its imposing façade (a former church) contrasts with the glass walls of the new Omni leisure complex of which it is a part; interiors are the height of contemporary chic.

Le Méridien Edinburgh I8

18–22 Royal Terrace, t (0131) 557 3222, f (0131) 557 5334, w www. lemeridien.com.

In a peaceful Georgian mansion designed by William Playfair, Le Méridien (formerly the Royal Terrace Hotel) offers an outside courtyard, a pool and a gym.

The Old Waverley H9

43 Princes St, t (0131) 556 4648, f (0131) 557 6316, e oldwaverley reservations@paramount-hotels.co.uk, w www.paramount-hotels.co.uk.

This is one of those hotels that's been around almost as long as Princes Street itself. You pay for location rather than style, though it's perfectly comfortable, and rooms with views over Princes Street Gardens don't cost extra.

Parliament House H8

15 Calton Hill, t (0131) 478 4000, f (0131) 478 4001, e phhadams@ aol.com, w www.scotland-hotels. co.uk.

Occupying a Jacobean, Georgian and modern building tucked into the side of Calton Hill, this hotel has rooms overlooking Leith and the Firth of Forth. MP's is a laid-back bistro with an international menu; room service is also available during restaurant hours.

Rick's G8

55a Frederick St, t (0131) 622 7800, f (0131) 622 7801, e info@ ricksedinburgh.co.uk, w www. ricksedinburgh.co.uk.

Ten stylish rooms above the trendy bar and restaurant of the same name (*see* p.167 and p.176). On Sundays guests can enjoy all-day breakfasts in the restaurant.

Roxburghe Hotel F9

38 Charlotte Square, t (0131) 240 5500, f (0131) 240 5555, w www.macdonaldhotels.com.

This landmark on the corner of George Street and Charlotte Square, aimed at business travellers as much as tourists, has been refurbished as part of its incorporation into the Macdonald's hotel chain (which also owns the new Holyrood Hotel, *see* p.150). The result is a successful marriage of original Georgian detailing and modern luxury. There's a gym and swimming pool.

Royal Scots Club G8

30 Abercromby Place, t (0131) 556 4270, f (0131) 558 3769, e royalscotsclub@sol.co.uk, w www.scotsclub.co.uk.

Founded in 1919 as a war memorial to the soldiers of the Royal Scots, this retains just enough of its clubby character to set it apart from a straightforward hotel (including a gym in the old shooting range). The grand breakfast and dining room has a fine view of Queen Street Gardens, though the food is fairly basic. The colonel of the regiment, the Princess Royal, regularly stays here when visiting the city. There's also a self-catering mews cottage at the back, sleeping six.

17 Abercromby Place G8

17 Abercromby Place, t (0131) 557 8036, f (0131) 558 3453, e eirlys. lloyd@virgin.net, w www. abercrombyhouse.com.

Ten lovely rooms in William Playfair's old house, which has been restored to its 19th-century glory. Non-smoking and very New Town, with parking too.

Moderate

Castle Guest House F9

38 Castle St, t (0131) 225 1975, f (0131) 225 1975, e info@ castleguesthouse.com, w www.castleguesthouse.com.

Seven en-suite rooms and two rooms with shared facilities, all non-smoking, in a prime location just off George Street. There's a quaint breakfast room with tartan tablecloths but no wheelchair access (it's on the third floor of a Georgian townhouse).

Frederick House Hotel G9

42 Frederick St, t (0131) 226 1999, f (0131) 624 7064, e frederick house@ednet.co.uk, w www. townhousehotels.co.uk.

A very central, cheerful hotel owned by the same group as the Ailsa Craig and the Greenside (*see* p.153), with 44 four-star rooms (some ground-floor) furnished in red, green and beige in keeping with the Georgian building.

Greens D9

24 Eglinton Crescent, t 08700 507711, f (0131) 346 2990, e greens@british-trust-hotels.com, w www.british-trust-hotels.com.

A three-star hotel with 55 low-key, relatively tasteful rooms in a series of four Georgian town-houses, Greens represents good value for money.

Grosvenor Gardens Hotel D10
1 Grosvenor Gardens, t (0131) 313 3415, f (0131) 346 8732, e info@ stayinedinburgh.com, w www. stayinedinburgh.com.
A small, quiet, family-run hotel in a Victorian house just around the corner from St Mary's Episcopal Cathedral, with nine lavish family and single rooms.

16 Lynedoch Place E9
16 Lynedoch Place, t (0131) 225 5507, f (0131) 226 4185, e susie. lynedoch@btinternet.com, w www.16lynedochplace.co.uk.
Six elegant non-smoking en-suite rooms in a listed Georgian terraced house mere seconds from Princes Street. The plush dining room has views over Dean Bridge. Dogs are welcome.

Walton Hotel G8
79 Dundas St, t (0131) 556 1137, f (0131) 557 8367, e enquiries@ waltonhotel.com, w www. waltonhotel.com.
A recently refurbished three-star guesthouse in a central position, with ten fairly modern en-suite rooms on the ground floor and in the basement, a traditional dining room for breakfasts and a car park.

West End Hotel E10
35 Palmerston Place, t (0131) 225 3656, f (0131) 225 4393, e west-endhotel@btconnect.com.
A small, good-value, traditionally Scottish, family-run hotel with eight bedrooms and great break-fasts (lunch is also available, but not dinner). The lively evening folk sessions in the little bar (Wed–Sat) are popular with locals as well as tourists.

Inexpensive

Ailsa Craig Hotel I8
24 Royal Terrace, t (0131) 556 1022, f (0131) 556 6055, e ailsacraighotel @ednet.co.uk, w www.townhouse hotels.co.uk.

Like its sister hotel the Greenside (*see* below), the Ailsa Craig is an old-fashioned, family-run, basic hotel in a grandly set Georgian townhouse designed by William Playfair. All rooms are en-suite.

Greenside Hotel I8
9 Royal Terrace, t (0131) 557 0121, f (0131) 557 0022, e greensidehotel @ednet.co.uk, w www.townhouse hotels.co.uk.
The Greenside is very similar to its sister hotel, Ailsa Craig. There's a small residents' bar, a comfortable dining room and a lovely private garden. Popular with tourists.

Marrakech H7
30 London St, t (0131) 556 4444, f (0131) 557 3615.
A characterful central hotel run by a Moroccan family, with 11 rooms above a cheap and cheerful North African restaurant that also offers room service (*see* p.168).

Mrs L Collie B&B F8
37 Howe St, t/f (0131) 557 3487.
One large, good-value double room in a garden flat (not easily wheelchair accessible). Early booking advised for the summer. No children or dogs.

Dean Village and Stockbridge

Expensive

Channings D8
15 South Learmonth Gardens, t (0131) 332 3232, f (0131) 332 9631, e reserve@channings.co.uk, w www.channings.co.uk.
Though it's the least expensive and least central of the Town House Hotels group, this Edwardian terrace house has just as much character as the Howard and the Bonham (*see* p.151), while the West End is only a 10-minute walk away and Stockbridge is a short trot down the hill. Genteel in atmosphere, it has a very good Scottish brasserie and a convivial bar. Ground-floor rooms are avail-able. There's also free on-street car parking. Brigitte Bardot once stayed here.

Moderate

6 Mary's Place E7
6 Mary's Place, off Raeburn Place, t (0131) 332 8965, f (0131) 624 7060, e info@sixmarysplace.co.uk, w www.sixmarysplace.co.uk.
Eight rooms (including a garden flat) in a comfy, vegetarian, non-smoking Georgian house. A recent refurbishment has resulted in exceptionally pleasant bright, modern rooms.

Inexpensive

Galloway Guest House E8
22 Dean Park Crescent, t (0131) 332 3672, f (0131) 332 3672, e galloway-theclarks@hotmail.com.
Thirteen rooms, some en-suite and some on the ground floor. Dinner is available on request, and dogs are welcome.

Raeburn House Hotel E7
112 Raeburn Place, t (0131) 332 2348, f (0131) 315 2381, e raeburn@ festival-inns.co.uk, w www. festival-inns.co.uk.
Nine rooms with shared facilities in a fine 18th-century stone building with a large front garden, a rear beer garden and a secure car park. Major extension and refurbishment work was in the pipeline as we went to press.

St Bernard's Guest House E8
22 St Bernard's Crescent, t (0131) 332 2339, f (0131) 332 8842, e alexstbernards@aol.com.
Four en-suite rooms and four standard rooms in a grand house situated in a beautiful Georgian crescent just 10mins' walk from Princes Street. Early booking is highly advisable for weekends and essential for the Festival and New Year.

12 Belford Terrace D9
12 Belford Terrace, t (0131) 332 2413, e Carolyn.Crabbie@virgin.net.
A good-value, family-friendly B&B a few seconds from the National Gallery of Modern Art. There's a large garden (dogs are welcome) and private parking. Bedrooms are non-smoking.

Ocean Terminal

250 m
220 yards

N

H · **I** · **J** · **K**

3 · **4** · **5** · **6** · **7**

Outside the Centre

Luxury

Dundas Castle Off maps
South Queensferry, **t** *(0131) 319 2039,* **f** *(0131) 319 2068,* **w** *www.dundascastle.co.uk.*
Designed by William Burn in 1818, the stately home of Sir Jack and Lady Stewart-Clark is a grand but friendly private residence complete with an early 15th-century keep overlooking the Firth of Forth. To have the run of the place will cost you about £2,000 a night (Mon–Thurs; four bedrooms), excluding VAT, but up to 28 people can be accommodated (extra bedrooms are £200 per night each).

Sheraton Grand Hotel F10
1 Festival Square, **t** *(0131) 229 9131,* **f** *(0131) 229 6254,* **e** *grandedinburgh. sheraton@sheraton.com,* **w** *www. sheraton.com.*
A plush but bland business favourite next to the International Conference Centre, offering three restaurants, a swimming pool and the wonderful new ONE spa, designed by Sir Terry Farrell (*see* p.188). The rooms boasting views of Usher Hall and the Castle are worth the extra cost.

Expensive

Apex European D10
90 Haymarket Terrace, **t** *0845 608 3456,* **f** *(0131) 474 3400,* **e** *european@apexhotels.co.uk,* **w** *www.apexhotels.co.uk.*
Part of the revamped Apex group (*see* Apex International, p.151, and Apex City, p.150), the European offers the same cool modern aesthetic of its sisters on a smaller scale, though from the outside it's the most unprepossessing. Its 70 rooms include such amenities as satellite TV and in-house movies, and its Metro West End Brasserie is a vibrant space.

The Borough Hotel I12
72–80 Causewayside, **t** *(0131) 668 2255,* **f** *(0131) 667 6622,*

e bookings@edin-borough.co.uk,
w www.edin-borough.co.uk.
Voted one of the coolest new
hotels in Britain by Condé Nast
Traveller when it opened in 2001,
this discreet and stylish boutique
hotel in a former snooker hall has
just ten immaculately designed
rooms, including one big family
room. All comforts are provided,
from duck-down duvets and
pillows and Molton Brown
toiletries to free DVD and book
loans. There's also a swish bar and
a restaurant serving the likes of
organic haggis (see p.169).

Malmaison J4
1 Tower Place, Leith, t (0131) 468
5000, f (0131) 468 5002,
e edinburgh@malmaison.com,
w www.malmaison.com.
An award-winning designer hotel
in a superb dockside location
(making it a good alternative to
being in the heart of the city), the
original Malmaison (there are
others in Glasgow, Manchester
and elsewhere, and more in the
pipeline in London and Brussels) –
is still deservedly popular with the
in-crowd. A £4-million refurbishment completed in summer 2002
added 40 rooms (bringing the
total to 100) and a new lobby area
and gave a more modern look to
the bar and brasserie.

Point Hotel F10
34 Bread St, t (0131) 221 5555,
f (0131) 221 9929, e sales@
point-hotel.co.uk, w www.
point-hotel.co.uk.
A great marriage of architectural
vision and entertainment value,
offering the minimum of fuss or
ornament in its 140 rooms yet full
four-star comfort. For pure hedo-
nism go for one of the five jacuzzi
suites. Most rooms have castle
views. The slick restaurant (see
p.171) is unbeatable value;
Monboddo bar (see p.178) is buzzy.

Prestonfield House Off maps
Priestfield Rd, t (0131) 668 3346,
f (0131) 668 3976, e info@
prestonfieldhouse.com,
w www.prestonfieldhouse.com.
Located close to Duddingston,
right in the shadow of Arthur's

Seat, Prestonfield House is an
attractive historic building, part of
which dates from the 17th century
(see p.34). Attractions on offer
include magnificent grounds
(including access to a golf course)
and a restaurant with an excellent
reputation. Ground-floor rooms
are available.

Moderate

Allison House Off maps
15–17 Mayfield Gardens, t (0131)
667 8049, f (0131) 667 5001,
e info@allisonhousehotel.com,
w www.allisonhousehotel.com.
Traditional family-run B&B a mile
south of the centre; 23 en-suite
rooms, an inexpensive restaurant
that's open to the public, a residents' honesty bar and parking.

Avenue Hotel Off maps
4 Murrayfield Avenue, t (0131) 346
7270, e avenue.hotel@virgin.net,
w www.aboutscotland.com/edin/
avenue.
A nine-bedroom B&B located near
Murrayfield Stadium, 10mins by
bus from the city centre. All rooms
have private bathrooms. Dogs
are welcome.

Original Raj C10
6 West Coates, t (0131) 346 1333,
f (0131) 337 6688, e originalrajhotel
@aol.com, w www.aboutscotland.
com/edin/raj.
With its exotic furniture (including
a silver Jaipuri elephant throne in
the dining room), colourful
embroidered fabrics and 17
spacious rooms (among them the
Bollywood Suite), this Indian-run
hotel in a Victorian house is a
good-value choice for those
seeking something a little
different. Breakfast includes
samosas and pakora in addition to
the usual continental fare, and
mehndi (henna hand- and foot-
painting) is an unusual extra.

Stuart House H7
12 East Claremont St, t (0131) 557
9030, f (0131) 557 0563, june@
stuartguesthouse.com, w www.
stuarthouse.pwp.blueyonder.co.uk.
Ten minutes' walk from Princes
Street, this has five attractive and

well-maintained doubles and
twins with en-suite bathroom and
two single rooms with private
bathrooms. Breakfast is included.
No ground-floor rooms.

Inexpensive

Abbotsford Guest House I6
36 Pilrig St, t (0131) 554 2706,
e info@abbotsfordguesthouse.co.
uk, w abbotsfordguesthouse.co.uk.
This spacious and comfortable
little Italian-owned guesthouse is
situated between Broughton and
Leith. It has just eight rooms, six of
which are en-suite, and represents
very good value.

Balfour House I6
90 Pilrig St, t (0131) 554 2106,
f (0131) 554 3887.
The Balfour has 20 basic rooms
with showers, four with en-suite
bathrooms. Some of the rooms at
the back are quieter. There's a
communal TV lounge.

Claremont Hotel H7
14–15 Claremont Crescent, t (0131)
556 1487, f (0131) 556 7077.
An excellent-value family-run
Georgian townhouse a 5min walk
north of Broughton Street. Some
of the 24 recently refurbished en-
suite rooms are family-size, and
kids are welcome.

Classic House Off maps
50 Mayfield Rd, t (0131) 667 5847,
w www.classichouse.demon.co.uk.
A pleasant, non-smoking B&B set
in a Victorian house a 10-minute
bus ride south of the centre.
Breakfasts are of the hearty
Scottish variety.

Express by Holiday Inn I3
Britannia Way, Ocean Drive, Leith,
t (0870) 744 2163, f (0131) 555 4646,
e info@hiex-edinburgh.com,
w www.hiex-edinburgh.com.
Boasting unbeatable views of the
relocated Former Royal Yacht
Britannia (see p.118), this is an
affordable if rather soulless
option. In lieu of room service a
delivery service is laid on by
several local restaurants, and the
shopping and leisure facilities of
the Ocean Terminal are right
next door.

Java K4
*48–50 Constitution St, Leith,
t (0131) 553 2020, w www.
javabedandbreakfast.co.uk.*
Situated above the lively Bar Java
bistro and beer garden, which
offer good food and live music,
this has ten rooms and a
communal TV lounge.

Portobello House Off maps
*2 Pittville Street, Portobello,
t (0131) 669 6067, f (0131) 657 9194,
e athena@portobelloguesthouse.
co.uk, w www.portobelloguest
house.co.uk.*
A charming B&B in a Victorian
villa seconds from the shore, with
superb organic breakfasts served
in its airy dining room. Most
rooms are en-suite.

San Marco Guest House
Off maps
*24 Mayfield Gardens, t (0131) 667
8982, f (0131) 662 1945,
e san.marco@ukgateway.net.*
Some way outside of the town
centre to the south, this is a
pleasant enough guesthouse with
several en-suite rooms.

Smith's Guest House Off maps
*77 Mayfield Rd, t (0131) 667 2524,
f (0131) 668 4455, e mail@smithsgh.
com, w www.smithsgh.com.*
A two-star B&B in a Victorian
townhouse a 10min bus ride
south of the centre. Rooms, some
of which are en-suite, are spick
and span, breakfasts are Scottish.

Straven Guest House Off maps
*3 Brunstane Rd North, Portobello,
t (0131) 669 5580, f (0131) 657 2517,
e book@stravenguesthouse.com,
w www.stravenguesthouse.com.*
A 15-minute bus ride from central
Edinburgh, this has seven quiet
rooms, all en-suite, one with a
seaview. No children under 12.

B&B Agencies

In addition to the specialist
agencies listed here, the **Tourist
Information Office** (*t (0131) 473
3800*) can make a B&B reservation
on your behalf for a £3 booking
fee and £10 deposit. Alternatively,
see *w www.aboutscotland.com*.

Festival Beds F8
*38 Moray Place, t (0131) 225 1101,
f (0131) 225 2724, e info@festival
beds.co.uk, w www.festivalbeds.
co.uk.*
An agency sourcing B&B accommodation during the Festival.

First Option Leisure Breaks H9
*Unit 3, Platform 1, Waverley
Station, t (0131) 557 0034,
w www.firstoption.co.uk.*
First Option charges a £5 booking
fee but is conveniently located.
There's also a desk in the airport
arrivals lounge (*t (0131) 333 5119*).

Isabel Thomas & Associates D8
136 Queensferry Rd, t (0131) 343 2298.
A no-fee agency offering same-
day bookings if needed.

Murray Accommodation
Off maps
*108 Broomfield Crescent, t (0131)
477 3339/08707 509808, w www.
murray-accommodation.com.*
A recommended no-fee agency.

Student Halls of Residence

During the **Festival**, central
student residences can be booked
through Eglinton Youth Hostel
(*see p.157*) or by calling **t** (01786)
891400. Rates are £20 a night for a
single room with shared facilities.

Leonard Turner Hall Off maps
*Heriot Watt University, Rickerton,
t (0131) 451 3669.*
Some way out of town (it's close
to the Pentland Hills) but good
parking facilities. For B&B expect
to pay about £37.50 for a single,
£55 for a double or twin.

Napier University C11
*Dalry and other locations, t (0131)
455 4211.*
A reasonable location (most of the
rooms are in Dalry, 20mins' walk
from the centre), with single
student rooms for about £28.

**University of Edinburgh
Pollock Halls of Residence** J11
*Contact Edinburgh First:
t (0131) 651 2007.*
This is easily the best option thanks
to its location in landscaped

grounds on the edge of Holyrood
Park, so book well ahead. B&B
accommodation in a single room
with shared facilities is about £27,
a double room with private facilities about £69. Breakfast is served
in the refectory in the John
MacIntyre Building, where there is
also an ATM, shop and bar.

Youth Hostels

Argyle Backpackers Hotel G11
*14 Argyle Pl, t (0131) 667 9991, f (0131)
662 0002, e argyle@sol.co.uk.*
A Marchmont hostel with doubles
for £30–£40, dorm beds for £10.

The Belford D9
*6–8 Douglas Gardens, t (0131) 225
6209, e info@hoppo.com, w www.
hoppo.com.*
The West End sister hostel to
Edinburgh Backpackers is in an old
church by the Water of Leith. Dorm
beds cost from £12 a night; twins
and doubles are also available.

Brodies Backpackers Hostel H9
*12 High St, t (0131) 556 6770,
e reception@brodieshostels.co.uk,
w www.brodieshostels.co.uk.*
Right on the Royal Mile, this has
four dorms with 56 beds costing
from £10.50 per night. There are
also 24-hour hot showers, a small
common room with an open fire,
internet access and CCTV.

Bruntsfield Youth Hostel
Off maps
*7 Bruntsfield Crescent, t 0871 330
8515, f (0131) 452 8588, w www.
syha.org.uk.*
Nicely situated near Bruntsfield
Links, this has 150 beds costing
from £10.25. There's a £1 fee for
non-members and a 2am curfew.

Castle Rock Hostel G9
*15 Johnston Terrace, t (0131) 225
9666, f (0131) 226 5078, e castle-
rock@scotlands-top-hostels.com,
w www.scotlands-top-hostels.com.*
A large hostel (170 rooms, with
beds starting at £11 a night) with
in-your-face views of the Castle.

Edinburgh Backpackers H9
*65 Cockburn St, t (0131) 220 1717,
e info@hoppo.com, w www.
hoppo.com.*

A popular central hostel that fills up by 10am every day. Dorm beds cost from £13. Double and twin rooms are housed in a self-catering apartment with a fully equipped kitchen and a bathroom. The hostel has its own bistro.

Edinburgh Central SYHA H10
*Robertson's Close, **t** 0871 330 8517, **w** www.syha.org.uk.*
Just off the Royal Mile, this summer-only (June 30–Aug 27) hostel has single rooms only, costing £17.50–£20.

Eglinton Youth Hostel D10
*18 Eglinton Crescent, **t** (0131) 337 1120, **f** (0131) 313 2053, **w** www.syha.org.uk.*
A large West End hostel (158 rooms) charging a £1 fee for non-members, and during July and August. Beds cost from £10.25 per night. No curfew.

High Street Hostel H9
*8 Blackfriars St, **t** (0131) 557 3984, **f** (0131) 556 2981, **e** highstreet@scotlands-top-hostels.com, **w** www.scotlands-top-hostels.com.*
An Old Town hostel with 16 dorms and 156 beds (£11–£13), a full self-catering kitchen, laundry facilities, 24-hour hot showers, two lounges and a pool table. Free tours of the Old Town are laid on each morning.

Princes Street East Backpackers H8
*5 West Register St, **t** (0131) 556 6894, **f** (0131) 557 3236, **e** reception@edinburghbackpackers.com, **w** www.edinburghbackpackers.com.*
A no-curfew, central hostel with 120 beds at £11 a pop in a dorm and £30 for a double room (seventh night free). There's also a movie room, and a 24-hour shop and internet facility.

Royal Mile Backpackers H9
*105 High St, **t** (0131) 557 6120, **e** royal-mile@scotlands-top-hostels.com, **w** www.scotlands-top-hostels.com.*
A small, 38-bed hostel in the heart of the tourist district, with dorm beds costing from £11 a night.

St Christopher's Inn H9
*9–13 Market St, **t** (0131) 226 1446, **f** (0131) 226 1447, **e** bookings@st-christophers.co.uk, **w** www.st-christophers.co.uk/edinburgh.htm.*

A relatively large hostel (123 beds) right by Waverley Station, with two bars. Doubles are £40–£46, dorm beds £11–£17.

Self-catering

Albany Rentals H8
*37b Albany Street and 24a York Place, **t** (0131) 557 9030, **f** (0131) 557 0563, **e** info@albanyrentals.co.uk, **w** www.albanyrentals.co.uk.*
Two new, non-smoking basement flats in the New Town, each with private parking, run by the same couple as Stuart House (see p.155). Situated in a Georgian building that was originally the Bank of Scotland counting house, York Place has a tasteful modern interior, with beech flooring, and sleeps up to four people in two en-suite double bedrooms. Albany Street, which has more chintzy décor, sleeps up to six. Three nights' minimum stay.

Calton Apartments I7
*44 Annandale Street, **t/f** (0131) 556 3221, **e** caltonapts@ednet.co.uk, **w** www.townhousehotels.co.uk/calton.html.*
Clean and bright accommodation in the heart of Broughton, run by the same company as Frederick House Hotel (see p.152). The flats each have one double bedroom, one twin bedroom, a bathroom with bath and power shower, a lounge with a double sofa bed and dining area, a fully fitted kitchen, and private parking.

Candlemaker Row Self-Catering Flat H10
*c/o Dr Julie Watt, 630 Lanark Rd, EH14, **t** (0131) 538 0352, **f** (0131) 453 4088, **e** julie.watt@virgin.net.*
A flat in a superb position near the university, with a rear view of Greyfriars Kirkyard. The pleasantly furnished bedroom and kitchen area are not very wheelchair friendly, and there's no parking, but early booking is advisable (at least a year in advance for the Festival and New Year). It sleeps two to four people at £40–£150 per night, depending on the time of year.

Gladstone's Land G9
*Lawnmarket, **t** (0131) 243 9331, **w** www.nts.org.uk.*
Experience life in a 17th-century house but with modern comforts in this National Trust property (see p.65) on the Royal Mile. There's a fourth-floor one-bedroom flat, accessed via a steep spiral staircase, and costing £400 a week in high season, and a second-floor twin-bedded flat.

Sibbet House Apartments G8
*28a Northumberland St and 26 Abercromby Place, **t** (0131) 624 0084, **e** veroniquejohnston@yahoo.co.uk, **w** www.26abercrombyplace.co.uk.*
Two central, no-smoking flats: Northumberland St costs from £100 a night and can accommodate up to 6 people in 2 double/twin rooms and a single room, all en-suite. Its kitchen and sitting room overlook a pretty, private walled garden. Abercromby Place (from £90 per night) is an elegant, high-ceilinged flat with a double bedroom and a large sitting room with 2 single beds in a screened off area. A 2- to 3-night minimum stay is generally required for both.

Camping

Camping here is a relatively expensive and inconvenient option that you'll probably only want to consider if the hostels are full.

The Monks' Muir Off maps
*Haddington, **t** (01620) 860 340, **w** www.monksmuir.co.uk.*
An award-winning environmental campsite a 15-minute drive from the outskirts of Edinburgh.

Mortonhall Caravan Park Off maps
*Frogston Rd East, **t** (0131) 664 1533.*
Four miles outside the city centre, this is the most central option.

Slatebarns Caravan Park Off maps
*Slatebarns Farm, Roslin, **t** (0131) 440 2192.*
A reasonably priced choice southwest of the city but not very well connected to it by bus.

Eating Out

Never Mind the Haggis

Edinburgh has been accused of being slow to join in the UK's recent gastro-boom, with even top-notch places such as The Atrium, (fitz)Henry, The Marque, The Pompadour and Le Café St Honoré unable to compete with similar places in London, and with only one Michelin Star for the city to boast of, for Restaurant Martin Wishart (see p.170). On the other hand, the best restaurants in town are often less expensive than their southern counterparts, and their customers can delight in the superior quality of local ingredients.

A more justified criticism might be that there are too many places of a similar tone both in food and atmosphere: the Auld Alliance is certainly alive and well in kitchens all over the city, doing Scottish takes on French cuisine. However, there are also a number of excellent, moderately priced places specializing in **Scottish food** – fish, game and, yes, haggis – including the local Howie's chain (see p.163) and Martin's (see p.165).

There are also some fine **Indian restaurants**, even if some are cast in a rather tired colonial style, and the strong Italian community in Edinburgh ensures that good **Italian cooking** is very much on the menu. **Mexican, Thai, Chinese and American cuisines** are also well represented, and Edinburgh is one the best cities in the UK in which to be a **vegetarian or vegan**. In fact, anyone who can't find something to suit their mood, wallet or inclination isn't really trying.

Popular areas for eating out include the **West End** (at the western end of the New Town) and **Broughton** just outside the city centre. Further afield, the once-depressed port of **Leith** has become one of the hippest spots for restaurants in the city. There are also a few good-value place south of the Old Town, around **Bruntsfield** and **Tollcross**.

Practicalities

Many restaurants close on Sundays and some on Mondays. Most change their hours and a few their entire character during the Festival.

When it comes to paying, look carefully at your bill to see if **service** is included; if it's not, leave an extra 10–15% of the total, preferably in cash. All but the cheapest establishments take cheques and/or credit cards. If you are paying with plastic, the total box will almost inevitably be left for you to fill, in anticipation of a fat tip. Don't feel under any pressure, especially if service is already included.

Note on payment: when we state in the listings that a restaurant takes 'all cards', we mean AmEx, Diners Club (DC), MasterCard (MC) and Visa (V). When one of these cards is not accepted, we state its absence.

Price Categories

Categories are based on the price of a two-course evening meal (lunch is usually considerably cheaper) for one person without wine and service.

expensive	above £20
moderate	£10–20
inexpensive	under £10

The Old Town

Restaurants

Expensive

Creelers H9

3 Hunter Square, **t** *(0131) 220 4447,* **w** *www.creelers.co.uk; wheelchair accessible.* **Open** *Mon–Fri noon–2.30pm and 5.30–10pm, Fri and Sat 12.30–3pm and 5.30–11pm.* **Payment:** *all cards.*

The airy and newly refurbished yet traditional setting allows this very central piscivore's heaven to double as a bistro and a more formal dining spot. The ultra-fresh fish and game are simply prepared.

The Dial H10

44–46 George IV Bridge, **t** *(0131) 225 7179.* **Open** *Mon–Sat noon–3pm and 6–11pm, Sun noon–3pm and 7–11pm.* **Payment:** *all cards.*

A lovely dining room with designer notes and a subterranean feel, although in fact it's in the body of George IV Bridge. Well-meaning if sometimes shambolic service delivers an ever-changing range of interesting Scottish dishes.

Dubh Prais H9

123B High St, **t** *(0131) 557 5732,* **w** *www.bencraighouse.co.uk.* **Open** *Tues–Fri noon–2pm and 6.30–10.30pm, Sat 6.30–10.30pm.* **Payment:** *DC not accepted.*

A small subterranean restaurant specializing in succulent venison, game and smoked haddock. The inventiveness of the recipes and the friendly service rarely disappoint either locals or tourists. Booking essential.

La Garrigue H9

31 Jeffrey St, **t** *(0131) 557 3032; wheelchair accessible.* **Open** *Tues–Sat noon–2.30pm and 6.30–10.30pm, Sun noon–2.30pm.* **Payment:** *all cards.*

A relative newcomer to the Jeffrey Street restaurant strip, La Garrigue has quickly established a reputation for top-notch French country cooking in a relaxed and informal setting. It's just the kind of restaurant that Edinburgh does best: somewhere to enjoy an easy-going evening over carefully prepared cuisine. Child-friendly.

Grain Store G9

30 Victoria St, **t** *(0131) 225 7635.* **Open** *Mon–Thurs noon–2pm and 6–10pm, Fri and Sat noon–3pm and 6–11pm, Sun noon–3pm and 6–10pm.* **Payment:** *all cards.*

This underrated restaurant is hard to categorize, serving as it does fresh Scottish food, modern British dishes and a range of vegetarian options, all cooked to order. Its atmospheric, old-fashioned first-floor rooms attract a widely varied clientele. Booking is essential from Thursday to Saturday.

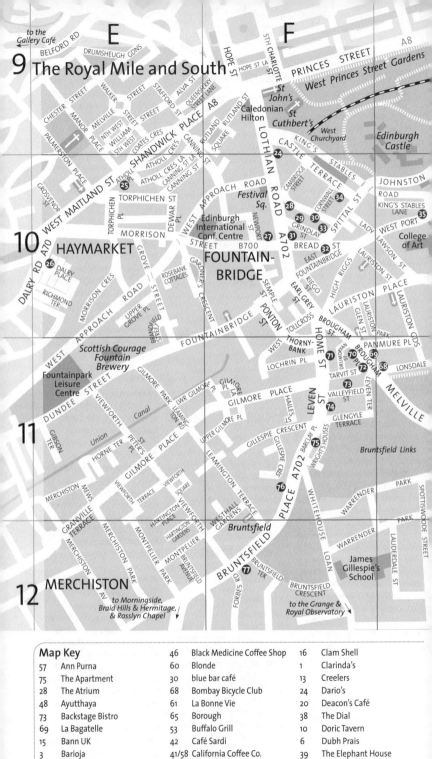

10 HAYMARKET

FOUNTAIN-BRIDGE

11

12 MERCHISTON

to the
Gallery Café

to Morningside,
Braid Hills & Hermitage,
& Rosslyn Chapel

to the Grange &
Royal Observatory

Edinburgh
Castle

Festival
Sq.

Edinburgh
International
Conf. Centre

Scottish Courage
Fountain
Brewery

Fountainpark
Leisure
Centre

Bruntsfield Links

Bruntsfield

James
Gillespie's
School

College
of Art

Caledonian
Hilton

St
John's

St
Cuthbert's

West
Churchyard

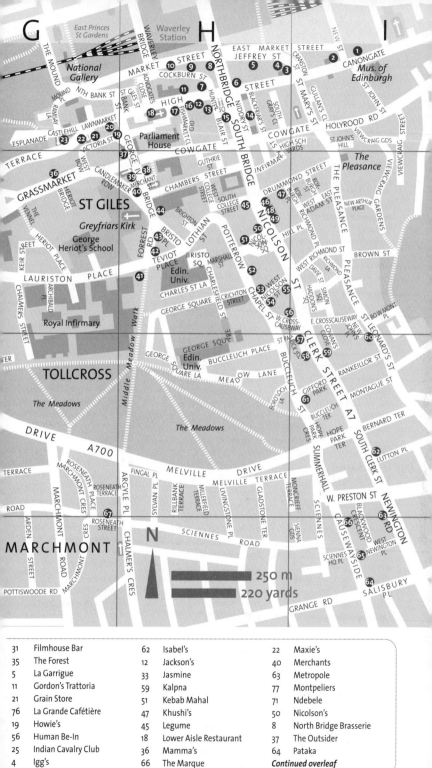

Map Key (cont'd)

55	Phenecia	70	Shamiana	44	The Tower
54	Pigs Bistro	7	Southern Cross Café	26	The Verandah
2	Plaisir du Chocolat	72	Sukhothai	8	Vermilion
32	Point Restaurant	49	Suruchi	9	Viva Mexico
27	Rogue	67	Sweet Melinda's	23	The Witchery by the Castle
17	Le Sept	43	Tapas Olé		and the Secret Garden
		29	Thai Orchid	52	Wok Bar

Igg's H9
*15 Jeffrey St, t (0131) 557 8184;
wheelchair accessible.* **Open**
*Mon–Sat noon–2.30pm and
6–10.30pm.* **Payment:** *all cards.*
Popular with the media set and
local celebs (so expect plenty of
attitude), Igg's offers Spanish
tapas at lunch and Scottish food
in the evenings.

Jackson's H9
*209 High St, t (0131) 225 1793,
w www.jacksons-restaurant.co.uk. .*
Open *daily noon–2.30pm and
6–10.30pm.* **Payment:** *all cards.*
A laid-back atmosphere prevails in
this child-friendly Scottish old-
timer snugly located in a rough
stone basement just off the Royal
Mile. The food itself – the likes of
haggis in whisky sauce and fine
game – is wholesome and served
by good-humoured staff. Booking
is advisable in summer.

Merchants H10
*17 Merchant St, t (0131) 225 4009,
w www.merchantsrestaurant.co.uk;
wheelchair accessible and toilet.*
Open *Mon–Fri noon–2pm,
6–10pm, Sat 6.30pm–10pm.*
Payment: *all cards.*
Globally influenced Scottish food
in bright surroundings, despite
the gloomy location beneath
George IV Bridge. Booking essential Fridays and Saturdays.

North Bridge Brasserie H9
*The Scotsman Hotel, 20 North
Bridge, t (0131) 556 5565, w www.
thescotsmanhotel.co.uk; wheelchair accessible and toilet.* **Open**
*daily 12.15–2.30pm and 6.15–
10.30pm.* **Payment:** *all cards.*
Classic British fare, funky salads
and recipes from further afield. In
the stylish hotel (see p.150). As
much a bar as a brasserie, it has a
balcony area that's great for
people-watching.

Le Sept H9
*7 Old Fishmarket Close, t (0131) 225
5428, w www.lesept.co.uk.* **Open**
*Mon–Thurs noon–2pm and
6–10.30pm, Fri and Sat noon–11pm,
Sun 12.30–10pm.* **Payment:** *all cards.*
A French-style institution in the
olde-worlde atmosphere of Old
Fishmarket Close, appropriately
enough offering an excellent
daily-changing fish and seafood
menu. The regular menu also has
lots of meat dishes.

The Tower H10
*Museum of Scotland, t (0131) 225
3003, w www.tower-restaurant.
com; wheelchair accessible and
toilet.* **Open** *daily 10am–11pm.*
Payment: *all cards.*
Situated on the 5th floor of the
Museum of Scotland and boasting
superb views, this is a smart place
run by the same people as The
Witchery (see below). The Scottish
dishes are reliable, but service can
be a little offhand. No smoking.

Vermilion H9
*The Scotsman Hotel, 20 North
Bridge, t (0131) 556 5565;
w www.thescotsmanhotel.co.uk;
wheelchair accessible and toilet.*
*Open daily 12.15–2.30pm and
6.15–10.30pm. Payment: all cards.*
The Scotsman hotel's restaurant
has simple but sophisticated
contemporary décor. The food,
based around fresh local ingredients, is worth every penny.

**The Witchery by the Castle
and the Secret Garden** g9
*Boswell's Close, Castlehill, t (0131)
225 5613, w www.thewitchery.com.
Open daily noon–4pm and
5.30–11.30pm. Payment: all cards.*
Luxurious, exotic décor upstairs in
the Witchery and a stone-flagged
basement giving on to a 'secret
garden' are the settings for some
rich, rather expensive Franco-

Scottish recipes complemented by
an exceptional wine list. It also
has six plush suites (see p.151).

Moderate

Ann Purna I11
*45 St Patrick Square, t (0131) 662
1807; wheelchair accessible.* **Open**
*Mon–Fri noon–2pm and 5.30–
10.30pm, Sat and Sun 5.30–
10.30pm.* **Payment:** *No AmEx .*
Reliable Nepalese vegetarian
cooking served up in basic but
serviceable surroundings, with
extremely attentive service.
Booking is essential.

Ayutthaya H10
14 Nicolson St, t (0131) 556 9351.
Open *daily noon–2.30pm,
5.30–11pm.* **Payment:** *all cards.*
A child-friendly northeastern Thai
restaurant that is very popular
with vegetarians and couples
enjoying a reasonably priced meal
before heading for the Festival
Theatre over the road.

Bann UK H9
*5 Hunter Square, t (0131) 226 1112,
w www.urbann.co.uk.* **Open** *daily
11am–11pm.* **Payment:** *all cards.*
A stylish veggie restaurant/café
famous for innovative recipes.
Kids are welcome.

Barioja H9
*19 Jeffrey St, t (0131) 557 3622;
wheelchair accessible.* **Open** *Mon–
Sat 11am–11pm.* **Payment:** *all cards.*
A lively, child-friendly Spanish
tapas joint run by the same people
as Igg's (see above). Book from
Thursday to Saturday in summer.

Black Bo's H9
57 Blackfriars St, t (0131) 557 6136.
Open *Fri and Sat noon–2pm and
6–10.30pm, Sun–Thurs 6–10.30pm.*
Payment: *all cards.*
A candle-lit vegetarian restaurant
offering rich, well-prepared dishes.
It also has a lively bar.

Blonde I11

75 St Leonard's St, t (0131) 668 2917; wheelchair accessible and toilet. **Open** *Mon 6–10pm, Tues–Sun noon–2pm and 6–10pm.* **Payment:** *all cards.*

A breakaway from Howie's (*see* below), Blonde offers Scottish dishes using local ingredients. It's laid back and popular with locals (booking essential at weekends).

La Bonne Vie I11

113 Buccleuch St, t (0131) 667 1110; wheelchair accessible and toilet. **Open** *Mon 6–10pm, Tues–Sat noon–2pm and 6–10pm, Sun noon–2pm.* **Payment:** *all cards.*

An enduring, child-friendly French country restaurant with an open fire and friendly staff. Booking is essential on Fridays and Saturdays.

Buffalo Grill H10

12–14 Chapel St, t (0131) 667 7427, w www.buffalogrill.co.uk; wheelchair accessible. **Open** *Mon–Fri noon–2pm and 6–10.15pm, Sat 6–10.15pm, Sun 5–10pm.* **Payment:** *DC and AmEx not accepted.*

Chicken, Scottish beef steaks and burgers. Booking is essential. BYOB, or there's a licensed branch at 1 Raeburn Place (*t (0131) 332 3864*).

Café Sardi H10

18–20 Forrest Rd, t (0131) 220 5553; wheelchair accessible and toilet. **Open** *Mon–Thurs 10am–11pm, Fri and Sat 10am–midnight, Sun 5–11pm.* **Payment:** *all cards.*

A good-value, child-friendly Italian with a traditional trattoria menu and great coffee. Licensed or BYOB.

Doric Tavern H9

15 Market St, t (0131) 225 1084, w www.thedoric.co.uk. **Open** *Mon–Sat 11.30am–10.30pm (April–Oct also Sun 12.30–10.30pm).* **Payment:** *all cards.*

An excellent bistro and wine bar beloved of journos, academics and arty types (Joni Mitchell was once thrown out). Booking advisable.

Gordon's Trattoria H9

231 High St, t (0131) 225 7992; wheelchair accessible. **Open** *Mon–Thurs and Sun noon–midnight, Fri and Sat noon–3am.* **Payment:** *all cards.*

This bustling, child-friendly trattoria is useful late at night at the weekend, for filling, reasonably priced pastas, pizzas and the like. Booking advisable in summer.

Howie's G9

10 Victoria Street, t (0131) 225 1721, w www.howies.uk.com. **Open** *daily noon–2.30pm and 6–10.30pm.* **Payment:** *all cards.*

A very popular local chain offering Franco-Scottish dishes in a lively and informal 'countrified' atmosphere. Prices are very reasonable. Kids' menus are available. There are branches at 208 Bruntsfield Place, t (0131) 221 1777, 4–6 Glanville Place (on Hamilton Place), t (0131) 225 5553, and 29 Waterloo Place, t (0131) 556 5766.

Human Be-In I10

2–8 West Crosscuseway, t (0131) 662 8860, w www.humanbe-in. co.uk, wheelchair accessible. **Open** *daily 11am–1am.* **Payment:** *all cards.*

A trendy student haunt serving a mix of modern Scottish and global food. Side orders are available until late, and there are great Sunday brunches. Live jazz on Tuesday and Wednesday nights.

Kalpna I11

2 St Patrick Square, t (0131) 667 9890. **Open** *Mon–Sat noon–2.30pm and 5.30–10pm, Sun 5.30–10pm.* **Payment:** *all cards.*

A time-honoured Indian offering very good veggie dishes. Booking essential Thursday–Saturday.

Legume H10

11 South College St, t (0131) 667 1597. **Open** *Mon–Sat noon–2pm and 5.30–10pm.* **Payment:** *all cards.*

A small French restaurant serving mainly vegetarian cuisine, with faintly twee décor but charming and attentive service.

Mamma's G10

28 Grassmarket, t (0131) 225 6464, w www.mammas.co.uk; wheelchair accessible. **Open** *Mon–Fri and Sun 10am–11pm, Sat 10am–midnight.* **Payment:** *DC and AmEx not accepted.*

A local American pizza parlour popular with students. A kids' menu is available. There are also branches at 2 Broughton Place, t (0131) 558 8868, and 1 Howard Street, t (0131) 558 7177.

Maxie's G9

5 Johnston Terrace, t (0131) 226 7770, w www.maxies.co.uk. **Open** *daily 11am–11pm.* **Payment:** *all cards.*

A cosy and convivial subterranean lair for reasonably priced lunches, good seafood and fine wines. The sunny back terrace overlooking Victoria Street and Grassmarket is a great spot for coffee.

Nicolson's H10

6a Nicolson St, t (0131) 557 4567; wheelchair accessible and toilet. **Open** *Mon–Sat noon–3pm and 5–11pm.* **Payment:** *DC not accepted.*

This 80-seater restaurant offers mainly Mediterranean cooking. Booking is advisable on Fridays and Saturdays.

The Outsider G10

15–16 George IV Bridge, t (0131) 226 3131; wheelchair accessible and toilet. **Open** *daily noon–11pm (bar until 1am).* **Payment:** *AmEx and DC not accepted.*

The latest venture by Malcolm Innes, who was also behind The Apartment (*see* p.170), offers a well-priced international fusion menu (the likes of mussels in bacon and cream, and squid with lime and green chillies) in spacious, modern rooms that boast great views of the Castle out the back. Child-friendly.

Phenecia H10

55 West Nicolson St, t (0131) 662 4493. **Open** *Mon–Sat noon–2pm and 6–10.30pm.* **Payment:** *AmEx not accepted.*

A wide variety of accomplished North African and Mediterranean dishes in a bright and friendly environment. Licensed or BYOB.

Pigs Bistro H10

41 West Nicolson St, t (0131) 667 6676. **Open** *Mon–Fri noon–2pm and 6–10pm, Sat 6–10pm.* **Payment:** *all cards.*

A quirky little BYOB place that's popular among local students. The good-value, eclectic menu includes pasta dishes and steak and chips.

Southern Cross Café H9
63a Cockburn St, *t (0131) 622 0622.*
Open *Tues and Wed 10.30am–6pm,*
Thurs 10.30am–11pm, Fri 10.30am–
midnight, Sat 8am–midnight, Sun
8am–6pm. **Payment:** *all cards.*
The child-friendly Southern Cross
has a wide-ranging bistro menu at
lunchtime but is more of a restaurant at night, with music, sushi
starters and global fusion food.

Suruchi H10
14a Nicolson St, *t (0131) 556 6583.*
Open *Mon–Sat noon–2pm and*
5.30–11.30pm, Sun 5–11.30pm.
Payment: *DC not accepted.*
A wide-ranging Indian menu –
including lots of veggie dishes –
with Scottish translations. It's
always busy (booking essential
Friday and Saturday), but the food
isn't always top notch. There's a
new outpost at 121 Constitution
Street (*t (0131) 554 3268*).

Tapas Olé H10
4a Forrest Road, *t (0131) 225 7069,*
w www.tapasolé.com. **Open**
Mon–Wed noon–3pm and 6–10pm,
Thur–Sat noon–10pm and Sun
5–10pm. **Payment:** *all cards.*
A lively, child-friendly tapas
restaurant with a sister restaurant
at 10 Eyre Place (*t (0131) 556 2754*).

Viva Mexico H9
41 Cockburn St, *t (0131) 226 5145,*
w www.viva-mexico.co.uk.
Open *Mon–Sat noon–2pm and*
6–10.30pm, Sun 6.30–10pm.
Payment: *all cards.*
A popular Mexican with good
veggie options, cheery staff and
great margaritas. It's apparently
one of Irvine Welsh's favourites.
Book on Fridays and Saturdays.

Wok Bar H10
30 Potterrow, *t (0131) 667 8594;*
wheelchair accessible. **Open** *Mon–*
Wed noon–10.30pm, Thurs–Sat
noon–11.30pm, Sun 5–10.30pm.
Payment: *AmEx not accepted.*
Reasonably priced noodles and
curries popular with students.

Inexpensive

Clam Shell H9
148 High St, *t (0131) 225 4338.*
Open *Mon–Thurs and Sun*

11am–12.30am, Fri and Sat
11am–2am. **Payment:** *no cards.*
The Clam Shell is a handy, central
spot when you want some late-
night fish and chips.

Kebab Mahal H10
7 Nicolson Square, *t (0131) 667 5214.*
Open *Mon–Thurs and Sun noon–*
midnight, Fri and Sat noon–2am.
Payment: *all cards.*
A basic but cheerful kebab joint in
the Old Town.

Khushi's H10
16 Drummond St, *t (0131) 556 8996.*
Open *Mon–Thurs and Sun*
noon–3pm and 5–9pm, Fri and Sat
noon–3pm and 5–9.30pm.
Payment: *no cards.*
A basic Indian canteen, one of the
first in the city. BYOB.

Lower Aisle Restaurant H9
High Kirk of St Giles, High St,
t (0131) 225 5147. **Open** *Mon–Fri*
8.30am–4.30pm, Sun 9.30am–
1.30pm; wheelchair accessible.
Payment: *no cards.*
Basic breakfasts and wholesome
lunches are served up in this
atmospheric, smoky café beneath
the cathedral.

Cafés and Teahouses

Black Medicine Coffee Shop H10
2 Nicolson St, *t (0131) 622 7209.*
Open *daily 8am–8pm.* **Payment:**
DC and AmEx not accepted.
Seriously strong coffee, decent
breakfasts and snack lunches in a
log-cabin-style café.

California Coffee Co H10/I11
Middle Meadow Walk/St Patrick
Square, *t (0131) 667 2366.* **Open**
Mon–Fri 7am–9pm, Sat and Sun
10am–9pm. **Payment:** *no cards.*
Good coffee and excellent cake
served up in converted police
boxes. There are also branches in
the New Town – in Rose Street,
behind Marks & Spencer, and
George Street (on the corner with
Hanover Street).

Clarinda's I9
69 Canongate, *t (0131) 557 1888.*
Open *Mon–Sat 9am–4.45pm, Sun*
10am–4.45pm. **Payment:** *no cards.*

Couples' City
Woo in style or rekindle an old
flame in one of the following
atmospheric restaurants or cafés.
The Atrium (*see p.169*), **Café
Royal Oyster Bar** (*see p.165*),
fitz(Henry) (*see p.169*), **Plaisir du
Chocolat** (*see below*), **The Secret
Garden** (*see p.162*), **The Vintner's
Rooms** (*see p.170*).

A delightful non-smoking, old-
fashioned teashop. No bookings
are taken.

Deacon's Café H9
3 Brodie's Close, off Lawnmarket,
t (0131) 226 1894. **Open** *daily*
9am–4pm. **Payment:** *all cards.*
Part of the kitchens of Deacon
Brodie's old house (*see p.67*), this is
a small tearoom serving light
daytime snacks.

The Elephant House H10
21 George IV Bridge, *t (0131) 220*
5355, w www.elephant-house.co.uk;
wheelchair toilet. **Open** *Mon–Fri*
8am–11pm, Sat and Sun
9am–11pm. **Payment:** *DC and*
AmEx not accepted.
Popular with students from the
libraries and university, this is an
efficient but often very busy café
that has a back room with an
unexpected view of the Castle.

The Forest G10
9 West Port, *t (0131) 221 0237.*
Open *daily noon–10pm.* **Payment:**
DC and AmEx not accepted.
A tremendously laid-back and
scruffy vegetarian and vegan café
providing wholesome food at low
prices. Unsurprisingly, it's something of a centre for the city's
alternative scene.

Plaisir du Chocolat I9
251–53 Canongate, *t (0131) 556*
9524; wheelchair accessible.
Open *Tues, Wed and Sun 10am–*
6pm, Thurs–Sat 10am–10.30pm.
Payment: *DC not accepted.*
A much-loved spot for some very
fine teas (no less than 185 varieties) and delicious hot chocolate
(15 types), as well as homemade
truffles and cakes. Le Petit Plaisir
over the road is a more informal
chocolate bar with an off licence.

The New Town

Restaurants

Expensive

Café Royal Oyster Bar H9
18 West Register St, **t** (0131) 556 4124; wheelchair accessible. **Open** daily noon–2pm and 7–10pm. **Payment**: all cards.
A very civilized rendezvous for rich seafood, oysters and game in a grand Victorian dining room.

Le Café St Honoré G8
34 Thistle St, North West Lane, **t** (0131) 226 2211; wheelchair accessible. **Open** Mon–Fri noon–2.15pm and 5–10pm, Sat noon–2.15pm and 6–10pm. **Payment**: all cards.
There's a laid-back French atmosphere at this delightful, hidden-away, upmarket brasserie. Top-quality local produce is used to make the Scottish food, but veggie options are not standard. The wine list also has a good reputation. Pre-theatre menus available (5–7pm Mon–Fri). No smoking except at the bar.

Le Chambertin G8
George Intercontinental Hotel, 19–21 George St, **t** (0131) 240 7198, **w** www.intercontinental.com. **Open** Mon–Fri 12.30–2pm and 7–10pm, Sat 7–10pm. **Payment**: all cards.
Classical French dishes with Scottish influences are served in the grand but not overly formal surroundings of the George Intercontinental Hotel (see p.152). Plenty of game and shellfish, and very good wines, are enjoyed by a respectable older clientele.

Cosmo F9
58 North Castle St, **t** (0131) 226 6743, **w** www.cosmo-restaurant. co.uk; wheelchair accessible. **Open** Mon–Fri 12.30–2.15pm and 7–10.45pm, Sat 7–10.45pm. **Payment**: DC not accepted.
This smart Italian restaurant relies mainly on regulars, who appreciate the robust recipes and traditional standards of service. It's been around for a long time but only shows its age in its pace and decorum. Smart dress.

Fisher's in the City G8
58 Thistle Street, **t** (0131) 225 5109, **w** www.fishersbistros.co.uk; wheelchair accessible and toilet. **Open** Mon–Sat noon–10.30pm, Sun 12.30–10.30pm. **Payment**: DC not accepted.
A newish, swish branch of the famous Leith fish restaurant (see p.169), doing similarly imaginative things with seafood, as well as offering vegetarian options and steak. Booking is highly advisable.

Haldanes H8
39 Albany St, **t** (0131) 556 8407. **Open** Mon–Fri noon–1.30pm and 6–9.30pm, Sat and Sun 6–9.30pm. **Payment**: all cards.
A well-regarded traditional Scottish menu in what feels like a country-house hotel dining room.

Harvey Nichols Forth Floor Restaurant, Bar and Brasserie H8
30–34 St Andrew Square, **t** (0131) 524 8388, **w** www.harveynichols. com; wheelchair accessible and toilet. **Open** restaurant Tues–Sat noon–3pm and 6–10.30pm; brasserie Mon 10am–6pm, Tues–Sat 10am–10.30pm, Sun 10am–5pm. **Payment**: all cards.
A trendy new eaterie in the chic department store, serving traditional Franco-Scottish fare. The brasserie offers similar but less expensive fare throughout the day. Child-friendly.

Kweilin G8
19–21 Dundas St, **t** (0131) 557 1875, **w** www.kweilin.co.uk; wheelchair accessible. **Open** Tues–Thurs noon–2pm and 5–11pm, Fri and Sat, noon–2pm and 5pm–midnight, Sun 5–11pm. **Payment**: all cards.
A fairly formal Cantonese restaurant that's popular with lunching businessmen from nearby offices. The food is of a high standard, with dim sum, fresh fish and lobster specialities.

Librizzi's F9
69 North Castle St, **t** (0131) 226 1155. **Open** Mon–Sat noon–2pm, 5.30–11pm. **Payment**: all cards.
A Sicilian restaurant in grand premises and specializing in fish.

Martin's F9
70 Rose St North Lane, **t** (0131) 225 3106; wheelchair accessible. **Open** Tues–Fri noon–2pm and 7–10pm, Sat 7–10pm. **Payment**: all cards.
A bright and friendly restaurant in spite of its obscure location, serving award-winning variations on Scottish dishes, including delicious game in season. The local cheese board is famous. Fixed-price and à la carte menus are available. Booking highly advised.

Number One H9
Balmoral Hotel, 1 Princes St, **t** (0131) 557 6727, **w** www. thebalmoralhotel.com; wheelchair accessible and toilet. **Open** Mon–Fri noon–2pm, 7–10.30pm, Fri and Sat 7–10.30pm, Sun 7–10pm. **Payment**: all cards.
A grand mahogany dining room with a cocktail bar, set in the city's most luxurious hotel (see p.151). The top-class menu, which is both classical and modern, is served in private booths or at the generously spaced tables. Child-friendly.

Oloroso F9
33 Castle St, **t** (0131) 226 7614, **w** www.oloroso.co.uk; wheelchair accessible and toilet. **Open** daily noon–2.30pm and 6–10.30pm. **Payment**: all cards.
A new designer restaurant and bar (see p.176) that has had local foodies reaching for superlatives, especially about its rooftop location and suave décor. The modern European dishes can be enjoyed on the terrace in summer, and good-value bar snacks are available until 1am. Booking essential.

The Pompadour F9
Caledonian Hilton Hotel, Princes St, **t** (0131) 222 8888, **w** www. caledonian.hilton.com; wheelchair accessible and toilet. **Open** Tues–Fri 12.30–2.30pm and 7–10pm, Sat 7–10pm. **Payment**: all cards.
Very traditional service in grand surroundings and a reliably impressive Franco-Scottish menu and wine list combine to create one of the most luxurious dining experiences in Edinburgh (though it's child-friendly). Dress smart.

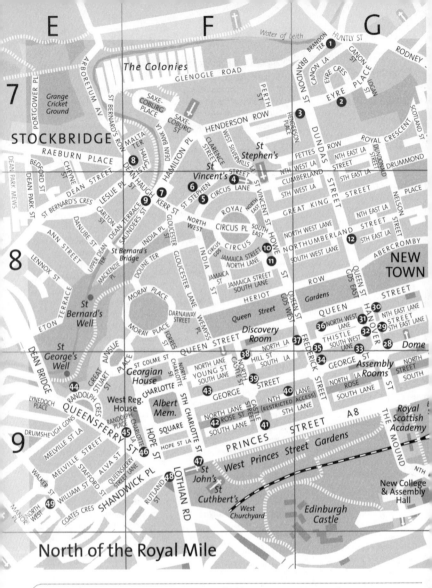

North of the Royal Mile

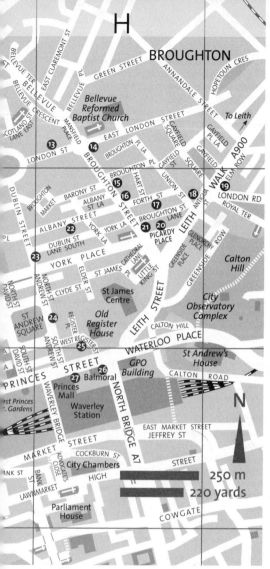

Stac Polly H8

*29–33 Dublin St, **t** (0131) 556 2231, **w** www.stacpolly.com. **Open** Mon–Fri noon–2pm and 6–10pm, Sat and Sun 6–10pm. **Payment**: all cards.*
Named after a mountain, this basement restaurant has a slightly contrived Scottish atmosphere, and the food sometimes tries too hard, but the smiling service adds to its romantic charm. Popular with tourists, and child-friendly. There's a branch at 8–10 Grindlay Street (**t** (0131) 229 5405).

Moderate

Bamboo Garden G8

*57 Frederick St, **t** (0131) 225 2382. **Open** Mon and Wed–Sat noon–2pm and 5.30–11pm, Sun 5.30–11pm. **Payment**: DC not accepted.*
A medium-sized, child-friendly basement Hong Kong Chinese specializing in fresh seafood but also serving great crispy duck and Hong Kong dim sum. Booking is advisable Fridays and Saturdays.

BiSi E9

*Randolph Place, **t** (0131) 225 6060, **w** www.bisi.co.uk; wheelchair accessible. **Open** Mon–Sat noon–2.30pm and 5.30–10pm. **Payment**: all cards.*
This stylish, airy and innovative pasta joint tucked away behind Charlotte Square has won itself a loyal young following and feels intimate even when it's busy.

Café Rouge G9

*43 Frederick St, **t** (0131) 225 4515; wheelchair accessible and toilet. **Open** Mon–Sat 10am–11pm, Sun 10am–10.30pm. **Payment**: all cards.*
The Edinburgh branch of this British chain does decent French food at acceptable prices in a lively cosmopolitan décor. A kids' menu is available.

La Cuisine d'Odile E9

*French Institute, 13 Randolph Crescent, **t** (0131) 225 5685. **Open** Tues–Sat noon–2pm. **Payment**: no cards.*
A select, changing lunch menu of delicious French dishes that can be enjoyed in the small garden in summer. BYOB. Booking is advised.

Rick's G8

*55 Frederick St, **t** (0131) 622 7800, **w** www.ricksedinburgh.co.uk. **Open** Thurs–Sat 7am–11pm, Sun–Wed 7am–10pm. **Payment**: No DC.*
As trendy a restaurant and bar (with bedrooms too; see p.152) as the city can provide, Rick's is a great place for breakfast, and is usually buzzing lunchtimes and evenings too, with people tucking into the well-presented fusion food. Book from Thursdays to Saturdays, especially if you want to snare a quieter corner away from the scrum.

Late Eats

For post-midnight meals or snacks, head for one of the following restaurants or cafés:

Bar Roma (see below), **Clam Shell** (see p.164), **Dario's** (see p.171), **Favorit** (see p.172), **Gordon's Trattoria** (see p.163), **Human Be-In** (see p.163), **Jasmine** (see p.171), **Kebab Mahal** (see p.164), **Rapido** (see p.172).

Est Est Est F9
135 George St, t (0131) 225 2555, w www.estestest.co.uk; wheelchair accessible and toilet. *Open* Mon–Sat noon–11pm, Sun noon–10.30pm. *Payment:* all cards.

This sleek, spacious branch of the English chain doing *nouvelle* Italian cuisine can get very loud. A kids' menu is available. Booking is essential at night. No smoking.

Mussel Inn F9
61–65 Rose St, t (0131) 225 5979, w www.mussel-inn.com; wheelchair accessible and toilet. *Open* daily noon–10pm. *Payment:* all cards.

An all-round treat for seafood lovers, the Mussel Inn has big windows looking out on to pedestrianized Rose Street, an open kitchen and a bright, breezy, modern atmosphere. The gloriously fresh shellfish from the Scottish coasts is accompanied by a variety of interesting sauces. A children's menu is available. Booking is advisable.

Nargile G8
73 Hanover St, t (0131) 225 5755, w www.nargile.co.uk; wheelchair accessible and toilet. *Open* Mon–Thurs noon–2pm and 5.30–10.30pm, Fri and Sat noon–2pm and 5.30–11pm. *Payment:* DC not accepted.

A newish Turkish restaurant that has quickly become a firm favourite among New Towners because of its good-value mezes and restrained ambience.

Peter's Cellars E9
11a William St, t (0131) 226 3161. *Open* Mon–Sat noon–2.30pm and 6–10.30pm, Sun 12.30–2.30pm and 6–10pm. *Payment:* all cards.

A convivial West End basement restaurant serving mainly Scottish brasserie food and popular with locals. Licensed and BYOB.

A Room in the Town F8
88 Howe St, t (0131) 225 8204, w www.aroomin.co.uk/thetown. *Open* daily noon–2.30pm, 5.30pm–midnight. *Payment:* AmEx not accepted.

A Room offers simple, reasonably priced Scottish food for well-paid office workers by day (there are daily-changing lunch deals) and is often lively by night too (the dinner menu changes monthly). Booking is advised Thursday to Saturday. BYOB and licensed.

Siam Erawan F8
48 Howe St, t (0131) 226 3675. *Open* daily noon–2.30pm and 6–11pm. *Payment:* DC not accepted. Excellent Thai food in cool, atmospheric surroundings that are always packed at weekends. There's a newer branch, Erewan Oriental, at 14 South St Andrew Street (t (0131) 556 4242).

Inexpensive

Henderson's Salad Table G8
94 Hanover St, t (0131) 225 2131, w www.hendersonsofedinburgh. co.uk. *Open* Mon–Sat 8am–10pm. *Payment:* DC not accepted.

A good-value veggie favourite with 180 seats, famous for its great bread and self-service salads. A children's menu is available.

Marrakech H7
30 London St, t (0131) 556 7293. *Open* Thurs–Sat 6–10pm. *Payment:* AmEx and DC not accepted.

A quirky Moroccan restaurant and hotel (see p.153), this is the place to come for couscous and tagines. It's BYOB, hence popular with students. A kids' menu is available.

Cafés and Teahouses

Bar Roma F9
Queensferry St, t (0131) 226 2977, w www.barroma.co.uk, wheelchair accessible and toilet. *Open* Mon–Thurs and Sun noon–midnight, Fri and Sat noon–1am. *Payment:* all cards.

A large Italian café-bar with good coffee and snacks, Roma gets very busy in the evenings. A kids' menu is available.

Cornerstone Café F9
St John's Church, Princes St, t (0131) 229 0212; wheelchair accessible. *Open* Mon–Sat 9.30am–4pm. *Payment:* no cards.

A charming, child-friendly veggie café beneath St John's Church.

Duck's de la Gare H8
Waverley Steps, Princes St, t (0131) 557 8887, wheelchair accessible. *Open* Mon–Fri 7am–7pm, Sat 9am–6pm, Sun 11am–5pm. *Payment:* AmEx and DC not accepted.

An excellent Frenchified coffeeshop that was set up by the people behind Duck's at Le Marché Noir (see p.169), with good-value sandwiches, croissants and cakes. It's conveniently located for the station.

Juniper's G8
117a–121 Hanover St, t (0131) 225 1552. *Open* Mon–Wed 8am–8pm, Thurs–Sat 8am–9.45pm. *Payment:* all cards.

An organic deli, takeaway and restaurant in the atmospheric basement that was once the Laigh Bake House. Very good homemade soups, stews and salads are served, plus kedgeree and great bacon rolls for breakfast.

Ottokar's Café G9
57 George St, t (0131) 225 4495. *Open* Mon–Sat 9am–5pm. *Payment:* No DC or AmEx.

The haunt of literary shoppers seeking simple refreshments in pleasant rooms overlooking George Street.

Palm Court H9
Balmoral Hotel, 1 Princes St, t (0131) 557 6727, w www.thebalmoralhotel. com; wheelchair accessible and toilet. *Open* daily 10am–6pm (tea served from 3pm). *Payment:* all cards.

This grand lounge at the heart of one of Edinburgh's smartest hotels is the perfect setting for traditional afternoon teas.

Dean Village and Stockbridge

Restaurants

Expensive

Duck's at Le Marché Noir G7
2–4 Eyre Place, **t** (0131) 558 1608,
w www.ducks.co.uk; wheelchair
accessible. **Open** Mon 7–10.30pm,
Tues–Fri noon–2.30pm and
7–10.30pm, Sat and Sun 7–10pm.
Payment: all cards.
Candlelight and white linen set
the scene for fine French food
using Scottish ingredients, accompanied by an impressive wine list.

Stockbridge Restaurant F8
54 St Stephen Street, **t** (0131) 226
6766. **Open** Tues–Sat 7–9.30pm.
Payment: AmEx not accepted.
A pleasant basement restaurant
with a laid-back café style and
ambience that belie the high
quality of the Scottish cuisine.
There's a fixed-price menu.

Moderate

Blue Parrot Cantina F8
49 St Stephen St, **t** (0131) 225 2941.
Open Mon–Thurs 5–11pm, Fri and
Sat noon–11pm, Sun 5–10.30pm.
Payment: all cards.
An intimate Mexican basement
with a regularly changing menu
and sensational guacamole. BYOB.

Hector's F7
47 Deanhaugh St, **t** (0131) 343 1735;
wheelchair accessible and toilet.
Open Mon–Fri noon–3pm and
6–9.30pm, Sat noon–1am, Sun
noon–midnight. **Payment:** all cards.
A stylish local brasserie/cocktail
bar serving pasta and French-style
meals, plus weekend brunches.

Lancer's F8
5 Hamilton Place, **t** (0131) 332 3444.
Open daily noon–2.30pm and
5.30–11.30pm. **Payment:** all cards.
An Indian restaurant and local
institution in an old police station.

Inexpensive

L'Alba Doro G7
5 Henderson Row, **t** (0131) 557 2580.
Open Mon–Fri 11.30am–1.30pm
and 5pm–midnight, Sat and Sun
5pm–midnight. **Payment:** no cards.
A long-standing local fish and
chip takeaway doing every kind of
deep-fried supper that you, if not
your heart, might desire.

Unicorn Inn F18
112 St Stephen St, **t** (0131) 220 4799.
Open Mon, Sat and Sun 5.30–
10.30pm, Tues–Fri noon–2pm,
5.30–10.30pm. **Payment:** all cards.
This small Chinese restaurant is a
firm favourite with locals and
always needs to be booked at
weekends. Takeaways available.

Cafés and Teahouses

Au Gourmand
1 Brandon Terrace, **t** (0131 624 4666),
w www.augourmand.co.uk,
wheelchair accessible. **Open** Mon
and Tues 9am–6pm, Wed–Sat
9am–6pm and 7–10.30pm, Sun
10am–5pm. **Payment:** all cards.
A top-notch, child-friendly French
café and deli situated near the
river in Canonmills, doing a
selection of very good soups,
sandwiches and cheeses for the
local office population during the
day and transforming itself into a
superior, idiosyncratic haute-
cuisine restaurant in the evenings
later in the week.

The Gallery Café C9
Scottish National Gallery of Modern
Art, 74 Belford Rd, **t** (0131) 332 8600;
wheelchair accessible and toilet.
Open daily 10am–4.30pm. **Payment:**
AmEx and DC not accepted.
A bustling, child-friendly, non-
smoking canteen-style café with a
wonderful sun-trap of a terrace.
The freshly made soups, sweets
and main meals include whole-
some veggie options.

Sabor Criollo F8
36 Deanhaugh St, **t** (0131) 332 3322.
Open daily 11am–11pm. **Payment:**
all cards.
A colourful and authentic, child-
friendly South American café and
restaurant. The lunchtime set
menus (three courses for about
£6) are particularly good value.

Outside the Centre

Restaurants

Expensive

The Atrium F10
10 Cambridge St, **t** (0131) 228 8882,
w www.atriumrestaurant.co.uk;
wheelchair accessible and toilet.
Open Mon–Fri noon–2pm, 6–10pm,
Sat 6–10pm. **Payment:** all cards.
One of the most highly regarded
restaurants in the city, offering the
finest Scottish dishes backed up
by an excellent wine list. The set
menu is good value at £25. The
theatrical atmosphere (it's above
the Traverse Theatre; see p.181) is
completed by handmade oil-
burning lamps. Child-friendly.

La Bagatelle G11
22 Brougham Place, Tollcross, **t** (0131)
229 0869; wheelchair accessible.
Open Mon–Sat noon–2pm and
6.30–10.30pm. **Payment:** No DC.
Excellent, rich French cuisine in a
child-friendly setting. The set
lunches are good value. Booking is
advisable on Saturdays.

Borough I12
72–80 Causewayside, **t** (0131) 668
2255, **w** www.edin-borough.co.uk,
wheelchair accessible. **Open** Mon–
Thurs 12.30–2.30pm, Fri and Sat 6–
10pm. **Payment:** DC not accepted.
A discreet hotel restaurant south
of The Meadows, serving fusion
food in an immaculate setting.

Fisher's Bistro J4
1 The Shore, Leith, **t** (0131) 554 5666,
w www.fishersbistros.co.uk;
wheelchair accessible and toilet.
Open Mon–Sat noon–10.30pm, Sun
12.30–10.30pm. **Payment:** all cards.
Regarded as the best seafood
restaurant in the city, Fisher's
is in the windmill and watchtower
at the end of the harbour.
Booking is essential, especially
at weekends.

(fitz)Henry J4
19 Shore Place, Leith, **t** (0131) 555
6625; wheelchair accessible and
toilet. **Open** Mon–Fri noon–2.30pm
and 6.30–10.30pm, Sat 6.30–
10.30pm. **Payment:** DC not accepted.

A romantic converted warehouse, specializing in the cuisine of southern France. Good-value 3-course weekday set menu for £16.

The Marque I12

19–21 Causewayside, t (0131) 466 6660. Open Tues–Thurs noon–2pm and 6–10pm, Fri noon–2pm and 6–11pm, Sat 12.30–2pm and 6–11pm, Sun 12.30–2pm and 6–10pm. Payment: all cards.

Set up by emigrants from the Atrium (see p.169), this smart, non-smoking restaurant just south of The Meadows may not have perfectly balanced cutlery and the vegetable side orders might be superfluous, but it has established itself as one of most adventurous Scottish restaurants in the city. Booking is essential. There are good-value pre- and post-theatre menus. The Marque Central is an offshoot next to the Lyceum Theatre at 30b Grindlay Street (*t (0131) 220 9859*).

Restaurant Martin Wishart J4

54 The Shore, Leith, t (0131) 553 3557, w www.martin-wishart.co.uk; wheelchair accessible and toilet. Open Tues–Fri noon–2pm and 7–10pm, Sat 7–10pm. Payment: DC and AmEx not accepted.

A small place decorated in yellow with purple banquettes, serving French-style food based on Scottish ingredients (Wishart used to work at Le Gavroche in London and established the reputation of Hadrian's at the Balmoral Hotel). It well deserves Edinburgh's only Michelin star. No smoking until the coffee arrives. Booking essential.

The Rock

78 Commercial St, Leith, t (0131) 555 2225; wheelchair accessible and toilet. Open Tues–Fri 6–10pm, Sat 11am–4pm and 6–10pm, Sun 11am–3pm and 6–10pm. Payment: DC not accepted.

A stone-walled, fairly formal (though child-friendly) modern Scottish restaurant with plain white tablecloths and fresh flowers. Its excellent reputation makes booking essential, especially at weekends.

Rogue F10

Scottish Widows Building, 67 Morrison St, t (0131) 228 2700, w www.rogues-uk.com; wheelchair accessible and toilet. Open Mon–Sat noon–3pm and 6–11pm. Payment: DC not accepted.

The latest venture by David Ramsden of (fitz)Henry (see p.169) is 'an expensive restaurant where you can eat cheaply', with a menu ranging from delicately prepared bar snacks to full three-course modern Scottish meals. The wine list is a conversation piece too, and the space modern and theatrical. It's close to Haymarket Station. Booking advised.

Sweet Melinda's G11

11 Roseneath St, t (0131) 229 7953; wheelchair accessible. Open Mon 7–10pm, Tues–Sat noon–2pm and 7–10pm. Payment: DC and AmEx not accepted.

A cosy, candle-lit, child-friendly Scottish seafood and game restaurant situated to the south of the Old Town in Marchmont, with a good wine list. Booking is essential at weekends.

The Vintner's Rooms J5

The Vaults, 87 Giles St, Leith, t (0131) 554 6767, w www.thevintnersrooms.demon.co.uk; wheelchair accessible. Open Mon–Sat noon–2pm and 7–9.30pm. Payment: DC not accepted.

Fine French provincial cuisine served up in a candle-lit 16th-century room and enhanced by the homemade puddings and excellent wine list.

The Waterfront J4

1 Dock Place, Leith, t (0131) 554 7427, w www.sjf.co.uk; wheelchair accessible and toilet. Open Mon–Thurs noon–9.30pm, Fri and Sat noon–10pm, Sun 12.30–9.30pm. Payment: DC not accepted.

A maze of rooms with a vaguely nautical/French theme, including a dockside pontoon, is the setting for some thoroughly Frenchified food. The Waterfront, which also has a wine bar, was at the vanguard of Leith's restaurant boom. Child-friendly.

Moderate

The Apartment F11

7–13 Barclay Place, Bruntsfield, t (0131) 228 6456; wheelchair accessible. Open Mon–Fri 6–11pm, Sat and Sun noon–3pm, 6–11pm. Payment: DC and AmEx not accepted.

Lively and informal, this is one of the city's most popular restaurants (booking is essential). The chatty staff serve up a wide-ranging, healthy, international menu with an Asian and Mediterranean emphasis.

Backstage Bistro F11

22 Valleyfield St, Tollcross, t (0131) 229 1978; wheelchair accessible. Open daily noon–10pm. Payment: all cards.

An inviting little place behind the King's Theatre. Specialities include a starter of *pastilla*, north African chicken with honey and almonds, and an unlikely combination of salmon and haggis. BYOB.

blue bar café F10

10 Cambridge St, t (0131) 221 1222, w www.bluebarcafe.com; wheelchair accessible and toilet. Open Mon–Sat noon–3pm and 6–11pm. Payment: all cards.

A roomy, minimalist café-bar above The Atrium (see p.169) and the Traverse Theatre, with a reliable menu of modern European favourites. It can get loud and busy, but the staff's laid-back attitude ensures that eating here is a pleasant experience. A kids' menu is available. Booking essential Friday and Saturday.

The Camargue J4

23 Commercial St, Leith, t (0131) 554 9999, w www.camcameo.co.uk. Open daily noon–2pm and 6–10pm. Payment: all cards.

A simple set seafood menu amidst simple décor; a kids' menu is available. The adjoining Cameo Bar (see p.177) is open during the day.

Il Castello F9

35 Castle Terrace, t (0131) 229 2730, wheelchair accessible and toilet. Open daily noon–2pm, 5–11pm. Payment: DC not accepted.

A cheery, child-friendly, traditional pizza and pasta place in the shadow of the castle, beloved of the natives and handy for Traverse or Lyceum theatregoers. Booking essential Fridays and Saturdays.

Daniel's Bistro J4
88 Commercial St, Leith, t (0131) 553 5933; wheelchair accessible and toilet. Open daily 10am–10pm. Payment: DC not accepted.
Offering French provincial cooking, Daniel's has succeeded on a strip where many other restaurants have failed, by keeping a loyal following while drawing in the tourists. The set lunches are excellent value, and the glass frontage makes the place light and airy. Child-friendly.

Dario's F9
85–87 Lothian Rd, t (0131) 229 9625. Open daily noon–5am. Payment: all cards.
A late-night, traditional pizzeria and something of an Edinburgh institution. Booking advised.

Harry Ramsden's H3
5 Newhaven Place, t (0131) 551 5566; wheelchair accessible and toilet. Open daily noon–9pm. Payment: AmEx not accepted.
Britain's most successful fish and chip chain opened this first branch in the old Newhaven fish-market some time ago and still does brisk business year round. All manner of quite pricey deep-fried fish are eaten off chequered table-cloths, and there's a kids' menu.

Indian Cavalry Club E10
3 Atholl Place, t (0131) 228 3282; wheelchair accessible. Open daily noon–2pm, 5.30–11.30pm. Payment: all cards.
An upmarket Indian near Haymarket Station, with décor harking back to the days of the Raj and wonderful food. Booking is advised on Fridays and Saturdays.

Jasmine F10
32 Grindlay Street, t (0131) 229 5757; wheelchair accessible. Open Mon–Thurs noon–2pm and 5–11.30pm, Fri noon–2pm and 5pm–12.30am, Sat 2pm–12.30am, Sun 2–11.30pm. Payment: DC not accepted.

This reliable, modern little Chinese offering carefully presented delicacies is convenient for the theatres and concert halls off the Lothian Road. Booking is essential on Fridays and Saturdays.

Montpeliers F12
159–61 Bruntsfield Place, Bruntsfield, t (0131) 229 3115, w www.montpeliersedinburgh. co.uk; wheelchair accessible. Open daily 9am–1pm (bar until 1am). Payment: all cards.
An Edinburgh institution, this bistro and bar, owned by the same people as Rick's (see p.167), serves up reliable 'Scottish international' fare in comfy, convivial surroundings, plus good cocktails. Booking is advisable Fridays and Saturdays.

Point Restaurant F10
Point Hotel, 34 Bread St, t (0131) 221 5555, w www.point-hotel.co.uk; wheelchair accessible and toilet. Open Mon–Thurs noon–2pm and 6–10pm, Fri noon–2pm and 6–11pm, Sat 6–11pm, Sun 6–9pm. Payment: all cards.
A surprisingly good-value, child-friendly restaurant in the designer hotel (see p.155), with occasional live jazz. The food (£15 for three courses) almost lives up to the hotel's glamorous aspirations.

The Raj Restaurant J4
89–91 Henderson St, Leith, t (0131) 553 3980; wheelchair accessible and toilet. Open Mon–Thurs and Sun noon–2.30pm and 5.30–11.30pm, Fri and Sat noon–2.30pm and 5.30pm–midnight. Payment: DC not accepted.
A famous, high-quality Bengali restaurant overlooking Leith harbour, with bargain deals from Sunday to Thursday.

Shamiana F11
14 Brougham Place, Tollcross, t (0131) 228 2265, wheelchair accessible. Open Mon–Thurs 6–9pm, Fri and Sat 6–9.30pm, Sun 6–8pm. Payment: all cards.
A chic Indian restaurant that specializes in Kashmiri dishes. The chef was once voted the best in Britain by the *Curry Cooker*. Booking is required.

Vegetarian Eats
Being veggie is not a problem in this student-filled city: most, if not all, restaurants offer meat-free choices these days. When a non-vegetarian restaurant offers interesting veggie alternatives, we say so. The following restaurants and cafés offer exclusively or mainly vegetarian fare:
Black Bo's (see p.162), **Cornerstone Café** (see p.168), **The Forest** (see p.164), **Henderson's Salad Table** (see p.168), **Isabel's** (see p.172), **Kalpna** (see p.163), **Legume** (see p.163).

Skippers J4
1a Dock Place, Leith, t (0131) 554 1018, w www.skippers.co.uk; wheelchair accessible and toilet. Open Mon–Sat 12.30–2pm and 7–10pm, Sun 12.30–2.30pm and 7–10pm. Payment: all cards.
Simple fresh seafood, and home-made puddings to follow, in a nautical nook that really does smack of the sea.

Smoke Stack H8
53–55 Broughton St, Broughton, t (0131) 556 6032, w www.base ment.org; wheelchair accessible. Open Mon–Fri noon–2.30pm and 6–10.30pm, Sat noon–10.30pm, Sun 6–10.30pm. Payment: all cards.
A mellow, low-lit environment where all manner of chargrilled food is served. Main courses are massive. Advance booking is essential at weekends.

Sukhothai F11
23 Brougham Place, Tollcross, t (0131) 229 1537; wheelchair accessible. Open daily noon–2.30pm, 5.30pm–11pm. Payment: all cards.
A popular Thai restaurant near The Meadows. Booking is advised on Fridays and Saturdays.

Tapas Tree H8
1 Forth St, Broughton, t (0131) 556 7118, w www.tapastree.co.uk. Open daily 11am–11pm. Payment: all cards.
A busy, child-friendly tapas bar on two levels with live guitar music on Wednesdays and flamenco on Thursdays. Booking is essential.

Thai Orchid F10

44 Grindlay St, t (0131) 228 4438.
Open *Mon–Fri noon–2.30pm and
5.30pm–midnight, Sat and Sun
5.30pm–midnight.* **Payment:**
all cards.
A wide choice of Thai food; try the
coconut and peanut *mooaloi*.
Convenient for the theatres.

Tinelli J7

139 Easter Rd, t (0131) 652 1932.
Open *Tues–Sat noon–2.30pm and
6.30–11pm.* **Payment:** *all cards.*
A small Italian restaurant off the
beaten track behind Calton Hill
but such good value that it draws
hungry hordes from miles around.

The Verandah E10

17 Dalry Rd, t (0131) 337 5828.
Open *daily noon–2.15pm and
5pm–midnight.* **Payment:** *all cards.*
A popular Indian restaurant not
far from Haymarket Station.

Zinc Bar and Grill I3

*Ocean Terminal, Ocean Drive, Leith,
t (0131) 553 8070, w www.conran.
com; wheelchair accessible and
toilet.* **Open** *daily noon–11pm.*
Payment: *all cards.*
A Conran restaurant with great
views. Daytime dishes might
include grilled sardines or fish and
chips; the evening menu is more
sophisticated. *Prix fixe* and kids'
menus are available.

Inexpensive

Bombay Bicycle Club G11

*6 Brougham Place, Tollcross, t (0131)
229 3839.* **Open** *daily noon–2pm
and 5.30pm–midnight.* **Payment:**
all cards.
A slightly upmarket Indian to the
west of The Meadows.

Ferri's H8

*1 Antigua St, Broughton, t (0131)
556 5592.* **Open** *Mon–Sat noon–
2.30pm and 5pm–midnight, Sun
5pm–midnight.* **Payment:** *all cards.*
Filling pizza and pasta in a hectic
but child-friendly atmosphere.

Pataka I12

*190 Causewayside, t (0131) 668
1167, w www.pataka.co.uk;
wheelchair accessible.* **Open** *daily
noon–2pm and 5.30–11.30pm.*
Payment: *all cards.*

A Bengali Indian restaurant south
of The Meadows, with a good
reputation for dishes such as
green herb chicken.

Rapido H8

*79 Broughton St, Broughton, t (0131)
556 2041.* **Open** *Mon–Thurs
10am–1pm, Fri and Sat 10am–2am,
Sun 4.30pm–1am.* **Payment:** *AmEx
and DC not accepted.*
A classic late-night takeaway
chippie. It also sells pasta, toasted
ciabattas, Ben & Jerry's ice cream,
tobacco, sweets and soft drinks.

Cafés and Teahouses

Favorit F11

*30–32 Leven St, t (0131) 221 1800,
w www.favoritedinburgh.co.uk.*
Open *daily 8am–1am.* **Payment**
DC not accepted.
A no-nonsense, airy café-bar with
long opening hours, serving freshly
prepared snacks and specials. The
Teviot Place branch (*t (0131) 220
6880*), is popular with students.

Filmhouse Bar F10

*88 Lothian Rd, t (0131) 229 5932,
w www.filmhousecinema.com;
wheelchair accessible and toilet.*
Open *10am–10pm.* **Payment:**
all cards.
A very pleasant place to stop for a
coffee or reasonably priced sandwich or cake, with exhibitions of
contemporary art held in the non-
smoking section and friendly staff.

La Grande Cafétière F11

*184 Bruntsfield Place, Bruntsfield,
t (0131) 228 1188; wheelchair accessible.* **Open** *Mon–Wed 9am–11pm,
Thurs–Sat 9am–midnight, Sun
10am–11pm.* **Payment:** *all cards.*
A charming little place serving
Scottish dishes, pasta, quiches and
steak and chips. A children's menu
is available.

Isabel's I11

83 South Clerk St, t (0131) 662 4014.
Open *Mon–Sat 11.30am–5.30pm.*
Payment: *no cards.*
A child-friendly vegetarian and
vegan café beneath a wholefood
shop just east of The Meadows.
Non smoking; BYOB.

Lost Sock Diner H7

*11 East London St, Broughton,
t (0131) 557 6097.* **Open** *Mon 9am–
4pm, Tues–Sat 9am–9.30pm, Sun
11am–4.30pm.* **Payment:** *no cards.*
A laid-back, funky café with an
attached launderette, where some
of Broughton's in-crowd like to
hang out to dry. Child-friendly.

Mediterraneo H8

*73 Broughton St, Broughton, t (0131)
557 6900.* **Open** *Mon–Sat 8am–
6pm, Sun 9am–5pm.* **Payment:**
DC and AmEx not accepted.
Excellent sandwiches and beautifully prepared light meals in
colourful surroundings.

Metropole I11

*33 Newington Rd, t (0131) 668
4999.* **Open** *daily 9am–10pm.*
Payment: *no cards.*
A trendy, non-smoking Art Deco
brasserie in a former bank. Good
for light lunches and for its huge
choice of coffees and teas. There
are also newspapers to read.

Ndebele F11

*57 Home St, Tollcross, t (0131) 221
1141, w www.ndebele.co.uk;
wheelchair accessible.* **Open**
daily 10am–10pm. **Payment:**
DC not accepted.
Popular with students and child-
friendly, this lively café offers a
wide range of interesting African
food and sandwiches.

PopRokit H8

*2 Picardy Place, Broughton, t (0131)
556 4272; wheelchair accessible.*
Open *daily noon–7pm (bar
11am–1am).* **Payment:** *no cards.*
A stylish, bare-essentials café with
outside tables and a lively basement bar.

Valvona & Crolla I8

*19 Elm Row, t (0131) 556 6066,
w www.valvonacrolla.com;
wheelchair accessible and toilet.*
Open *Mon–Sat 8am–6.30pm.*
Payment: *DC not accepted.*
A famous, fairly expensive Italian
café and deli doing exceptional
pâtisserie plus more substantial
dishes and superb coffee. Booking
is advisable, but none are taken on
Saturdays so come early to get a
table. Non-smoking; child-friendly.

Nightlife

Pubs and Bars

Although today **whisky** is Scotland's national drink, Scotland was more a nation of wine-lovers, renowned for their ability to nose out a good claret, until late into the 18th century, when their pleasures were curtailed by British taxes on French imports. At that time the 'water of life' was freely available from innumerable illicit stills all over the country, which were rapidly turned into licensed revenue-raising ventures. Now whisky is a multi-billion-pound export industry and is only sold in tiny quantities, a 'wee dram' usually being a fifth of a gill.

Until as recently as the 1950s, though, Edinburgh was the centre of a massive beer-brewing industry, and it is still one of the world's best places to discover the delights of **real ale**. Scottish brews are usually denominated simply by the amount that they needed to be taxed, according to their alcohol content, from 70 shilling (the weakest), through 80 shilling, to 90 shilling (the strongest).

The places where these drinks can be enjoyed have changed hugely in the last decade or so. Before then, the 'howff' or tavern was a forbidding place, either underground or with blanked-out windows and always inimical to women. In the 1970s Scotland was the willing subject of a British experiment that allowed pubs to stay open all day and well into the night. Now the rest of the UK has followed suit, but Edinburgh's lead can still be appreciated in the confidence, variety and character of some of its pubs and bars.

Different parts of the city have distinct drinking identities: the **Old Town** is popular with students; **Stockbridge** caters for young professionals; **Broughton** has the hippest designer bars and restaurants and is the heart of the city's gay scene, especially around Broughton Street; and **Leith** has become just about everyone's favourite watering hole.

The Old Town

Bam Bou H10
66–67 South Bridge, t (0131) 556 0200. Open Mon–Sat 11am–1am, Sun noon–1am.
A new café/bar/restaurant with loud and lively pre-club DJ warm-up nights. Right opposite the Old College, it's popular with students.

Bannerman's H8
212 Cowgate, t (0131) 556 3254. Open daily noon–1am.
This old-timer, recently refurbished and kitted out with a giant football screen, now caters more for students than the crumpled intellectuals who once haunted its warren of cellars.

Bar Kohl H10
54–55 George IV Bridge, t (0131) 225 6936. Open 11.30am–1am daily.
A designer drinking bar next door to the National Library, with up-to-the-minute dance sounds and good-value happy hours.

Beluga H10
30a Chambers St, t (0131) 624 4545. Open daily 9am–1am.
A low-lit lair reached via a spiral staircase, Beluga has plenty of room for lounging on its chocolate leather seating. DJs play until late.

Biblos H10
1a Chambers St, t (0131) 226 7177. Open daily 8am–1am.
This decent student hangout is a popular coffee spot by day and lively bar by night.

Biddy Mulligan's G10
94 Grassmarket, t (0131) 220 1246. Open daily 9am–1am.
A noisy student favourite at the top of the Grassmarket.

Bow Bar G10
80 West Bow, t (0131) 226 7667. Open Mon–Sat noon–11.30pm, Sun 12.30pm–11.30pm.
A small, traditional pub with award-winning beer and whisky. It's usually standing room only.

Brass Monkey H10
14 Drummond St, t (0131) 556 1961. Open daily 11am–1am.
A Victorian bar that's made no concessions to the modern day.

Canon's Gait I9
232 Canongate, t (0131) 556 4481. Open Mon–Wed and Sun noon–11pm, Thurs–Sat noon–1am.
Canon's Gait offers lively contemporary Scottish music sessions, and, on its comfortable first floor, board games and decent beer.

City Café H9
19 Blair St, t (0131) 220 0127. Open daily 11am–1am.
Once the trendiest bar in the entire city, this is an American-style place that has largely retained its appeal to a youthful contingent. Immortalized by the writer Irvine Welsh, it is apparently little changed since he patronized it.

Deacon Brodie's G9
435 Lawnmarket, t (0131) 225 6531. Open 10am–1am daily.
Popular with tourists, this is a handy meeting place at the top of The Mound and George IV Bridge. The beer is nothing special and it can get very noisy.

Doric Bar H9
16 Market St, t (0131) 225 1084. Open noon–1am daily.
The boisterous downstairs part of the Doric Tavern (see p.163).

EH1 H9
197 High St, t (0131) 220 5277. Open daily 9am–1am.
A newish style bar on the Mile, with DJ stints at the weekends.

Frankenstein H10
26 George IV Bridge, t (0131) 622 1818. Open 10am–1am daily.
A roomy theme pub popular with students and tourists, serving vaguely Tex Mex food from 10am to 9pm. The pints are good value.

Halfway House H9
24 Fleshmarket Close, t (0131) 225 7101. Open Mon, Tues and Sun 11am–11pm, Wed–Sat 11am–1am (if busy).
A tiny, old-fashioned locals' bar with a railway theme.

Hebrides H9
17 Market St, t (0131) 220 4213. Open Mon–Thurs and Sun 11am–midnight, Fri and Sat 11am–1am.
Handy for the station, Hebrides offers folk music sessions.

Jolly Judge G9

*7 James Court, **t** (0131) 225 2669.*
***Open** Mon noon–midnight, Tues
and Wed noon–11pm, Thurs–Sat
noon–midnight, Sun 12.30pm–11pm.*
Tucked away down a narrow close
off Lawnmarket and popular with
literary tour groups, the Jolly
Judge with its recreation of a
painted 17th-century ceiling offers
a friendly atmosphere and good-
value toasted sandwiches.

Logie Baird's Bar H9

*Bank Hotel, 1 South Bridge, **t** (0131)
556 9043. **Open** daily 9am–1am.*
More impressive outside than in,
this nonetheless pleasant bar in
Bank Hotel (*see* p.151) is furnished
like a pub and has a gallery area.

Meadow Bar H11

*Moo Bar, 42–44 Buccleuch St,
t (0131) 667 6907. **Open** daily
11am–1am.*
A lively student haunt affectionately known as the Moo Bar, with
a club night at weekends and late
hours. Every second Monday at
9pm there's a free comedy quiz
with comedian Reg Anderson.

The Mitre H9

*133 High St, **t** (0131) 524 0071.
Open daily 11am–1am.*
A traditional pub that's undergone
a rather bland refurbishment but
that does what it does well.

Negociant's H10

*45 Lothian St, **t** (0131) 225 6313.
Open Mon–Thurs 9am–1am,
Fri and Sat 9am–3am.*
A large, trendy brasserie-bar with
reasonably priced food and
outside tables in summer.

Pear Tree House H10

*38 West Nicolson St, **t** (0131) 667
7533. **Open** Mon–Thurs 11am–
midnight, Fri and Sat 11am–1am,
Sun 12.30pm–midnight.*
A pub with the largest beer
garden in central Edinburgh;
inside can get somewhat rowdy.

Royal MacGregor H9

*154 High St, **t** (0131) 225 7064.
Open 10am–11pm daily.*
A snug little boozer that was once
the rather run-down Covenanter.
It's still popular with both locals
and tourists.

Rutherford's H10

*Drummond St, no phone.
Open noon–11pm daily.*
This Victorian pub was Robert Louis
Stevenson's favourite and looks to
have changed little since his day.

Southsider I10

*3–5 West Richmond St, **t** (0131) 667
2003. **Open** Mon–Wed 11am–
midnight, Thurs–Sat 11am–1am.*
In many ways a typical Edinburgh
pub, this is pretty basic, does
excellent beer and is frequented
by a wide cross-section of people.

Tolbooth Tavern I9

*167 Canongate, **t** (0131) 556 5348.
Open Mon–Wed 8am–11pm,
Thurs and Fri 8am–midnight,
Sat 8am–11.45pm, Sun 12.30–11pm.*
Atmospheric to the point of dingi-
ness, this has dusty mock-ups of
scenes from the Tolbooth's history.

Waverley Bar I9

*St Mary's St, no phone. **Open** Mon–
Sat 10am–11pm, Sun 12.30–11pm.*
One of the main venues for the
Edinburgh folk revival of the '60s,
this cosy pub also reinvented itself
as a centre for Scottish storytelling.
Bands still play here occasionally.

White Horse I9

*266 Canongate, **t** (0131) 556 3628.
Open daily 11am–11pm.*
Unchanged in aeons, this takes its
name from the old coaching inn at
the bottom of Canongate. There's
live music on Saturday afternoons.

World's End H9

*4 High St, **t** (0131) 556 3628.
Open Mon–Fri 11am–1pm,
Sat and Sun 10am–1am.*
A busy pub serving very good beer
(try the Belhaven Best) in fairly
cramped conditions at the top of
fashionable St Mary's Street.

The New Town

Abbotsford G9

*3 Rose St, **t** (0131) 225 5276.
Open Mon–Sat 11am–11pm.*
This Victorian drinking palace has
changed little since it was the
rendezvous of the literati leading
the Scottish renaissance. Great
lunches, and the beer has never
been known to disappoint.

**Café Royal Circle Bar
and Bistro Bar** H8

*17–19 West Register St, **t** (0131) 556
1884. **Open** Mon–Thurs and Sun
11am–11pm, Fri and Sat 11am–1am.*
The Circle Bar is a wonderful, quite
smart place popular with lawyers
and bankers, with green leather
seats, Doulton portrait tiles on the
walls and a huge island bar. The
Bistro Bar has a similar but more
restrained Edwardian style.

Clark's Bar G8

*142 Dundas St, **t** (0131) 556 1067.
Open Mon–Wed 11am–11pm,
Thurs–Sat 11am–midnight,
Sun 12.30pm–11pm.*
An old-fashioned pub fitted out
with black wood and red leather,
popular with workers in the Bank
of Scotland computer department
over the road. There's good beer
and a snug little room at the back.

The Cumberland Bar G7

*1 Cumberland St, **t** (0131) 553 3134.
Open daily 11am–1am.*
This pub has a tremendous reno-
vated Victorian interior where you
can enjoy great real ales, plus a
leafy courtyard beer garden.

**The Dome and Frazer's
Cocktail Bar** G8

*14 George St, **t** (0131) 624 8624.
Open Mon–Thurs 10am–midnight,
Fri and Sat 10am–12.45am,
Sun 10am–11pm.*
Once the Commercial Bank, hence
its huge domed ceiling, the Dome
has space for a round central bar
and a restaurant, both of which
are glitzy in a slightly tacky way.
Frazer's, done up like the cocktail
bar of a 1920s ocean-going liner, is
usually quieter.

80 Queen Street F9

*80 Queen St, **t** (0131) 538 8111. **Open**
Mon–Thurs 11.30am–midnight,
Fri and Sat 11.30am–1am.*
A clubby, old-style, upmarket
Edwardian bar popular with suits.

The Gordon Arms F9

*133 Rose St, **t** (0131) 226 0911. **Open**
Mon–Wed 11am–11pm, Thurs–Sat
11am–midnight, Sun 12.30–11pm.*
A basic boozer that courageously
defies the street's imperative to
pander to tourists and lager louts.

Great Grog G9

*43 Rose St, t (0131) 225 1616. **Open** Mon–Thurs and Sun 10am–11pm, Fri and Sat 10am–midnight.*

This upmarket winebar offshoot of a wine warehouse (*33–41 Radcliffe Terrace, off Causewayside, t (0131) 662 4777*) is a refreshing find in beer-crazy Rose Street. It offers about 100 wines by the bottle and around 30 by the glass. There are electric-blue benches on which to enjoy them.

Guildford Arms H8

*West Register St, t (0131) 556 4312. **Open** Mon–Thurs and Sun 11am–11pm, Fri and Sat 11am–midnight.*

This is probably the best beer-drinkers' pub in the city centre, with an amazing coffered ceiling, a gallery and, in one corner, a peculiar sunken round velvet bench. It's often crowded but is much loved by good-humoured locals.

Indigo (Yard) F9

*7 Charlotte Lane, t (0131) 220 5603. **Open** daily 8.30am–1am.*

A stylish, two-level place marrying contemporary design with an old building. The food is expensive but interesting, the service bright and efficient. Cocktails, rather than beer, are the order of the day. There are tables outside in summer.

Kay's Bar F8

*39 Jamaica St, t (0131) 225 1858. **Open** Mon–Thurs 11am–midnight, Fri and Sat 11am–1am, Sun 11am–11pm.*

Popular with visiting Highlanders and various New Town characters, this cosy red-walled pub pulls a good pint of ale and has a wide selection of malt whiskies.

Mathers F9

*1 Queensferry St, t (0131) 225 3549. **Open** Mon–Thurs 11am–midnight, Fri and Sat 11am–1am, Sun 12.30–11pm.*

Basic, but full of character and old men, Mathers offers great whiskies.

Mezz H7

*49–51 London St, t (0131) 556 9808. **Open** Mon–Sat 11am–1am, Sun 12.30–1am.*

A colourful, cheerful, loud new bar on the site of the scruffy old Bellevue pub. Reliable bar meals

of the pitta bread and fusion food variety are served until 7.30pm, and snappy CD sounds keep a mix of students and young professionals happy until late.

Milne's Bar G9

*35 Hanover St, t (0131) 225 1858. **Open** Mon–Thurs 11am–midnight, Fri and Sat 11am–1pm, Sun 12.30pm–midnight.*

Now trading almost exclusively on its reputation as the one-time haunt of Scots poets such as Hugh MacDiarmid and Norman MacCaig, this rambling place has several subterranean levels.

Oloroso F9

*33 Castle St, t (0131 226 7614), w www.oloroso.co.uk. **Open** daily noon–2.30pm and 6–10.30pm.*

A rooftop bar and restaurant (*see also p.165*) with designer décor. The long bar serves snacks (about £8) until 1am.

Opal Lounge G9

*51 George St, t (0131) 226 2275. **Open** daily noon–3am.*

A newish, hip place run by the same team as Montpeliers (*see p.171*), with beautiful staff, exotic cocktails, DJs spinning tunes until late, and a slightly pretentious restaurant serving Asian fusion food in finger-bowls. Entry is £3 after 10pm from Monday to Thursday and on Sundays, £5 on Fridays and Saturdays.

Oxford Bar F9

*8 Young St, t (0131) 539 7119. **Open** Mon–Sat 11am–1am, Sun 12.30pm–12.30am.*

A defiantly basic pub much loved by detectives in the afternoon (it's the favoured haunt of Ian Rankin's Inspector Rebus), lawyers after work, and regulars all day.

Penny Black H8

*17 West Register St, t (0131) 556 1106. **Open** 5am–3pm.*

This very basic city institution opens at the crack of dawn for night-shift workers.

Pivo Café H9

*2–6 Calton Rd, t (0131) 557 2925. **Open** daily 4pm–3am.*

A Czech theme bar doing Central European lagers and food.

Rick's G9

*55 Frederick St, t (0131) 622 7800, w www.ricksedinburgh.co.uk. **Open** Mon–Wed and Sun 7am–10pm, Thurs–Sat 7am–11pm.*

One of the New Town's biggest bar openings in a while. The expertly concocted premium-brand cocktails cost £3–7. Rick's is also a restaurant (*see p.167*) and a small boutique hotel (*see p.152*).

Rose Street Brewery G9

*55 Rose St, t (0131) 220 1227. **Open** Mon–Sat 11am–1am, Sun 12.30–11pm.*

The Brewery has a sunken, barrel-filled ground floor where bar snacks can be enjoyed and a decent restaurant upstairs.

Ryan's F9

*2 Hope St, t (0131) 226 7005. **Open** Mon–Thurs and Sun 10am–midnight, Fri and Sat 10am–1am (coffee bar 7.30–10am daily).*

A large bar off the western end of Princes Street, popular with club-bers warming up for the night. The piano bar and bistro downstairs has live music at weekends.

Standing Order G9

*62–66 George St, t (0131) 225 4460. **Open** daily 10am–1am.*

A Wetherspoon's bank conversion complete with a non-smoking area and reasonable food at bargain prices. It's large and often busy but always convivial.

The Wally Dug G8

*32 Northumberland St, t (0131) 556 3271. **Open** Mon–Wed 11am–midnight, Fri and Sat 11am–1am, Sun 12.30pm–midnight.*

A basement bar named after the china spaniels that once graced many an Edinburgh mantelpiece, this is a welcoming retreat from the New Town's windy rectangles. The back bar is favoured by rugby-playing public-school types who know their beer, and there's an great little study alcove. It's run by the same people as the Antiquary in Stockbridge (*see p.177*).

Whigham's Wine Cellars F9

*13 Hope St, t (0131) 225 9717. **Open** Mon–Thurs noon–midnight, Fri and Sat noon–1am.*

An 18th-century-style wine bar with delicious local seafood, flagons of excellent claret and a woody, convivial atmosphere.

Yo! Below F9

*66 Rose St, t (0131) 220 6040. **Open** Mon–Thurs and Sun 5pm–1am, Fri and Sat noon–1am.*

An pre-club bar with attitude below Yo! Sushi, part of the conveyor-belt sushi chain. Singers, masseuses, tarot card readers and other acts jolly things along.

Dean Village and Stockbridge

Antiquary F8

*77–78 St Stephen St, t (0131) 225 2858. **Open** Mon–Wed and Sun 11.30am–12.30am, Thurs–Sat 11.30am–1am.*

Popular with students, this refurbished pub used to be one of Stockbridge's bohemian basement bars. There are lively late-night folk sessions on Thursdays.

The Bailie Bar F8

*2–4 St Stephen St, t (0131) 225 4673. **Open** Mon–Thurs 11am–midnight, Fri and Sat 11am–1pm, Sun 12.30–11pm.*

A coal fire, cosy red-leather seating and good food at reasonable prices make this popular with a cross-section of locals, from army types to English students.

Bert's Bar E7

*2–4 Raeburn Place, t (0131) 332 6345. **Open** Mon–Thurs 11am–midnight, Fri and Sat 11am–1am, Sun 11am–11pm.*

Done up as an old-style Edinburgh 'howff', Bert's is renowned for the number of things it can do with a pie. There's a more 'distressed' branch at 29 William Street in the New Town, t (0131) 225 5748.

Granary Bar D9

*Menzies Belford Hotel, 69 Belford Rd, t (0131) 332 2545. **Open** daily 11am–11pm.*

This is hardly a destination bar, but it's somewhere to drop in to if you happen to be walking along the Water of Leith. It has decent beer but is quite expensive.

Northern Bar G7

*1 Howard Place, t (0131) 556 1558. **Open** Mon–Thurs noon–midnight, Fri and Sat noon–1am, Sun 12.30–11pm.*

This unreconstructed Victorian boozer, which is handy for the Botanic Garden, is as impressive inside as out. It does pub food and pumps good beers.

Smithie's Ale House G7

*43 Eyre Place, t (0131) 556 9805. **Open** daily 11am–12.30am.*

A traditional boozer that manages to draw in sleek media types from the offices around while maintaining local custom.

Vincent's F8

*St Stephen St, t (0131) 225 7447. **Open** daily 11am–12.30am.*

A basement pub offering games, good beers and a comprehensive range of whiskies. It's often packed out with students warming up for a night out in the New Town or Stockbridge.

The Watershed F8

*44 St Stephen St, t (0131) 220 3774. **Open** Mon–Wed and Sun 11.30am–midnight, Thurs–Sat 11.30am–1am.*

A surprisingly light and airy basement bar and café, popular with students and clubbers.

Outside the Centre

Auld Toll Bar F11

*39 Leven St, Tollcross, t (0131) 229 1010. **Open** Mon–Thurs 9am–11.30pm, Fri and Sat 9am–12.30pm, Sun 12.30pm–midnight.*

A down-to-earth pub situated opposite the King's Theatre, with a few real ales.

Barony Bar H8

*81–5 Broughton St, Broughton, t (0131) 557 0546. **Open** Mon–Thurs 11am–midnight, Fri and Sat 11am–12.30am, Sun 12.30pm–11pm.*

One of the street's more traditional pubs, the Barony has a woody interior, a large open-plan floorspace and decent beer.

The Basement H8

*10–12 Broughton St, Broughton, t (0131) 557 0097. **Open** daily noon–12.45am.*

> ## Literary City
>
> The following pubs and bars all have literary associations of one kind or another:
>
> **Abbotsford** (*see p.175*), **City Café** (*see p.174*), **Jolly Judge** (*see p.175*), **Milne's Bar** (*see p.176*), **Oxford Bar** (*see p.176*), **Rutherford's** (*see p.175*), **Waverley Bar** (*see p.175*).

Possibly the trendiest bar on trendy Broughton Street, The Basement offers loud club music and designer lagers.

Bennet's Bar F11

*8 Leven St, Tollcross, t (0131) 229 5143. **Open** Mon–Wed 11am–12.15am, Thurs–Sat 11am–1am, Sun 12.30pm–11.30pm.*

The mirrored interior and fine selection of malts makes this place worth travelling to.

Caledonian Ale House D10

*1–3 Haymarket Terrace, t (0131) 337 1006. **Open** Mon–Wed and Sun 12.30pm–11.30pm, Thurs–Sat 11am–1am.*

This big, noisy place near Haymarket Station is a useful rendezvous point. There is a range of good beers from the Caledonian Brewery, and a restaurant upstairs.

Cameo Bar J4

*Commercial St, Leith, t (0131) 553 7639. **Open** daily 10am–1am.*

A bar-cum-pub offering oysters and other delicacies from the attached restaurant, The Camargue (*see p.170*). There are board games for rainy afternoons.

Cask and Barrel H7

*115 Broughton St, Broughton, t (0131) 556 3132. **Open** Mon–Wed and Sun 11am–12.30am, Thurs–Sat 11am–1pm.*

A very good alehouse at the bottom of the street, popular among beer aficionados. There's no music and plenty of seats.

Cloisters F11

*Brougham Place, Tollcross, t (0131) 221 9997. **Open** Mon–Thurs 11am–midnight, Fri and Sat 11am–1am, Sun 12.30–11pm.*

Reasonable food and good beer, plus great Bloody Marys, in a converted church.

Victorian Charm

The following watering-holes are noteworthy for their impressive Victorian interiors.

Abbotsford (see p.175), **Brass Monkey** (see p.174), **The Cumberland Bar** (see p.175), **Leslie's** (see p.178), **Northern Bar** (see p.177), **Rutherford's** (see p.175).

Drew Nichol's at the Old Chain Pier F3
*1 Trinity Crescent, Newhaven, t (0131) 552 1233. **Open** Mon–Wed noon–11pm, Thurs–Sat noon–midnight.*
The food served at Drew Nichol's is good value, but people really come for here the location – the bar is situated in the ticket office of the now non-existent pier, almost in the Firth of Forth itself (at high tide the windows are flecked with seaspray).

Golf Tavern F11
*31 Wright's Houses, Bruntsfield, t (0131) 229 3235. **Open** daily 11am–1am.*
A refurbished but still historic ancient pub overlooking Bruntsfield Links (from April to September you can hire pitch and putt equipment here).

Hogshead Alehouse F10
*30 Bread St, t (0131) 221 0575. **Open** Mon–Sat 11am–1am, Sun 12.30pm–1am.*
A roomy, lively Whitbread establishment down towards Tollcross, doing decent beer.

International Bar F11
*15 Brougham Place, Tollcross, t (0131) 229 6815. **Open** daily 11am–1am.*
Popular with students, the dark, cosy and often loud International has a certain scruffy charm and boasts the best Guinness in town.

Iso-bar J4
*7 Bernard St, Leith, t (0131) 467 8904. **Open** daily 10am–1am.*
A convivial and lively bar with long narrow benches and tables, famous for its full breakfasts at weekends. It also offers delicious burgers, panini and wraps and very good tea and coffee.

King's Wark J4
*36 The Shore, Leith, t (0131) 554 9260. **Open** Mon–Thurs 11am–11pm, Fri and Sat 11am–midnight, Sun 12.30–11pm.*
Good food in the traditional surroundings of one of the oldest buildings on The Shore.

Leslie's Off maps
*45 Ratcliffe Terrace, t (0131) 667 5957. **Open** noon–11pm daily.*
A few minutes' walk south of The Meadows, Leslie's has coal fires and a splendid Victorian interior with eye-level peep-holes (so the quality wouldn't have to look across the bar at the quantity). The Diplomats of Jazz play on Monday nights.

Malmaison J4
*1 Tower Place, Leith, t (0131) 555 6898. **Open** Mon–Thurs 11am–11pm, Fri and Sat 11am–midnight, Sun 12.30–11pm.*
This bar of the stylish hotel (see p.155), with its low lighting and refined ambience, is a great place for swish cocktails before a meal out in Leith.

Malt and Hops J4
*6 The Shore, Leith, t (0131) 555 0083. **Open** Mon and Tues 11am–11pm, Wed and Thurs 11am–midnight, Fri and Sat 11am–1am, Sun 12.30–11pm.*
An old pub with a reputation for its real ales. Popular with locals.

Monboddo F10
*Point Hotel, 34 Bread St, t (0131) 221 5555. **Open** Mon–Sat 11am–1am, Sun noon–1am.*
This trendy hotel bar (see p.155), gets packed with bright young things at weekends, has decent food and designer lagers.

Ocean Bar I3
*Ocean Terminal, t (0131) 553 8073. **Open** daily noon–midnight.*
A shiny Terence Conran bar situated on the terminal concourse itself and part of the Zinc restaurant complex (see p.172).

Port of Leith K4
*58 Constitution St, Leith, t (0131) 554 3568. **Open** daily 8am–1am.*
Unique and much loved by a wide variety of people, the Port has flags from around the world decking out the ceiling and ship-shaped lampshades.

Sheep Heid Inn Off maps
*43 The Causeway, Duddingston, t (0131) 656 6951. **Open** Mon–Sat 11am–11.30pm, Sun 12.30pm–11pm.*
This unashamedly locals' village boozer is one of the oldest pubs in Edinburgh. At weekends it fills rapidly with walkers from Arthur's Seat enjoying the filling pub grub and rustic atmosphere.

The Shore Bar J4
*3–4 The Shore, Leith, t (0131) 553 5080. **Open** Mon–Sat 11am–midnight, Sun 12.30–11pm.*
Right on the old harbour, this traditional, atmospheric pub and dining room moved upmarket from a spit-and-sawdust sailors' gaff some time ago. There's good beer, and Scottish fish and shellfish from a daily-changing blackboard menu.

Starbank Inn G3
*64 Laverockbank Rd, Newhaven, t (0131) 552 4141. **Open** Mon–Sat 11am–midnight, Sun 12.30pm–midnight.*
A large, traditional pub in a fine position on the Newhaven waterfront, with a reputation for real ales and good food.

Timberbush K4
*28 Bernard St, Leith, t (0131) 476 8080. **Open** Mon–Thurs and Sun 10am–11pm, Fri and Sat 10am–1am.*
A newish and airy bistro-type café bar in a converted bank. Laid-back staff mix great cocktails and serve burgers, tortillas and the like.

Traverse Theatre Bar F10
*10 Cambridge St, t (0131) 228 5383. **Open** daily 11am–midnight.*
A spacious basement bar and café where the movers and shakers of the theatre world congregate. The café section serves home-made hot meals, the bar is well stocked and there are occasional gigs by up-and-coming jazz bands.

Volunteer Arms/ Cannyman's Off maps
*237 Morningside Rd, t (0131) 447 1484. **Open** Mon–Thurs noon–midnight, Fri noon–1pm, Sun noon–11.30pm.*

A destination pub of some note: expect to pay over the odds for drinks, but it's worth it.

Ye Olde Peacock Inn I3
Lindsay Road, Newhaven, t (0131) 552 8707. Open Mon–Sat 11am–11pm, Sun 12.30pm–11pm.
An old-fashioned tourist trap of considerable charm, complete with photographs of Newhaven in days gone by and a scale model of a sailing ship. It's also one of the very few establishments to advertise a separate menu for women.

Clubs

Late-night Edinburgh has been dancing into the wee small hours for considerably longer than most other places in the UK, and the sheer variety of different options can bamboozle the most avid night owl. Maybe it's the effect of the long winter nights, or the result of the city's more amenable licensing laws, but after dark throughout the year the city gets into gear and enjoys itself – anywhere from sweaty hardcore clubs to genteel drinking palaces. Beware, though – draconian local legislation means everywhere has to shut down at 3am.

Despite the recent fire, which claimed several venues, **Cowgate** remains one of the city's liveliest streets in terms of nightlife, with a plethora of different places vying for the not-so-studious student clubbers' attentions.

As we went to press, **La Belle Angele** on Cowgate was closed for an indefinite period after severe damage in the fire. Live music dates were being transferred to The Venue (*see* below), and alternatives were being sought for the club nights. See www.la-belle-angele.co.uk for developments.

For more club nights, *see* Studio 24 on p.182. For predominantly **gay-orientated venues**, *see* p.201.

Bongo Club I9
14 New St, t (0131) 556 5204. Open Thurs–Sat 10.30pm–3am.
A variety of regular club nights take place at the Bongo Club,

including roots, reggae, dub and ska, in a bohemian space that also operates as an exhibition space for Urban Art Official.

Cabaret Voltaire H9
36–38 Blair St, t (0131) 220 6176, w www.cabaret-voltaire.co.uk. Open daily 5pm–3am.
Located in the two-floor venue that was The Honeycomb and then Peppermint Lounge, Voltaire has a cerebral vibe. Mondays host Acoustica (live acoustic bands) and Wednesdays live bands, while on Friday and Saturday you're likely to encounter either Popcorn (cheesy underground sound), Ultragroove (a DJ-driven dance night) or Get-Together (live music and DJs spinning breakbeats).

The Cavendish F10
3 West Tollcross, t (0131) 228 3252, w www.thecav.co.uk. Open Tues, Wed and Sun 10pm–3am, Fri 4pm–3am.
The Cavendish has a top-floor dancefloor playing music from 1960 to 1985 and a ground-floor space playing music from 1985 on. It's over-25s only on Wednesday and Friday, and students only on Tuesdays and Sundays. Smart dress only (no denims or trainers).

Club Ego H8
12 Picardy Place, t (0131) 478 7434. Open Fri and Sat 10pm–3am and occasional other nights.
This Broughton venue has two dancefloors – a big one upstairs and a cosier, more intimate one downstairs. It hosts a variety of nights, mixed and gay (*see* p.201).

The Honeycomb H9
15 Niddry St, t (0131) 556 2442. Open Fri and Sat 10.30pm–3am, occasional other nights.
An eclectic mix of club nights, from breaks and house to grunge and cheese.

The Liquid Room G9
9c Victoria St, t (0131) 225 2564, w www.liquidroom.com. Open daily 10pm–3am.
A wide variety of very popular club nights and occasional live bands in this loud, popular and fairly cramped Old Town club.

The Massa H9
36 Market St, t (0131) 226 4224. Open daily 10pm–3am.
Formerly Club Mercado, The Massa hosts a variety of club nights, the best known of which is the ever-popular dressed-up TV night Tackno (*see* p.201).

Peppermint Lounge H10
1a Chambers St, t (0131) 225 5209. Open daily 10am–3am.
The house and dance music club has moved into the space below Biblos (*see* p.174) that used to be the Beat Jazz Basement before the December 2002 fire.

Po Na Na G9
43b Frederick St, t (0131) 226 4224, w www.ponana.com. Open Mon and Wed–Sat 10pm–3am, Tues 8pm–2am.
A crowded, loud but funky nightspot in the New Town. Monday is Bibido (soul, funk, disco and Mexican food), Tuesday is Yerba Buena (global Latin, house and funk), Wednesday Bling (mainstream hiphop), Thursday TLC (house and mainstream chart music), Friday Roadblock (funk, disco, R&B) and Saturday Funky (sensual, soulful house).

The Venue H9
17–21 Calton Rd, t (0131) 557 3073, Open Fri and Sat 10.30pm–3am and occasional other nights.
A three-storey New Town venue hosting a variety of club nights (hiphop, soul, funk, digital techno, drum 'n' bass, grungey house) and live events (indie, alt pop, punk, ska, and occasional folk).

The Wee Red Bar G10
Edinburgh College of Art, Lauriston Place, t (0131) 229 1442. Open Fri and Sat 10pm–3am.
Indie, 1960s tunes and whatever takes the DJ's fancy for members, students and their guests.

Entertainment

The **Edinburgh Festival** (*see* p.38) has had a beneficial impact on the city's arts scene as a whole: you can now enjoy year-round drama and dance in at least five large theatres, films on more than 50 screens, and music both live and DJ-driven in countless pubs, clubs, restaurants and bars (Edinburgh is still at the epicentre of Scottish folk music).

The fortnightly *The List: Glasgow and Edinburgh Events Guide* (£2.20) is the best source of information about upcoming events and concerts. The *Gig Guide*, available at outlets all over the city, is a free monthly broadsheet with basic listings (there's an online version at *www. gigguide.co.uk*). The *Edinburgh News*, Edinburgh's local daily paper, run by *The Scotsman*, contains details of daily entertainment and events, as well as some trenchant theatre and cinema reviews (*see also www. edinburghnews.com*). Lastly, the tourist board publishes a comprehensive events diary, available at the TIC (*see* p.56) or on-line at *www.edinburgh.org*.

Edinburgh is not large enough to require centralized **booking agencies**, though The Hub (*see* p.183) and the Assembly Rooms (*see* p.182) manage tickets for a variety of venues year round.

Theatre and Performance Arts

Edinburgh's good selection of theatres large and small keep the dramatic spirit alive year round.

The **Assembly Rooms** (*see* p.101 and p.182) also host a number of touring modern dance productions and shows by medium-scale theatre companies.

Bedlam Theatre H10
2 Forrest Rd, t (0131) 225 9893.
The university's main theatre, set in a converted church on a prominent corner site near the Museum of Scotland, is still going strong despite threats of closure.

Brunton Theatre Off maps
Ladywell Way, Musselburgh, t (0131) 665 2240.
This out-of-town venue hosts popular middle-scale touring shows and boasts an acclaimed in-house production company.

Church Hill Theatre Off maps
33a Morningside Rd, t (0131) 220 4349.
A former church south of the city where you can catch amateur dramatics and touring shows.

Dance Base G10
National Centre for Dance, 14–16 Grassmarket, t (0131) 225 5525, w www.dancebase.co.uk.
An exciting new lottery-funded building in the Old Town, and a new venue on the Edinburgh Fringe (there are plans for regular performances in the future). Classes are run for beginners, amateurs and professionals.

Edinburgh Festival Theatre H10
13–29 Nicolson St, t (0131) 529 6000, w www.eft.co.uk.
An opera house and theatre with Europe's largest stage, catering for a range of tastes from variety to ballet. Behind the new glass frontage, the auditorium was once the Empire Theatre music hall. *See also* p.182.

Gateway Theatre I8
Elm Row, t (0131) 317 3939.
A small studio theatre near the Playhouse in Broughton.

King's Theatre F11
2 Leven St, t (0131) 220 4349, box office t (0131) 529 6000, w www.eft.co.uk.
This grand red sandstone building near Tollcross teamed up with the Edinburgh Festival Theatre several years ago, and the pair divide most of the prestige touring productions between them.

Netherbow Arts Centre H9
43 High St, t (0131) 556 9579.
This medium-sized theatre right on the Royal Mile, run by the Church of Scotland, stages anything from community theatre to modern dance.

Playhouse Theatre H8
18–22 Greenside Place, t (0131) 557 2590.
A huge old theatre off Picardy Place, usually the venue for large-scale visiting musicals and operas.

Royal Lyceum F10
Grindlay St, t (0131) 248 4848, w www.lyceum.org.uk.
A small, plush, Victorian auditorium behind the Castle, with a striking glass foyer. The resident company puts on a fairly adventurous mix of crowd-pleasing classics, lesser-known plays and new – and often distinctly Scottish – writing.

Theatre Workshop F7
34 Hamilton Place, t (0131) 226 5425.
Edinburgh's alternative theatre space in Stockbridge features community-based local productions and visiting small and middle-scale touring companies.

Traverse Theatre F10
10 Cambridge St, t (0131) 228 1404, w www.traverse.co.uk.
Since the 1960s this theatre in superb modern premises behind the castle has been the most vibrant in the city, with a reputation for showcasing new Scottish writing and directing talent.

Music

Rock and Pop

As a large university town, Edinburgh should have a thriving music scene, but sadly the temptations of Glasgow are too close to resist for most of Edinburgh's emerging stars. With the glorious exception of the Bay City Rollers in the 1970s (who were only discovered in the first place because a US record producer's flight was diverted from Glasgow), the city has never produced its own big names, and it doesn't even have a venue that's large enough to host big international acts.

On the other hand, Edinburgh's compact character and enthusiastic student population ensure there's never any shortage of effort. Venues are likely to be jumping most at weekends, while pubs keep at it all week.

Other venues hosting occasional rock, pop and indie concerts include the Bongo Club (see p.179), the Edinburgh Festival Theatre (see p.183), the Liquid Room (see p.179), the Playhouse Theatre (see p.181), The Pleasance Cabaret Bar (see p.183), Usher Hall (see p.183) and The Venue (see p.179).

As we went to press, the Bridge Jazz Bar, La Belle Angele and the Gilded Balloon remained closed after the Cowgate fire.

The Blue Blazer F10
2 Spittal St, t (0131) 229 5030.
Sunday night is songwriters' night in this busy little pub behind the castle.

Corn Exchange Off maps
11 Newmarket Rd, t (0131) 477 3500,
w www.ece.uk.com.
Situated down in Slateford and run by the De Marco's Leisure Group, the Exchange features big-name bands.

The Maltings Off maps
81–85 St Leonard's St, t (0131) 667 5946.
A cheerful studenty pub on the edge of the Old Town, with indie bands on Saturday nights plus occasional folk nights.

The Mercat E10
28 West Maitland St, t (0131) 225 3861.
This venue near Haymarket Station has indie bands on Saturday nights and occasional country and western nights during the week.

Studio 24 H9
24–26 Calton Rd, t (0131) 558 3758.
Mainly a live music venue hosting performances by heavy rock bands, Studio One also puts on occasional hard-dance club nights.

The Tron H9
9 Hunter Square, t (0131) 226 0931.
Lively and crowded indie and folk and sessions – sometimes with free entry for punters in fancy dress – take place in this loud and busy basement bar situated just off the High Street.

The Village I5
16 South Fort St, Leith, t (0131) 478 7810.
Regular singers and bands perform at this gallery/food pub in Leith.

Whistle Binkies H9
4–6 South Bridge, t (0131) 557 5114,
w www.whistlebinkies.com.
A popular, sometimes deafening, late-night live music pub in a series of caverns beneath South Bridge. There's always a queue later in the evening, so arrive by ten o'clock (entry is £2–3 after midnight on Fridays and Saturdays).

Jazz

Famous names in Edinburgh jazz include the world-renowned saxophonist Tommy Smith and guitarist Martin Taylor. Look out also for the Brian Kellock Trio, the Alex Shaw Trio, Toto and the Dexters, and Madaline Eastman.

The Human Be-In (see p.163), Leslie's (see p.178), the Queen's Hall (see p.183) and the Traverse Theatre Bar (see p.178) also host jazz events.

Café Royal Bistro Bar H8
17 West Register St, t (0131) 557 4792.
Thursday-night jazz piano and vocals in a refined Edwardian ambience in the New Town.

The Dome Bar and Grill G8
14 George St, t (0131) 624 8624,
w www.thedomeedinburgh.com.
Sunday-afternoon easy-listening with a pianist and singer in this flashy New Town venue.

Henderson's G8
94 Hanover St, t (0131) 225 2131.
Every evening this veggie salad bar in the New Town (see also p.168) hosts live piano jazz/bands.

Henry's Cellar Bar F10
8 Morrison St, t (0131) 538 7385.
Live jazz and music nights (Wednesday–Sunday, about £5) in a boho underground lair between Haymarket and Fountainbridge.

Malt Shovel H9
11–15 Cockburn St, t (0131) 225 6843.
Swing 2003 play every Tuesday night at 9pm at this large Cockburn Street institution.

Folk

Edinburgh was the centre of the Scottish folk revival in the 1960s and 1970s, and some musicians and singers such as Dick Gaughan who started out playing at small get-togethers above the Waverley Arms have gone on to achieve international acclaim for their driven, politicized and heartfelt performances and recordings.

Today, acts such as the Wrigley Sisters, demon fiddlers from Orkney, have adopted Edinburgh as their home and often team up with other virtuosos such as Alasdair Fraser to give scorching performances in the city. The Battlefield Band have taken their song-based, electrified and bagpipe sounds around the world, while Shooglenifty were one of the first bands to incorporate driving rhythms and house beats with more traditional tunes at the currently defunct La Belle Angele.

There's plenty of folk to be heard at the Fringe, and New Year celebrations have also developed a folky slant. See 'Edinburgh's Festivals' (p.40) for details of the Ceilidh Culture Festival, which includes folk music.

Other venues where you can hear folk include Antiquary (see p.177), The Tron (see above) and The Venue (see p.179).

Assembly Rooms G9
54 George St, t (0131) 220 4349,
w www.assemblyroomsedinburgh.co.uk.
The monthly ceilidhs held here each month from October to May are one of the best Scottish folk experiences, though they sell out way in advance.

Caledonian Brewery C12
Slateford Rd, t (0131) 623 8066.
Regular lively ceilidhs and folk sessions in a brewery south-west of the town centre (see p.122).

Ensign Ewart G9
Lawnmarket, t (0131) 225 7440.
Live folk on Saturdays and Sundays until midnight, in a venue at the top of the Royal Mile.

The Hub G9
*348 Castlehill, **t** (0131) 473 2000, **w** www.eif.co.uk.*
Fairly regular folk café-concerts and occasional performances by big players take place in the main hall of the International Festival HQ (*see also* p.65).

The Pleasance Cabaret Bar I10
*60 The Pleasance, **t** (0131) 650 2349.*
The Edinburgh University student union is home to the Edinburgh Folk Club, who do occasional sessions here and elsewhere. Rock/pop acts sometimes appear too.

Royal Oak H10
*1 Infirmary St, **t** (0131) 557 2976.*
One of the Old Town's two famous folk pubs (*see also* Sandy Bell's, below), this has been in the same hands for as long as its regulars care to remember. There are lively jams upstairs in the week and visiting performers in the downstairs bar on Fridays and Saturdays until late, and on Sundays.

Sandy Bell's H10
*25 Forrest Rd, **t** (0131) 225 2751.*
The original folk music pub (formerly called the Forrest Hill Bar), this has retained much of its cachet and is a good place to catch the rising stars of the folk world. Music starts at 9pm, and there are also Saturday and Sunday afternoon sessions.

West End Hotel E10
*35 Palmerston Place, **t** (0131) 225 3656.*
Lively, informal folk sessions beloved by the regulars at this little hotel bar in the New Town (*see also* p.153).

Classical

Edinburgh has long been a city of music-lovers. The main resident orchestra, the Scottish Chamber Orchestra (SCO), is based at the Queen's Hall, but there are plenty of smaller groups worth a listen in a wide range of venues. Keep an eye out for performances in churches, and concerts by the Edinburgh University Faculty of Music in the Reid Concert Hall and St Cecilia's Hall.

Large-scale visiting operas are sometimes hosted by the Playhouse Theatre (*see* p.181).

Edinburgh Festival Theatre H10
*13–29 Nicolson St, **t** (0131) 529 6000, **w** www.eft.co.uk.*
The home to Scottish Opera and Royal Scottish National Orchestra (RSNO) productions, plus performances by large touring orchestras. *See also* p.181.

High Kirk of St Giles H9
*Parliament Square, **t** (0131) 225 9442.*
A spectacular-sounding modern organ is put through its paces here on a regular basis, in concert and during services. *See also* p.67.

Queen's Hall H11
*Clerk St, **t** (0131) 668 2019.*
Scottish Chamber Orchestra concerts (Thursdays and Saturdays from September to May), plus four performances a year by the Scottish Ensemble. Smaller events and comedians also feature, and the bigger noises in jazz sometimes play here.

Reid Concert Hall H10
*Bristo Square, **t** (0131) 650 4367.*
Free lunchtime concerts in the Old Town, on Tuesdays in termtime.

St Cecilia's Hall H9
*Niddry St, Cowgate, **t** (0131) 650 2805, **w** www.music.ed.ac.uk/russell/.*
St Cecilia's (*see also* p.80) is famous for its wonderful acoustics and its approximately thrice-yearly concerts on authentic period instruments, which are organized by the Edinburgh University Faculty of Music (**t** (0131) 650 2423).

St Mary's Episcopal Cathedral E9
*Palmerston Place, **t** (0131) 225 6293.*
Regular organ recitals and a very fine choir can be enjoyed in this New Town venue. *See also* p.106.

Usher Hall F10
*Lothian Rd, **t** (0131) 228 1155, **w** www.usherhall.co.uk.*
Built by brewer Andrew Usher and recently overhauled, this is Edinburgh's premier concert venue. The RSNO's winter season is a highlight.

> ### The Edinburgh Lectures
>
> A legacy of the UK's presidency of the European Union in 1992, the annual Edinburgh Lectures provide a world-class forum in which to hear movers and shakers speak about some of the more pressing issues of the day. Each year, on about a dozen different dates between October and February, at various venues around the city (some not usually open to the public), eminent politicians, academics, broadcasters, journalists and even royals are asked to deliver lectures on a chosen theme. In 2002/3 it was 'Freedoms', with contributions from, among others, the Secretary General of NATO, Lord Robertson, Princess Basma bint Talal of Jordan, and special BBC correspondent Fergal Keane.
>
> Organized with the support of a broad spectrum of institutions and organizations across Edinburgh – the university, the Royal Society, the City Council and the Scottish Parliament to name but a few – the lectures are free, are open to all and provide an ideal opportunity to enjoy the city's famous spirit of enlightenment and debate at its best.
>
> For details of the current year's series, contact the Usher Hall Box Office, **t** (0131) 228 1155, or visit **w** www.edinburghlectures.org.

Comedy

This is a city that only takes stand-up comedy seriously during the Festival, although there are a few places that present young native talent throughout the rest of the year. Don't be surprised, however, if some of the jokes are incomprehensible to tourists or the English.

At the time of writing, comedy and performance poetry events in the Gilded Saloon (the bar of the Gilded Balloon) and La Belle Angele had been put on hold after the venues were heavily damaged in the 2002 fire.

Fin MacCool's F10
161 Lothian Rd, t (0131) 622 7109.
Friday-night comedy (9pm, £3) in
a venue just beyond the Old Town,
with Reg Anderson (*see also* p.175,
Meadow Bar) introducing a
variety of British acts.

Jongleurs H8
Omni Complex, Greenside Place,
t 0870 787 0707, w www.jongleurs.
com.
A mainstream comedy venue in
the new leisure centre.

The Stand Comedy Club H8
5 York Place, t (0131) 558 7272,
w www.thestand.co.uk.
Easily the best place for comedy in
the city, this New Town basement
venue regularly sells out and gets
so packed that it's worth arriving
early to get a table. There's a gay
night on the second Tuesday of
each month (9–11pm).

Cinema

Edinburgh has been used as
the location for some very
successful – and very different
– films. *Trainspotting*, the 1995
adaptation of Irvine Welsh's hit
novel about the sordid lives of
some of the city's heroin abusers,
has become easily the most
famous film set in the city. A few
years earlier, the same production
team made *Shallow Grave*, which
was also set in Edinburgh but
mainly filmed in Glasgow.

In the 1980s the city was used
as a backdrop for the Oscar-
winning film *Chariots of Fire*, in
which the Christian athlete Eric
Liddell can be seen running past
the John Knox statue on The
Mound and walking in Holyrood
Park with his sister, and Jewish
athlete Harold Abrahams is
shown taking tea with his sweet-
heart in the Café Royal.

Further back, in the 1960s,
Edinburgh was associated with
another Oscar-winning perform-
ance when it played a deservedly
central role in *The Prime of Miss
Jean Brodie*, written by Muriel
Spark and starring Dame
Maggie Smith.

Cameo F11
38 Home St, t (0131) 228 4141,
recorded information t (0131) 228
2800, w www.cameocinema.co.uk.
Cult classics and interesting
programming on three screens
down by Tollcross.

Dominion Cinema Off maps
18 Newbattle Terrace, t (0131)
447 4771, recorded information
t (0131) 447 2660.
A tremendous Art Deco, family-
run cinema outside the city centre
in Morningside.

Filmhouse F10
88 Lothian Rd, t (0131) 228 2688.
The pick of the bunch for movie
buffs, just beyond the Old Town,
this is the venue for film festivals.

Odeon I11
7 Clerk Street, t (0131) 667 0971.
Mainstream releases on five
screens in the Old Town.

Ster Century I3
Ocean Terminal, Ocean Drive, Leith,
t (0131) 553 0700.
A twelve-screen multiplex in the
new waterside mall in Leith.

UGC Fountainpark E11
Fountainpark Leisure Centre,
Dundee St, t 0870 902 0417.
An eleven-screen multiplex situ-
ated in Fountainbridge to the
southwest of town.

Warner Village Cinema H8
Omni Complex, Greenside Place,
t 0870 240 6020, w www.
warnervillage.co.uk
A central new multiplex with 12
screens showing mainstream
releases. Three screens are 'gold
class' (leather seats, with drinks
and nibbles thrown in).

Shopping

Until quite recently, Edinburgh's shopkeepers could boast expert knowledge of their specialized but extensive stock, but though examples of this can still be found in the city centre – at Robert Cresser's broom shop (see p.189) and Mr Wood's Fossils (see p.190), for instance – such dedication is becoming unusual. Like misfits in the school playground, those quirky shops that have survived tend to be clustered together: in Canongate on the Royal Mile; around Cowgatehead and the bottom of Victoria Street; and on the fringes of the New Town around Broughton Street and St Stephen Street.

One of the joys of shopping in this city is that whole streets have retained their character. Sadly, Princes Street was one of the first places to fall prey to the creeping homogeneity of high streets and shopping malls across the land and is now full of national and international chain-stores, with the grand exception of Jenners, the oldest department store in the world. Nearby George Street is still home to several distinctive independent retailers, including outfitters Aitken and Niven (see below) and jewellers Hamilton and Inches (see p.187).

Opening times are usually 9am or 10am to 5pm or 6pm (later on Thursdays in some cases). Many are closed on Sundays.

Books, Maps and Stationery

For second-hand books, see also Duncan & Reid on p.189. For details of the city's annual Book Festival, see p.39.

Beyond Words H9
42 Cockburn St, t (0131) 226 6636, w www.beyondwords.co.uk.
An extensive independent stock of monographs and photographic art books, and interesting postcards.

Blackwell's H10
53 South Bridge, t (0131) 556 6743, w www.blackwell.co.uk.

Until recently James Thin, the original Edinburgh University bookshop, Blackwell's still has the most comprehensive stock in the city, as well as a very good classical music section.

The Cook's Bookshop G10
118 West Bow, t (0131) 226 4445.
An Old Town shop set up by Clarissa Dickson-Wright of Two Fat Ladies fame.

Edinburgh Pen Shop F9
194 Rose St, t (0131) 226 3624, w www.edinburghpenshop.com.
Scribblers' heaven, with a huge variety of writing implements, especially smart fountain pens and their accessories.

Helios Fountain G10
7 Grassmarket, t (0131) 229 7884, w www.helios-fountain.co.uk.
Offbeat books, beads, candles and unusual gifts in the Old Town.

International Newsagents H9
351 High St, t (0131) 225 4827.
A Royal Mile newsagents with an enormous selection of newspapers from around the world.

McNaughtan's Bookshop I7
3a & 4a Haddington Place (on Leith Walk), t (0131) 556 5897.
A second-hand and antiquarian bookseller in Broughton, with a strong Scottish section.

Ottokar's G9
59 George St, t (0131) 225 4495, w www.ottokars.co.uk.
A general chain bookshop in the New Town, with a good tea shop (see p.168).

Peter Bell G10
68 West Port, t (0131) 229 0562, w www.peterbell.net.
A second-hand and rare books specialist in the Old Town.

Second Edition G7
9 Howard Street, t (0131) 556 9403.
Located in Stockbridge, this shop specializes in second-hand books on travel, military history, the fine arts and Scotland.

Stationery Office Bookshop F10
71 Lothian Rd, t (0870) 606 55 66.
Ordnance Survey maps and government handbooks are sold here, just beyond the Old Town.

West Port Books G10
145–47 West Port, t (0131) 229 4431, w www.portbooks.freeserve.co.uk.
An Old Town shop selling second-hand books. Particularly strong on local topography.

Word Power H10
43 West Nicolson St, t (0131) 662 9112., w www.word-power.co.uk.
A purveyor of alternative books down in the Southside area.

Children

Aha Ha Ha G10
99 West Bow, t (0131) 220 5252.
This Old Town store specializes in joke items and fancy dress.

Edinburgh Bear Company H9
46 High St, t (0131) 557 9564, w www.edinburghbear.co.uk.
All kinds of furry friends are available in this Royal Mile shop.

Monkey Business E10
167 Morrison St, t (0131) 228 6636.
Monkey Business offers fancy dress hire near Haymarket Station.

Mulberry Bush Off maps
77 Morningside Rd, t (0131) 447 5145.
Wooden toys, rocking horses and dolls' houses in Marchmont.

New & Junior Profile E7
88 Raeburn Place, t (0131) 332 7928.
A Stockbridge shop sellling babywear and wooden toys.

Wonderland F10
97 Lothian Rd, t (0131) 229 6428, w www.wonderlandmodels.com.
Build-your-own models, radio-controlled planes, boats and cars sold just beyond the Old Town.

Clothes and Accessories

Aitken & Niven F9
79 George St, t (0131) 225 1461, w www.aitken-niven.co.uk.
A venerable gentlemen's, ladies' and schools' outfitters located in the New Town.

Argentium F9
105 Rose St, t (0131) 225 8057.
A New Town shop selling hand-made contemporary Scottish and international jewellery.

Armstrongs G10
83 Grassmarket, t (0131) 220 5557.
A well-known vintage clothes
emporium. There's a second
branch at 64–66 Clerk Street
(*t (0131) 667 3056*).

Big Ideas G10
96 West Bow, t (0131) 226 2532,
w www.bigideasforladies.co.uk.
An Old Town shop specializing in
clothes for larger women.

Bill Baber G10
66 Grassmarket, t (0131) 225 3249,
w www.billbaber.com.
A shop/workshop in the Old Town,
selling bright handmade sweaters.

Corniche H9
2 Jeffrey St, t (0131) 556 3707.
Women's designerwear on the
Royal Mile, by the likes of Vivienne
Westwood, Yohji Yamamoto and
Comme des Garçons. Next door is
menswear by Gaultier, McQueen
and their ilk (*t (0131) 557 8333*).

Cruise I9
14 St Mary's St, t (0131) 556 2532.
A designer clothes paradise off
the Royal Mile. This main branch
sells jeans; there's another branch
at 94 George Street (*t (0131) 556
2532*) and a womenswear-only
store at 31 Castle Street (*t (0131)
220 4441*).

Cult Clothing H9
7–9 North Bridge, t (0131) 556 5003.
One of the most fashionable
streetwear shops in the city,
stocking labels such as Bench,
Freshjive, Komodo and Carhartt.

Extra Inch E9
12 William St, t (0131) 226 3303.
A West End boutique selling larger
sizes for women.

Geoffrey (Tailor)
Highland Crafts H9
57–59 High St, t (0131) 557 0256,
w www.geoffreykilts.co.uk.
Kilts and sporrans galore on the
Royal Mile.

Get Shirty F9
134 Rose St, t (0131) 220 4628,
w www.getshirty.com.
Shirts, ties and kilts and other
fairly formal menswear, plus a few
casual lines, in the New Town.

Grass Hatters G10
13 West Bow, t (0131) 229 0500.
An Old Town shop selling interesting hats.

Hamilton & Inches G9
87 George St, t (0131) 225 4898,
w www.hamiltonandinches.com.
An old-established jewellers,
silversmiths and clock specialists.

Hawick Cashmere Co G10
71–81 Grassmarket, t (0131) 225 8634,
w www.hawickcashmere.com.
Scarves, hats, skirts and dresses in
cashmere, lambswool and merino
are sold in this Old Town shop.

Herman Brown G10
151 West Port, t (0131) 228 2589,
w www.hermanbrown.co.uk.
Quirky, mainly women's second-
hand clothing, both retro and
modern, in very good condition,
plus jewellery and accessories.

Jigsaw F9
49 George St, t (0131) 225 4501.
Mid-priced, well-made
womenswear with its finger
firmly on the pulse of fashion.

Joseph Bonar G8
72 Thistle St, t (0131) 226 2811.
An antique jewellery shop in the
New Town.

Kinloch Anderson J4
Dock St, Leith, t (0131) 555 1390,
w www.kinlochanderson.com.
Bespoke and ready-to-wear kilts,
plus a variety of tartan accessories. There's a museum too.

McCalls of the Royal Mile H9
11 High St, t (0131) 557 3979,
w www.mccalls.co.uk.
A kilt hire company.

Montresor F8
35 St Stephen St, t (0131) 220 6877.
An antique and costume jewellery
shop in Stockbridge.

Number Two F8
2 St Stephen Place, t (0131) 225 6257.
A Stockbridge store selling own-
brand hand-knitted Fair Isle
jumpers and traditional Scottish
and modern British knitwear.

Ragamuffin I9
278 Canongate, t (0131) 557 6007.
A shop selling woolly jumpers and
cardigans, mainly for women, on
the Royal Mile.

The Rusty Zip H10
14 Teviot Place, t (0131) 226 4634.
An Old Town vintage fashion and
accessories outlet run by the
same people as Armstrongs.

Schuh G9
6 Frederick St, t (0131) 220 0290,
w www.schuh.co.uk.
A New Town branch of the fashionable Scottish women's, men's
and children's shoe chain.

Scoosh I9
30 St Mary's St, t (0131) 557 6600,
w www.scoosh.co.uk.
Eccentric and upbeat fashions 'for
mature women'.

Scottish Gems H9
24 High St, t (0131) 557 5731.
Modern and Celtic jewellery
designs on the Royal Mile.

Troon H8
1 York Place, t (0131) 557 4045.
Closed Mon.
Individualist women's clothes.

Walker and Slater G9
20 Victoria St, t (0131) 220 2636,
w www.walkerslater.co.uk.
Men's fashion, own brand and
made-to-measure, in the Old Town.

Whistles G9
97 George St, t (0131) 226 4398.
Distinctive, ultra-fashionable,
expensive women's clothing.

Department Stores

Harvey Nichols H8
*30–34 St Andrew Square, t (0131) 524
8388, w www.harveynichols.com.*
Though it doesn't sell the full
range of Harvey Nicks must-have
goodies (there's not much
bedding for example), this new
store in a converted bus station
stocks big fashion names such as
Prada and Gucci. Locals have also
been flocking to the Forth Floor
restaurant (*see p.165*) and the less
expensive bar and brasserie.

Jenners G9
48 Princes St, t (0131) 225 2442,
w www.jenners.com.
The granddaddy of them all, much
loved by locals but facing stiff
competition from Harvey Nicks.

John Lewis H8
St James Centre, t (0131) 556 9121,
w www.johnlewis.com.
The Edinburgh branch of the
British middle-class favourite.

Marks & Spencer G9
54 and 91 Princes St, t (0131) 225 2301,
w www.marks-and-spencer.co.uk.
Menswear, childrenswear and the
food hall at No.54, womenwswear
at No.91. There's another branch in
the Gyle Centre (*see* p.189).

Food and Drink

See also the renowned Italian
café/deli Valvona and Crolla, p.172.

Better Beverage Company E10
204 Morrison St, t (0131) 476 2600.
A highly regarded specialist tea
and coffee merchant.

Cadenheads Whisky Shop I9
172 Canongate, t (0131) 556 5864.
A huge stock of single malts and
blended whiskies, as well as some
rare finds.

Casey's I9
52 St Mary's St, t (0131) 556 6082.
A traditional confectioners with
jars of boiled sweets and the like.

Crombies of Edinburgh H8
97 Broughton St, t (0131) 557 0111,
w www.sausages.co.uk.
Some of the best sausages in the
world and a serious selection of
prime Scottish beef, pork, eggs,
poultry and game.

The Fudge House I9
197 Canongate, t (0131) 556 4172,
w www.fudgehouse.co.uk.
Raymond Disotto's famous Royal
Mile fudge shop and café.

Iain Mellis: Cheesemonger G9
30a Victoria St, t (0131) 226 6215,
w www.ijmellischeesemonger.com.
Fine cheeses sold in the heart of
the Old Town. There are other
branches of the shop at 205
Bruntsfield Place (*t (0131) 447
8889*), and at 6 Bakers Place in
Stockbridge (*t (0131) 225 6566*).

Mr Boni's F11
*4 Lochrin Buildings, off Leven
Street, t (0131) 229 5319.*
Very good ice cream sold by an old
family firm in Tollcross.

Nature's Gate I11
83 Clerk St, t (0131) 668 2067.
A wholefood store just east of The
Meadows.

Peter Green and Co G11
*37a Warrender Park Rd, t (0131)
229 5925.*
A reliable Scottish wine merchant
in Marchmont.

**Raeburn Fine Wine
and Flowers** E7
23 Comely Bank Rd, t (0131) 343 1159.
A well-respected Stockbridge
vintner and flower shop.

Real Foods H8
37 Broughton St, t (0131) 557 1911,
w www.realfoods.co.uk.
Wholesome foodstuffs, mostly
organic, in Broughton.

**Scotch Malt Whisky
Society** J5
*The Vaults, 87 Giles St, Leith, t 554
3451, w www.smws.com.*
The membership fee for the
SMWS (£75 for the first year, £25
thereafter) includes a £30 bottle
of Scotch and great deals on fine
malts, as well as the use of the
comfortable club-like members'
room and accommodation.

Health and Beauty

For a **late-night chemist**, *see* p.53.

Cheynes Hairdresser E9
*3 Drumsheugh Place, t (0131)
225 2234.*
The most central branch of the
local unisex salon chain.

Jo Malone G9
93 George St, t (0131) 478 8555,
w www.jomalone.co.uk.
Fragrance, skincare and scented
candles by the London beautician
extraordinaire. Hand and arm
massages are available, as are
individual skin consultations.

Lush G9
44 Princes St, t (0131) 557 3177,
w www.lush.co.uk.
Fresh handmade cosmetics and
bath ballistics made using essential oils and the like.

Napiers Herbalists H10
18 Bristo Place, t (0131) 225 5542,
w www.napiers.net.

Established in 1860, this Old Town
clinic and dispensary is the oldest
herbal medicine store in the UK
and the only one in Scotland.
There's another branch at 35
Hamilton Place in Stockbridge
(*t (0131) 315 2130*).

Neal's Yard Remedies G8
102 Hanover St, t (0131) 226 3223,
w www.nealsyardremedies.com.
A top-quality and justly renowned
herbal remedies and potions shop
with a therapy room.

ONE F10
*Sheraton Grand Hotel, 8 Conference
Square, t (0131) 221 7777, w www.
one-spa.com.*
A split-level, beech and glass spa
designed by Sir Terry Farrell and
offering a sophisticated selection
of therapies, plus a bio sauna and
outdoor hydropool.

Space NK G9
97–103 George St, t (0131) 225 6371,
w www.spacenk.co.uk.
A cutting-edge cosmetics store
selling brands that are usually
unavailable on the high street,
such as Kiehl's.

The Whole Works H9
Jackson's Close, t (0131) 225 8092,
w www.thewholeworks.co.uk.
An old-fashioned complementary
medicine centre on the Royal Mile.
By appointment only.

Interiors

The Adam Pottery F7
76 Henderson Row, t (0131) 557 3978.
Janet Adam's Stockbridge show-
room full of attractive handmade
stoneware and porcelain thrown
by herself and other ceramicists.

Anta Scotland H9
32 High St, t (0131) 557 8300,
w www.anta.co.uk.
Ceramics and textiles in a range of
modern tartan designs.

Bonhams Auctioneers F9
65 George St, t (0131) 225 2266,
w www.bonhams.com.
Anything and everything can go
under the hammer here; usually
it's fine art, jewellery, antiques and
collectables that are up for grabs.

Duncan & Reid G7
5 Tanfield, t (0131) 556 4591.
Interesting antiques and second-hand books in Canonmills.

Edinburgh Architectural Salvage Yard I4
Unit 6, Couper St, Leith, t (0131) 554 7077, w www.easy-arch-salv.co.uk.
Reclaimed fireplaces, church pews, stained glass, lights and suchlike.

Halibut and Herring F12
108 Bruntsfield Place, t (0131) 229 2669.
A quirky local bathroom products and accessories chain, with smelly soothing things aplenty, including the sought-after Aran aromatic bath range. Good giftboxes are another highlight. There are other central branches in Raeburn Place (t (0131) 332 5687) and West Bow (t (0131) 226 7472).

Inhouse F8
28 Howe St, t (0131) 225 2888.
Contemporary furniture and home accessories by the likes of Philippe Starck, Achille Castiglione and Charles Eames.

Mayfield Studios Off maps
14 Springvalley Gardens, t (0131) 466 7014.
A Marchmont pottery studio.

The Meadows Pottery I11
1a Summerhall Place, t (0131) 662 4064.
Junko Shibe and Paul Tebble throw a range of colourful pots and dishes on their premises just south of The Meadows.

Retro Interiors I9
36 St Mary's St, t (0131) 558 9090.
Closed Mon. No credit cards.
Two floors of household accessories and designer furnishings from the second half of the last century.

Robert Cresser G9
40 Victoria St, t (0131) 225 2181.
All you could ever need in the way of brooms and brushes is stocked in this Old Town shop.

Studio One Off maps
71 Morningside Rd, t (0131) 447 0452.
An upmarket store for cooks, selling ceramics, woodware, electrical goods, utensils and more.

The Whistling Tortoise F7
42a Hamilton Place, t (0131) 225 6365, w www.whistlingtortoise.com.
'Anything to make life easier' promises this Stockbridge store, whether it be extending grabs, corkscrews, non-slip bathmats or shooting sticks.

Markets

Farmers' Market F10
Castle Terrace.
Exceptional and interesting organic foods from local suppliers, on the first and third Saturday of every month (9am–2pm).

Indoor Sunday Market I9
New St.
A Sunday bric-a-brac and clothes market that takes place off the Royal Mile, lasting from 10am to about 4pm.

Ingliston Market Off maps
Next to Edinburgh Airport and the Royal Highland Centre.
An informal outdoor market held every Sunday from 10am onwards. The most interesting part is the car boot section.

Music

Avalanche Records H9
63 Cockburn St, t (0131) 225 3939.
New and second-hand indie, metal and punk CDs and LPs are sold here, as well as chart and dance music.

Blackfriars Folk Music Shop H9
49 Blackfriars St, t (0131) 557 3090, w www.blackfriarsmusic.com.
Scottish music and books on the subject, as well as instruments.

Coda H9
12 Bank St, t (0131) 622 7246, w www.codamusic.co.uk.
An Old Town folk and Scottish music specialist. Coda Music at Unit 14, Princes Mall (t (0131) 557 4694) stocks more general popular music.

Fopp H9
55 Cockburn St, t (0131) 220 0133, w www.fopp.co.uk.
A rock, pop and dance music shop on the Royal Mile.

McAlister Matheson F10
1 Grindlay Street, t (0131) 228 3827.
The best place to come for classical music and opera.

Ripping Music and Tickets H10
91 South Bridge, t (0131) 226 7010, w www.rippingrecords.com.
An Old Town rock music shop that also sells concert tickets.

Vinyl Villains I8
5 Elm Row, t (0131) 558 1170.
Second-hand records and CDs behind Calton Hill.

Shopping Centres

Edinburgh has its fair share of malls, and, though they may not be the most exciting of retail environments, the weather in the city often enhances their overall appeal.

Cameron Toll Shopping Centre Off maps
6 Lady Rd, t (0131) 666 2777, w www.camerontoll.co.uk.
To the south of the city centre, towards Craigmillar, this is Edinburgh's largest shopping centre, with a Sainsbury's supermarket and all the usual suspects.

Fort Kinnaird Shopping Park Off maps
Newcraighall Road, t (0131) 669 4784, w www.fortkinnaird.co.uk.
Five miles out of town off the A1, this is the UK's largest shopping park, with 55 big-name outlets on an open-air site, clustered around a 10-screen multiplex cinema and with various food outlets.

Gyle Centre Off maps
South Gyle Broadway, t (0131) 539 9000, w www.gyleshopping.com.
Way out west on the way to the airport, the Gyle Centre contains a Safeway supermarket, a branch of Marks and Spencer, and host of high-street names.

Ocean Terminal I3
Ocean Drive, Leith, w www.oceanterminal.com.
A relatively recent arrival on the waterfront at Leith, Sir Terence Conran's multi-million-pound redevelopment of the dockside

contains the obligatory Conran restaurant (*see* Zinc Bar and Grill, p.172), a multiplex cinema (*see* p.184), and more than 50 shops, including branches of Debenhams, Bhs and M&S Simply Food and smaller concerns such as Schuh (*see* p.187). It's also home to the mighty Former Royal Yacht *Britannia* (*see* p.118).

Princes Mall H9
Princes St, t (0131) 557 3759.
A relatively small mall but the most central (it's above Waverley Station), Princes Mall is packed with high-street clothes and jewellery shops and fast-food outlets, including a branch of Harry Ramsden's fish and chip shop (*see* p.171).

St James Centre H8
Leith St, t (0131) 557 0050, w www.thestjames.com.
A notoriously ugly, central shopping mall that's home to the Edinburgh branch of John Lewis (*see* p.188) and a wealth of high-street names.

Specialist Retailers

Alexander Leven F11
31 Leven St, t (0131) 229 0000.
An independent specialist tobacconist in Tollcross, selling pipes, cigars and rare cigarettes for those who still smoke.

Henderson Art Shop E7
28a Raeburn Place, t (0131) 332 7800.
A Stockbridge supplier of oil paints and sketching materials.

Mr Wood's Fossils G10
5 Cowgatehead, Grassmarket, t (0131) 220 1344, w www.mrwoodsfossils.co.uk.
Long-dead things, mainly found in limestone, costing anything from £1 to £2,000.

Sports and Outdoor Pursuits

Blacks Outdoor Leisure G9
24 Frederick St, t (0131) 225 8686, w www.outdoorgroup.com.
Hiking clothes and accessories for camping. A basic alternative to Graham Tiso (*see* below).

Boardwise F10
4 Lady Lawson St, t (0131) 229 5887, w www.boardwise.com.
An Old Town purveyor of boards of the snow, surf and skate variety.

Graham Tiso F9
123–25 Rose St, t (0131) 225 9486, w www.tiso.co.uk.
Camping, hiking, skiiing and mountaineering gear in the New Town. A specialist, highly regarded shop for people who take the great outdoors seriously.

John Dickson G9
21 Frederick St, t (0131) 225 4218, w www.gunandline.co.uk.
A New Town hunting, shooting and fishing gear shop.

Momentum Surf Shop F11
22 Bruntsfield Place, t (0131) 229 6665.
Skate and surfboard clothing, plus all the accessories.

Wind Things G10
11 Cowgatehead, Grassmarket, t (0131) 622 7032, w www.windthings.co.uk.
An Old Town shop stocking kites, frisbees and juggling equipment.

Sports and
Green Spaces

Spectator Sports

The Scots are even more obsessed with **football** than the rest of Britain, and Edinburgh is no exception. Its teams may not have the worldwide reputation of Glasgow's Rangers or Celtic, but they are followed just as passionately. Watching a match at either Tynecastle or Easter Road is bound to be memorable, if not necessarily for the quality of the football then certainly for the fans' commitment to the game, and thankfully not at all for the reasons that have made football crowds notorious.

Rugby arouses similar emotions, but they're only really in evidence at the internationals held at Murrayfield Stadium. The Scottish rivalry with the English is particularly vocalized.

Golf has a long and venerable history in the city, which is home to possibly the oldest golf club in the world, and there are some 30 courses within the city boundaries.

Football

Edinburgh has two teams in the Scottish Premier League: **Heart of Midlothian** and **Hibernian**. Heart of Midlothian (Hearts), founded in 1873, seems to have been named after a dancehall not far from where the city's Tolbooth, the 'Heart of Midlothian', once stood. A heart in the cobblestones in the High Street still shows where the Tolbooth was located.

In November 1914, the entire first team and many of their supporters volunteered for military service. Of the 16 players who signed up, six did not return – they are commemorated at the club's war memorial at Haymarket. Hearts won the Scottish League, the Scottish Cup and the League Cup (twice) in the late 1950s, and in 1998 they again won the Scottish Cup, beating Glasgow Rangers in the final.

Hibernian (Hibs) were formed two years after Hearts and drew support from Edinburgh's Irish community. Though rivalry with Hearts is keen, it generally lacks the sectarian edge that is still found in Glasgow between Rangers and Celtic.

Hibs' golden age was the post-1945 period, when they won three league championships in five years. Their stars were forwards – the 'Famous Five' (Gordon Smith, Bobby Johnstone, Lawrie Reilly, Eddie Turnbull and Willie Ormond) who now have a stand named after them. Hibs were relegated in 1998 – the year Hearts won the Scottish Cup – but won the First Division with a record number of points in 1999 to return to the Premier League.

Major Events

At the time of writing, Hearts and Hibs both play in the **Scottish Premier League**. The season runs from the end of July to May, with a winter break in January. Games are usually played on Saturdays at 3pm, although there are some on midweek evenings and Sundays. Both stadia have shops.

Major Venues

Easter Road Stadium K7
Albion Place, t (0131) 661 2159, tickets t (0131) 661 1875, w www.hibs.co.uk. The home ground of Hibernian FC.

Tynecastle Stadium Off maps *Gorgie Rd, t (0131) 200 7200, tickets t (0131) 200 7201, w www.heartsfc.co.uk.* The home ground of Heart of Midlothian FC. Tours of the stadium are available.

Rugby Union

Rougher and more complex than football, rugby union is played with an oval ball, features 15-man teams and allows hand as well as foot contact. The **Six Nations Championship** is competed for every spring by England, France, Ireland, Scotland, Wales and Italy (who in 2000 joined what used to be the Five Nations Championship). Scotland won the final Five Nations Championship in 1999.

Major Events

Six Nations games are played at Murrayfield on varying dates in spring, and the **Calcutta Cup** game between England and Scotland – the oldest international rugby fixture in the world – is played there in even years (in odd years it's at Twickenham).

Major Venues

Murrayfield Stadium Off maps *Roseburn St, t (0131) 346 5000.* The home of the Scottish Rugby Union and venue for Six Nations matches and friendlies, a mile to the west of Haymarket Station.

Golf

Major Events

The **Open** visits Scotland on a regular basis, often using the seaside course at Muirfield, home of the Honourable Company of Edinburgh Golfers, in the town of Gullane (see p.144). The courses at St Andrews and Troon are also Open venues. For the most up-to-date information, see *www.opengolf.com.*

The **Scottish Open** is a newer competition that began in 1996 and is played in stunning surroundings on the shores of Loch Lomond just north of Glasgow. The modern course is set on the ancestral estate of the chiefs of Clan Colquhoun, which is also home to two sites of Special Scientific Interest, two scheduled ancient monuments and 10 listed buildings, including the ruins of Rossdhu Castle, behind the 18th-green and Rossdhu House, the course clubhouse. *See www.thescottishopenatlochlomond.com* for information.

Cricket

Cricket has been popular in Scotland for more than two centuries. Notable Edinburgh clubs include Carlton, Grange and Watsonians. For information on matches call the **Scottish Cricket Union** (*t (0131) 317 7247*).

Horse Racing

Musselburgh Races Off maps
*Linkfield Rd, Musselburgh, t (0131)
665 2859, f (0131) 653 2083.*
Scotland's oldest racecourse, five
miles east of the city, is classed as
Class D for Flat and National Hunt
racing, and is 10 furlongs in length
with a 4 furlong run-in.

Cycling

Edinburgh boasts one of the UK's
best competitive cycling teams,
which practises at theVelodrome
at **Meadowbank Stadium** (*139
London Rd, t (0131) 652 0895*).

Activities

Scottish Sports Council
*Caledonia House, 1 Redheughs Rigg,
t (0131) 317 7200.*
Several Scottish sport associations, such as athletics and
basketball, have their headquarters here, and staff deal with
sports queries in general.

Sports Centres

Public sports centres, pools and
golf courses have peak and off-
peak times when different prices
apply. The **Leisure Card** gives
cheaper prices for most facilities,
but is aimed at residents, costing
£29 (£5 concessions) for a year.

**Meadowbank Sports
Centre** L8
*139 London Rd, t (0131) 661 5351.
Open Mon 9.30am–11pm, Tues–
Sun 9am–11pm.*
Close to Meadowbank Stadium,
this has an athletics track, indoor
halls, a climbing wall, a gym, all-
weather pitches, squash courts, a
cricket/archery range and an aerobics studio. Classes are available
for other activities, including
badminton and martial arts.

Cycling

Mountain biking is big in
Edinburgh; enthusiasts head out
to the Pentland Hills for some

challenging climbs. Bikes can be
hired at the following outlets:

BikeTrax F11
*11 Lochrin Place, t (0131) 228 6633/
3686, w www.biketrax.co.uk.*
A well-established Tollcross sales
and rental outlet, with hire
costing from £10 a day. Also offers
touring packages, from Edinburgh
day trips to Highland tours.

**Great Bikes,
No Bull/Recycling** J7
*25 Iona St, t (0131) 467 7775/
553 1130.*
Touring and off-road bikes for hire
for £5–20 a day or £25–50 a week.
A £50–100 deposit is required.

Golf

In 1744 the Honourable Company
of Edinburgh Golfers (possibly the
world's oldest golf club) played its
first competition at Leith Links.
Meanwhile, the Edinburgh Burgess
Golfing Society has records dating
from 1773, and the Bruntsfield
Links Golf Club dates from 1787.
Both played initially on Bruntsfield
Links, to the south of the city and
not a true links (a seaside course)
at all. Their clubhouse, the Golf
Tavern (*see p.178*), is still there,
although much altered.

The clubs moved to Musselburgh,
east of the city, then to adjacent
courses west of it, at Barnton and
Davidson's Mains. In the mid 19th
century, the nine-hole course at
Musselburgh held six Open championships, but in 1891 the oldest
club, the Honourable Company,
moved to Muirfield and took the
Open with them (*see p.192*). In
recent years the Musselburgh
course has been modified to meet
the needs of the adjacent racecourse, despite the outcry of
golfers around the world.

A **discount golf pass** available
from the Edinburgh and Lothians
Tourist Board gives discounts at
20 courses in Lothians, four of
them in Edinburgh. There are
several private golf clubs, many of
which welcome visitors. Note that
Leith Links and Bruntsfield Links
are not proper golf courses.

Braid Hills Golf Course Off maps
*Braid Hills Approach, t (0131)
447 6666.*

Carrick Knowe Golf Course
Off maps
Glendevon Park, t (0131) 337 1096.

Craigentinny Golf Course
Off maps
*Craigentinny Avenue, Restalrig,
t (0131) 554 7501.*

Lothianburn Golf Club Off maps
106a Biggar Rd, t (0131) 445 5067.

**Melville Golf Course,
Range & Shop** Off maps
*South Melville, Lasswade, t (0131)
663 8038.*

Musselburgh Links Off maps
*Balcarres Road, Musselburgh,
t (0131) 665 5438.*

Portobello Golf Course Off maps
*Stanley St, Portobello, t (0131)
669 4361.*

Silverknowes Golf Club
Off maps
*Silverknowes Parkway, t (0131)
336 3843.*

Gyms

If you're in Edinburgh for any
length of time, enquire about
membership rates at the
following central health clubs.

Bannatyne Health Club G8
43 Queen St, t (0131) 225 8384.

Carlton Club H9
19 North Bridge, t (0131) 472 3133.

Claremont Health Club H7
*53 East Claremont St, t (0131) 557
0349.*

The Edinburgh Club I8
*1–2 Hillside Crescent, t (0131)
556 8845.*

Fitness First G8
*30 Abercromby Place, t (0131)
558 7887.*

Holmes Place H8
*Omni Centre, Greenside Place,
t (0131) 550 1650, w www.
holmesplace.co.uk.*

The Ladies Club I7
*15-17 Windsor St Lane, t (0131)
558 9200.*

Lady in Leisure F10
57–59 Bread St, t (0131) 228 8990.

**Pelican Health
& Leisure Club** F9
*Roxburghe Hotel, 38 Charlotte
Square, t (0131) 225 3921.*

**Royal Terrace Health
& Leisure Club** I8
22 Royal Terrace, t (0131) 556 5879.

Horse Riding

**Pentland Hills Icelandic
Trekking Centre** Off maps
*Windy Gowl Farm, Carlops, t 01968
661095, w www.phicelandics.co.uk.*
Off-road riding over spectacular
Border countryside, on the UK's
largest herd of Icelandic horses.

Indoor Rock Climbing

There's also a climbing wall at
the **Meadowbank Sports Centre**,
see p.193.

Alien Rock G3
*Old St Andrew's Church, 8a Pier
Place, Newhaven, t (0131) 552 7211,
w www.alienrock.co.uk.*
A top indoor climbing centre.
The recent extension at 37 West
Bowling Green Street (*t (0131) 555
3650*) boasts Scotland's biggest
indoor bouldering wall.

Jogging

Edinburgh could have been
designed with joggers in mind:
the pavements are wide, the hills
are challenging, and most of its
green spaces can be easily linked
together on a jog.

The most popular jogging spot
is **Holyrood Park** and its peak,
Arthur's Seat (*see below*). Other
refreshing routes include the
Water of Leith footpath (*see
p.130*), the **Hermitage of Braid** in
Morningside, and **Princes Street
Gardens** (*see below*).

Skiing and Ice Skating

Midlothian Ski Centre Off maps
Hillend, Biggar Rd, t (0131) 445 4433.
An artificial ski slope in the south
of the city.

Murrayfield Ice Rink Off maps
*13 Riversdale Crescent, t (0131)
337 6933.*
A rink west of the city centre, next
to Murrayfield Stadium.

Swimming and Watersports

See also **Leith Waterworld**, p.197.

Swimming Pools

Glenogle Swim Centre F7
3 Glenogle Rd, t (0131) 343 6376.
Tiled Victorian baths in Stockbridge.

Portobello Swim Centre
Off maps
*57 Promenade, Portobello, t (0131)
669 6888.*
A refurbished Victorian pool in the
city's foremost seaside resort.

Royal Commonwealth Pool J11
21 Dalkeith Rd, t (0131) 667 7211.
Built for the 1970 Commonwealth
Games on the edges of Holyrood
Park, this has a 50m pool, a diving
pool, a children's pool, flumes, a
pulse centre gym, aerobics facilities and a crèche.

Watersports

**Port Edgar Sailing School
and Marina** Off maps
*Shore Rd, South Queensferry,
t (0131) 331 3330.*
Windsurfing, canoeing and
sailing facilities.

Tennis

**Craiglockhart Tennis and
Sports Centre** Off maps
*177 Colinton Rd, t (0131) 444 1969
(tennis), t (0131) 443 0101
(other sports).*
The courts at this sports hall are
used for the summer Scottish
Championships (it's the HQ of the
Scottish Lawn Tennis Association).
Gym, squash, badminton and
table tennis facilities and aerobics
classes are also available.

Yoga and Pilates

Some **gyms**, including the new
Holmes Place (*see p.193*), also offer
Pilates classes.

**The Brigid McCarthy
Pilates Studio** E9
*16 Canning St, t (0131) 221 1131,
w www.mccarthypilates.co.uk.*
'Matwork' (non-equipment-based
Pilates) with an emphasis on individual programmes.

Edinburgh Pilates Centre F9
45a George St, t (0131) 226 1815.
A New Town facility offering
Pilates classes for all levels.

The Yoga Centre G11
*1 Meadow Place, t (0131) 221 9697,
w www.theyogacentre.co.uk.*
Specializing in astanga vinyasa,
this is Europe's largest purpose-
built yoga studio.

Green Spaces

Braid Hills and Hermitage
Off maps
See p.121.
With great views over the polite
suburbs of Morningside, the Braid
Hills provide good gentle walks on
the city's outskirts. At their feet,
the Braid burn winds through a
wooded dell laced with nature
trails, known as the Hermitage.
The path beside the stream, which
is particularly lovely in autumn,
eventually leads up onto Blackford
Hill and the Royal Observatory,
another great viewpoint.

**Calton Hill and
Regents Gardens** I8
See p.99.
Dotted with a striking mish-mash
of monuments and follies, Calton
Hill is one of the city's best viewpoints. During the day the
relatively easy stroll up from
Waterloo Place affords a
panoramic overview of the new
Scottish Parliament building
beneath Arthur's Seat, Princes
Street heading dead straight west,
and the Firth of Forth and blue
hills of Fife glimmering off to the
north. At dusk it becomes a faintly
threatening gay cruising ground.

Corstorphine Hill Off maps
See p.122.
Home to Edinburgh Zoo,
Corstorphine Hill is a short bus
ride from the western end of

Princes Street. One of the city's less well-known green spaces, it allows for woodland walks that give sudden views of the Firth and its bridges to the north and to the south towards the Pentland Hills, snow-capped in winter. There's a spooky folly tower in the middle of the woods, constructed in memory of Sir Walter Scott.

Cramond Island Off maps
See p.123.
This rocky little island situated in the Firth of Forth can be reached across a half mile of tidal causeway and makes for an excellent picnic destination after an inspection of Edinburgh's only Roman remains in the attractive little village of Cramond itself. There are great views of the bridges to the west and docks to the east, but be careful not to be cut off by the rapid tide, especially in high winds.

Holyrood Park and Arthur's Seat J9–K11
See p.128.
A royal park since the days of King James, Holyrood Park is home to Edinburgh's extinct volcano, Arthur's Seat. Rough grass and gorse cover its rocky flanks, crisscrossed by paths that give some of the most wonderful views of the city. Explore prehistoric geology, spot rare wildlife and enjoy breezy strolls around the city's most surprising natural asset.

Lauriston Castle Off maps
See p.123.
The gardens of Lauriston Castle, a few miles west of the city centre, provide charming walks along the shores of the Firth of Forth, with rhodendrons and azaleas bursting with colour in season. Little-changed since the early 20th century, the gardens can be visited even when the house is closed.

The Meadows and Bruntsfield Links F11–H11
See p.87.
A flat area of playing fields to the south of the city centre, The Meadows are a popular spot for informal ball games. The site of the city's Great Exhibition in the mid-19th century, it has imposing stone gateposts giving on to tree-lined avenues and a riot of blossom in the spring. A little further south, the sloping greens of Bruntsfield Links, a city centre pitch and putt course (*see* p.193), reputedly cover the site of an old plague pit.

Pentland Hills Off maps
See p.125.
The most serious hills within easy reach of the city, the Pentlands are good for wild and lonely walks with nothing but sheep and birds for company, and afford views over chilly reservoirs. Some parts are popular with mountain bikers, and the dry ski slope of the Midlothian Ski Centre (*see* p.194)

just north of Robert Louis Stevenson's childhood holiday home at Swanston is a prominent landmark, especially when floodlit at night.

Princes Street Gardens F9–G9
See p.92.
Formed by the draining of the Nor'Loch in the 18th century, these formal gardens in the middle of town form the south side of Princes Street. West Princes Street Gardens, home to the Ross Bandstand, a café and the graveyards of St Cuthbert's and St John's churches, are the largest. Bridges over the railway lead to more secluded spots beneath the castle crag. East of The Mound and the National Gallery, East Princes Street Gardens are much smaller but boast superb views up to the High Street from the Scott Monument.

Royal Botanic Garden E6–F6
See p.113.
Just north of the New Town, the Botanic Garden is a heaven for horticulturalists but also provides great views of the city skyline and is the setting for some delightful walks. As well as the glasshouses, rockeries and Chinese garden, there's a reasonable canteen-style café and an impressive contemporary art gallery in Inverleith House at the heart of the gardens.

Children's and Teenagers' Edinburgh

Children

Despite its traditionally rather dour reputation, Edinburgh is actually ideal for kids, as its citizens have long appreciated. As well as a clutch of world-class attractions that are largely tailored to the interests of the under-10s – notably, Our Dynamic Earth, Deep Sea World and Edinburgh Zoo – the city as a whole is very child-friendly. Most restaurants are used to catering for kids; many of the museums, especially the Museum of Scotland and the People's Story, are well practised at keeping them interested, and the city's open townscape and wide streets make it easy to keep track of little ones during exploratory walks.

Museums and Attractions

The following attractions listed in the main neighbourhood or Day Trips chapters also appeal to children as well as adults: **Brass Rubbing Centre** (see p.72), **Camera Obscura and World of Illusions** (see p.64), the **Museum of Childhood** (see p.72), the **Museum of Flight** (see p.146), **Newhaven Heritage Museum** (see p.119), the **Royal Museum** (see p.84) and the **Museum of Scotland** (see p.85), and the **Royal Observatory** (see p.121).

Deep Sea World Off maps
North Queensferry, t (01383) 411 411, w www.deepseaworld.com.
Open *April–Oct daily 10am–6pm, Nov–March Mon–Fri 11am–5pm, Sat, Sun 10am–6pm;* **adm** *£7.50, children £5.50 (special family rates also available).*
Though this is some way outside the city in North Queensferry (see p.125), the ride here across the Forth Rail Bridge is a thrill in itself. Scotland's second most popular tourist attraction, it has fearsome sandtiger sharks and conger eels, plus the world's longest underwater tunnel, at 367ft.

Edinburgh Butterfly and Insect World Off maps
In Dobbies Gardening World, Lasswade, t (0131) 663 4932, w www.edinburgh-butterfly-world.co.uk.
Open *daily April–Oct 10am–5.30pm, Nov–March 10am–5pm;* **adm** *£4.35, children aged 3–15 £3.35 (special family rates also available).*
Huge butterflies and moths, 16ft pythons and free-roaming iguanas are just some of the beasties on show here. The main attraction is the handling sessions of pythons, millipedes and spiders, at noon and 3pm every day. The Edinburgh Bird of Prey Centre is also in Dobbies Gardening World.

Edinburgh Castle G9
See p.59.
The firing of the One O'Clock Gun is always a hit with kids.

Edinburgh Dungeon H9
31 Market St, t (0131) 240 1000, w www.edinburghdungeon.com.
Open *daily April–Oct 10am–5pm, Nov–March 11am–4pm;* **adm** *£9.50, children aged 4–14 £6.50.*
The dungeon offers a noisy 85-minute promenade through the darker side of the city, with grim displays and a lot of shrieking.

Edinburgh Zoo Off maps
Corstorphine Rd, t (0131) 334 9171, w www.edinburghzoo.org.uk.
Open *April–Sept Mon–Sat 9am–6pm and Sun 9.30am–6pm, Oct–March Mon–Sat 9am–4.30pm and Sun 9.30am–4.30pm;* **adm** *£7.50, children aged 3–14 £4.50.*
This spectacularly sited zoo with its view of the Pentland Hills is famous for its penguins (fed daily at 2pm from March to October). There are also rhinos, lots of monkeys, an 'African safari' with a zebra and an antelope, and a new otter enclosure. It's even open on Christmas Day.

Gorgie City Farm Off maps
Gorgie Rd, t (0131) 623 7031. **Open** *daily March–Oct 9.30am–4.30pm, Nov–Feb 9.30am–4pm;* **adm** *free.*
A very popular attraction among younger children, who get the chance to go 'aaah' over small animals and livestock.

Leith Waterworld J5
377 Easter Rd, t (0131) 555 6000.
Open *summer daily 10am–7pm, winter Fri–Sun 10am–5pm;* **adm** *£3.20, children over 5 £2.20.*
Slides, flumes, wave machines and other state-of-the-art aquatic thrills and spills.

Our Dynamic Earth J9
Holyrood Rd, t (0131) 550 7800, w www.dynamicearth.co.uk.
Open *April–Oct daily 10am–6pm (last adm 4.50pm), Nov–March Wed–Sat 10am–5pm (last adm 3.50pm); closed 24–26 Dec, 31 Dec;* **adm** *£8.45, children over 5 £4.95.*
In the shadow of Arthur's Seat, beneath Scotland's very own little 'dome', this high-tech audiovisual celebration of the earth's geology is a hit with kids, who can count down to their descent in 'the time machine' elevator, get shaken on an earthquake simulator, and gaze in wonder at wraparound polar phenomena. These 'experiences' are part of the timed guided tours, after which you can explore the galleries – six signposted areas telling the story of our natural environment – at your leisure. The climaxes are a simulated rainforest, complete with tropical downpours and twitching snakes, and the biosphere: images from the past few millennia projected on to a planetarium-style dome giving a salutary lesson in ecological and humanitarian awareness.

The Outdoors

The **Royal Botanic Garden** (see p.113) is a delightful, dog-free zone in which toddlers can safely ramble. Also in central Edinburgh, **Calton Hill** (see p.99) and the **Scott Monument** (see p.96) afford stunning views of the surrounds.

To the west, **Corstorphine Hill**, home to **Edinburgh Zoo** (see above), is a good place for woodland walks and also provides splendid vistas north towards the Firth and south towards the Pentland Hills. To the north of it, **Cramond Island** (see p.123), with its ruined fortifications and the possibility of being marooned, makes a great destination for the over-5s. Further into the Forth, the ruined abbey on **Inchcolm Island** (see p.126) is a similarly wonderful place for kids to explore.

To the east, **Holyrood Park** (see p.128) is perfect if you have energetic children who need to let off steam, though Arthur's Seat is challenging. Blackford Hill, home to the child-orientated **Royal Observatory** (see p.121), is an easier climb with views that are almost as wonderful. The nearby **Hermitage of Braid** (see p.121) is good for educational nature walks.

Further afield, **Seacliff** (take the A198 to Dirleton) is a lovely bay with dramatic views of **Bass Rock** and the spooky sandstone ruins of **Tantallon Castle** (see p.145). The **Scottish Seabird Centre** (see p.145) in nearby North Berwick relays live pictures of puffins, gannets and the like on Bass Rock.

Of the several **beaches** within easy travelling distance of Edinburgh, the best is probably **Portobello** (see p.120), with its donkeys, funfair and promenade.

Festivals

See also the **Scottish International Storytelling Festival**, p.42.

Scottish International Children's Festival
Information: 45a George St, EH2 2HT, t (0131) 225 8050, f (0131) 225 6440, w www.imaginate.org.uk. Date last wk May–1st wk June. Britain's biggest performing arts festival for children (roughly 3–12-year-olds), including shows by the world's leading children's theatre companies. The event takes place in Inverleith Park.

Restaurants and Cafés

The majority of Edinburgh eateries are used to dealing with children and happy to do so; in our 'Eating Out' chapter (see p.158) we have indicated where a restaurant or café offers a separate kids'

menu, and where an establishment is child-friendly in general.

In addition to the places listed below, **blue bar café** (see p.170), **The Hub** (see p.65) and **Mamma's** (see p.163) are particularly recommended for those with kids in tow.

Giuliano's on the Shore J4
1 Commercial St, Leith, t (0131) 554 5272. Open daily noon–10.30pm. This no-nonsense Italian restaurant specializing in seafood is especially good with kids. Accordion music is played from Monday to Wednesday.

Umberto's I5
2 Bonnington Rd Lane, Leith, t (0131) 554 1314; wheelchair accessible and toilet. Open Mon–Sat noon–2pm, 5–10pm, Sun noon–7pm. Payment: DC not accepted. Umberto's first-floor family bistro (the ground floor offers serious Italian-Scottish food) has won the District Council's award for the most child-friendly restaurant in the city for several years running.

Babysitting

Edinburgh Creche Co-op
297 Easter Rd, t (0131) 553 2116. Childminders (registered with and vetted by Disclosure Scotland) to look after your baby or children in your hotel room. About £12 an hour.

Reference

Child Friendly Guide to Edinburgh
The district council publishes this free booklet, which is available from most bookshops.

Children's Library
Next door to the Central Library on George IV Bridge, t (0131) 242 8027. Open Mon and Wed 1–8pm, Tues, Thurs and Fri 10am–5pm, Sat 9am–1pm.

Edinburgh for Under Fives, A Handbook for Parents
A veritable mine of information, published by local members of the National Childbirth Trust and designed as much for residents as visitors. Available from most bookshops, priced £5.95.

Take the Kids Travelling
(Helen Truszkowski, Cadogan)
General information on roaming with babies and children, available in good bookshops (£12.99).

Teenagers

13–18-year-olds are unlikely to get bored during a trip to Edinburgh. The city's fairly hard-nosed attitude is generally appreciated by the age group as a whole, while most attractions are mercifully free of patronizing attitudes towards younger visitors; the **Museum of Scotland** (see p.85) is a shining example of this, especially with regard to the lower teens. Meanwhile, the huge number of **students** in the city is likely to thrill and inspire the top end of the age range.

Edinburgh Castle (see p.59) is likely to impress everyone, with its spectacular views and hidden corners, as well as its National War Memorial and military museums, while the holographic tricks at the nearby **Camera Obscura** (see p.64) will appeal to teenage boys. Mature girls might prefer the **Georgian House** (see p.102) in Charlotte Square or the city's Baroque graveyards: try **Dean Cemetery** (see p.111) or the **Old Calton Burial Ground** (see p.98) for size.

Teenagers are also likely to appreciate bohemian **Stockbridge** (see p.112), which boasts a range of quirky shops. To the southwest, the Surrealist art on display at the **Dean Gallery** (see p.111) generally proves a hit with anyone over 15, while to the northeast **Lady Haig's Poppy Factory** (see p.134), where former servicemen make the paper poppies that commemorate the world wars, makes for an unusual outing.

Leith (see p.118) is also a good bet, with the **Former Royal Yacht Britannia** and **Ocean Terminal** allowing for readily accessible and enjoyable days out for teenagers of both sexes.

Gay and Lesbian Edinburgh

With an estimated 15,000 to 20,000 gays and lesbians living here, Edinburgh has a vibrant gay community. Much of the action centres on the 'Pink Triangle', the area between Broughton Street, Calton Hill and Drummond Place. Calton Hill is popular for cruising, especially at sunset, but it's dangerous after dark; it's better to stick to Regent Road and London Road, though attacks on gay men have been known there too. Warriston Cemetery is quite a safe cruising ground during the day but not after dark.

Scotland's annual gay pride march alternates between Edinburgh (odd years) and Glasgow (even years). Scotsgay (w www.scotsgay.co.uk) is the best place to find out what's going on throughout the rest of the year, not just on the scene but also in quieter parts of town.

Organizations and Helplines

Edinburgh Lesbian, Gay and Bisexual Centre H8
60 Broughton St, t (0131) 478 7069. This centre provides meeting and noticeboard space for a number of les/bi/gay organizations. Private mailboxes are available.

Equality Network H8
58a Broughton St, t 07020 933952. A campaigning group for lesbian and gay issues.

Lothian Gay and Lesbian Switchboard
t (0131) 556 4049, w www.lgls.org. Operates 7.30–10pm nightly.

Lothian Lesbian Line
t (0131) 557 0751.
The Lesbian Line operates from Monday to Thursday from 7.30pm to 10pm.

Solas HIV/AIDS Information Centre J8
2–4 Abbeymount, t (0131) 661 0982, w www.waverleycare.org.
Open 9pm–5pm.
An HIV/AIDS support and information centre with a friendly café (see below).

Accommodation

Amaryllis F11
21 Gilmore Place, t (0131) 229 3293, w www.amaryllisguesthouse.com.
Payment: no DC or AmEx.
A gay-friendly guesthouse in Fountainbridge, with five double rooms costing £50 a night.

Armadillo F11
12 Gilmore Place, t (0131) 229 6457.
Payment: no DC or AmEx.
Another Fountainbridge guesthouse that welcomes gay couples, charging £50 a night for a double room. It also has a refurbished self-catering flat sleeping 4 people for a minimum booking of 3 nights.

Garland Guest House I6
48 Pilrig St, Leith, t (0131) 554 4205, w www.garlands.demon.co.uk.
Payment: no DC or AmEx.
A Leith guesthouse welcoming gay and straight couples and singles. Doubles are £90 a night in the high season, £65 in the low season.

Mansfield House Guesthouse G8
57 Dublin St, t (0131) 556 7980.
Payment: no DC or AmEx.
An exclusively gay and lesbian B&B in the New Town, with double rooms for £50 (£90 for superior rooms).

Cafés and Restaurants

Black Bo's (see p.162) is another very gay-friendly eatery.

Blue Moon Café H8
36 Broughton St, t (0131) 556 2788.
Open Mon–Fri 11am–10pm, Sat and Sun 9.30am–10pm.
This long-established gay-run café in Broughton welcomes all comers (including kids, for whom there's a special menu). It serves good-value toasted sandwiches, soups and light meals. Local artists' work adorns the walls.

Claremont Restaurant and Bar H6
135 East Claremont St, t (0131) 556 5662. Open bar Mon–Sat 11am–1am, Sun 12.30pm–1am; restaurant Mon–Wed 11.30am–2.30pm and 6–10pm, Thurs–Sat 11.30am–10pm, Sun 12.30–10pm.
Gay-owned and renowned for its courteous service and comfort, the Claremont offers good food and men-only nights on the first and third Saturdays of the month (from 8pm).

Easy Internet Café F9
58 Rose St, t (0131) 220 3580.
Open Mon–Sat 7am–11pm, Sun 8am–11pm.
A large New Town internet café popular with gay men.

Sala H8
60 Broughton St, t (0131) 478 7069.
Open daily 11am–11pm.
Internet access and decent food beneath the Lesbian, Gay and Bisexual Centre (see above). The basement houses Massage for Health, a gay massage parlour.

Solas Café J8
2–4 Abbeymount, t (0131) 661 0982. Open Mon, Wed and Fri–Sun 11am–4pm, Tues and Thurs 11am–7.30pm.
Home-made food for both vegetarians and carnivores is served up in the café of the Solas HIV/AIDS Information Centre (see above) behind Calton Hill.

Web 13 Internet Café F10
13 Bread St, t (0131) 229 8883.
Open Mon–Fri 10am–8pm, Sat 10am–6pm, Sun noon–6pm.
An informal mixed cybercafé just beyond the Old Town, with friendly staff.

Pubs and Bars

Frenchie's Bar F9
89 Rose St Lane North, t (0131) 225 7651. Open Mon–Sat 1pm–1am, Sun 2pm–midnight.
The original Edinburgh gay bar, situated in the New Town, has a daily happy hour (6–8pm).

Habana H8
22 Greenside Place, t (0131) 558 1270. Open Mon–Sat noon–1am, Sun 12.30pm–1am.
A popular pre-club bar close to the Edinburgh Playhouse, good for meeting people.

Holyrood Tavern I9
9a Holyrood Rd, **t** *(0131) 556 5044.*
Open *daily noon–12.30am.*
An rare gay-friendly real ale dispensary (CAMRA's Lesbian and Gay Real Ale Drinkers meet here on the first Monday of the month), this scruffy pub does reasonably priced food. Goths meet every Wednesday from 9pm (all welcome).

Laughing Duck F8
24 Howe St, **t** *(0131) 220 2376.*
Open *Mon–Wed noon–11pm, Thurs and Sun noon–midnight, Fri and Sat noon–1am.*
The New Town's most prominent and popular gay pub has been through various manifestations in its time, most recently as the Oirish theme pub Fibber Magee's. Now it's out with the fake snug cubicles and in with a cream paint job. The atmosphere is lively and there's loud music. Popular club nights take place downstairs. Food is served until 7.30pm.

New Town Bar G8
26B Dublin St, **t** *(0131) 538 7775.* **Open** *Mon–Thurs noon–1am, Fri–Sat noon–2am, Sun 12.30pm–1am.*
A men-only dive bar. On Fridays and Saturdays there's a downstairs bar with a resident DJ from 10pm to 2am.

Planet Out I8
6 Baxter's Place, off Leith Walk,
t *(0131) 524 0061.* **Open** *daily 4pm–1am.*
Formerly called Route 66, this friendly, laidback pub located on the other side of Leith Walk from Broughton is one of the epicentres of the area's gay community, though the clientele is mixed. DJ Trendy Wendy spins discs every Monday night.

Clubs

There's a monthly gay comedy night, OOT on Tuesday, at **The Stand Comedy Club**, *see* p.184.

CC Blooms H8
23 Greenside Place, **t** *(0131) 556 9331.* **Open** *Mon–Sat 7pm–3am, Sun 8pm–3am.*
Just down from the Playhouse behind Calton Hill, this two-storey gay club has karaoke capers on Thursdays and and occasional striptease nights. DJ Blondie presides over the extremely hectic Friday and Saturday nights.

L—vely and Taste at The Liquid Room G9
See p.179.
L—vely is a dance music night (from house to hard house) held one Saturday each month. Taste (**w** *www.taste-clubs.com*) is a very popular mixed progressive house night on Sundays.

Mingin' at Studio 24 H9
See p.182. **Open** *11pm–3am alternate Sats.*
Progressive house and garage at this New Town live-music venue.

Tackno at The Massa H9
See p.179. **Open** *10pm–3am last Sun of month.*
Popular dressed-up transvestite and mixed disco nights in the former Club Mercado on the Royal Mile, orchestrated by Trendy Wendy.

Vibe at Club Ego H8
See p.179; **w** *www.vibetuesdays. com.* **Open** *Tues 11pm–Sat.*
Mainstream sounds in this fashionable Broughton club. Also look out for the monthly Saturday-nighters Wiggle and Joy (**w** *www. clubjoy.co.uk*) and the more

commercialized Lush! (**w** *www. clublush.co.uk*) on the last Friday of each month.

Shops

Bobbie's Bookshop E10
220 Morrison St, **t** *(0131) 538 7069.*
A mixed bookshop selling British and imported gay magazines and videos, as well as second-hand and new books, at the Dalry end of Morrison Street.

Leather and Lace J7
25 Easter Rd, **t** *(0131) 623 6969,*
w *www.leatherlace.co.uk.*
Fetish gear, lingerie, sex toys and gay videos and magazines north of the city centre. There are other branches at 8 Drummond Street in the New Town (**t** *(0131) 622 6969*) and south of the centre at 368–370 Gorgie Road (**t** *(0131) 478 6969*).

Out of the Blue H8
Downstairs at the Blue Moon Café,
t *(0131) 478 7048.* **Open** *Mon–Fri 11am–7pm, Sat 11am–6pm, Sun noon–6pm.*
A gay and lesbian store selling books, mags, videos and toys.

Saunas

18 Albert Place I7
18 Albert Place, **t** *(0131) 553 3222.*
Open *daily noon–10pm.*
A good sauna for gay men just across Leith Walk from Broughton. Admission is £9.

The Townhouse H7
53 East Claremont St, **t** *(0131) 556 6116.* **Open** *Mon–Thurs noon–11pm, Fri and Sat noon–midnight.*
A Broughton sauna costing £10 a session (membership is £2).

Language

Scots is more than just another dialect of English: it is a language in itself that has been gradually compromised by the overbearing influence of English for more than 400 years. At least that's the official Scottish Nationalist line, and it makes the history of the Scots language the direct opposite of the history of the American language, which has steadily established itself as a separate tongue over a similar period. Like English itself, Scots is now changing under the influence of the American language, though perhaps less readily.

Glossary

These are just a smattering of the Scots words and phrases still in everyday use in Edinburgh that may not be immediately familiar, either in themselves or in the way they're used, to English or American ears.

advocate barrister, counsel

ain own, as in 'on my ain'

all your puff all your life

Auld Alliance 6th-century French and Scottish political ties

Auld Enemy England

Auld Reekie Edinburgh, 'Old Smokey'

bampot reckless idiot (slightly admiring)

bauchle (n. and adj.) shabby person

bawheid someone with a big round face

bevvy any alcohol drink, also 'bevvy merchant': big drinker

birling spinning or turning; 'go on a birl': make a trip

blether (n. and vb.) nonsense, to talk nonsense

blootered very drunk, also 'stotious'

boke throw up, as in 'give me the dry boke': makes me retch

bridie a folded-over pie

on the broo on the dole

cairy-oot takeaway, alcohol and food

cannae cannot

canny cunning, or good, as in 'a canny tin-opener'

ceilidh informal knees-up

champit mashed

chronic teenage term of approval

chum accompany, as in 'I'll chum you to the bus stop' or 'I'll give you a chum'

clapshot potatoes and swedes mashed together

cludgie toilet

couthy friendly and down-to-earth

crabbit grumpy

cry call, as in 'what do you cry that?'

douce genteel, from the French for gentle

dyke stone wall

Embra Edinburgh

fae from, as in 'fae Embra'

fash bother, or worry, as in 'dinnae fash yerself'

fiscal a cross between a coroner and Director of Public Prosecutions

fitbaw football

folk people

furth of outside

Gael any Gaelic speaker

gallus cheeky

gie give, as in 'gie's': give us, or 'gie it laldy': give it your all

glaikit affectionately

greetin weeping

haar sea mist on land

haddie haddock, as in a Finnan haddie

haver talk nonsense

Hearts Heart of Midlothian Football Club

heavy any keg beer (i.e. not cask real ale) that isn't lager

Hibs Hibernian FC

Hibbie Hibs fan

hoachin busy or crowded

Jambo fan of the Jam Tarts (Hearts)

keechie dirty and smelly, as in 'a keechie pub'

ken as in 'you know'; 'well kent': well known

loan path

mental over-excited/exciting; also mad

mince bad or useless

mingin smelly or nasty

MSP Member of the Scottish Parliament

Munro any mountain over 3,000ft

nae bother no trouble, as in 'no worries'

neb nose

neeps mashed turnip (actually swede)

out of your box off your head

outwith outside

oxter armpit

panelling punching

pants rubbish

pinkie little finger

pish piss, or 'on the pish': going drinking

plouter splash

poke a bag, as in 'poke of chips'

presbytery a Scottish church council procurator

radge (n. and adj.) mad or mad person

rammy fight

reek (n. and vb.) smoke

salt 'n' sauce instead of salt and vinegar, the sauce being brown but definitely not HP

sannies plimsolls

schemie someone from a housing estate

scunnered revolted; also 'take a scunner to someone'

sett the repeated square pattern in tartan

shan unfair

shilpit scrawny

shooglie shaky or wobbly

smokie salted and smoked haddock, as in Arbroath Smokie

SNP Scottish National Party

supper anything with chips, e.g. 'fish supper'; also evening snack

swally a drink

swithering dithering

tattie potato

tea supper

teuchter highlander (derog.)

yer ma! nonsense!

Index

Numbers in **bold** indicate main references. Numbers in *italic* indicate maps.

AVAILABLE FROM CADOGAN GUIDES...

Italy

Italy
Bay of Naples & Southern Italy
Bologna & Emilia-Romagna
Central Italy
Italian Riviera
Lombardy & the Italian Lakes
Northeast Italy
Rome, Venice, Florence
Sardinia
Sicily
Tuscany, Umbria & the Marches
Tuscany
Umbria

France

France
Brittany
Corsica
Côte d'Azur
Dordogne & the Lot
Gascony & the Pyrenees
Loire
South of France
Short Breaks in Northern France
Take the Kids: Paris & Disneyland®
   Resort Paris
Take the Kids: South of France

Spain

Spain
Andalucía
Bilbao & the Basque Lands
Northern Spain
Granada, Seville, Cordoba

Greece

Greece
Greek Islands
Crete

The UK and Ireland

London–Paris
London Markets
Take the Kids: England
Take the Kids: London
Scotland
Scotland's Highlands & Islands
Ireland
Southwest Ireland
Take the Kids: Ireland

Other Europe

Madeira & Porto Santo
Malta, Gozo & Comino
Portugal

City Guides

Amsterdam
Barcelona
Bruges
Brussels
Edinburgh
Florence
London
Madrid
Milan
Paris
Prague
Rome
Venice

Flying Visits

Flying Visits: France
Flying Visits: Italy
Flying Visits: Spain

Buying a Property

Buying a Property: France
Buying a Property: Italy
Buying a Property: Spain

*Cadogan Guides are available from good bookshops, or via **Littlehampton Book Services Ltd.**, Faraday Close, Durrington, Worthing, West Sussex, BN13 3RB, **t** (01903) 828 503, **f** (01903) 828 802, **e** mailorder@lbsltd.co.uk; and **The Globe Pequot Press**, 246 Goose Lane, PO Box 480, Guilford, Connecticut 06437–0480, **t** (800) 458 4500/ **f** (203) 458 4500, **t** (203) 458 4603. **w** www.cadoganguides.com*

Edinburgh Street Maps

	A	B	C	D	E	F	G	H	I	J	K	L	M
1													
2									Leith		Firth of Forth		
3			❶		LOWER CRANTON ROAD A901				Ocean Terminal				❷
4	PILTON		GRANTON		TRINITY		NEWHAVEN	COMMERCIAL STREET A199		LEITH			
5			FERRY ROAD A902				FERRY ROAD A902		Leith Links				SEAFIELD ROAD
6			INVERLEITH	Royal Botanic Garden			CANONMILLS						
7			❸ STOCKBRIDGE				BROUGHTON			Hibernian F.C. ❹			
8		QUEENSFERRY ROAD A90	DEAN VILLAGE	NEW TOWN					CALTON				
9	MURRAYFIELD	DEAN	Scottish National Gallery Of Modern Art	PRINCES STREET A8	Waverley Station	Edinburgh Castle		Palace of Holyroodhouse & Holyrood Abbey				WILLOWBRAE
10	CORSTORPHINE ROAD A8	Murrayfield Stadium	HAYMARKET	FOUNTAIN-BRIDGE	ST. GILES	Royal Infirmary		Holyrood Park				
11		Heart Of Midlothian F.C. (Tynecastle Park)	DALRY	Fountainpark Leisure Centre	TOLLCROSS						DUDDINGSTON VILLAGE		
12		GORGIE	MERCHISTON	PRESTONFIELD VILLA A702	MARCHMONT					PRESTONFIELD			

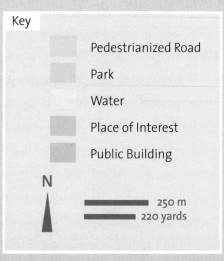

Key

	Pedestrianized Road
	Park
	Water
	Place of Interest
	Public Building

N

250 m
220 yards

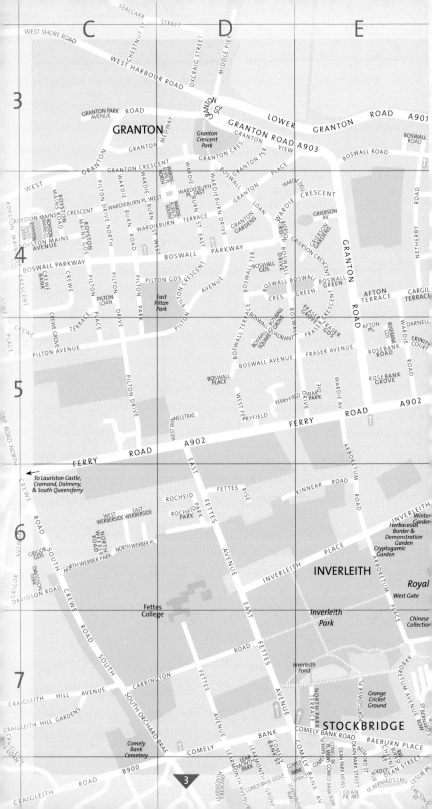

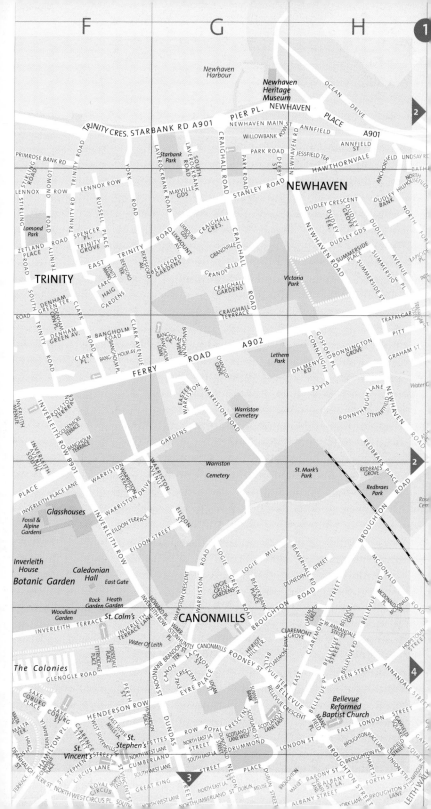

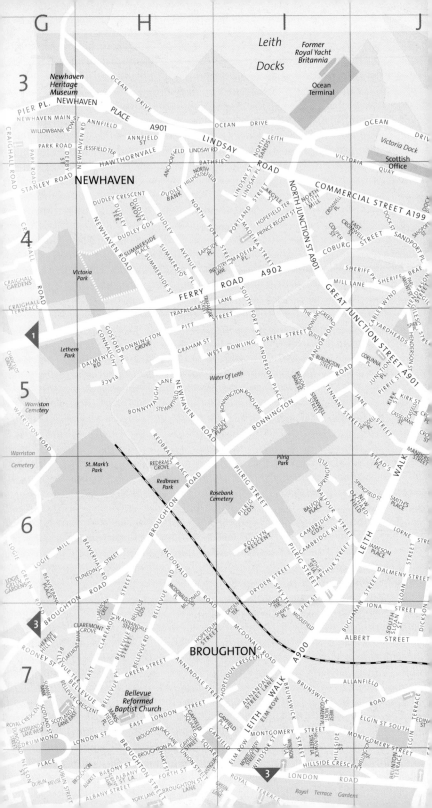

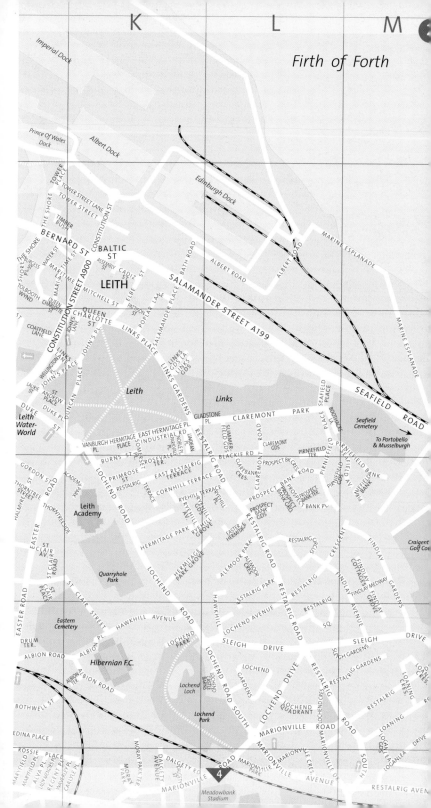

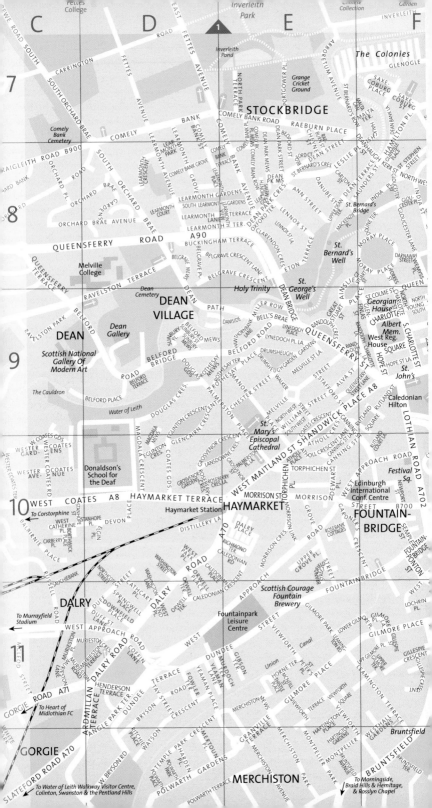

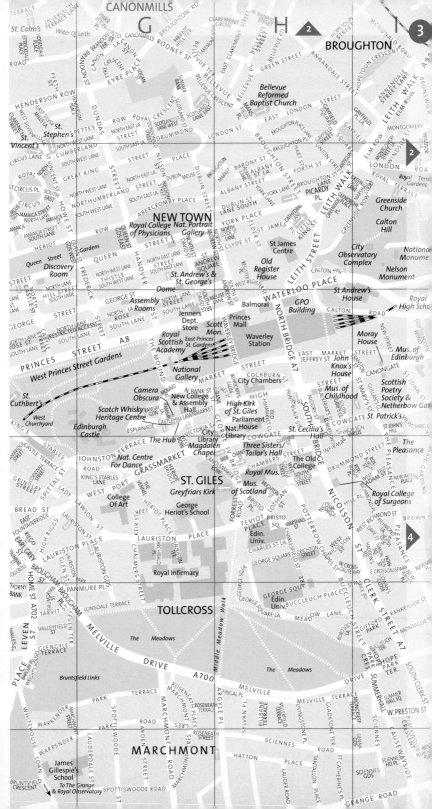

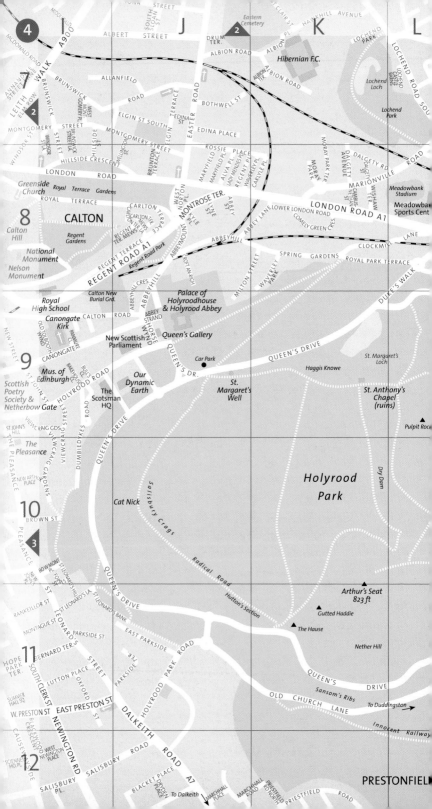